JET SET

Jet Set

The People, the Planes, the Glamour, and the Romance in Aviation's Glory Years

William Stadiem

BALLANTINE BOOKS • NEW YORK

Published in the United States by Ballantine Books, an imprint of Random House, a division of Random House LLC, a Penguin Random House Company, New York.

BALLANTINE and the HOUSE colophon are registered trademarks of Random House LLC.

ISBN 978-0-345-53695-2
eBook ISBN 978-0-345-53697-6

Printed in the United States of America on acid-free paper

www.ballantinebooks.com

123456789

First Edition

Book design by Susan Turner

Contents

Introduction

T HE PASSENGER JET WAS, AND STILL IS, ONE OF THE WONDERS OF THE WORLD, A
world whose other wonders the jet made accessible. Along with the
personal computer, it ranks as the greatest technological innovation of
the second half of the twentieth century. The computer turned your
lowly desk into a cross between Harvard and Hollywood. The jet turned
you into an adventurer. It freed you from the shackles of that desk and
set you free to roam the world, to become a Lindbergh, an Earhart, a
James Bond, and, if you had enough money and time, a jet-setter.

On October 26, 1958, Pan Am made history when it launched the
Boeing 707 on its first commercial flight from New York's Idlewild Airport to Paris's Le Bourget. The plane, called the *Clipper America,* had just
been christened a week before in Washington, D.C., by first lady Mamie
Eisenhower, and it was as different from its airborne antecedents as
Jackie Kennedy soon would be from Mamie, as Jack from Ike. Before the
707, the king of the skies and the way to Europe was President Eisenhower's own *Air Force One* (before the appellation), the Lockheed Con-

stellation. Ike had two of these "Connies," named *Columbine II* and
Columbine III.

The Connie, developed by the eccentric billionaire aviator/mogul
Howard Hughes for his airline, TWA, with the same zeal for design that
he had lavished on Jane Russell's brassiere in *The Outlaw* (a movie that
he produced), was instantly recognizable for its curvy dolphin-shaped
fuselage, its four huge, brutal propellers, and its trident tail, which
looked like a gladiatorial weapon from *Spartacus*. At its maximum speed
of 376 miles per hour, it seemed incredibly big and fast, able to transport
sixty-six passengers from New York to Europe in a mere fourteen hours.
Before the Connie, the trip had taken more than twenty-one hours, with
stops in Gander, Reykjavík, and Shannon before reaching the Old World.

The 707 made the Connie look like the proverbial "ninety-seven-
pound weakling" so famous in the advertising of the age. With its four
grand Pratt & Whitney jet pods, the 707 cut the transatlantic time to a
good night's sleep of seven hours. Not only did the jet take half the time,

DREAM MACHINE. The first version of the Boeing 707, which started crossing the Atlantic
in 1958.

at over 600 miles per hour, it also doubled the load, to 120 passengers. The sleek, shimmering silver rocket-bomber-shaped craft weighed 100,000 pounds more than the Connie and was 30 percent longer, at 144 feet, but it was exceptionally light on its toes, flying "above the weather" at 40,000 feet, compared to the Connie's ceiling of 25,000. Gone was the bone-rattling propeller vibration; gone was the stomach-churning turbulence. Now Pan Am's first-class passengers could savor the gourmet meals of foie gras and lobster thermidor and Mouton Roths-child catered by Maxim's of Paris without recourse to the airsick bags. Pan Am was taking haute cuisine as high as it could go.

The world of 1958 was in the Space Age, and the 707 was in every sense a futuristic spacecraft, Tomorrowland today. The subdued lighting, the ventilation, the individual controls, the Eames-like modernist seats, the relative silence, all instantly belied the 707's whimsical motif of hot-air balloons decorating the panels that separated deluxe from economy. "Tourist," Pan Am had decided, was a dirty word, and first class meant that there was a second. No one wanted to be second, not at Pan Am, which made a fetish and a legend out of always being first. Every traveler was to be treated as an explorer. They were all Phileas Foggs, and the 707 was their beautiful balloon.

Suffice it to say that a trip on the new 707 was a special event. The pilots were straight out of central casting, John Waynes who could rise to any occasion, not that "occasions" were expected ever to befall this mir-acle of technology. The stewardesses were sexistly stunning, pure *Coffee, Tea or Me?* avian goddesses, yet there was no hauteur, just a crisp, omni-competent cheeriness befitting your favorite schoolteacher. The passen-gers felt impelled to dress the part, coats and ties for the men, suits and pearls and heels for the women. It was a sky party, and you were honored to be on the guest list.

Furthermore, the price was right: $909 round-trip deluxe, $489 economy, the same fares as on the now-snailish Connie. Those prices, which would go down the more jets went up, were definitely doable for the American middle class, who in 1958 could buy a snazzy Chevrolet Impala for $2,700 and a home for a national median price of $12,750.

Even at $10 a day, which was twice the price on which Arthur Frommer would make his name and fame, a three-week European adventure of a lifetime would cost under $1,000. That may have been the deal of the century.

Within two years of Pan Am's inaugural flight, virtually all the world's major airlines would make the big switch from props to jets. Pan Am quickly expanded its initial service to Paris to include daily nonstops from New York to the other capitals of the grand tour, London and Rome. In early 1959 Air France began flying the 707 across the Atlantic, while TWA and American Airlines began jetting coast-to-coast in under five hours, compared to the Connie's endless eight. Also in 1959, Boeing's rival Douglas Aircraft introduced its own jet, the DC-8, which was so similar to the 707 that it was instantly relegated to "copycat" status, despite becoming the jet of choice for such giants as United, Swissair, KLM, and Japan Air Lines.

By 1960 BOAC (the

THE WORLD ON SALE. An early Air France jet ad. The prices for globe-trotting were too low to stay home.

forerunner of British Airways), Lufthansa, Air India, and Qantas had all jumped on the 707 bandwagon, giving the Boeing product a synonymy with jet travel that Douglas could never equal. Whichever plane they took, travelers were the beneficiaries of a newly accessible world. In 1958, 500,000 American tourists visited Europe. A decade of jets later, the figure had gone up to 2,000,000, an increase of 400 percent. The growth rate was so enormous that it rendered the 707 obsoletely small in record time and led to the development of the leviathan 747.

The Jet Set of this book is not merely the boldfaced names who populated the slopes of Gstaad, the topless beaches of Saint-Tropez, the tables of Maxim's, the dance floor of Regine's, and, of course, the gossip columns of the world. These people were traveling to all the right places long before the 707 was on the drawing board. They didn't need the jets. But the jets needed them, as the shock troops of fantasy, the stuff of dreams—and of ticket sales. Call them the uppercase Jet Set. The lower-case jet set were all the real people in the back of the plane. They might not have made the columns, but they were having the time of their lives. And they fueled the big, big business of aviation. This "real" jet set put the planes in the sky.

There was one further dichotomy in the concept of the Jet Set, upper- and lowercase. That was the division between the Jet, which was business, and the Set, which was social. The emperors of the air, and the airlines, and the aerospace companies, were among the most powerful men on the planet, but they were high-leverage, low-visibility. You didn't see them in Saint-Tropez. You didn't read about them in the columns. Without them, there would be no jet, and hence no set. Yet the world could not live on jet fuel alone. Fantasy was essential to the combustion that would create a new generation of travelers, as global mobility, in one amazing decade, became a new but integral part of the American Dream.

JET SET

1

The Flying Châteaux

THE POSTER BOY FOR THE JET SET HAD A BIG SECRET. FRANK SINATRA WAS AFRAID of flying. His 1958 album *Come Fly with Me* had become the soundtrack for the new jet age that had kicked off that same year in October with Pan Am's 707 service between New York and Paris. Yet Sinatra wouldn't be caught dead on Pan Am or TWA or even Air France, no matter how good the meals, catered by La Tour d'Argent, were supposed to be. "Dead" was the operative word for Sinatra, that most distrustful of all superstars. He simply didn't believe the airlines were careful enough. That was why he had his own plane, a big dual-prop Martin 404 called, in those days before political correctness, *El Dago*. Before the advent of the jets, the Martin was state-of-the art, air-conditioned, pressurized, and customized for his hard-drinking Rat Pack show-business buddies, with a piano and a central bar almost as long as the one at Chasen's. Hollywood felt at home here in the air, though for the nervous Sinatra, the *El Dago* bar was a necessity rather than a status symbol.

Aside from insisting on war-hero private pilots, Sinatra obsessively had his valet, ex–navy man George Jacobs, spend even more time checking weather reports and communicating with all the airports on their prospective routes to make sure there would be no nasty surprises than Jacobs did in arranging starlet assignations for his master. Sinatra once threw a fit when Jacobs arranged a post-dinner screening of the classic airline near-disaster film, *The High and the Mighty,* notwithstanding John Wayne's saving the day—and the plane. And he confided in Jacobs that he had a recurring nightmare inspired by *The Glenn Miller Story,* wherein the big bandleader disappeared over the foggy Channel on a flight from England to Paris. Moreover, Sinatra was still haunted by having bailed out, at the last second, of a 1958 cross-country flight with *Around the World in 80 Days* impresario and Elizabeth Taylor husband Mike Todd on his plane *The Lucky Liz,* which went down in a fireball in a New Mexico cornfield.

Such high anxiety was not the stuff of American legends, especially that of the swaggering, carefree, ring-a-ding variety that Sinatra apotheosized. He knew he had to get with the program, the jet program. After all, he was supposed to *be* the program. Accordingly, in 1962, when the ocean liners were still carrying more passengers across the Atlantic than the new jets, Sinatra did more than anyone thus far to emblazon the jet fantasy in the still-sedentary imagination of America. His high-profile grand gesture was chartering his own 707 for a three-month round-the-world tour to benefit children's charities in the countries he would visit. He would fly from L.A. to Tokyo, to Hong Kong, then across the globe to Israel, Greece, Italy, France, England, a swinging, speedy update of the grand tour for the Sputnik era.

What the world didn't realize was that, for all his ostensible altruism, Sinatra's charity began at home. The new commercial jets may have needed passengers, but Sinatra needed something, too: a makeover of a Mafia image occasioned by his guilt-by-association relationship with Chicago Mob boss Sam Giancana. While Giancana may have been instrumental in stealing Illinois, and the presidency, for John F. Kennedy in 1960, it was a debt that Attorney General Bobby Kennedy was intent on wiping from the ledger, even if that meant obliterating the playboy friendship between Sinatra and his brother. Bobby was so down on Sinatra, who had reconstructed his Palm Springs compound to become JFK's own Western White House, that he pressured his brother into rejecting the Sinatra hospitality and bunking instead chez Bing Crosby, Sinatra's archrival and an even archer Republican.

Humiliated, Sinatra, at the advice of his master-strategist lawyer, Mickey Rudin, decided to get out of Dodge—all the way out to Tokyo, as far as a 707 would take him. His entourage wasn't comprised of the usual Jet Set suspects, ultramobile international legends like Onassis, Agnelli, Rubirosa, or even Jacqueline Kennedy herself, whose high-profile Francophilia was proving to be a greater gesture of Franco-American comity than the Statue of Liberty. No, instead of the global nomads, Sinatra filled his 707 with his regiment of musicians and his best local buddies. The latter included his favorite Beverly Hills restaurateur, "Prince" Mike Romanoff, everyone's favorite charlatan, on whom Sinatra counted to get him the best tables on earth; his personal banker, Al Hart, head of Beverly Hills's City National and the man who financed Sinatra's comeback film, *From Here to Eternity*, to pay the freight; his songwriter and sexmeister Jimmy Van Heusen, himself an accomplished pilot, to get the girls; and legendary New York Giants baseball manager Leo "The Lip" Durocher, to provide all-American ballpark ballast amid the anticipated dislocations and alienations of the long foreign journey.

While not exactly the Ugly American, Sinatra provided plenty of his own homegrown ballast. For all his previous international performances and global exposure, Sinatra had almost no interest in foreign cultures, except for the women. He couldn't have cared less about the Louvre or Versailles, classic architecture or haute cuisine. In fact, he had George Jacobs stock the 707 with a three-month supply of his favorite snack, Campbell's franks and beans, which he would devour cold, straight from the tin. This was soul food, Hoboken-style. God forbid Sinatra would have to ingest sushi or chop suey or foie gras or, even on his ostensible home turf, spaghetti alla vongole. Even in Italy, the star invariably rejected the *alta cucina* grand-hotel fare of Rome's Excelsior and Milan's Principe di Savoia. Instead, he insisted that Jacobs, an accomplished navy cook whom Sinatra's mother Dolly had taught to "do" bridge-and-

(used inline below)

tunnel red-gravy transplant-*paisan* food, prepare his Jersey favorites in the kitchen of his suite.

Sinatra left for Tokyo in April 1962, perfect for cherry-blossom time. His tour instantly generated massive worldwide news coverage, just as lawyer Rudin had promised. Every day the still-powerful syndicated gossip columns, led by Hearst's "Cholly Knickerbocker," the nom de plume of the worldly and genuine Russian count Igor Cassini, featured breathlessly glamorous dispatches on Sinatra's mix of good deeds and high life, visiting a Buddhist monastery on Mount Fuji, endowing a youth center on the Sea of Galilee, cruising the Mediterranean on Onassian yachts, serenading his *High Society* costar Princess Grace at a series of "Chinchilla and Diamonds" concert benefits at the Sporting Club in Monte Carlo designed to soak high rollers for the benefit of poor kids.

Sinatra had *El Dago* flown over to Europe to replace the 707 for short intercontinental hops, though in a nod to his quest to sanitize his

COME FLY WITH ME. Frank Sinatra at London's Heathrow Airport in 1961. More than any other entertainer, Sinatra embodied and popularized jet travel.

escutcheon, it had been renamed the *Christina,* after his younger daughter. He posed with blind children in Greece and crippled children in Italy and orphans in England. He sang everywhere, from the Mikado Theater in Tokyo, to the Parthenon in Athens, to the Baths of Caracalla in Rome, to the Royal Festival Hall in London. He was feted by everyone from the emperor of Japan to Princess Grace to Princess Margaret (whom he tried, unsuccessfully, to bed) to General de Gaulle, who got over being not invited by Prince Rainier to the Monaco gala and decorated Sinatra as a chevalier of the Order of Public Health, an ironic honor given the unsalubrious post-concert orgies being carried on in the entertainer's imperial suite at the Hotel George V. The fantasy trip of a lifetime, Sinatra's "one man, one world" extravaganza underscored, as nothing before it, the jet-age miracle of making the planet seem, if not small, then certainly accessible.

The Sinatra coverage was proving an inspiration to another group of travelers who were planning their own trip-of-a-lifetime spring adventure to Europe, an odyssey that would be as long on culture as Sinatra's would be short. The Atlanta Art Association, which constituted the art- and music-loving elite of the capital of the Peach State and the symbol of a South that was rising again, was chartering an Air France 707 to take its members on a very grand tour of the Old World for the month of May. Just as the Sinatra world tour would become the most-reported-on celebrity superjunket of the sixties, the Atlanta art excursion would become the most-reported-on tour of "real people," although for entirely different reasons, as will be seen.

Sinatra was fantasy, Atlanta reality. Both captured the public imagination. The Art Association trip would be featured on the cover of *Life* as a paradigm of how the new jets were opening up the Old World to America's burgeoning middle class, and how travel was becoming both an affordable luxury and, for Americans in the Camelot era that prized sophistication, a cultural necessity. The Atlanta tour thus provides valuable insight into how Americans traveled at the dawn of the jet age and the joy it brought them. Sadly, the main reason it made *Life* was death, for the tour, realizing Sinatra's darkest fears, became the greatest disaster in aviation history.

In 1960, following its own assemblage of a jet fleet to compete with Pan Am and TWA in the war for the Atlantic, Air France had established a sales office in Atlanta. Its local manager was a suave and dashing Frenchman named Paul Dossans, who proved enormously attractive to the local country-club set who were Air France's target clientele. Dossans started small, donating a free jet round-trip ticket to Paris to the Art Association's 1960 charity auction. The prize turned out to be such a hit that Dossans decided next to go for not one seat but the whole plane. He joined forces with the local American Express office to assemble a tour and charter package exclusively for the Art Association.

Exclusivity, embodied in the Piedmont Driving Club, which had a large overlapping membership with the Art Association, was everything in Atlanta. The boomtown was still suffering from the century-old inferiority complex vis-à-vis the "Yankee" metropolises occasioned by General Sherman's having burned it to the ground. Atlanta didn't have anything like the Metropolitan Museum or the Metropolitan Opera, but it did have a *Gone with the Wind* gracious mystique, it had the global colossus of Coca-Cola, and it had a huge amount of new money that wanted to burnish itself with an "artistic" patina. It was a perfect target for Air France, and in teaming up with an Art Association grand dame named Anne Merritt, Paul Dossans hit the Dixie bull's-eye.

In return for a free first-class ticket, Dossans got Merritt, the wife of a Harvard-trained fertilizer broker, to fill up his plane with 120 of her society friends. Merritt was already a world traveler, though doing so from pre-707 Atlanta was a major pain, requiring numerous stopovers and basically twenty-four hours to reach Europe. That the new jet could do it in eight, with only one stop at New York's Idlewild, was a technological marvel, a magic carpet that Merritt couldn't wait to experience. As someone who loved to go places, she knew it would change her life.

Many of the women Anne Merritt recruited for the trip were Jackie Kennedy wannabes, her Yankee-ness notwithstanding. Few American women, north or south, east or west, had failed to be captivated by Jackie's accompanying JFK on a state visit to France, and the rest of Europe, in June 1961. The trip was extensively televised, and everyone was riveted. From the minute Jackie descended the gangway from the new 707 that had become *Air Force One,* and rode into Paris in her pillbox hat in a gleaming Simca cabriolet, it was clear that she had stolen the show from her husband. JFK admitted as much in his famous self-deprecatory introductory quote to the French, "I am the man who accompanied

Jacqueline Kennedy to Paris." General de Gaulle was so taken by Jackie's Miss Porter's–perfect French and her grasp of the culture that at the Élysée Palace, he gushed, "She knows more French history than any French-woman!"

In light of such glorious flattery, Jackie was unable to resist the siren call of French couture. Pressured by her husband to "dress American," she had brought with her a gown by Oleg Cassini, the fashion designer big brother of gossip lord Igor. However, while preparing for the grand ball at Versailles's Galerie des Glaces (Hall of Mirrors), Jackie was emboldened by a speed-laced "vitamin" injection from the family's Dr. Feelgood, the New York physician Max Jacobson, who traveled everywhere with the Kennedys, dispensing medicinal fixes the way George Jacobs dispensed culinary fixes for Frank Sinatra. Suddenly, recalling the De Gaulle encomium, Jackie decided she had to play to the local audience, as well as to her French Bouvier bloodlines. Accordingly, she switched to her backup rhinestone-studded white satin gown by Hubert de Givenchy. When she rose at Versailles in Givenchy splendor to sing the French national anthem, it was the most rousing performance "La Marseillaise" had gotten since it stole the show in *Casablanca*.

That Givenchy moment stuck in the mind of the Atlanta belles, who were easy marks for Anne Merritt. Some of her friends had, like Jackie, gone to Vassar. More had attended Agnes Scott, the Vassar of the South, outside of Atlanta. Even if they hadn't done their junior year in Paris, a year that made Jackie obsessed with all things French and fine, the ladies of Atlanta saw themselves as *culturati*. After all, they were the Art Association. Jackie *spoke* to them. Their good-old-boy husbands, a lot of whom were "rambling wrecks" from Georgia Tech or ex–big men on campuses like Charlottesville and Chapel Hill, may have preferred to stay home and play golf at Piedmont. However, they took a cue from President Kennedy and accepted the conjugal imperative. Merritt filled the charter in short order. Besides, the package—which the Art Association named "Trip to the Louvre"—was a good deal. Dossans, his airline, and American Express had come up with a bargain price for the monthlong tour, which included London, Paris, Amsterdam, Lucerne, Venice, Florence, Rome, and their own special visit to Versailles, for a rock-bottom $895. Normal first-class fare alone would have been $1,100.

For the independent travelers, who eschewed anything packaged and were confident to rely on that Bible of upper-bourgeois independent voyaging, *Fielding's Travel Guide to Europe,* Dossans offered the Atlantans an air-only price of $388, compared to the $632 economy fare of the day. The independents would still get the inside track at the Louvre and Versailles, meeting up with their fellow Atlantans at the end of the trip for a Paris blowout. Arthur Frommer's *Europe on 5 Dollars a Day* may have been infra dig for the Atlantans. But Fielding, basically *Europe on 50 Dollars a Day,* spoke the language of ritzy Peachtree Street. At $5 a day, the trip would have cost under $600, including airfare. That would have been beyond the dreams of the average American, whose median annual income in 1962 was $6,000. At the deluxe level of $50 a day, the monthlong trip would have cost $2,000. Coca-Cola executives were earning upward of $25,000 a year, as were the doctors and lawyers of Peachtree Street. At the top, then, these prices, for the trip of a lifetime (even factoring in inflation), were well within reach. Any way one went, travel then was a great deal, compared to the bank-breaker it would become. It paid to be a pioneer, a jet-setter even without one's name in the columns.

Temple Fielding, the most trusted man in travel, the Walter Cronkite of tourism, was a highly acerbic exception to the gush-and-fawn corps of travel writers who tended to subsist on airline and hotel freebies. He was no fan of Air France. He renamed it "Air Chance," justifying his anxieties by his observation that "on every flight I've taken with this line, at least one tray of champagne or still wine or cognac has gone up to the cockpit." A chauvinistic American advocate of our "don't drink and drive" ethos, Fielding wrote how he had approached Air France head honcho Max Hymans to discuss why French pilots were free to booze it up aloft while Americans were required to abstain from even a mug of beer within twelve hours prior to takeoff. Hymans's arrogant retort was basically that French pilots don't get drunk.

"He assured me that because the French pilot has grown up with wine," Fielding reported, "'a little wine' [the quotation marks were a piqued Fielding's] won't hurt him during the flight." This sent Fielding into one of his high dudgeons: "If Air France sincerely believes that the reflexes of their crews, after a glass or two of brandy or wine, are sufficiently razor-sharp to cope with instantaneous emergencies aloft, that's their affair . . . I regret that it's not the line for me." The Atlantans may have been put off by Fielding's warning, but they weren't about to change their plans. The price was right, and the champagne-drenched French mystique, so heavily promoted in Air France's "le bon voyage" advertising campaign, served to overcome any Fielding-induced trepidation.

The white, blue-striped Air France 707, named *Château d'Amboise* (the line's 707s were all named after Loire châteaux) with 20 passengers in first class and 102 others in "tourist," left Atlanta's brand-new terminal on May 8, 1962. The plane's name was pure Marie Antoinette, but the plane itself was pure Buck Rogers, endlessly long and sleek and a major step into the future from the boxier prop planes that had preceded it. The 707s were under three years old and still a novelty, though the local carrier Delta had recently begun flying the 707's rival, the Douglas DC-8, on the Atlanta–New York route, so many of the Art Association group had already enjoyed the unique and overwhelmingly modern jet experience.

Everyone dressed for the occasion, the men in their Southern preppy best, blue blazers, ties, and straw boaters; the women in Jackie-esque pillbox hats, silk dresses, high heels, and because these were Southern belles, white gloves. All plane trips then were special events, this overseas departure even more so. Almost all the women were wearing corsages, farewell gifts from the large crowd of well-wishers who, in an age before security checks, streamed out to the tarmac and toured the 707 before takeoff.

Finally, friends and family retreated to the sides of the runway to watch the flying *Château* commence its mighty roar and takeoff to Idlewild. The flight would take an hour and a half, a seeming split second in those days when most Southerners went to Manhattan via over-

night Pullman on the
Atlantic Coast Line. The
all-French stewardess staff
served a picnic lunch of
pâté et salade, and lots
of Moët & Chandon
champagne, *splendeur en
l'air,* to be sure. The supposedly brief New York
pit stop turned out to
be a five-hour delay due
to mechanical problems.
Not wanting to spoil
the multicourse gourmet
French meal they knew
was coming on the trans-
atlantic leg, the Geor-
gians trooped into the
Idlewild bars and bided
their time, hour upon
hour, over peanuts and
cocktails. By nine P.M.,

PARDON OUR FRENCH. A 1962 Air France promotion
that fused French hospitality with American technology
to entice tourists like those on the ill-fated Atlanta Art
Association charter.

the *Château* had been repaired. The ladies slithered out of their girdles,
kicked off their heels, and settled in for the flight and the night. Few
could sleep. The 707's launch campaign had stressed how "vibration-
free" the jet experience was, eliminating the grind of the propellers, and
how the new plane flew five miles "above the weather." The Boeing people never mentioned turbulence, and the choppy spring jet stream kept
most of the Georgians nervously awake throughout the seven-hour
journey.

Morning in Paris was more than worth the nocturnal bumps. The
weather was cool by Atlanta standards, in the midfifties, but the spring
flowers were in bloom, and the sights were magical. Whether they took
the tour or not, all the Art Association guests were treated to a compli-

mentary night at the Hôtel du Louvre, across from the vast palace museum. Those lodgings could be had for around five dollars a night, and the more fastidious travelers could note that Temple Fielding didn't even include the hotel in his guide. Such silence was not golden in a writer who cautioned his readers that the hotels he didn't mention were "pretty grim," and who trashed Sinatra's—and Hollywood's—favorite, the George V, thus:

> . . . the connecting doors between some of the bedrooms are so thin that even private personal activities carry through them like paper; some of the staff, too, couldn't seem to care less about answering that buzzer . . . I think that the George V is a very poor value for the money ($25 for a double)—but if you like the limelight and if you're happy in a frenzied, F-sharp atmosphere, you'll probably enjoy every minute of your stay in this hub of the restless American abroad.

Fielding was snide about the Jet Set's go-to abode in Paris without actually using the appellation "Jet Set." Fielding had his own words for the crowd, describing the grand hotel as "the French home away from home for the less self-conscious members of Broadway, Hollywood, Miami Beach and Main Street café society, most of them seeking lights, action and music in giddy determination." As for less than grand places like the Hôtel du Louvre, which catered to package tours, Fielding had the most withering disdain:

> Hoteliers in this city seem to spend their money on the ground floor, not in the bedrooms; upstairs you'll often find peeling paint, frayed carpets, screamingly lurid French wallpaper and toilet facilities that are so chummy, cozy and nonchalant that you'll either turn pale in horror or burst out laughing.

The group had no time to dwell on the shortcomings of their lodgings. They were whisked off by an American Express guide to the Louvre to see the *Mona Lisa*, the *Winged Victory*, and the group's favorite, Whis-

tler's Mother. Then they were herded onto a tour bus to see *Paris by
Night* and dine in what their trip brochure described as a "typical popular restaurant." The usual go-to of American Express was Au Mouton de
Panurge, an urban kitsch farmhouse on the right bank near the Opéra,
complete with wench-waitresses in medieval costumes and live sheep
grazing about. The restaurant, inspired by Rabelais's *Gargantua and Pan-
tagruel,* had been around since the thirties and was testimony to French
intellectualism; even the tourist traps had literary antecedents. This one
rubbed its customers' faces in it. The restaurant was named for a Rabe-
laisian sheep who followed other sheep off a cliff without regard to the
disastrous consequences. Sort of like tourists flocking to a bad restaurant
because lots of other tourists were there. Fielding described the ambience
as "startlingly pornographic," with phallic-shaped rolls and escargots
served in replicas of chamber pots. He hated the food, which cost a steep
$10 a head. Even worse were the boisterous and non-French clientele.
There were "so many Americans," Fielding wrote, "I could shut my eyes
and swear that I was back in Howard Johnson's."

After the first night, the tour left for the English Channel boat train
to London, while the independents checked out of the Louvre and in to
Fielding-approved caravanserais, where they followed the Fielding program of restaurants, nightclubs, and shops (he barely mentioned museums) designed for *his* tourists to feel vastly superior to *un-Fielding*
tourists. Fielding gave his readers the names of the owners of these places,
the concierges and maître d's, and insisted the readers drop them like
crazy. Royal treatment would be assured.

Fielding's number one Paris gourmet pick was the Tour d'Argent,
which had been founded by the proprietor of the George V, André Terrail, one of the giants of French hospitality and the favorite of *tout* Hollywood. His son, Claude, the current *patron* of the Tour, had become
part of filmland's inner circle by having been the lover of Ava Gardner
and Rita Hayworth, then marrying the daughter of movie mogul Jack
Warner. It was the one restaurant in Paris that could lure Sinatra away
from Campbell's, and similarly, it was able to lure American tourists,
such as the Georgians, away from their steaks and Scotch. For under

$10, including fine wine, it was easy to be seduced by the Tour, espe-
cially if you could see Sinatra, or Audrey Hepburn, or Gary Cooper, or
Jackie herself, across the dining room, silhouetted against the restaurant's
iconic vista of the flying buttresses of Notre Dame. Small wonder the
Fielding *Guide* became a must for the well-off traveler and, updated annually, sold in the millions.

However they traveled, organized or independent, all the Atlantans
had a wonderful month of May. Some of those who didn't take the tour
had done the highlights before and now went as far afield as Greece,
Egypt, and Israel. They all reassembled in Paris on May 30, loaded to the
gills with treasures from across the Continent. Their common concern
was how to circumvent the low $100-per-person customs exemption.
Some spent their remaining four days in the City of Light at the post
offices, dividing their spoils into many packages with low declarations,
and shipping them to a lot of varied addresses, to beat the duty.

Otherwise, they took Paris by storm, eating, drinking, shopping, but
always putting culture first. They went back to the Louvre and savored a
perfect full day at Versailles, made more memorable by the presence of a
large troupe of thespians dressed in Louis XIV regalia, shooting a film
called *Angélique and the King*. The actors and actresses of this French
costume epic, starring Michèle Mercier and Jean Rochefort, posed with
the Atlantans throughout the palace. What photos they had to show the
folks back at home.

Finally, it was time to go. June 3, 1962, was a glorious Sunday,
cloudless blue skies, a brilliant sun. It was a perfect day to fly. But it was
also a perfect day for Paris. A lot of Georgians hated to leave, hated to go
back to hush puppies and Cokes after croissants and café au lait. How,
indeed, were you gonna keep 'em down on the farm, or even the new
Lenox Square Mall, the grandest shopping center in America, after they'd
seen Paree? They took one last glance at the Eiffel Tower and wistfully
filed into the American Express coaches that transported the group, past
Notre Dame, past the Île Saint-Louis, past the Tour d'Argent, out to the
gleaming modern American-style terminal at Orly Airport to board their
return chartered 707. This one was named the *Château de Sully* and was

designated Air France Flight 007. *Dr. No,* the first of the James Bond series films, would not debut until October of that year in England, the following year in America. But several of the men in the group were fans of the Ian Fleming books, inspired perhaps by big fan John F. Kennedy, and in light of their recent transcontinental derring-dos, they may have made some hay of the jet's secret agent–sounding appellation.

Paul Dossans had flown over from Atlanta just to make sure the trip ended well, and was flying back with the Art Association. The goodwill and word of mouth his brainstorm promised to generate was enormous, guaranteeing Air France a special place in the heart of haute Atlanta and hopefully giving it a big leg up against rivals Pan Am and TWA. One of the group's couples, who had three young children, insisted on traveling on separate jets. The wife was on the charter; the husband had booked a later Pan Am flight to New York, where he would switch to Delta and fly home. Dossans tried to talk him out of it. But the husband was too superstitious to change his plans.

The captain, thirty-nine-year-old Roland Hoche, personally welcomed each of the Atlantans onto his gleaming *Château,* which was only two years old. Dedicated to charter-only service, the *Château de Sully* had logged only five thousand flight hours, mostly carrying tour groups like this one across the Atlantic. There were seven French flight attendants, two in first and five in tourist. Hoche announced that the estimated flight time to New York would be a speedy seven and a half hours. There were no major headwinds expected. The stewardesses poured the champagne, and the Atlantans took one last look at the green French countryside. But it wasn't *adieu.* It was *à bientôt.* Everyone couldn't wait to come back. How could they not? It was cheap. It was fast. It was easy. It was *Europe.*

The *Sully* got off to a late start because several of the group lost track of time making last-minute purchases in the duty-free stores. Dossans combed Orly and rounded up the dilatory shopaholics and herded them to the jet. The stewardesses cosseted travelers with *International Herald Tribune*s and fine chocolates, made sure they were belted in, and recited safety instructions that no one was listening to. Then Hoche pulled back from the terminal and took the *Sully* to Runway 26 for takeoff. The Georgians had a number of friends at Orly saying goodbye, who watched the *Sully* start to accelerate. While the roar was mighty and the speed was lightning, the plane seemed to be taking too long to rise into the air. Finally, it did lift off, but only a few feet.

Then the *Sully*, hurtling toward the end of the runway, tried to stop. The reverse thrust and screeching brakes, sounding like a thousand banshees, were unable to stop the 140-ton craft. The runway ended and the *Sully* hurtled into a green field in the adjacent hamlet of Villeneuve-le-Roi. There it careened wildly. Upended, one of the wings hit the ground, and the plane began breaking apart. When the jet engines hit the earth, there were several massive explosions as the twenty thousand gallons of jet fuel ignited.

The *Sully* went up in what looked like a nuclear blast that disintegrated most of what was left of it. The thick black smoke was a miasma blotting out the bright sun. It was springtime, but it looked like autumn, when the fields were burned. One house nearby caught fire. But the residents were away. Miraculously, no one in the village, many of whom were enjoying Sunday picnics in the countryside following a parade honoring the 1944 liberation of French prisoners of war, was harmed. The Villeneuvians were inured to the noise of Orly. But they had never seen a crash, not like this. No one had. The failure of the *Sully* was the worst single-plane disaster in the history of aviation to that day.

One hundred thirty people perished. Only the two stewardesses and one steward, sitting at the tail of the plane, survived, having been hurled from the wreckage before the explosions. Everyone else was obliterated, the French crew, the Georgians, and Paul Dossans, who had striven so mightily to make everything on the "Trip to the Louvre" be perfection. Atlanta had not been so devastated since Sherman's March. The city was in shock, too dazed to mourn. Its progressive Kennedy-esque, newly elected mayor Ivan Allen dropped everything to fly via New York to Paris and help identify the bodies, if such a task were possible. Many of the dead were his good friends.

Despite the tragedy, Allen was not one to blame Air France. In fact, he took the New York–to–Paris Air France flight, on which the captain invited him, his deputy mayor, and his press secretary to spend an hour in the cockpit and see the marvel of technology firsthand. The horror was brought home at Orly when French authorities, led by an emissary of President de Gaulle, gave Mayor Allen and company a tour of the wreckage, the *Sully*'s intact tail section standing sentinel over the still-smoldering carnage. The bodies may have been burned beyond recognition, but a lot of the inanimate objects remained. Allen spotted a necktie he had given one of the passengers as a Christmas gift. He recognized mink stoles, party dresses, necklaces the women had worn to dances at the Piedmont Driving Club. He saw labels from Atlanta's top stores. But he couldn't see his friends.

The darkest commentary on the dark day came from sunny Los Angeles, where Nation of Islam leader Malcolm X literally jumped for joy at the tragic news. "I got a wire from God today," he exulted to his audience, "well, all right, somebody came and told me that he had really answered our prayers over in France. He dropped an airplane out of the sky with over 120 white people on it because the Muslims believe in an eye for an eye and a tooth for a tooth. But thanks to God, or Jehovah, or Allah, we will continue to pray, and we hope that every day another plane falls out of the sky." Malcolm X was denounced by Los Angeles Mayor Sam Yorty as a "fiend," which only added fuel to the fire and succeeded in getting X the front-page recognition he had been seeking. The Atlantan Martin Luther King, Jr., was appalled. Reverend King had been working hand in hand with Mayor Allen, a born-again integrationist, to change the ways of Atlanta. This was not his method.

Frank Sinatra was in London when the crash occurred. He had flown there from Rome in *El Dago* (now *Christina*) to stay at the Savoy and do a benefit command performance for Princess Margaret at the Royal Festival Hall. At the Hall, he did a thirty-song set, culminating in "Come Fly with Me." And then he flew off to Paris, to the George V, to prepare for shows at the Olympia Music Hall and at the Lido, flanked by the super-cabaret's Bluebells, Paris's topless answer to Radio City Music Hall's Rockettes. The first Lido show was June 4, one day after the Sunday crash, and it is notable that "Come Fly with Me," Sinatra's standard closer, had been dropped from the playlist. Sinatra concluded his performance with "The Lady Is a Tramp."

It had been a terrible period for the 707, which had gone for its first two years without a crash. The bad luck started in February 1961, when a Sabena 707 en route to Brussels from New York crashed on landing at Brussels, killing seventy-two, including the entire American figure-skating team, traveling to the world championships in Prague. In March 1962, an automatic-pilot defect caused American Airlines Flight 1, from New York to Los Angeles, to crash into Jamaica Bay on takeoff, killing several major tycoons, including hotel magnate Arnold Kirkeby and oil magnate W. Alton Jones, a close friend of President Eisenhower. A $10,000 bill was found in Jones's wallet. Sinatra had even more doubts about flying commercial after that one.

On May 22, 1962, when Sinatra was performing in Rome, Continental Airlines Flight 11, going from Chicago to Kansas City, exploded over Centerville, Iowa, killing all forty-five people aboard. At first it was suspected that the plane had been downed by heavy thunderstorms. However, an investigation led to the discovery of sabotage. One of the passengers had bought $300,000 of insurance right before the flight. He had also purchased six sticks of dynamite for twenty-nine cents apiece. He jerry-rigged a bomb and planted it in the 707's rear lavatory. The bomb worked. So did the plot, which became the basis of Arthur Hailey's 1968 bestseller *Airport*.

And now, less than two weeks later, the *Château de Sully* became the fourth ill-fated 707. Once Atlantans recovered enough, people began speculating. Some articulated the Temple Fielding "Air Chance" notion that the crew members were drinking before takeoff. But the predominant hypothesis was that the Art Association voyagers were victims of their own acquisitiveness. Because the *Sully* was a private charter, baggage weight restrictions may have been honored in the breach. Despite enduring the long lines at the Paris post offices to minimize customs duties, the Atlantans may have been carrying back so many antiques, paintings, and clothes that, combined with the heavy fuel load to make it across the Atlantic, and the full capacity, the *Sully* could have been a victim of its own weight. The Art Association may have literally "shopped till they dropped," a ghastly possibility.

It wasn't until 1965 that the seemingly endless investigation of the *Sully* crash was concluded. In February of that year, the International Civil Aviation Organization (ICAO) issued its long-awaited report. The lawyers for the decedents' families were already in a legal war with Air France, hiding behind the shield of the pre–World War II Warsaw Convention, which capped any family's recovery at $8,291. This added up to under $1 million for the whole plane. The plaintiffs' lawyers were seeking upward of $20 million. The ICAO's report was curtains for Air France, which was blamed for both pilot error and mechanical failure (of something called the trim tabs, before the name was commandeered by a vitamin company). The litigation dragged on for several more years until, after the death of the plaintiffs' lead counsel, his successors quietly settled with Air France for around $5 million, or about $85,000 per family. It was the largest settlement in history for a single airplane crash, but to the victims' families, it seemed like peanuts.

The government of France, knowing it had gotten a great deal, tried to make it up to Atlanta by donating a Rodin sculpture to become the centerpiece of the city's new Municipal Arts Center, opened in 1968 as a memorial to the Art Association victims. The statue was called *L'Ombre,* or *The Shade.* In his presentation, the French ambassador described the Rodin as "a reconciliation of death and destiny." Atlantans, famed for their courtesy and Southern hospitality, accepted the goodwill gesture and refrained from blaming France or its airline. The premier exhibit of the new High Art Museum was a tribute called "The Taste of Paris," featuring three centuries of art loaned by French museums. The "Trip to the Louvre" would never be forgotten.

As for Frank Sinatra, the ultimate Jet Setter kept on jetting, albeit privately and nervously. He stayed off Air France. He stayed off Pan Am. If he needed a 707, he would charter it and do it "his way." In 1964, he signed a contract with the Learjet Corporation to buy one of their first-generation private jets. Lear congratulated Sinatra on purchasing "the world's finest business machine." By 1964 Sinatra, nearing fifty, was chairman of Reprise, his own record label; he also oversaw his film company, his huge real estate holdings, and a major investment in a missile parts manufacturer. Sinatra was now a Big Businessman, and a Learjet, the ultimate corporate tool, was as natural a component of his portfolio as his cellar full of Jack Daniel's. He tastefully named the Lear the *Christina II*. The Hoboken swagger had been replaced by a Wall Street stride.

Not that the Rat Pack party days were completely behind him. He used the Lear—which seated only six and had no bar—mostly to shuttle his pals between Los Angeles, Palm Springs, and Las Vegas. For the long hauls and the concert tours, he still chartered the big 707s. But he loved showing off the Lear as the party favor for a Hollywood that had everything. He flew a wide-eyed Mia Farrow on it to Palm Springs for their first date, and to the Côte d'Azur for their 1966 honeymoon. He snowed Michael Caine, when Caine was dating Sinatra's daughter Nancy, by Lear-ing him to Vegas, just the two guys, heart-to-heart, to make sure Caine's intentions were honorable. Sinatra assumed that the truth would be spoken at 30,000 feet. Sinatra lent the Lear to Sammy Davis, Jr., and Marlon Brando to fly to Mississippi to join Martin Luther King, Jr., on a freedom march. He lent it to Elvis Presley, whom he once despised as vulgar but came to embrace, for the King and Priscilla Beaulieu to fly from Palm Springs to Las Vegas to get hitched by a justice of the peace. He lent it to the Beatles. And in 1967, having been instrumental in making the Learjet the millionaire's favorite status symbol, he sold it, trading up to the new Gulfstream GII, which did have room for a bar, though not as big as *El Dago*'s. By now the chairman was drinking less. In 1972, he bought his very own 707, one originally built for Australia's Qantas.

In January 1977, the ultimate irony befell Sinatra. He was about to fly his entourage on his current jet from Palm Springs to his opening night at Caesar's Palace. But his beloved mother, Dolly, visiting from New Jersey, couldn't stand Sinatra's new wife, Barbara Marx, and refused to fly with her. So Sinatra simply chartered Dolly her own Learjet for the twenty-minute flight to Las Vegas. The plane was overflowing with a cornucopia of luxury food and amenities, as if destined for Paris.

It was one of those rare winter days when it was cloudy in Palm Springs. The pilot, who had flown the short route countless times, was undeterred. But, like the pilot of the *Château de Sully*, this pilot was in error. The clouds became a blinding blizzard, and the Lear crashed into the massive Mount San Gorgonio, instantly killing Dolly, her friend, and the Lear's crew.

The pallbearers at Dolly Sinatra's funeral included Frank's old flying buddies Jimmy Van Heusen, Leo Durocher, and Dean Martin. Frank was so traumatized by the loss that he reembraced his long-lost Catholicism and forced his wife, Barbara, to convert. But no religion could restore his shaken faith in private jet aviation, or his faith in himself as always being in control, that his way was the safe way. He could never believe that the anxieties he'd fought so hard could come true, that a Sinatra could die in a plane crash. "She was a woman who flew maybe five times a year," he mumbled incredulously to the press. "I could understand if it happened to me . . ."

But that tragedy was decades away. At the dawn of the jet age, the utter glamour and flash of Sinatra's own historic "Come Fly with Me" spring tour ultimately proved to be an effective counterweight to make the world forget the disaster of the Atlanta "Trip to the Louvre." It transformed 1962 from what could have been an annus horribilis into what Sinatra would deem "a very good year," emblazoning the concept of the Jet Set in the public consciousness and inculcating a national belief in another famous Sinatra lyric, "Fairy tales can come true, they can happen to you." Nevertheless, there was a nightmare of fiery destruction lurking in the wings, the specter that the magic carpet of jet travel could unravel. It was the genius of the airlines, the myth-making machinery, and the power of positive thinking, that the Jet Set, and not fear of flying, took a pole position in the sixties' version of the American Dream.

2

Set Designer

THERE WAS NO CHICKEN/EGG CONUNDRUM IN THE ETYMOLOGY OF THE PHRASE "Jet Set." First came the Set, then came the Jet. The Set was all about people, in the sixties called "the beautiful people," an elite of fine visage and deep pockets and great networks the "regular people" thought had it made, because the Set were in all the right places, at all the right times, always together, always looking fantastic. They had always *been* around, but now they *got* around a lot more and a lot faster. The Jet was all about technology, a great scientific leap forward that enabled the Set to live even higher and larger at a pace and a scope theretofore unimaginable. But more important than propelling the Set to suddenly convenient exotic places for its conspicuous consumption, the jet propelled the mass public into a whole new level of aspiration. In the process, the Jet Set became far more than the sum of its celebrities.

The Jet Set proved to be a fantasy of great distance and glamorous surroundings and memorable company that was totally within reach. This wasn't some Depression reverie where people from the apple lines went to watch Astaire and Rogers do the Continental in art deco splen-

ADVANCE MAN. Igor Cassini, the columnist who coined the phrase "Jet Set," with his jet-settiest friends John and Jacqueline Kennedy, 1962.

dor. This was a new reality where anyone could be Flying Down to Rio, could become an American in Paris, could have a Roman Holiday. At its core, the Jet Set was a brilliantly inadvertent joint venture of celebrity, technology, and media, whose confluence ended up transforming not only all three elements but the entire society as well.

So first the Set. In its sixties heyday, the jet set (lowercase) was defined by Webster's as "an international social group of wealthy individuals who frequent fashionable resorts." Note that the definition does not mention the conveyance at all. While credit for the first early-sixties coinage of the phrase unofficially went to Igor Cassini, "jet set" was first used in 1951 in Hearst's *San Francisco Examiner*. While the first military jet was flown in 1942, and jets were frequently used to fight the Korean War, extreme speed and extreme luxury had not previously been paired to connote extreme glamour. It took a while for glamour to catch up.

The *Examiner*'s context was one of beachgoing, and it referred to altitude, not to class. "You're strictly jet set if you stake your claim in the dunes . . . Never descend to ocean level except for a quick dunk." Later, in 1956, while the passenger jet was still a gleam in Boeing's eye, *The New York Times* reported the term—for the first time in a social context, albeit far from high (altitude or class) society—in an article about rebellious Communist teenagers when such rebellion was still high-risk. "The term was originated by a young member of a foreign embassy staff in Moscow and refers to the Soviet youth who are attracted to things foreign."

Before that maiden Pan Am flight to Paris in October 1958, the nucleus of the in-crowd who would become associated with the Boeing 707 and the nipping-at-its heels Douglas DC-8 was already formed in the public consciousness, in the pages of *Life* and *Look*, in the gossip columns, on television. Basically, these were superrich people with money who got around, people like Joseph Kennedy of the U.S., Aristotle Onassis and Stavros Niarchos of Greece, Gianni Agnelli of Italy, Aly Khan of France, "Baby" Pignatari of Brazil, all of whom lived the lives that got the press by traveling, not on planes, but on superluxurious yachts.

You didn't necessarily have to be rich to be in this pre–jet set, the "yacht lot," but you needed special qualities that gave you unique access to the tycoons' floating palaces. Frank Sinatra was in the mix because he was the coolest singer/swinger in the world; Porfirio Rubirosa because the Dominican diplomat/polo-playing stud had married both of the two richest heiresses of the era, Doris Duke and Barbara Hutton. But Cary Grant, who was the coolest movie star and had preceded Rubirosa down the aisle with Hutton, was not, because of his obsessive desire for privacy.

Women, for the most part, were in the yacht lot only as decorative appurtenances, unless like Duke or Hutton, they could afford the yachts themselves. Olivia de Havilland and her sister, Joan Fontaine, whose family were the eponymous British jet manufacturers, should have been in this pre–jet set by double virtue of their pedigree and multi-Oscar movie stardom. But they weren't interested in the high life, whether in the sky or in the sea lanes. The most pre–jet set person of all was Howard Hughes, who owned two sets of magic initials, RKO and TWA, a studio and an airline, but he was too paranoid to do anything beyond a party of two, and eventually, two would become a crowd. No set for him.

The Rothschilds were too exclusive to join any set but their own. Notwithstanding those high-profile gallivants the Duke and Duchess of Windsor, English aristocrats, shooting in the moors, tended to be out of the mix, though the consummate Englishman Winston Churchill was an enthusiastic fixture on the Onassis yacht, in one of the unlikeliest friendships of the fifties. And no one was more pre–jet set than mogul Darryl F. Zanuck, who shot glamorous films all over Europe, living like an unholy Roman emperor in the process. The Wahoo, Nebraska, naïf, who broke in to Hollywood writing scripts for *Rin Tin Tin,* was living proof that when it came to defining an aristocracy in the fifties, blood-lines could be offset by lines at the box office.

The roots of the Jet Set are all about this displacement of pedigree by flash, and can be traced to 350 Fifth Avenue, the current site of the Empire State Building. This edifice had its own unique relationship to aviation, not just in the climax of *King Kong* but also through its 1945 front-page encounter with a B-25 Bomber that crashed into the sky-scraper's seventy-ninth floor in a thick fog. But it wasn't this precursor to the airborne terror of 9/11 that links the site to the jet age and its attendant social order: 350 Fifth was the address of the mansion of Mrs. William Backhouse Astor, the richest grande dame of America's Gilded Age, the period from the 1870s to the 1890s. The four hundred people who could fit into Mrs. Astor's grand ballroom (every Fifth Avenue mansion had to have one, like fallout shelters in the 1950s) were designated America's high society, and every change in what was considered America's in-crowd was an evolution—or, in some cases, a deviation—from this original model.

Mrs. Astor, née Caroline "Lina" Schermerhorn, was Old New York, a charter member of Gotham's Dutch founding elite. Her husband was the grandson of John Jacob Astor, the German-descended fur baron and America's first multimillionaire. But in the post–Civil War boom that saw the rise of the robber barons, a couple of generations were sufficient to separate the nobs from the swells, and the Astors could confidently look down on the Vanderbilts and other "new money" as upstart and uncouth. In reality, Mrs. Astor was just a convenient front for the machinations of her Rasputin-like best friend and party planner Ward McAllister, who in 1888 labeled her circle of friends "The 400," the first appellation of a seemingly impenetrable elite that became the lodestar of every outsider who had the dream to rise and shine.

Ward McAllister was the first public snob, the Marquess of Queensbury of social climbing. In setting the rules of the postbellum game of ambition, he put snobbery on the map and turned upward mobility into an imperative. The Martha Stewart/Robin Leach of his day, he installed the rich and their lifestyle onto a national pedestal. A Savannah, Georgia, grandee, McAllister himself was a precursor of Jet Set mobility. His father was a prominent lawyer/politician who lost a campaign for governor of Georgia by less than a thousand votes because his blood was too blue for the increasingly populist populace. Ward's brother Hall sailed around South America to California during the gold rush and made a fortune as a prospectors' attorney in San Francisco, where a major street was named for him. Ward, too, went west and joined the firm, but he hated the relative rigors of forty-niner life. He quickly fled back east, where he found and married a steamboat heiress who was an Astor cousin. Soon after the nuptials, he left his new homebody bride on her horse farm in New Jersey and took off to Europe for a grand tour, traveling in style with his own personal physician.

When Ward returned after a year of continental sophistication, the McAllisters set up a townhouse on Sixteenth Street in Manhattan and a country house, Bayside Farm, in Newport, Rhode Island. Formerly a summer escape for Southern planters, Newport was transformed into the American Riviera by McAllister, renowned for his *fêtes champêtres*, multicourse picnics worthy of the French Impressionists. At his urgings, the great robber-baron families built their summer mansions there, calling them "cottages" because one of McAllister's edicts was that big money was never supposed to blow its own horn. Back in New York, he started a dancing school, created the opera season, and pioneered the then-alien concept of entertaining at public restaurants, rather than at home or in

clubs. He made Delmonico's—just down Sixteenth Street from his pied-
à-terre—the most famous restaurant in America.

Alas, Mrs. McAllister was a homebody who was ailing much of the
time. She hated her husband's extravaganzas, his foxhunts, his carriage
rides, his nights at the opera. So McAllister found a soul mate in Lina
Astor, whose husband avoided partying as much as McAllister's wife did.
Notwithstanding her wealth and position, Mrs. Astor was no beauty.
She was often described, behind her back, as having the visage of an
orangutan. But McAllister made her feel like Venus. He called her his
"Mystic Rose" and used her enormous resources to give what were widely
considered to be the most extravagant parties this side of Versailles. What
were these fetes like? Here's McAllister's description of his "Dresden
Quadrille," held in the Astor ballroom on March 26, 1883:

> The ladies wore white satin, with powdered hair, and the gentlemen
> white satin knee breeches and powdered wigs, with the Dresden
> mark, crossed swords, on each of them . . . The most remarkable cos-
> tume was that of a cat; the dress being of a cat's tails and white cat's
> heads, and a bell with "PUSS" on it in large letters. The Hostess
> (Mrs. Astor) appeared as a Venetian Princess, with a superb jeweled
> peacock in her hair. The host was the Duc de Guise. The host's elder
> brother wore a costume of Louis XVI. His wife appeared as "The
> Electric Light," her head one blaze of diamonds.

McAllister's obvious specialty was theme parties, meticulously re-
searched. He organized a Pinafore quadrille, where everyone dressed as
sailors, and a Mother Goose quadrille, in which all the men wore pink
and sang nursery rhymes. Whatever the theme, the message was the
same: "Let them eat cake." He had even less of an inkling than Louis
XIV that, *après lui,* there might be a deluge.

During his social dictatorship, McAllister became a genuine celebrity in his own right. Newspapers, including the august *New York Times,*
followed his every diktat. Who were the 400? Mostly millionaires like
the Astors themselves, plus a lot of genteel *nouveau pauvre* post–Civil

War Southerners who came north to marry off their polished trophy children to the robber barony. Families like the "Marrying Wilsons," Memphis transplants whose four daughters hit a conjugal jackpot by wedding, respectively, an Astor (Mystic Rose's son); a Vanderbilt; a Goelet, who was Knickerbocker royalty; and, for good measure, a Herbert, who was British royalty.

McAllister, nostalgic for his Savannah plantation past, had a soft spot for Southerners, whom he regarded with far more esteem than the uncouth Northern moneymen. There were few white-collar types in the 400, almost no lawyers, no doctors, just a lot of very big businessmen and very old money: in short, a fairly dull, guarded lot. He had no use whatsoever for artists, writers, singers, even opera stars, other than as hired entertainment. "Remember that Broadway only cuts across Fifth Avenue. It never parallels it," he was fond of saying.

Known as "the Autocrat of Drawing Rooms," McAllister, who placed himself squarely on the 400 list, was surely the most colorful of all. In 1890, he published his bestseller, *Society as I Have Found It*. By then he may have gotten too big for his morning coat. The book was a paean to Southern aristocracy and a broadside against Yankee parvenuity. The book basically lampooned the "society" McAllister had created above the Mason-Dixon Line, biting the many white-gloved hands that had fed him champagne and caviar. Typically, he wrote about the Southern view "that they alone lived well, and that there was no such thing as good society in New York or other Northern cities, that New Yorkers and other people are simply a lot of tradespeople, having no antecedents, springing up like the mushroom, who did not know how to live."

While McAllister had done his best to "educate" New York in the ways of the Old South, he declared that the rest of the rapidly industrializing United States was basically a lost cause. He decried "the sharp character of Chicago magnates . . . Their growth has been too rapid to allow them to acquire both wealth and culture. Their leaders of society are the successful Stock Yard magnates, cottolene manufacturers, soupmakers, Chicago gas trust speculators and dry good princes . . ." The hog butchers of the world soon ganged up to turn Ward McAllister into bacon.

Under pressure from her friends, and not just from Chicago, McAllister's Mystic Rose severed their long relationship. Mrs. Astor informed her grand vizier that from now on, she would populate her own ballroom and create her own guest lists.

Bereft, McAllister withdrew from society, telling the press "it's more of a bore than a pleasure to me. I merely perform my functions, you understand." In the bitter winter of 1895, he died of the grippe after dining, all by himself, at the Union Club. He was sixty-eight. He would have found consolation that his funeral at Grace Church on Broadway, the temple of high society, was packed even tighter than Mrs. Astor's ballroom, with the Episcopal bishop of Mississippi leading the service, a thirty-voice choir, and a society ballroom orchestra to dance the blues away.

Despite the rise of the tabloidish "yellow press" and the epic battles between William Randolph Hearst and Joseph Pulitzer to capture a national imagination that was stirred like nothing else by images of wealth and excess, Ward McAllister's unique position as the ultimate social arbiter somehow stayed vacant until 1921. With the rise of the giant monopolistic trusts that so exercised Teddy Roosevelt and other reformers, big money became front-page news. However, society, such as it was, had taken too religiously to McAllister's commands of tastefulness to make for riveting copy. The muckraked excesses of the big businesses were far more fascinating than the excesses of the big businessmen outside the boardrooms.

Tiptoeing into the McAllister void was a failed gunsmith and dairy farmer named Louis Keller, who found some success as a golf course developer. He finally hit the jackpot by tapping in to McAllister's discovery of the power of exclusionary lists. Keller created the black-and-red *Social Register,* a small, handsome, annually printed hardcover book that enumerated the names, addresses, schools, and clubs of the "right people," as defined by Keller. The *Social Register* had reached its peak of influence by the time of Keller's death at sixty-five in 1922. The problem with the *Register* was that while it played to the egos of its listees, it did nothing for the imaginations of everyone else. It was so rigid, stuffy, and intolerant, with a divorce or a marriage to a Jew or a thespian, or, God forbid, a showgirl, grounds for expulsion, that it might as well have been called the *Book of the Dead*. But then Keller dropped dead, the movies emerged as the national pastime, and Prohibition turned America into a nation of hypocritical, hip-flask-toting, technically illegal party animals. Society, at last, began to loosen up.

There to report it was the country's first great but unlikely gossip columnist, a tubby teetotaler who lived with his mother; his name was Maury Henry Biddle Paul. That third name was Paul's main claim to Main Line social fame, along with his three years at the University of Pennsylvania. But the Biddles never claimed Paul, and neither did Penn. After dropping out, he worked for a while in a machine foundry and then sold costume jewelry door-to-door before finding his niche as a Philadelphia society columnist, listing weddings, charity balls, and the like for *The Philadelphia Inquirer*.

When his editor at that journal decamped for New York in 1914, Paul, then twenty-four, followed him, finding piecework at four Manhattan rags and writing under a different pseudonym at each one. He made his first Manhattan faux pas while covering an opening night at the Metropolitan Opera. Not knowing Who Was Who on his new turf, he created a list of first-nighters by copying the names on the brass donors' plaques in the prime boxes. What he didn't realize was that most of these aristocratic donors were not live at the Met but buried at Woodlawn Cemetery, Gotham's graveyard of the rich. His understanding editor gave Paul credit for his efforts and another chance.

Paul's big break came in 1919 when William Randolph Hearst was trying to get the attention of his mistress Marion Davies, who was engrossed in a newspaper that Hearst did not own. "What are you reading?" Hearst demanded. "Dolly Madison," the actress replied. "Get Dolly" was Hearst's command. What he got was not what he expected: Dolly was Maury Paul. Hearst didn't care. If "Dolly" was good enough for his mistress, he was good enough for the chief. Hearst hired Paul at a salary said to be higher than that of Edward Douglass White, the chief justice of the Supreme Court, and Paul became the hanging judge of the new order he named "Café Society." Not bad for an under-thirty drop-out. The column was called "Cholly Knickerbocker," a play on the Washington Irving character Diedrich Knickerbocker, a pretentious Dutch historian whom Irving had created in the early 1800s as the author of Irving's *A History of New York,* a satire on Yankee pomposity. Cholly was the way fancy New Yorkers pronounced "Charlie," as in Good Time Charlie.

A born list-o-phile, Maury Paul, who loved coining phrases, divided New York into two warring camps, pitching his Café Society against what he called the "Old Guard," the Mrs. Astor set. Not that the Café people were Sacco and Vanzetti or a bunch of avant-garde artists. Rather, they tended to be Old Guard types who, instead of sitting in their clubs or drawing rooms, liked going out to restaurants and speakeasies and, when they were there, were not too snobbish to mix with new money whom they probably wouldn't have invited into their mansions. They weren't all that different from the nobs McAllister entertained at Delmonico's, just a bit younger and looser. And, unlike the Old Guard who eschewed all notoriety beyond weddings, funerals, and debuts, Café Society liked, really liked, getting their names in the papers. With the rise of the tabloid press and the movies, the hypnotic power of the image became the civilized world's leitmotif. Publicity became the drug, fame the cure, and Maury Paul the doctor to New Society.

Paul, too, became a major celebrity, just as Ward McAllister had, as famous as most of the swells his constant repetition in his column turned into household names, people like Jock Whitney, "Little" Gloria Vanderbilt, Barbara Hutton, Doris Duke, and superdeb Brenda Frazier. One of the wittier of his endless witty headlines was a profile of the Duchess of Windsor's first husband, Ernest Simpson, entitled "The Unimportance of Being Ernest." Many of the clichés Paul used over and over would enter the lexicon of the period, such as "chitchat," "glamour girl," "Longuyland," "Reno-vation" (for a divorce), "snobility," "oodles of ducats," "heir-conditioned," "yours truly."

Paul was featured out and about on his nightly rounds in huge magazine spreads such as a 1941 issue of *Life,* showing him dressing in black tie and drenching himself in cologne in his East Side penthouse (his live-in mother wasn't mentioned), with Rubenses and heraldic crests on his walls and houseboys at his beck and call. Once groomed, he hit every-thing from debutante balls to El Morocco, sitting with the Vanderbilts, Condé Nast, Brenda Frazier, nixing the champagne and sipping his own special tea blend, all the while collecting a then-behemoth annual $100,000 Hearst salary for what most post-Depression Americans had to think was the coolest writing job in the world. He had pulled a fast one, getting paid oodles of ducats to live the Fred and Ginger life. Paul was syndicated in more than a hundred newspapers and had five million readers.

Even if Maury Paul had gotten his start in the gossip business pre-tending to be "Dolly Madison," there were almost no women whatso-ever in the gossip trade. Yes, there were female "society editors" at many newspapers, but the trench warfare that was gossip itself, no matter how gilded, was effectively off-limits for the fairer sex. The glass ceiling here was shattered by Elsa Maxwell, who, in addition to becoming the great-est "party professional" of the century, became one of the leading gossip writers and an autocratic social arbiter who might have put Ward McAl-lister on her own waiting list.

Maxwell's background for her position was even less likely than that of Maury Paul. Elsa Maxwell, a poor and portly girl from Keokuk, Iowa, was born in a box at the theater when her pregnant culture-vulture mother couldn't bear to miss the next act at the opera. The homeschooled daughter of an insurance broker who eventually moved the family to San Francisco, Elsa never got over her parents' being snubbed for the guest list of a party honoring a California senator's daughter who was marry-ing a Vanderbilt. A woman who would become famous for her grudges against the rich and famous, Maxwell started with the Vanderbilts, vow-ing, according to her memoirs, "that no one would give more parties, with less Vanderbilts, than I would."

To that end, Maxwell, who had learned to play the piano, hired her-self out to a traveling vaudeville company. She went as far as South Af-rica, and toured Europe before World War I. Along the way, she became

cleverly sophisticated, a quality she brought back to New York and used
to ingratiate herself with the reigning queen of Manhattan society, Mrs.
Oliver Hazard Perry Vanderbilt Belmont, née Alva Smith. Alva was an
upwardly mobile belle from Mobile, Alabama, whose mother had come
to post–Civil War New York to run a boardinghouse. The rentals paid
for the Worth gowns she dressed her daughter in. Alva's mother's sacri-
fices paid off as Alva married, in succession, a Vanderbilt and a Belmont,
two of America's greatest fortunes.

The cheeky, witty Alva came to adore the cheeky, witty Elsa, in
whom she had found a kindred spirit. Alva was a proto-feminist, as was
Elsa, who kept a beautiful lesbian companion (but no sex ever, she
claimed), "Dickie" Fellowes-Gordon, from 1912 until her death in
1963. Maxwell had an uncanny knack for betting on the right horses. As
with Alva Belmont, she was close to Jane Campbell from Bernardsville,
New Jersey, who went to Europe, like Elsa, and, unlike Elsa, went the
wedding-belle route, becoming the Countess di San Faustino and the
grandmother of Fiat auto mogul Gianni Agnelli, assuring Elsa Maxwell's
tenure through three generations of Euro-glamour, from steamship, to
the propeller-driven flying boats, to the jets. Ensuring her Jet Set inevitability, Elsa did not tether herself to high society alone. She "discovered"
a young Cole Porter and sang his songs at parties where he played before
he was famous. She staged concerts at Venice's Lido by Porter and Noël
Coward, whom she had befriended in her London vaudeville days. She
was pals with Fanny Brice, George Gershwin, Vladimir Horowitz, all of
whom she got to play at the parties she became famous for giving, so
famous that she would charge socialites a small fortune for giving them.
Her scavenger hunts, started in Paris during the Jazz Age, were her trademark. She became the greatest freeloader in history, traveling the world
first-class, first by ship, then by plane, and paying for nothing except
with her connections.

Maury Paul died at the height of his power in 1942, at fifty-two, of
a heart ailment. Into the breach stepped Elsa Maxwell, who was quickly
syndicated in twenty papers and given her own radio show, *Party Line*.
Her high-water mark occurred in October 1944, when she gave the

party of the year in Hollywood, "Free France," to celebrate the liberation of Paris. Renting a mansion in Beverly Hills, she assembled 130 stars; it was the first time most of them had donned evening clothes since Pearl Harbor. It was a classic melding of society, Hollywood, and the higher arts. The pianist Arthur Rubinstein played accordion while Danny Kaye played bass and Elsa dominated the piano. Barbara Hutton and Cary Grant, just divorced, were there, separate but equal, Grant dancing with Anita Colby, the highest-paid model of her generation.

Barbara Hutton, again the most eligible woman in the country, hoofed with Igor Cassini's brother, Oleg. Igor was still off at war as an army sergeant in Paris (where else?). A rising gossip columnist in Washington, D.C., Igor had been tapped by Hearst in 1943 to replace Maury Paul as the new Cholly Knickerbocker, assuming he got back in one piece and not in a box. Oleg was then a struggling designer who had hit the showbiz jackpot by marrying movie star Gene Tierney (*Laura*), who, that magic Maxwell night, was busy socializing with Orson Welles and Rita Hayworth and Lana Turner and the Charles Boyers. Both Judy Garland and Frank Sinatra performed—for free. Elsa Maxwell never paid anyone but herself. Maxwell admitted that while this fete was her "pièce de résistance," she tantalized the world by promising that her next one would be atop the Acropolis. She kept that promise, and kept the public panting for more.

Elsa Maxwell's best friend in Beverly Hills and the woman who footed the bills for most of Maxwell's parties was Countess Dorothy di Frasso, who was without question the most proto–Jet Set woman on earth. Her life was so dizzyingly mobile that it seemed the 707 had been designed specifically for her. Like Jane Campbell, Dorothy Caldwell Taylor was a Jersey girl who dreamed of living overseas. Unlike Jane Campbell, she was an heiress-socialite, having inherited $12 million from her leather-tycoon father. Her brother was the youngest governor of the New York Stock Exchange. She quickly took the money and ran abroad. Entranced by the new romance of aviation, Dorothy chose as her first husband a pioneer British pilot, Claude Grahame-White, famous for making the first night flight from London to Manchester and the first flight over the White House on a barnstorming visit to Washington in 1910. He was also an RAF hero in World War I, the English answer to the German Red Baron.

When the aviation marriage crashed and burned, Dorothy, wanting to remain in Europe, went the royal route, marrying in 1923 the Italian count Carlo di Frasso, thirty years her senior. They lived north of Rome in Renaissance splendor at the Villa Madama, which was designed by Raphael. The "madama" for whom the villa was named was Margaret of Austria, the bastard daughter of the Holy Roman Emperor who was engaged at age five and married at ten to Alessandro de' Medici, himself the illegitimate son of a pope and an African servant. When Alessandro was assassinated in his twenties, Margaret, then fifteen, remarried the thirteen-year-old Ottavio Farnese, the Duke of Parma. Who ever said that the sexual revolution had to wait for the Jet Set?

Dorothy di Frasso was as liberated as they came. She and the count had a fairly open marriage, and she used the villa as an aphrodisiac, luring in the likes of Gary Cooper and Cary Grant for long-term torrid affairs. But the love of her life was the gangster Benjamin ("Never call me 'Bugsy'") Siegel, whom she had met in Hollywood and invited to Rome to visit the Villa Madama in 1938. There were two other houseguests, on a visit to Mussolini: Joseph Goebbels, Hitler's minister of propaganda; and Hermann Göring, who headed the Luftwaffe and was Hitler's designated successor. Siegel, who was well aware of Hitler's rabid anti-Semitism, was set to kill both men right there at the Villa Madama. If he had, World War II might never have happened. But Dorothy had a soft spot for Göring, who had been a World War I flying ace like her ex-husband. And she had a softer spot for her husband, who tolerated her endless indiscretions and whom she was certain Mussolini would blame and kill for whatever Siegel did to his Axis partners. So she talked Siegel back to bed and out of war.

Dorothy died at sixty-eight in 1954, right after spending a wild New Year's holiday with Marlene Dietrich in Las Vegas at the El Rancho Hotel. Siegel, who was shot to death in Beverly Hills in 1947, had taught Dorothy to love the desert oasis he built. Accompanied by actor Clifton

Webb, she took the Union Pacific's Los Angeles Limited back to L.A. She was found dead in her roomette wearing $250,000 worth of jewelry and a mink coat, with an empty bottle of nitroglycerin pills by her side. She had been felled by a heart attack.

The countess's death naturally got major play in the Cholly Knickerbocker column, whose new Cholly, Igor Cassini, had made the world all but forget his predecessor Maury Paul. Cassini, who did dote on his adored mother and her every word, nonetheless did not live with her, like his predecessor did with his. Igor was a stud, a real stud, yet one with brains and wit. He was a genuinely titled European royal playboy bon vivant, the scion of a distinguished line of diplomats. For probably the first time in the history of gossip, the columnist *was* what he was writing about. Furthermore, this one actually set the agenda that his subjects followed. He was the real deal. Yet he got no respect. Because of the absurdities of his predecessors—the pomposity of McAllister, the effeminacy of Paul, the avarice of Maxwell, Cassini became the whipping boy of the serious press. His investiture in November 1945 as Cholly, at the jealousy-stirring age of thirty, was duly noted in the then-august *Time*, but oh so snidely.

EAGER IGOR was the headline. "Anything can happen in America," *Time* wrote. "Less than ten years ago, slight, pompadoured little Igor Loiewski-Cassini landed in the U.S. with only $10, a hint of a titled past, and a lean and hungry look. By last week, at 30, as the new Cholly Knickerbocker . . . he had reached the peak in his particular field." Asked about his standards for his new position, Igor told *Time* he planned to concentrate on what he called the "International Smart Set." Trying to show the world he was no Paulian stuffed shirt, Igor declared, "I think it is very important not to develop a pot belly." Then he mused on being home from war, "Peace, it's wonderful! What a change from the muddy boots, the shivering cold, the caked blood . . ." The article closed with Igor's exuberant forecast, "We're in for an era of mad spending and fun-making."

Igor's first column in *The New York Journal-American* was his declaration of independence from the perfumed ghost of Maury Paul. Instead of aiming his poison pen at the Old Guard in Mrs. Astor's ballroom, the new Cholly expanded his purview to include, as he enumerated in his first column, "dispossessed dukes and diplomats, broken down eighteen carat European aristocrats and upcoming foreign phonies, bored businessmen dragged out of their offices by their fun-loving, socially ambitious wives, to say nothing of long-haired artists, writers, actors, cover girls with perfectly painted faces and impeccable legs, eager 'Souz-Americanos' with pockets full of pesetas and an eye for pretty girls, and people whose only social introduction is that they can buy themselves a ringside table." Add the 707 to the mix, and a decade or so later, you would have the Jet Set.

Even then, after his Jet Set had taken off and Cassini had become more powerful than Paul and Maxwell combined—and nearly as ubiquitous in the media as the syndicated gossip columnist and radio broadcaster Walter Winchell, who had an audience of over fifty million worldwide—he still continued to get no respect. That Elsa Maxwell did not mention his name once in her 1954 memoir, *RSVP,* can be written off to their rivalry. But the preeminent social historian Cleveland Amory's Siberianization of Igor to one brief mention in his weighty 1962 tome *Who Killed Society?* was a commentary on the virulent column envy Igor Cassini engendered. Amory's thesis was that "Society" had been elbowed out by what he called "Publi-ciety," in which celebrity ruled and the ultimate validation was getting one's name in the paper or, even better, on television. Amory was clearly nostalgic for the Old Guard. By making Igor Cassini virtually unmentionable, Amory was trying to give the upstart the worst dose of his own medicine: anonymity. That Igor could engender such a reaction was testimony to his remarkable influence as a celebrity-maker in an age when fame was becoming the ultimate reward.

Just who was this intrepid future pilot of the Jet Set? Or, as the Old Guard viewed him, the terrorist hijacker of the Good Ship Society? He was born Igor Aleksandrovich Loiewski Cassini in Sebastopol, in the Crimea, sometime around 1916 (he was never specific), on the eve of the Bolshevik Revolution that would transform his diplomatic family into international nomads, the precursors of what became known derisively as Eurotrash. In fact, much like Countess Dorothy di Frasso and other fellow travelers, they were "Jet Set" decades before the 707 was a figment of Pan Am founder Juan Trippe's soaring imagination.

Igor's mastery of networking was genetic, inherited from his mother, Marguerite. A Russian countess whose father had been the tsar's minister to Peking and then to Washington, fluent in six languages, Marguerite became the instant toast of the embassy circuit. Her best friends were the future Alice Longworth, Teddy Roosevelt's daughter; Helen Hay, daughter of Secretary of State John Hay, who would marry tycoon and über-philanthropist Payne Whitney; and Cissy Patterson, heiress to the Medill-McCormick Chicago newspaper dynasty. Patterson would give Igor Cassini his first newspaper job, as a favor to "Maman."

Countess Cassini followed her father to his newest post in Madrid, then decamped to Paris to study voice. There was a lot of Café Society in Old Guard Marguerite, who embraced Paris and married significantly below her station. The lucky man was also royalty, albeit Polish royalty. He was Count Alexander Loiewski, a spoiled clotheshorse and bon vivant whose father—a lawyer who made his living finding lost heirs of large unclaimed inheritances—shot himself when a make-or-break case fell through. The young count worked in low-level diplomatic posts that took him to the Crimea, after which the 1917 Bolshevik Revolution put him out of business.

The Loiewskis, hocking a Fabergé cross and other imperial trinkets, escaped to Montreux, Switzerland, then to Florence, where Marguerite ran a boutique on the Via Tornabuoni, the Fifth Avenue of Florence. Oleg and Ghighi, as Igor was called (hard G's as opposed to the soft ones of Colette's *Gigi*), were educated at a school run by Jesuit friars, with the goal of their becoming Florentine gentlemen. It was a big challenge, as the two young counts (they each inherited their father's title at birth) were known as "the little Cossacks" in a city where every chauffeur seemed to have a Russian title. While Oleg was tall and thin and Ghighi much smaller, both boys became great skiers, horseback riders, tennis players, and ballroom dancers, as well as piano players, skills that would come in handy in their social conquest of America. In the summer, the family went to Forte dei Marmi, the Tuscan version of the Hamptons, where the boys' beachmates included Gianni Agnelli and Emilio Pucci.

Even as children, the Cassini boys, goaded by their ultra-ambitious mother, were all about contacts and networking. To ensure that the boys were perfectly equipped to network at the very top, the countess hired as their tutors a former officer in the Russian Imperial Guards and a displaced Georgian prince, to give the boys a spit and polish that even the toniest American prep schools, like Groton and St. Paul's, could never touch. In his memoir, Igor fondly recalled his teachers and reduced their lessons into six basis precepts: "1. Never speak to grown-ups until they speak to you. 2. Know how to bow correctly. 3. Remember to kiss the hands of married ladies. 4. Know how to use which fork for what. 5. Wear white gloves when dancing with royal princesses. 6. Never lie and never show any fear."

The schooling finished, the countess dispatched Oleg to Rome to study fashion design, in hopes that they would have a business together one day. Meanwhile, Igor, who lacked Oleg's visual sense, was whistling Dixie. Having spent a few desultory months in Paris studying international law, always with the idea of becoming a diplomat, Igor decided the Old World was for old people like his parents. America had become his goal, especially after he was smitten with a Richmond, Virginia, belle who had the quintessentially Southern name of Archer Coke. Miss Coke was going to an international finishing school in Florence called Miss May's. Igor dropped the law. Arming himself with his father's tuxedo and Charvet formal shirts and his mother's high-society friends' calling cards, he finagled a free passage to New York in 1933 on a cargo ship owned by a family contact. The countess gave him the grand allowance of two dollars a day for several months. It was the Depression. He was lucky as hell to be traveling at all.

Igor was as entranced by Richmond as he had been by Archer Coke, who was now at home on the deb circuit. Even before the novel came out in 1936, he loved the whole *Gone with the Wind* ambience, the Cokes' Tara-like columned residence, the liveried black retainers, the mint juleps, the fragrance of the magnolias. Sadly for Igor, Archer Coke was much less taken with him in Richmond than she had seemed to be in Florence. At one cotillion, when he was supposed to be waltzing, Igor decided to show off with a wild and crazy Cossack dance, kicking his legs out from a squatting position. All Archer could see was red. Which was worse, Igor's lack of decorum or the big holes in the soles of his shoes? Archer sent the Russian packing to Yankeeland, where he found the cheapest lodgings in New York at Columbia University's International House and set out to network with his mother's important friends.

Again disaster. No one called him back, no Whitneys, no Roosevelts, no one. Igor's salvation came from an Italian, his beach-boy friend Emilio Pucci, who, also entranced with all things antebellum, had enrolled at the University of Georgia in Athens on an exchange program. Pucci told Igor to jump the first train from Penn Station to Georgia. There was an opening for a tennis coach at the university, and Igor could play. Thus Igor came to Athens and, in a match that his future depended on, managed to defeat the college champion and got the job. He also ending up tutoring, along with backhand, Italian and French.

Pucci and Cassini couldn't have been happier at Harvard, which couldn't match the weather or the women, not to mention the Southern hospitality. The Italian boys were lionized on campus as the experts in the emerging European fascism. The governor of Georgia, Eugene Talmadge, was a big fan of the seemingly crackerjack efficiency expert Mussolini, and the tidbit that Igor's brother was designing dresses for Il Duce's daughter helped make Igor big man on campus. His Southern exposure also made him big man in Rome when he went back to Italy in 1934 to visit his family. Oleg, the family fashion plate, was wowed by Igor's new Joe College style: camel coats, porkpie hats, white bucks, and gray flannels. Plus, Igor could do the fox-trot and the dip. Igor brought Oleg a copy of the single "Moon Over Miami," which Oleg couldn't stop playing. Now Oleg wanted his turn in America.

At a tennis tournament in Venice, Oleg found an American sponsor, a newspaperman named Victor Ridder. Ridder published the German *Zeitung* in New York; it would become the nucleus of the Knight-Ridder print colossus. Declaring he had friends at Saks Fifth Avenue, Ridder promised Oleg a job in the rag trade. Igor got Oleg the American uniform of a gray flannel suit and a porkpie hat. That, his dinner jacket, and his tennis racket, Igor assured him, were all he would need. In 1936 the brothers set out together to make their mark in the Brave New World. Assuming that mark would be made quickly, the parents—armed with visas gotten for them by one of Marguerite's old beaux who had become the French ambassador to Italy—planned their arrival for the next year.

Ridder couldn't get Oleg in to Saks, but he did get him a post as a very junior designer for Jo Copeland, a major manufacturer on Seventh Avenue, who quickly fired him. Igor's own term at Georgia had come to an end, and the two brothers found cold-water digs over a smelly delicatessen on far West Fifty-first Street for fifty cents a day. The two Euro-gourmets subsisted on hot dogs at Nedick's, a chain they dubbed "La Salle Orange." Igor, like Oleg, needed a job. He still had fantasies of becoming a diplomat, but his reality was hawking cold cream door-to-door.

Nonetheless, Igor was indefatigable. He was already a young master at mobilizing royal contacts. He soon connected with another Italian count, who was trying to introduce the bidet to Park Avenue. His new friend failed, because the device was viewed by Puritans as impure, but not before introducing Igor to the Italo-American Tammany power broker, Generoso Pope. Pope was the owner-publisher of *Il Progresso,* the largest Italian newspaper in the country, and a pivotal supporter of Franklin Roosevelt. Pope was also a big Mussolini fan, but so were lots of Americans when Il Duce was doing nothing more sinister than making the trains run on time. Pope's son, Generoso Jr., would go on to found *The National Enquirer.*

Thus, early on, the Cassini boys were knee-deep in newsprint's upper reaches. Igor was literally covered in newsprint. He had thought Mr. Pope was going to make him a reporter. Instead, Pope made him a night-shift proofreader at $30 a week. Igor supplemented that with an even lower-paying day job at the Italian Tourist Office as a ticket clerk. Meanwhile, Oleg, who couldn't find anything that paid, simply played a lot of tennis, as well as Ping-Pong, becoming a local champion. The boys certainly weren't in the best shape to receive their parents, who arrived in 1937 and settled in gloomy walk-up digs in the predominantly German Yorkville, the most unfashionable precinct of the Upper East Side.

To support his parents in the style to which they once were accustomed, Igor sold a bust of Nicolas II, which the tsar himself had given to his grandfather, to the antique emporium A La Vieille Russie for $500. Much of that money the brothers squandered on outings to the Stork Club, just to remind themselves why they had decided to come to New York in the first place. At the same time, while father Cassini moped around the flat in Yorkville, making borscht and pierogis on his hot plate, the countess took to riding the escalators at Macy's, up and down, up and down, hours at a time.

Her own depression notwithstanding, Marguerite Cassini, now fifty-five, was not going to allow her sons' occupational torpor to continue. Accordingly, she traveled to Washington, D.C., to call in a favor from Eleanor "Cissy" Medill Patterson, the Chicago newspaper heiress who herself, in a tour de force of early feminism, had used her fortune to purchase two Washington papers from William Randolph Hearst; merge them into one, *The Washington Times-Herald;* and run it by herself. Cissy had a private railway car, gave legendary parties, and was a stunning and stylish redhead, but her main claim to fame now was that she was a working girl. Marguerite asked her to give Igor a job.

Cissy acceded, though she didn't hold much hope for the tryout. But Igor seized the opportunity, for it may have been his last. He got his very first scoop by discovering that Vittorio Mussolini, the cineast son of the dictator who published his own movie magazine, was visiting Chevy Chase. He tracked him down, played his Italian royalty card—not revealing his press ties—and got him to open up. The result was a big article and Igor's first byline: Igor Loiewski-Cassini. The editor couldn't understand the L-word and dropped it. Igor Cassini was on his way, and he never looked back.

Igor started work in 1938. A year later, despite his byline, he was languishing on the obituaries desk. Despite all his and his mother's contacts, there was no room at the top at Cissy Patterson's paper, which had two established society columnists covering embassy parties and the like. The ever enterprising Igor thus decided to create his own niche: the *young* society column, the smart junior set, of which he, in his early twenties, was a member, cutting his swath though deb-land. Cissy gave him a shot, naming the column "Petit Point," which locals derided as "petticoat."

Aiding Igor was his new girlfriend, a sleek titian-tressed debutante from the Middleburg, Virginia, hunt country outside the capital. Austine "Bootsie" McDonnell, the daughter of a career army officer, was Igor's opportunity to recapture the lost love of his first Virginia belle, Archer Coke. Bootsie was great-looking, popular, and a major source of gossip; plus, she could help Igor with his accented English. However, Bootsie's various and sundry charms made her a prime object of local desire, and the competition for her hand was more than figuratively fierce. Igor's fatal attraction to Southern beauties proved nearly that when, in June 1939, three of his local rivals for Bootsie lay in wait for Igor outside a country club dance, beat him senseless, stripped him, and covered him with heating oil used to pave the roads. Two of the boys were the sons of a woman about whom Igor had written sarcastically in his column.

The previously unknown little foreigner suddenly became front-page news all over the country. The press romanticized the attack as "tar and feathering," the stuff Old Virginians did to damn Yankees, "foreigners," and other objects of their xenophobia, and sprang to Igor's defense, elevating him from petty gossip columnist to fearless crusading journalist. Among the celebrated fellow columnists who took up his cause were Walter Winchell and Maury Paul, who then reigned supreme as Hearst's Cholly Knickerbocker. Paul's encomium to young Cassini concluded, "Until you find a bomb every night in your car, until people wait in the street to beat you up, until you be chased from every club and are the fear of every hostess, you will not be a newspaperman." For now, Igor seemed like the most intrepid newsman around.

The trial, which took place in Warrenton in November 1939, pitted the Old World against the Old South. The three defendant/assailants, two Montgomerys and a Calvert, great Virginia names, were portrayed by their lawyer, a state senator of the high-bombast school, as flowers of post-Confederate manhood, heirs to the noble Old Dominion traditions of Robert E. Lee, standing up for the honor of their family and their community against this uppity foreign "count" who was now a "chit-chat" columnist.

The Virginia boys were accused of such un-Leeish, loutish behavior as looting Igor's wallet when he was being tarred, as well as threatening to castrate him. Despite the senator's summation that Igor had not been harmed physically, only humiliated, and that the boys "had done a public service to this community," the three were convicted of "constituting a mob" and committing assault and fined several hundred dollars. More important, the national publicity the case generated had made the copy-boy into a star.

A few months after the verdict, the woman who wrote the social column "These Charming People" for the *Times-Herald* married the *New York Times* D.C. bureau chief and stepped down. Immediately, Cissy Patterson summoned Igor Cassini to step up. She gave him the column and raised his weekly salary from $30 to $100, and he proceeded to transform the column, as he said, from "saccharin to sarcasm," oblivious to any risks of tar and feathers.

Igor's big raise impelled him to take Bootsie McDonnell off a market whose competitiveness was demonstrated by the tar affair. This time Igor was up against far bigger sharks than the local gentry. Howard Hughes himself had invited Bootsie to Hollywood and offered to put her under contract. She had already won a bit part in a big Broadway musical, *Two for the Show,* where Hughes discovered her. Once he learned that she had eloped with Igor, in April 1940, Hughes just as quickly undiscovered her. He never picked up her contract, and Bootsie slunk back to George-town, where Igor had bought them a little love nest that realtors had described to him as a "Negro shack." He had put down $1,500 against the $5,000 price. After World War II, he would sell it for six times that.

During the war, Igor hit his stride as the bête noire of the New Deal.

At one 1942 holiday event given by high financier Bernard Baruch in honor of Roosevelt right hand Harry Hopkins, a major prophet of austerity, Igor regaled his readers with the buffet of foie gras, caviar, "truite en gelée," and "homard en aspic" devoured by such guests as Hollywood's Darryl Zanuck and Melvyn Douglas and told them the price tag of $3,000 for the event, or as he put it, "88,200 bullets." That particular exposé infuriated the White House so much Igor believed his subsequent draft notice was an act of retaliation. He was quickly and mysteriously reclassified 1-A (cannon fodder) after having hypochondriac-ed his way to a 4-F deferment the year before by getting wasted beyond life itself the evening before his physical.

The war was initially déjà vu to the war-weary Cassini and his endlessly displaced family, the same old same old Euro game of nations (the genocide horrors hadn't come out yet). He was all for isolation, all for partying, all for furthering his booming career. The "Uncle Sam Wants You" notice was particularly inopportune because, just before the Hopkins scoop, Igor had gotten the chance to make the career move of a lifetime.

It was fall 1942 in Manhattan when a beautiful woman accosted Igor on Fifth Avenue and introduced herself as Lorelle Hearst, the wife of William Randolph Hearst, Jr., son of *Citizen Kane* himself. Hearst Sr. was still the most powerful news mogul in America. Lorelle, a Dallas actress turned war correspondent thanks to her husband's patronage, was a huge fan of Igor's saucy style, so huge that they began a secret affair that weekend. Between the sheets, she suggested that Igor send some of his clippings to her father-in-law, Big Bill. Maury Paul, Cholly Knickerbocker, the king of gossip, had just died in July. Wags feigned surprise that this ruthless arbiter of society even had a heart to fail, and other, more cerebral outlets, such as *Time* magazine, predicted the concurrent death of both "society" and the frivolous social gossip column, in the context of the deadly seriousness of the war effort at hand. Lorelle Hearst knew better. Convinced there would always be a niche for gossip, she believed that no one writing was better equipped to fill it than her bedmate Igor Cassini.

Lorelle got her man in more ways than one. Just before Igor reported for his induction physical, he got the nod from Hearst's *Journal-American:* He was tapped to become the new Cholly Knickerbocker. They agreed to hold the post open for two years, presuming he would come back alive. If he did, he had a lot to live for. His salary would be $300 a week, plus another $100 for expenses. Cissy had seemed a high roller at $100. Now Igor was moving up to starland. Maury Paul himself was earning $2,000 a week when he died, the highest of any reporter in the world. All Igor had to do was survive to be able to get to that heaven.

Igor did not tell Cissy Patterson of his job offer. What if the war dragged on and he didn't get back in time? Fortunately, he had a perfect fallback in his wife. Inspired by Igor's success, Bootsie had decided that she, too, would like to be a gossip columnist, an Elsa Maxwell with looks. Igor thus convinced Cissy to let Bootsie realize these journalistic ambitions by taking over "These Charming People" in his absence. Theoretically, Bootsie was unaware of Igor's job-creating affair with Lorelle Hearst. However, she claimed she was so overwhelmed with her new job that she was unable to come to New York to meet her husband on his last weekend before being shipped overseas. Igor's mother came instead. The countess was always there for him.

Igor went to Europe aboard the *Mauretania,* which had been converted into a cattle-car troop ship whose D-deck, where he was billeted, he compared to "slow death in the Lincoln Tunnel, worse than any battle I later had to cover." That kind of hyperbole was what had won him the job as Cholly. After experiencing the buzz bombs of besieged London, he was sent to liberated Paris and found, as only Igor could find, a luxe apartment in the *seizième arrondissement* as his army digs. In Paris, in addition to a plum flat, he got a plum job, assigned to put his writerly skills to use on *Warweek,* the magazine component of *Stars and Stripes,* the official army newspaper.

Although he served with distinction and won several battle stars, the isolationist Igor still felt weird about being at war, fighting on the side of the Russian Communists who had ruined his family's life, fighting against his Italian countrymen. Because of his European roots and anti-

FDR politics, not to mention his curious draft reclassification, Igor suspected that Washington was somehow out to get him. That suspicion exploded into paranoia when, after the German surrender, he was reassigned to the Pacific theater, an extension of his tour of duty that would have cost him his Cholly future. Back in D.C. en route to Japan, Igor checked in to Walter Reed Army Medical Center complaining of "battle fatigue." Its chief manifestation, Igor told the doctors, was impotence. The doctors bought the pitch, and Igor got his discharge and his new identity as Cholly.

Igor summarized his new target as what he called "the Spotlighted Creatures," the prototype of which was none other than his brother. Oleg, growing more handsome and rakish as he aged, in the last five years had married, in succession, the gorgeous cough-syrup heiress Merry Fahrney, then the even more gorgeous movie star Gene Tierney. Oleg was now part of the Hollywood firmament, just as Igor was a key part of the Fifth Estate, a member of a gossipocracy led by Walter Winchell and Ed Sullivan in New York, and Hedda Hopper and Louella Parsons on the Cinema Coast. There, Oleg had had his own dustup with Hopper, who insinuated that he was a gigolo and called his mustache a symbol of his European immorality. Oleg sent her a famous telegram— "O.K., Hedda, you shave yours, I'll shave mine"—which forever short-circuited her vitriol toward him.

Igor hit the press running. His Oleg-showbiz inside track notwithstanding, he began his Cholly life focusing on the Newport/Hamptons/Manhattan/Palm Beach corridor, playing to the New Yorkers who were his core readers by profiling the leading members of the *Social Register*. *Time,* his nemesis, was not on his side, catching out "Eager Igor" for basically cribbing verbatim all his material from a scholarly book, *The Saga of American Society,* as well as recycling such hackneyed Maury Paul column-isms as "Reno-vation" and "Longuyland." Igor was impervious to any criticism. Seeing himself in print was the best revenge.

To be close to the action, Igor moved to New York, where Bootsie, who kept Igor's old column in Washington, would visit him on weekends. Igor's Manhattan circuit, aside from the endless charity balls, was a relatively tight one, controlled by great patrons. There were two restaurants, Henri Soulé's Le Pavillon and Gene Cavallero's Colony, and two nightclubs, John Perona's El Morocco and Sherman Billingsley's Stork Club, the latter the pinnacle of pinnacles where Winchell, the *capo di tutti capi* of gossip, held court in the Cub Room. Despite their opposite political inclinations, Winchell left and Cassini right, Winchell had a soft spot for Igor, thinking him more of a court jester than a rival for his throne, and tolerated his presence in their fraternity of vipers.

With Bootsie away, Ghighi would play, finding that the power of his column was definitely an aphrodisiac, just as it had been to Lorelle Hearst. But turnabout was foul play when, in 1947, Bootsie left Igor for *his* new boss, William Randolph Hearst, Jr. Hearst forsook his unfaithful Lorelle for Bootsie, giving the latter the ultimate gift for a columnist: He syndicated her Washington column in dozens of Hearst newspapers. But Hearst never dreamed of firing his new wife's ex. Igor was too good a Cholly to let go. Besides, there seemed to be no hard feelings. Love conquers all except circulation.

Igor salved whatever romantic wounds he had by remarrying the next year to Elizabeth Darrah Waters, a Grace Kelly–ish nineteen-year-old society girl from horsey Bedford, New York. In *Time*'s announcement of the nuptials, it continued to trash Igor, describing Darrah, who attended the Art Students League, as a "stately blonde" but her spouse as a "the squealy Hearst chitchatterer." Again, Igor loved being in *Time,* then at the height of its Lucean prestige. Forget the "squealy," he was Mighty Mouse. He even became friends with pompous Henry Luce's viciously witty wife, Clare Boothe Luce, who was as right-wing as Igor and Cissy Patterson and cottoned to the columnist's politics. Igor often wrote up journalism's first couple, referring to them as "Arsenic and Old Luce." Cholly gave as good as he got.

Before finding Darrah, Igor had flaunted his masculinity and soothed his ego—wounded from the loss of Bootsie—by stepping up his already formidable round of affairs, often with characters in his column. His weakness for Southern belles was augmented by an equal new weakness for big Swedes, who also tended to be carrying on with Cholly mainstays like Gianni Agnelli and Joe Kennedy. One such flame was Hjördis Genberg, a fashion model whom Igor first met at El Morocco on her honeymoon with a rich Stockholm industrialist. Honeymoons were no impediment to Igor, who invited her husband to play tennis in Palm Beach while making a big play for Hjördis off the court. They had a yearlong affair, during which Igor made the huge mistake of showing her off to his new best friend, Joe Kennedy. Old Joe exercised the *droit du seigneur*, having no compunction about acing Ghighi out and setting Hjördis up. But then Hjördis met David Niven. Neither Joe, having sold RKO decades before and with no Hollywood trump to play, nor Igor, whose column plugs were hardly the stuff of model dreams, was any match for movie star Niven, whom Hjördis married in 1948.

Igor had every reason to try to placate the ever powerful Joe Kennedy, sexually or otherwise, for in an early 1946 column, he had so offended the former SEC chairman and ambassador to Britain that Kennedy had called the boss of bosses, William Randolph Hearst himself, Senior not Junior, to get Igor fired. Cholly had reported that Joe's daughter Kathleen or "Kick," whose English husband, a marquess, had been killed in action during the war, was considering abandoning her Catholicism to marry a duke. Her late husband also was a Protestant, for whom Kick did not convert. But as Igor typically and cattily pointed out, a duke was higher than a marquess and worth switching for. Ironically, Kick used to work for Cissy Patterson alongside Igor as a society columnist for the *Times-Herald*. Neither the Igor-rumored conversion nor the marriage took place, but Kick did begin another romance with an earl (lower than a marquess), in which the only conversion that came up was Joe Kennedy's desire to convert Igor to the ranks of the unemployed.

To save his skin and his job, Igor gathered up Bootsie (this was before their split) and made a pilgrimage to San Simeon to meet, knees trembling, with the eightysomething Hearst. The chief, as Hearst was known, didn't break Igor's kneecaps, as Igor had feared. Conversely, encouraged by his mistress Marion Davies, who had taken to Igor, the chief raised his columnist's salary to $500 a week. And the next year, when

Igor finally encountered Joe Kennedy on a Palm Beach golf course, Joe, all hail-fellow-well-met, never mentioned the column that had so enraged him. Joe's son John had been elected to the House of Representatives in 1946, and Joe wanted him to get the best press that money could buy. Years later, Igor would recount Joe's retort to comments how JFK barely squeaked by Nixon: "Did you expect me to pay for a landslide?" It was the beginning of a genuine friendship and a symbiosis with those who would soon become America's royal family. Coincidentally, the same year Igor met Joe, 1947, Igor had discovered Joe's future daughter-in-law, at age eighteen at a Newport debutante ball, at least a year before she would meet Jack Kennedy on a train from Washington to New York. Igor trumpeted his find:

> This year, for the first time since our predecessor selected Brenda Frazier as the Queen of Glamour, we are ready to name the No. 1 Deb of the Year and the nine runners-up. Queen Deb of the Year is Jacqueline Bouvier, a regal debutante who has classic features and the daintiness of Dresden porcelain . . . Her family is strictly "Old Guard."

Through Joe Kennedy, Igor soon met Kennedy's new Palm Beach neighbors, the Charles B. Wrightsmans, who recently had purchased the oceanfront villa of Mona (Mrs. Harrison) Williams, once named the best-dressed woman in the world, courtesy of her public-utilities billionaire husband, who had such an eye for fashion that he'd had an affair with Coco Chanel, who dressed Mona. "I bought her taste," Wrightsman candidly admitted to Igor.

Mona, a poor Louisville girl who made very, very good, immortalized in song by Cole Porter and in art by Salvador Dalí, was a role model for the former Jayne Larkin, the L.A. shopgirl second wife (they wed in 1944) of the polo-playing Wrightsman, who controlled Standard Oil of Kansas. Wrightsman was a second-generation tycoon, an Okie who had been transformed by his taste of Ivy as a student at Exeter and Columbia, desperate to be accepted by society. The ultraconservative Wrightsmans saw Igor Cassini, with his all-validating Cholly column, as just the man for them to know. Igor played it to the hilt, calling Mr. Wrightsman "C.B.," as in DeMille.

When Igor was on his honeymoon with Darrah in Montego Bay, the Wrightsmans invited them to prolong the ecstasy in Palm Beach. It was then and there that the Wrightsmans' chubby, moody, solitary teenage daughter (from Charles's first marriage), Charlene, developed a mad crush on Igor, who, she said later, was the only man who had ever paid any attention to her, her father included. The Wrightsmans were surely distracted by the escapades of C.B.'s oldest daughter, Irene, who had been disinherited after eloping with the Australian sportsman-lothario Freddie McEvoy. "Suicide Freddie," as he was known, was a bobsled champion who had married several other heiresses, was the best friend of Errol Flynn, and raced Ferraris with Porfirio Rubirosa. The Wrightsmans, suffice it to say, were beside themselves.

They were even more beside themselves when Charlene, at seventeen in 1947, having finished finishing school at Foxcroft and dropping out of snooty Finch College, eloped with the Viennese B-actor Helmut Dantine. Dantine had played one of the young lovers trying to get exit visas in *Casablanca,* but despite his dashing looks, he ended up typecast as a Hollywood Nazi. That was ironic, given that both of his parents were anti-Hitlerians who died in a concentration camp. Helmut and Charlene had one son and divorced in 1950, Dantine going on to yet another heiress.

In 1952, in the endless society game of musical beds that filled the Cholly column, Igor lost his beloved Darrah to George Emmanuel, the indispensible consigliere of one of his column mainstays, Greek shipping tycoon Stavros Niarchos. It all took place that summer on the Côte d'Azur, where the Cassinis were freeloading at the Carlton, owned by the father of yet another column fixture, dashing British corporate raider Jimmy Goldsmith. In a cross between Holmesian whodunit and French farce, Igor at first suspected he was being cuckolded by one of two über-playboys: either Porfirio Rubirosa, whom he considered a dear friend; or Muslim billionaire-prince Aly Khan, another putative buddy who had

just split from Rita Hayworth. But his friends proved true blue, and Igor
was completely blindsided by the Greek connection.

In no time flat, Igor rebounded with marriage number three, to
none other than his former young idolator, Charlene Wrightsman Dantine, who had shed her baby fat and become a darkly chic beauty in the
mode of Jackie Kennedy. Before Charlene and Dantine split, the couple
would double-date with Igor and Darrah at El Morocco and take ski
holidays together. Marveling at Igor in action, Charlene rekindled her
teenage crush, and proximity fanned the flames. But Igor was getting
almost as close to Charlene's stepmother as to Charlene. It was a case of
all in the family, very cozy, if not incestuous. Jackie Kennedy herself had
taken Jayne Wrightsman as her role model in decorating and in fashion.
Although Jackie had no need to social-climb, Jayne proved such a brilliant society mountaineer that even the patrician Jackie was deeply impressed. Armed with her husband's fortune, Jayne proved to have
marvelous taste. Jayne had followed Mona Williams's inspiration to
eradicate all traces of her Flint, Michigan, roots to become the grandest
of all Palm Beach grande dames. A Europhile, Jayne adored Igor, who
could educate her in the ways of both the beau monde and the ancien
régime.

C. B. Wrightsman had been hanging out in Hollywood at the end of
World War II, attending parties and chasing starlets. However, he had
been getting too much sun on the Oklahoma oilfields, the Long Island
polo fields, the Malibu beaches. He developed a virulent squamous-cell
cancer on his lip. Wrightsman, suddenly feeling very mortal, decided he
needed a new wife to take care of him. Jayne Larkin was in the right
place at the right time.

When Charlene Wrightsman wanted to marry Igor, C.B. quickly
gave his blessing. How did Igor pass his tough muster? In Wrightsman's
worldview, columnists ranked way ahead of thespians like Flynn and
Dantine. Cholly Knickerbocker could convey the ultimate gift of fame,
or at least notoriety. What could an actor give but celluloid thrills? Furthermore, Cassini was a *count*. That title sealed the deal with C.B. Igor
and Charlene married in 1952 and settled down to be one of the future

Jet Set "A" couples. Igor had a daughter by Darrah named Marina. Charlene had a son by Helmut Dantine, Dana. The Cassinis raised them together, in Manhattan, in Palm Beach, in Hollywood, in Capri, anywhere on earth they wanted to go. Marrying a genuine heiress gave Igor Cassini "salon-cred," even more than his title or his exotic international heritage. He had hit the fiscal-social jackpot, practicing what he preached.

The Cholly column was a validation, and Igor's alliance with the Wrightsmans gave his validity even more heft and depth. The family was becoming the prime benefactor of the Metropolitan Museum of Art, the key route to social power in New York. Charles's lawyer was Allen Dulles, of the preeminent firm Sullivan & Cromwell, the lawyers for the Panama Canal, I. G. Farben of the Third Reich, and the most august bankers of Wall Street. Allen Dulles, Eisenhower's head of the CIA, and his brother John Foster, Ike's secretary of state, gave Igor access to the entire global power elite, from De Gaulle of France to the shah of Iran, whose beautiful but sullen East German–born wife, Soraya, was bored to death with everything but Igor's tales of Hollywood. Other fixtures at the Wrightsmans who Igor kept amused were the Duke and Duchess of Windsor.

The dowdy, split-level, suburban pre-jet Eisenhower era was a golden age for Cassini in particular and for glamour in general, because the "beautiful people," the Cholly people, were a tight little band who stood in dramatic relief to the gray-flannel-suited nine-to-five postwar masses. Igor saw himself as the ringmaster of a cozy circus of playboys, tycoons, and adventuresses that was small enough to fit if not into Mrs. Astor's ballroom, definitely into the Wrightsmans' Palm Beach backyard. The public lapped it up. By the dawn of the jet age, Igor had twenty million readers, not to mention a television show, *Igor Cassini's Million Dollar Showcase,* which reached millions more.

And who were Igor's beautiful people before that term, coined as a synonym for the Jet Set, entered the lexicon? Just look at Igor's ten best-dressed women list (like all great gossips, he used lists as his oxygen) for 1960. He presented them all as Mrs. Big, in her husband's name, rather than her own. Such was the sexism of the soon-to-be-changing times. Mrs. John F. Kennedy, of course, on the eve of her husband's inauguration. Mrs. Gianni Agnelli. Mrs. Stavros Niarchos. Mrs. Henry Ford. Mrs. William Paley. These were the usual suspects.

Less usual were: Mrs. Walter Moreira Salles, wife of the Brazilian billionaire banker and ambassador to Washington, and a close Cassini friend who often hosted him in Rio. Countess Rodolfo Crespi, another Rio connection, the American ex-supermodel (Consuelo O'Connor) wife of a Brazilian-Italian society publicist who fed Igor an endless plethora of column items. Vicomtesse Édouard de Ribes, a Paris aristocrat and Igor's chief French connection. Mrs. Charles Engelhard, the wife of the precious-metals king, co-owner of the De Beers diamond and precious metals consortium, who was Ian Fleming's inspiration for Auric Goldfinger and major host of Igor from Bernardsville to Johannesburg. Mrs. Edward Gilbert, the wife of the fiscal genius described by Igor as the "Boy Wonder of Wall Street," who was Christian Dior's number one client in America.

Here were the best-dressed men: England's Prince Phillip. Italy's Gianni Agnelli. Hollywood's Douglas Fairbanks, Jr. Diplomacy's Angier Biddle Duke. Stud-dom's Porfirio Rubirosa. Those were the famous. The more recherché were: Serge Obolensky, a fellow Russian aristocrat and prominent PR man who represented such blue-chip clients as Harry Winston and Hilton Hotels. Phillips Turnbull, president of Madison Avenue clothier Rogers

HOLLYWOOD ROYALTY. Grace Kelly, before she was a princess, and designer Oleg Cassini, who was always a count, during their torrid romance, 1954.

Peet. Christopher Dunphy, JFK's favorite golfing companion. Walter Shirley, Long Island real estate developer. And Oleg Cassini, that's who. Family pride was a good excuse for a plug.

It should be noted that Gilbert, Agnelli, Salles, Obolensky, Turnbull, and Shirley were all clients of Cassini's new (founded 1955) Madison Avenue public relations firm. The firm, named Martial (after his and Oleg's children, Marina, Tina, and Alex), was as high-profile as the rest of Igor's public-consumption high life. The notions of conflict of interest, or journalistic integrity, didn't seem to apply to gossip columnists. This was one former ink-stained wretch who had been transformed into a man in the gray flannel suit, custom-tailored for Igor at Rogers Peet. After all his years scrambling as a journalist, Igor adored the stability, the wealth, the power, and the respect of being a businessman, a Big Businessman. He viewed Martial as not only his cash cow but also his Trojan horse, which he hoped to ride into the Kennedy White House.

These wild ambitions would explode in Igor's face in what would be one of the seminal scandals of the sixties. But not now. As the jets began flying and world travel began to explode, Igor was riding high, as high as a new 707. Despite all of Igor's self-serving self-aggrandizement, his public, and it was a huge public, enjoyed his antics far too much to dream of censuring him, much less not reading him. Americans simply couldn't imagine living without Igor, for no other columnist could give them the same vicarious thrills that he did. Besides, for all his elitism and arrogance, the public *liked* Igor.

In contrast to Robin Leach, to come two decades later on *Lifestyles of the Rich and Famous,* Igor wasn't a poseur or a sycophant; he could just as easily lampoon his subjects as sing their praises. Most important, he came across as his readers' friend and confidant. He was the one and only count most Americans would probably ever think they knew, and he was taking them inside his otherwise forbidden world. Igor Cassini was both the chronicler of the Jet Set and its perfect role model and, at the same time, a tipster and buddy to the ordinary man and woman. He spoke Monte Carlo; he also spoke to Mayberry. "Le Jet Set, c'est moi," echoing

Louis XIV, might well have been the motto of this brilliant showman and surprisingly inclusive host of the party that was the jet age.

Like Igor, the entire Eisenhower era was obsessed with big business. While Igor and his column may have provided the software for the jet age, the publicity, the hype, the myth that got the public hooked on going places, the hardware was the plane, and that was the big feat that transformed the world. None of Igor's sizzle would have mattered were it not for the steak that was the jet plane itself. And the jet was, first and foremost, one of the great Wall Street power plays of all time, a tour de force of all-American capitalistic brains and brawn. Big business was what put the jets in the air, the jets that enabled Igor Cassini and his Jet Set, and his millions of vicarious-thrill-seeking readers, to live it up on the ground.

3

Skycoons

I T IS IRONIC THAT OF THE MIGHTY MOGULS BEHIND THE LAUNCH OF THE BOEING 707 and the Douglas DC-8, only maybe two or three of them ever appeared in Igor Cassini's Cholly Knickerbocker column. And not often. They might be on the cover of *Fortune* or *Time* or the front page of *The Wall Street Journal* or *The New York Times,* or on the television on *Huntley-Brinkley.* But as far as the social columns were concerned, this genuine jet set didn't warrant coverage. They weren't "fun" enough to be in Igor's world because they were too busy changing the real world.

The literal Jet Set comprised a tiny lot, beyond exclusivity: They were the corporate heads of the big American airlines and the airplane manufacturers. Call them the Skycoons. But just because they weren't in the gossip columns didn't mean they weren't colorful. Quite the contrary. These men were the folk heroes of capitalism. They were nothing like the fungible and interchangeable corporate suits who run the airlines today. The Skycoons didn't waste their time climbing corporate ladders. They created their companies out of blood, sweat, and propellers, and people climbed to reach *them.*

At the pinnacle of the aviation pyramid was Pan Am's Juan Trippe, the Yale preppy who built the colossus of the skies. Then there was TWA's Howard Hughes, the richest and most mysterious of all the air tycoons. American Airlines's prexy C. R. Smith was the opposite of Hughes. Both were Texans, but Smith, a CPA, was as grounded and bottom-line as Hughes was mercurial and madly brilliant. United Airlines's Pat Patterson grew up on a Hawaiian sugar plantation and got seasick every time he had to sail to the mainland. Cutting his corporate teeth as a Wells Fargo banker, he was obsessed with flying and, like his rival Smith, with keeping his airline flying above the red ink. Far more swashbuckling were Eastern's Eddie Rickenbacker, the World War I flying ace and Congressional Medal of Honor winner; Delta's C. E. Woolman, who worked his way up as a cotton-field crop duster; and Continental's Bob Six, a Waldo Pepper ish California stunt pilot who became so obsessed with Broadway that he married Ethel Merman.

Those were the heads of the airlines. Equally important were the two chief jet-maker rivals. Douglas's Donald Douglas was an Annapolis- and MIT-trained engineer whose boyhood inspiration to reach for the stars came from seeing Wilbur Wright fly. His adversary was Boeing's William Allen, a Harvard Law School–trained Montana cowboy who had a riverboat gambler's passion for risk. In leaving out these legends because they didn't hang out at the Stork Club or didn't seem "upperclawss," Igor Cassini simply didn't know what he was missing. Furthermore, these tycoons were, in effect, working for him. If Woodrow Wilson's mission had been to make the world safe for democracy, the mission of the Skycoons was to make the world safe for jetocracy.

The jet age's greatest missionary was undoubtedly Juan Trippe, the founder and chairman of its greatest airline, Pan Am. He was the one airman who was genuinely Old Guard, "listable" for Ward McAllister or Maury Paul, but way too much a relic of the quadrilles in the Astor Ballroom rather than the fox-trots of El Morocco to tickle the fancy of a Cholly addict. Conversely, Igor would have given a Fabergé egg— a whole henhouse of them—to have landed Pan Am as his public relations client. That would have been one of Madison Avenue's super-"gets." But Juan Trippe was beyond mortal celebrity.

Because the foundations of the Pan Am empire were laid in its pioneering routes to Cuba and then to South America, people often assumed that because of his first name, Juan Trippe was some sort of Latin fusion plutocrat. Not really. Juan Trippe was as American as the apple pie he relished in the refectory of the Hill School in Pottstown, Pennsylvania, where he was prepared for Yale and to follow his WASP father to his banking firm on Wall Street. The only border Juan had any connection south of was the Mason-Dixon Line, for his name came not from Ferdinand and Isabella but from his mother's beloved half sister, Juanita Terry, a Maryland blue blood who died young, speaking neither Spanish nor Portuguese.

Whatever the facts, the name alone made Juan seem more dashing than he first appeared. At Hill, he was so reserved that his classmates nicknamed him "the Mummy." At Yale, he was vastly overshadowed by such glittering schoolmates as *Time* cofounders Henry Luce and Briton Hadden and Cornelius Vanderbilt ("Sonny") Whitney, who would go on to finance *Gone with the Wind* and *The Searchers*. Trippe was a protonerd, enrolling in the university's Sheffield Scientific School to study unglamorous industrial engineering. He was tapped for Delta Psi, or St. Anthony's Hall, one of the lesser fraternities. Six feet and stocky, he did make guard on a weak football team that lost all its annual contests with Harvard and Princeton. Trippe clearly did not seem like secret-society Skull and Bones material.

Yet as a senior, he was tapped, along with Luce, Hadden, and Whitney. What changed things for the solid, stolid Trippe was World War I and the airplane. Trippe had always been fascinated by flying. As a ten-year-old he built a model plane, powered by rubber bands, that he flew in Central Park. That year his father took him to the Statue of Liberty to watch an air race between Wilbur Wright and Glenn Curtiss. The boy was hooked. In 1917 he took a leave from Yale to enter the Naval Reserve Force Flying Corps. He won his wings, but the war ended too soon for him to fulfill his fantasy of going "over there."

Instead, in 1919, he returned to New Haven, with new confidence derived from his naval spit and polish, if not combat decorations. He began writing for the Yale *Graphic*, the campus magazine. His first article, totally prescient, was about the future of the navy, flying giant seaplanes across the Atlantic. He soon rose to become the *Graphic*'s editor in chief, but most important, he helped found the Yale Aero Club, serving as secretary behind two returning World War I aces. He copiloted a plane that won a major race against eleven other colleges. While other Ivy boys in this Fitzgeraldian era were content to get their thrills in Stutz Bearcats, Trippe was clearly destined for a (literally) higher calling.

Trippe made a great name at Yale. He also made some great contacts. Many of his future investors in Pan Am were classmates. These were fellow Aero Club members Sonny Whitney and his cousin Bill Vanderbilt. There were his rich Delta Psi brothers, Alan Scaife, who would marry into the Pittsburgh Mellons; Tom Symington, a railway heir; and Theodore Weicker, a Squibb pharmaceutical scion. All wanted to fly. Vital as well was Trippe's buddy from the *Graphic*, Sam Pryor, who would become his number two at Pan Am. Alumni power brokers like Averell Harriman also proved true (Yale) blue to Trippe's aspirations. These school connections were valuable beyond any Ivy Leaguer's wildest dreams.

However, Trippe's dreams turned into nightmares when his father suddenly died at forty-seven of a supposedly tropical disease, typhoid fever, in East Hampton, during the summer of Trippe's twenty-first birthday. The enormous debts he left soon bankrupted his financial firm. Trippe's mother had to scrape and sacrifice to enable Juan to finish his senior year at Yale. When he did graduate in 1922, the fantasy of flight was foremost in his mind, but the burden of supporting his mother was squarely on his shoulders. Reality grounded the flyboy, who was hired by another Yale alumnus to become a bond salesman at the esteemed Boston–New York firm of Lee, Higginson & Co.

The gentleman's business of selling bonds to family and friends in the morning on Wall Street and then playing golf in the afternoon at the Apawamis Club in Westchester bored Trippe to death. His only fun was flying and doing stunts in a leaky used seaplane on weekends over Long

Island Sound. He endured banking until 1923, when he quit and announced that he was going into the aviation business. Flying was the Internet of its time, and the Roaring Twenties couldn't have been a more propitious era to find venture capital for a futuristic start-up, particularly for a man with Trippe's Yale connections to high finance.

He began on the cheap, using the Yale Club's address at 50 Vanderbilt Avenue for the nonexistent office of "J. Terry Trippe" (in those pre–Pan Am days he left out the Juan). When he eventually played the J-card to court the Latino market, *Time,* for one, with a typical white man's burden bias, called him on the carpet, noting that the only thing Latin about him was his "swarthy skin." What he didn't leave out were his old school ties. The New Haven Mafia provided him enough capital to buy some outdated navy planes and start Long Island Airways. Trippe's first company was basically a 1920s version of the Hampton Jitney, ferrying Gatsby-esque thrill-seekers to weekend parties, or sometimes just on romantic sightseeing dates flying around the Statue of Liberty. Trippe took on multiple roles, from president to pilot to mechanic. Effort didn't count. The venture failed.

Trippe was saved by the U.S. Post Office, which was about to open up its new airmail service to private bidders. What Trippe focused on was the potentially extremely lucrative Boston–New York corridor. To that end, Trippe hied himself to Sonny Whitney and William Rockefeller, yet another Yalie flying aficionado. They gave Trippe the backing he needed to float a $300,000 stock offering in Trippe's new company, Colonial Air Transport, which *The New York Times* described in 1925 as "the first definite adventure of important financial men into the field of commercial aviation." Until Trippe came along, most airlines were the creations of romantic but impractical ex–flying aces. Wall Street scorned these characters as "birdmen."

Trippe was only a closet birdman. When he called on money, he was a bottom-line Yale man. Yale ties financed Trippe in the air, just as they had financed Luce and Haddon on the ground. While Trippe might not have made Cholly Knickerbocker, the *Times* article was the way he wanted to see his name in print. Oddly enough, he *should* have made

Cholly for the courtship of his future blue-chip bride, which began around this time. The lady was Elizabeth Stettinius, the daughter of the great Morgan banker Edward Stettinius.

Again, capitalizing on college connections proved to be Juan Trippe's genius (and a great advertisement for an Ivy education). He met Elizabeth, a top debutante of the social season, through her brother Edward Jr., at the New York St. Anthony Hall alumni club. Edward had been a Delta Psi at the University of Virginia, a state where his mother was one of the FFVs (First Families of Virginia). His best friend there was his cousin David K. E. Bruce, who soon would marry the daughter of Andrew Mellon. The cousins both reached the pinnacle of American public service, Bruce as ambassador to France, Germany, and England; Stettinius as secretary of state, after heading U.S. Steel. Juan met Elizabeth at the Stettinius estate in Locust Valley. What won his heart was her power drive on the links at the Piping Rock Club. He wanted to marry her at first swing, but her family balked at giving their blessing until Juan Trippe proved that he could support a family.

Trippe quickly ascended to that challenge. Although the Boston mail route turned out to be much less lucrative than he had imagined, Trippe sold Colonial and began looking south and thinking internationally. He took his proceeds and went down to Cuba with John Hambleton, a rich Harvard friend from his intercollegiate flying days, to lobby the Cuban president Machado for the about-to-open Havana–Key West airmail route. Hambleton was from Baltimore, from a much tonier Maryland clan than Trippe, and that pedigree, plus his decorations as a World War I ace, put the often tongue-tied, malapropping Trippe in awe of the smoothly eloquent Harvard man. It was Hambleton who in 1927 muscled together a new, much bigger consortium of Ivy heirs and Wall Street wizards to create their newest venture, Aviation Corporation of America, which would win the Havana route and soon set off for South America and become Pan American Airways. Trippe was just about the only man in the group without deep family pockets. Accordingly, he did almost all the work. He was the tycoons' hired hand.

Trippe was more than grateful to have the opportunity. When on

October 28, 1927, his first "floatplane," *La Nina,* landed in the Havana harbor and unloaded its first load of 772 pounds of mail to a waiting boat, Trippe was there to telegraph Betty Stettinius, whom her parents had sent off to Paris to make her forget the loser Juan Trippe. The simple cable read, "First flight successful." But the message was clear. Juan Trippe had arrived. They married the next year, at a blowout for eight hundred guests at the Stettinius Locust Valley barony, after which they sailed to Europe on the S.S. *Rotterdam,* for London, Paris, and for Trippe, the highlight of all, the Berlin Air Show.

Meanwhile, John Hambleton pulled off the first publicity coup of Pan Am's young life. He bagged Charles Lindbergh to sign—in return for what became a fortune in Pan Am stock—an exclusive contract as the new airline's technical adviser. Nothing could instill confidence in flying like America's greatest hero, whom Trippe and Hambleton called "Slim." Still only twenty-seven at the time, Lindbergh was the pinnacle of trust, the ultimate seal of approval. Fifty thousand people turned out in Miami in February 1929 to watch Lindbergh, with Hambleton as his copilot, take off on the inaugural mail flight to the Canal Zone.

Hambleton was almost as charismatic as Lindy. At the outset of their venture, Trippe was languishing in his shadow as Pan Am's number two, running the office while Hambleton flew around the country, making deals. En route to Miami from New York on a small private plane, Hambleton broke one of his personal rules of never surrendering the controls of a plane to any pilot less skilled than Lindbergh or himself: Hambleton asked this so-honored pilot to make a brief stop in Wilmington, North Carolina, where his pregnant wife was visiting her family. It was a perfect day, as clear and sunny and springlike as the one that saw the doom decades later of the *Château de Sully.* Coming in for a landing, the plane simply fell three hundred feet from the sky, instantly crushing to death both Hambleton and his pilot. No cause was ever determined, though the speculation was that the little plane had hit an air pocket and was swept downward. It was a terrible loss for Juan Trippe. At the same time, it put all the responsibility for Pan Am solely in his court. Forced to step out of Hambleton's long shadow, Trippe had no choice but to overcome his natural reticence and his fear that being "pushy" was anathema to being a gentleman. The airline was his to make, and make it he did.

Trippe, who loathed publicity, was immediately pressed by Pan Am's investors to take a high profile. Given the airline's new focus on South America, its ad agency, New York's Doremus & Co., pressed "J. Terry Trippe" to trade on the "Juan." Trippe demurred. He hated the name, he told the agency. Ever since he was a boy, no one knew how to pronounce it. People called him "Wang." He preferred Trippy, his golfing moniker. He even preferred "Mummy." But Doremus had their way. "Juan" came out of mothballs, and a mythology about his Venezuelan ancestor was manufactured by the agency.

This was how the Trippe juggernaut began. It never stopped, as he quickly propelled Pan Am to world domination. Although he staffed the executive ranks of his airline with fellow Yalies, Pan Am was still a one-man show. Notwithstanding his hail-fellow-well-met, slightly bumbling demeanor, Trippe, who smoked cheap drugstore cigars and came to vastly prefer golf to travel, was totally in control, spinning his air web less on the fly than from his fifty-eighth-floor office in the Chrysler Building. He may have been even more secretive than Howard Hughes. He had to be. Such were the rigors and intrigues of the prewar thirties.

DON JUAN. Juan Trippe, the founder of Pan Am, in 1927. The emperor of the air.

Trippe outmaneuvered the Germans at the height of Nazi machinations in the South American air wars. He sneaked through the great walls of Chinese xenophobia toward foreign airlines by buying a controlling interest in China's leading carrier. He pitted Yankee ingenuity against British imperialism in taking control of the routes across the Atlantic. And he did it all single-handedly, without intervention from the State Department, despite his endless connections in the capital. Furthermore, no one other than Trippe and Pan Am had any interest in traversing the globe in the middle of the Depression. Accomplishing privately what surely would have gotten bogged down in the game of nations, Trippe, a diplomatic corps unto himself, was viewed by Washington as its Great White Hope to win the international air race.

After distinguished service lending its fleet of planes to the war effort around the world during World War II, Juan Trippe, always a visionary, began preparations for entering and, naturally, dominating the impending jet age. Trippe was always on the cutting edge, but sometimes that edge cut the wrong way. A case in point was the Boeing 314, a massive, elegant, long-range "flying boat" that could whiz around the world and land on water when there were no airports to receive it. This became the legendary Pan Am Clipper, whose one-class system was first class, pure luxury, all the way. He introduced it in 1939, bad timing for a passenger plane to span a world about to explode.

The seats were convertible into beds, thirty-six of them, for the journeys, slow by jet standards, at 188 miles per hour. It took over a day to fly from New York to Southampton, England. There were intermediate stops in New Brunswick, Newfoundland, Iceland, and Ireland. It took six days to fly from San Francisco to Hong Kong. To graciously pass the time, there were dressing rooms, a cocktail lounge, and a dining area for six-course meals, pioneered by Trippe, catered by top chefs recruited from grand hotels, and served on silver by white-coated stewards.

Transatlantic round-trip in 1939 cost $675, the equivalent of a future Concorde ticket. This was strictly a super-rich man's adventure, a conveyance for top-shelf Yale types. Still, Trippe wasn't dependent on putting fancy derrieres into fancy seats. Most of Pan Am's profits came from the government, from carrying the U.S. mail around the world. The Clippers, and their bon ton passengers, were what gave Pan Am its mystique but made many normal Americans see red. In addition to the incongruity of selling champagne fantasy when the reality was still bread lines, there was the even harsher reality of World War II.

After Pearl Harbor, the Clippers stopped commercial flights and were enlisted into military service, most famously transporting President Roosevelt to the Casablanca Conference. Winston Churchill was a huge fan of the flyboats. Nothing, not the *Super Chief* train, not the *Normandie* ship, could match their futuristic glamour. Unfortunately for seaplane devotee Trippe, the war saw not only the construction of countless airports but also the development of the Douglas DC-4 and the Lockheed Constellation, planes that were safer and easier to fly than the Boeing 314s. These "landplanes" made the seaplanes obsolete and cost Boeing a fortune in wasted development and production capacity devoted to Trippe's folly.

No folly could derail Juan Trippe from his godlike goal of ruling the skies. If landplanes must replace seaplanes, so be it. Pan Am bought the latest landplanes. It was number one or nothing. Even before the end of the war, Trippe foresaw the coming competition for his overseas routes from Howard Hughes's rising giant TWA. He wanted to stop it before it was fully risen. Pan Am had the prewar monopoly on America's foreign routes, the better to compete with the nationalized foreign carriers. Trippe saw Pan Am as America's "chosen instrument."

But Franklin Roosevelt, for all his aristocracy, was devoted to free trade and a policy called "open skies" that would end Trippe's "chosen" status. Once again, Trippe turned to Yale for a rescue, in the person of Congresswoman Clare Boothe Luce, wife of Trippe's fellow Bonesman Henry. Clare Boothe Luce added a new phrase to the language when she attacked FDR's open-skies policy as "globaloney." Notwithstanding the advocacy and wit of both Luces, on the floor of Congress and in the pages of *Time,* Roosevelt held the line on free competition, and not only TWA but also American Airlines began flying the North Atlantic after 1945. Pan Am remained the leader.

Despite Trippe's failure with his 314 and his turning to Douglas and Lockheed for postwar planes, Boeing could never turn its back on Pan

Am. And it wasn't because Boeing founder William Boeing was a Yale man, like Juan Trippe. Just as Trippe was beginning his ascent, Boeing was bailing out of the namesake company he had built. Boeing was the son of a millionaire German mining engineer/lumber baron from Detroit. Young William had left Yale and moved to Washington State to expand his father's barony on the Olympic peninsula. Before Yale, he had Anglicized his name from Wilhelm Boing.

Like Trippe, Boing/Boeing had been mesmerized by the early flying machines and decided that, as the boy who had everything, he wanted to build his own. He created not only Boeing Aircraft but also a passenger service with his Boeing planes that was the core of what would evolve into United Airlines. For all his energy, Boeing got caught in the sights of Franklin Roosevelt's trustbusters, led by future justice Hugo Black, who concluded that he had gone way beyond entrepreneurship to monopoly. The courts sundered Boeing's holdings into three great entities: Boeing, United Airlines (both based in Washington State), and Hartford-headquartered United Aircraft, which included engine colossus Pratt & Whitney and Sikorsky Helicopters. The pre-ruling Boeing certainly *looked* like a monopoly, notwithstanding the noble capitalist intent of its founder. Boeing left aviation for good and devoted the rest of his life to thoroughbred horse breeding. He died in 1956, shortly after his former company had shaken the world with its successful test flights of the 707.

Boeing, once its founder's one-man show, similar to that of Boeing's chief rival, Douglas Aircraft, now became faceless and totally corporate: similar, minus the Ivy, to the high-leverage, low-visibility financiers behind the Pan Am cult of Juan Trippe. Boeing was run largely by local engineers of Scandinavian descent, mostly trained at the University of Washington. Its head man was Philip Gustav Johnson, who, as *Time* described, "did his best to take the romance out of aviation."

An engineer who was the brains behind Boeing's wartime cash cow B-29 Superfortress, Johnson had a stroke and died at forty-nine while visiting Boeing's Wichita plant. He may have been unknown to Cholly Knickerbocker, but he was beloved by the assembly lines. His shoes seemed impossible to fill, especially given his demise at the end of the war, which meant the end of the huge demand for Boeing's specialty military machines. In addition to the loss of Johnson, 38,000 Boeing workers had already been laid off. The future now was passenger transport, and after the 314 Clipper fiasco, Boeing had gotten out of the passenger business. All of a sudden, peace was a bad thing. The manufacturer of America's most decorated wartime plane, the Flying Fortress, was finding itself besieged, in what looked like the start of Boeing's Alamo.

The man called in to save the day was a seemingly even more faceless character than Johnson. This was William M. Allen, a partner in the Seattle law firm that was Boeing's counsel. An evocation of Ichabod Crane, the tall, balding, archconservative Republican Allen was a dry man in many senses. He was born in Lolo, Montana, the son of a mining engineer and a suffragette-prohibitionist who took great pride in having closed three saloons and built one church in her hometown. Allen graduated from Montana State University, where he did so well that he married the daughter of the governor of Montana and went on to Harvard Law School for his LL.B. Harvard wasn't so easy. Allen got middling grades and was not recruited by Wall Street's white-shoe firms, the ones shuffling the papers behind Juan Trippe's

ROLE MODEL. William Allen, president of Boeing. Along with Trippe, the most powerful man in American aviation.

financings. Humbled, Allen came back west, to the "big town" of Seattle and Boeing's big law firm there.

Having risen to become Boeing's legal brains, Allen balked when the firm offered him its presidency. You don't need a lawyer at the controls, he demurred; you need an engineer. But Boeing persisted, and because his wife had just died of cancer, Allen took on the challenge in order to distract himself from the loss. His first effort nearly sent him back to the law. The long-range B-377 Stratocruiser, Boeing's commercial version of the B-29 big bomber, was a big bomb. The massive double-decker, with its lounge and berths, harked back to the luxuries of that earlier bomb, Trippe's B-314. But it was more expensive to operate than its now-entrenched Douglas and Lockheed competitors. Only Howard Hughes and Juan Trippe showed interest, but Hughes had money troubles, and Trippe was having second thoughts about selling airborne luxury in the midst of postwar austerity. Boeing was thus able to unload only a paltry fifty-five of the Stratocruisers. Luckily, Allen was able to recoup his R&D costs by reconfiguring the plane as a tanker version, which he sold to the military in great numbers.

The numbers were so good that Allen was emboldened to unleash his inner gambler and develop the radical idea of a jet tanker to refuel the new B-47 jets of the Strategic Air Command. Allen's big roll of the dice was to develop a passenger prototype of the B-47 jet as well, and in that, he was egged on by Juan Trippe, whose attitude was "If you bet your house, I'll bet mine." But Allen had been ready to roll ever since 1950, when he had taken his first ride in one of his jet B-47s to the Boeing Wichita plant, then switched to a DC-6 prop to a business meeting in Chicago. He found the prop plane impossibly slow. It was a case of when you're a jet, you're a jet all the way. It was love at first flight.

How could the jet, a seeming sure thing, be anything but a no-brainer? In a word, danger. In the early fifties, the passenger jet was perceived as a high-risk death machine. The British had long beaten the Americans to the punch, with their small (forty-nine seats) but beautiful De Havilland Comet, which entered commercial service in 1952, a tribute to British postwar resilience. But the Comet was better suited to the Museum of Modern Art than to the airways. The sleek silver birds just kept falling out of the sky, twice over India, twice over Italy. It took years to trace the disasters to metal fatigue, but pending the endless investigation, the British took the plane out of service, and despite an attempted comeback later in the decade, its fate was sealed.

Jets seemed hubristic to America's airline chiefs other than Hughes and Trippe. Based on the British experience, the Yanks felt they were witnessing a case of Icarus. The Brits were flying too fast, too soon. It could take years to work out the kinks. Meanwhile, the American airlines were planning to bet their houses on the halfway house that was the turboprop—that is, using a jet engine to turn a propeller. Lockheed was building one called the L-188 Electra, and both Eddie Rickenbacker of Eastern and C. R. Smith of American had just placed major orders. But Boeing's Allen was not deterred. His coffers brimming with armed-forces cash, and facing a huge tax bill, the balance-sheet lawyer decided he could take a big write-off and gave the green light to the passenger-jet prototype. It was assigned the model number 707.

The 707's specifications were impressive: a speed of 600 miles per hour, a capacity of up to 120 passengers, far superior to its nonjet predecessor the Stratocruiser (350 miles per hour, 80 passengers). It could fly as high as 50,000 feet, far above the weather. It would be able to reach Europe from the East Coast in just over six hours, compared to the current eleven. But there were still big problems to overcome, particularly fuel and noise. The 707 was a deafening machine, its screaming engines sure to be the bane of every airport-adjacent community. Furthermore, it was no cheap date. Each 707 had a prospective price tag of $4 million. C. R. Smith of American, the most hard-core realist of the Skycoons, poured ice water on Bill Allen's Dreamliner, justifying his turboprop order to *The New York Times* by declaring, "We can't go backward to the jet. I'm interested in cheap transportation and a more efficient machine, not in more expensive machines."

Smith was a great street fighter, the first airline chief to play the fear card. In 1937, he issued his notorious "Afraid to Fly?" ads, advertising American as "The Sunshine Route to the West" across the cloudless deserts of New Mexico and Arizona. The unstated here was that arch-competitor United's more northerly routes over the snowy, stormy Rockies were more dangerous. The low blow landed hard, and American doubled its revenues that year. Smith was perfectly capable of playing the safety ace again where the jets were concerned, and the British Comet disasters gave him a full hand.

Another powerful naysayer was, second to Lindbergh, the most respected man in aviation. This was Captain Eddie Rickenbacker, the head of Eastern, a key member of America's domestic "Big Four," with American, United, and TWA. The swashbuckling Rickenbacker had every intent of leading America's charge into the jet future. He had put his money where his mouth was by placing a huge $100 million order for thirty-five of the De Havilland Comets in 1952, far out-Trippe-ing Juan Trippe, who had just put his toe in the water by ordering three of the planes. When the Comets began crashing, Rickenbacker, the least

faint of heart of all Skycoons, canceled his commitment. He had legal grounds. The defective Comet had literally cooled his jets, and his cooling cooled the entire airline industry.

Rickenbacker was a genuine oracle. When he spoke about flying, the whole world listened. He was also the anti-Trippe, a sixth-grade dropout who didn't know Skull and Bones from skin and bones. Edward Reich-enbacher was born in

ACE HIGH. Eddie Rickenbacker, America's greatest air hero and president of Eastern Air Lines, 1920.

Columbus, Ohio, in 1890 to poor Swiss immigrant parents. His father was a construction worker. Rickenbacker changed the spelling of his name during World War I to improve his "war cred" in fighting the Germans, adding a middle name, Vernon, he said, for "a touch of class." But by then he was already famous as "Fast Eddie," one of the nation's highest-paid auto racers, after starting at the bottom as a lowly mechanic. In the war, he was the chief nemesis of "Red Baron" Manfred von Richthofen, and scored a record twenty-six "kills," shooting down twenty-two enemy planes and four dirigibles.

Just as Trippe had hired Lindbergh as a huge publicity coup, Eastern Air Transport, the struggling air arm of General Motors, in 1934 tapped Rickenbacker to give it a shot of fame in its unglamorous arm. The ex–World War I ace had been working as a sales manager for Cadillac after losing his own fortune in a car company that produced the first American auto with four-wheel brakes but failed nonetheless. Eastern controlled the highly lucrative New York–Miami route, from whence Pan Am jumped off into the Caribbean and points south. Rickenbacker came in and lent Eastern his name, his fame, and his expertise. In addition to his executive duties, from 1935 to 1940 Rickenbacker had his own comic strip about a self-styled aviator, *Ace Drummond*, which became a successful film and radio serial.

In 1941 and '42, Rickenbacker's great celebrity became even greater when he became an action hero not once but twice more. The first event came when an Eastern DC-3 that Rickenbacker was traveling in crashed in a Georgia forest on its landing approach to Atlanta's airport. Eight of the sixteen passengers died on impact. Rickenbacker, though fifty years old and critically injured with a skull fracture, countless broken bones, and a left eyeball knocked from its socket, located all the survivors, tended their wounds, and carried each of them to a forest clearing where ambulances could reach them.

Sixteen months later and barely recovered, he had another near-death experience when touring the Pacific theater for President Roosevelt and General MacArthur. His B-17 Flying Fortress had to ditch in the middle of the ocean, thousands of miles from anything. The eight survivors had to subsist at sea for twenty-four days, a real-life version of Hitchcock's *Lifeboat;* Rickenbacker took charge and kept everyone sane and alive. Their only provisions were four oranges, which Rickenbacker supplemented by catching fish as well as seagulls, and dividing the rainwater as it fell. Though America mourned the loss of its hero, who was reported dead, only one person actually perished before a navy plane spotted them and came to the rescue. A book recounting the adventure became a huge bestseller, enshrining Rickenbacker as a household name for courage.

At Eastern, Eddie Rickenbacker was anything but a publicity hire. Hands-on in every department, from advertising to maintenance to pilot training, he turned the airline into a cash machine. Although he was financed by Laurance Rockefeller, Rickenbacker never made Eastern glamorous; glamour wasn't his thing. He liked to say he was selling "seats and safety," not service. The aviator was running America's first no-frills airline, and it worked. He rescued Eastern from looming bankruptcy and transformed it into the most profitable of the Big Four. His modus operandi was simple: to fly the most planes, with the greatest capacity, at the least cost. His thumbs-down on the jet was as dispiriting as that of a Roman emperor at the Colosseum. And he put his money where his mouth was. He wrote a check to Lockheed for $100 million for fifty of its turboprop Constellations. The oracle had spoken. Who was going to listen to Bill Allen?

Just as realistic and as dispiriting as both Smith and Rickenbacker was Pat Patterson of United. As World War II ended, the ex-banker Patterson commissioned an in-depth study of the potential of foreign travel, with a special focus on what was called the "Blue Ribbon Route" across the North Atlantic. What he concluded was that if you somehow emptied all the first-class cabins of every great liner crossing the ocean and transformed these sailors into fliers, the whole rich lot would fit into a grand total of fifty planes. Patterson assumed Europe was a "millionaire's market," a big waste of time for the Big Four. Accordingly, he officially deferred to that darling of the millionaires, Juan Trippe. Let Pan Am be America's "chosen instrument," Patterson conceded, to compete with the nationalized foreign carriers, the BOACs and Air Frances and KLMs. Let Trippe have those headaches.

Juan Trippe didn't get headaches; he gave them. While he may have been the biggest dreamer in aviation, he also had an eye for statistics.

While Smith and Patterson were content to focus on domestic matters, what mattered to Trippe were foreign affairs. Trippe believed that where Patterson had gone wrong was by defining the European market through the demographics of the Yale Club. Trippe wasn't blinded by his residence in Greenwich. He was well aware of middle America and where it was going, which was up in the air. His 1952 brainstorm of cheaper-than-economy, advance-purchase "tourist fares" had caused a huge spike in air travel across the North Atlantic. In 1948, three quarters of a million people crossed that ocean, a third of them in planes, the rest in ships. By 1954, the air figure had doubled, and the ship crossings had declined to near-parity with the planes. Heartened, Trippe doubled down, creating a fly-now-pay-later installment plan; within a year, it generated another hundred thousand new Euro-fliers. Postwar Europe remained dirt-cheap; five dollars a day was a doable goal, and a European vacation had become as integral a part of the Eisenhower Dream as leaving your suburban split-level to see the U.S.A. in your Chevrolet. Trippe's dream was a big, fast plane to ferry lots and lots of these dreamers to their dream, and Bill Allen proved to be his genie in a bottle.

4

Jet Wars

THE 707 WAS KNOWN BY BOEING'S ENGINEERS AS THE DASH 80, AFTER ITS MILI-
tary model number, 367-80. Whatever they called it, the passenger
prototype was up in the air by 1954. Given the powerful naysayers like
C. R. Smith, Bill Allen knew he couldn't sell the jet on concept alone.
The plane had to be flown to be believed; *res ipsa loquitur,* "the thing
speaks for itself," was one of the jurisprudential buzz phrases that Harvard Law had instilled in Allen. It spoke even louder in August 1955,
when Boeing's chief test pilot, Alvin "Tex" Johnston, strapped himself in
at the controls of the canary yellow–chocolate brown, swept-wing 95-
ton Dash 80. He revved up its four behemoth state-of-the-art Pratt &
Whitney J-57 jet engines and taxied to the runway to show off the Dash
in a test flight before 350,000 people assembled for the Gold Cup hy-
droplane race, Seattle's answer to the Henley Regatta. Bill Allen was right
there, watching from a small boat, as proud as any new father as the ex-
barnstormer Johnston flew his $20 million baby into the heavens at 450
miles an hour, then plunged it back to earth, holding up at a mere 300
feet above the lake. Allen nearly died when Johnston threw the Dash

into a 360-degree complete belly roll. Allen turned to one of his companions, who had heart trouble, and asked if he could borrow one of his nitroglycerin tablets. The "thing," the 707, had spoken for itself.

Hearing that banshee whine a thousand miles away down the Pacific Coast in Santa Monica, California, was Bill Allen's only potential jet competitor, Donald Douglas. While Boeing's bread and butter had been the military, Douglas was the dominant figure in commercial aviation. Ever since the British Comets started flying, he had been playing for time. The great "decider" of aviation was for once as indecisive as Hamlet. Donald Douglas's problem was that he was a thrifty Scot. Yes, he was born in Brooklyn, but to first-generation Scottish parents. His father had the perfect cliché job for a Scotsman—a bank cashier.

Born in 1892, Donald Douglas had the genes of an accountant but the genius of an aeronautical engineer. Douglas earned one of the first degrees in that new field from the vaunted Massachusetts Institute of Technology in 1914, and he stayed on at the school for a year as an instructor. Douglas wore a kilt and played bagpipes for fun. He also slept with an adding machine next to his bed, so he could wake up and worry about numbers. Those $20 million for the Dash Eighty were sleepless numbers.

Douglas had worked his way up inch by inch to become the Flying Scotsman. He started at Annapolis, but after getting in trouble for hitting an admiral in the head with a toy glider he had built (shades of Juan Trippe in Central Park) and was flying from his dorm roof, he transferred to MIT. After MIT, he worked as an engineer for several airplane designers, including the top one, Glenn Martin, in Cleveland. But Douglas wanted to live in California, where the perfect weather meant flying year-round. Again in shades of Trippe, he found a rich backer, a young L.A. playboy named David Davis, who had the fantasy of becoming a pre-Lindbergh Lindbergh by flying nonstop across the United States. Opening an office in a barbershop on Pico Boulevard, the four D's, David Davis and Donald Douglas, started the Davis Douglas Co. in 1920. Douglas soon designed the plane called the Cloudster that would fly Davis into history. Davis put up the $40,000 to build it.

Sadly for Davis, the engine of the Cloudster conked out over Texas. A downcast Davis left the company. Nonetheless, the Cloudster entered the record books as the first plane to carry a payload greater than its own weight. Davis may not have been impressed, but the U.S. Navy was. They hired Douglas to design torpedo bombers for them. Douglas Aircraft was born. Its 1936 DC-3 was considered the first modern airliner. It seated 21, slept 16, had men's and women's lavatories, and could fly coast-to-coast, with just three refueling stops, in only fifteen hours. By 1939, 90 percent of all American passengers were flying on DC-3s.

However, Donald Douglas wanted not only America but the world. He wanted Boeing to do his dirty work, his legwork, for him. It had happened once before. In the early thirties, Boeing, while still part of the United monopoly, had developed the 247, the first all-metal (aluminum) plane. It had lots of first-ever features, such as retractable landing gear, deicers, autopilot, and trim tabs. The 247 was as radical a leap forward in its day as the 707 was now. However, because Boeing's entire

NEW DEAL. Donald Douglas, founder of Boeing's chief rival, Douglas Aviation, shaking hands with President Franklin Roosevelt, 1936.

production of the new plane was devoted to United, Donald Douglas was able to tap in to the demand of all the other airlines for the 247 by creating the DC-2, basically the same plane but 25 miles per hour faster (Boeing's speed was 180 miles per hour), which added up to an hour less on the New York–Chicago run. Time was money, lots of money, for Douglas, whose plane vastly outsold Boeing's and paved the way for his dominance with the DC-3, which was twice as fast as the 247. It wasn't patent infringement; Hollywood might have called it an homage. For a while Douglas sat back and tried to do it again, waiting for Boeing's jet prototype to make a few false moves that he could then improve on.

Juan Trippe wouldn't let Douglas get away with it this time, needling him with the motto on the Scottish coat of arms that dominated Douglas's Santa Monica office: *Jamais Arrière,* it read, *Never behind.* Trippe needed both Boeing and Douglas to fight it out, gladiator-style, for aerial Darwinism to generate the best survival-of-the-fittest result for Pan Am. Boeing was already in the game. To get Douglas in, Juan knew that he would have to show the Scotsman the money. Accordingly, Trippe went back to Wall Street and put together a consortium of insurance companies, which was where the big money was. With Metropolitan, on whose board Trippe conveniently sat, and Prudential giving him a thumbs-up, sixteen other insurers joined in to give Trippe a $60 million line of credit at 3.75 percent interest, to buy jets. Trippe assured the underwriters that the new planes were the best collateral their big money could buy.

Inspired by Trippe's newly deep pockets, Donald Douglas got off the dime. In 1955 he finally commissioned his own prototype for what he would call the DC-8, and the race was on. The DC-8 looked suspiciously, if not surprisingly, like Boeing's 707. Both planes had Pratt & Whitney J-57 jet engines. The problem for both companies was that there was only one prospective customer—Juan Trippe. All the other Skycoons passed, Rickenbacker with his $100 million bet on the Lockheed Electras, C. R. Smith with his $64 million wager on thirty-five of the Lockheed planes. Those numbers chilled both Allen and Douglas; each Skycoon knew he'd better jump through whatever hoops Trippe was demanding. The question was who, Allen or Douglas, would jump higher, because the loser could end up with the biggest embarrassment in the history of aviation, a very fast and fancy party to which nobody came.

The biggest contest was speed. Trippe declared that neither the Boeing nor the Douglas jet was fast enough. The populist Eddie Rickenbacker's avowed philosophy of flying the most planes with the most people wasn't that different from that of Trippe, the perceived elitist. The P&W J-57 engines, Trippe believed, were simply too weak to lift those loads of package tourists, the sugarplums that danced in Trippe's global head. Trippe always had aces up his sleeve, even if they were someone else's cards. In this case, he had inside information that P&W was developing a new and even more powerful jet engine, the J-75. He told Boeing that was what he wanted.

But Boeing was all set to fly with what it had. Allen told Trippe that even if the engines were more than just a gleam in P&W's eye, he couldn't afford to retool his entire plane around them. Even though the competing DC-8 was still on the drawing board, redesigning the 707 to make it faster might end up delaying the finished plane. Allen the gambler was gambling that Trippe would rather have a slow jet than no jet. He was also gambling that Douglas was so far behind the jet curve, with not even a plane but only a concept, that he could never catch up.

Not comprehending the word no, Trippe flew to Santa Monica to see Douglas again. Since the DC-8 hadn't been built, he pressed the Scotsman: Isn't this precisely what you wanted, to wait out Boeing and then make a better plane out of their design and hard work? Trippe laid it out plainly: Make your jet around the J-75 engines, and I'll buy it and not Allen's. Only with the J-75s could Pan Am live up to Trippe's desire to call itself the Intercontinental Airline, just as it was naming its new hotel chain InterContinental Hotels. Otherwise, the "weak" J-57s would have to make stops, and Juan Trippe viewed himself as a nonstop messiah. Douglas just sat there smoking his pipe. And then he did what few people ever did: Just like Bill Allen, he turned Juan

Trippe down. The J-75 was pure speculation. Trippe was talking Buck Rogers to him. It had never been flown at all. The Scotsman was no gambler. He wasn't about to commit his company's future to an untried engine that might never take his DC-8 off the ground.

Not one to be deterred, Trippe decided that if he could not bring the plane to the engines, he would bring the engines to the plane. He went directly to Hartford, Connecticut,

POWER ELITE. Frederick Rentschler (left), founder of Pratt & Whitney airplane engine manufacturer with Boeing founder, William Boeing, 1920s.

headquarters of Pratt & Whitney, to visit the company's chairman, Frederick Rentschler, a deity of airline technology in the same pantheon as Trippe. The two aging gods had a heart-to-heart. Trippe was fifty-six at the time, Rentschler sixty-six. Both had legacy on their minds. Rentschler was cut in the same patrician mold as Yale man Trippe, except that Rentschler had gone to Princeton. He was of privileged Germanic stock transplanted to the Midwest, similar to that of Wilhelm Boing, and just as rich. A plutocrat version of the Ohio German Edward Reichenbacher, who started his career as a car mechanic, Rentschler came from a dynasty, based in Hamilton, Ohio, that owned one of the first major automobile companies, Republic Motors. It was also a family of superachievers. Frederick's brother, Gordon, another Princetonian, went on to Wall Street to chair First National City Bank, the forerunner of Citicorp. A third Princeton man, George Rentschler, became the president of the mighty Baldwin Locomotive Company, overseeing the end of the railway era as his brother opened the one of flight.

Tall, blond, patrician, and Aryan, the sportsman Frederick Rentschler was central casting for the Red Baron. But underneath that *Übermensch* façade was a nerdy science whiz kid. Working at his father's auto plant as a machinist after Princeton, Rentschler went to war and served in Europe as an army captain. Afterward, like every young man of his generation obsessed with flight, he went to work at Wright Aviation (in name only; the brothers were long gone), where he designed the first air-cooled engine. Everyone thought he was crazy, believing that only water-cooled engines could fly planes. It took him five years, but eventually, the navy got with the Rentschler program and agreed to buy the motor. That purchase led to Rentschler's founding Pratt & Whitney in 1925. The engine became known as the Wasp and proved to be one of the seminal innovations of aviation.

When Rentschler decided to go beyond naval planes and convinced Bill Boeing to use the Wasp on his passenger craft, this led to their firms' combination into United Air Lines. It also led to the ire of Franklin Roosevelt and Hugo Black, whose commission calculated that Rentschler had made a profit of $21 million on an investment of under $300. Rentschler fought back, on the grounds of good old Yankee ingenuity. He had built the better mousetrap. Why shouldn't he reap the rewards? But one of his imperious, monopolistic comments backfired: "The air between the coasts is not big enough to be divided." Rentschler's eye-popping success created front-page headlines in the Depression.

The United/Boeing trust was busted under the Air Mail Act of 1934, forbidding the combine of airplane manufacturers and passenger airline fliers. Rentschler had to be content with Pratt & Whitney, where he made still another seminal move in creating a huge helicopter market with Igor Sikorsky. During World War II, Rentschler's Wasp engines powered America's great warplanes, the Hellcats and Thunderbolts, the Liberator bombers, the Skymaster transports. The war could not have been won without him, nor could the Cold War that followed. Rentschler's horsepower was the force behind the new Boeing Stratofortresses that were the backbone of the Strategic Air Command. Rentschler was not a speechmaker, but when he spoke, the world listened. "There is no such thing as a second best air force," he said. "There is the best, or nothing."

Both Trippe and Rentschler had graced the cover of *Time*, Trippe dubbed "Clipper Skipper," Rentschler "Mr. Horsepower." Now each cover boy exhorted the other to outdo himself. The J-75 was Trippe's dream engine. He tried to convince Rentschler that this engine could be even more seminal than the Wasp. Rentschler was cautious. A key part of his legacy was safety. The J-75 was still being tested in giant wind tunnels, in cold and heat, rain and sleet. Furthermore, the engine was intended first for military, not passenger planes. Rentschler didn't want any commercial passenger blood on his hands or his legacy.

Now Trippe came at Rentschler with a whole new approach. In late fall 1955, Trippe invited him down to New York to lunch at the Cloud Club, a triplex membership dining hall on the sixty-eighth floor of the Chrysler Building. Although the Chrysler was classic deco, the bar of the Cloud Club was classic Princeton-Yale, very baronial Olde English. Both men felt right at home drinking there, steeped in the nostalgia for their Ivy glory days.

But their business days were more glorious, and over lunch upstairs, Trippe pitched Rentschler that, for them, the best was yet to come. The setting of this pitch, the main dining room a floor above the bar, was pure Fred and Ginger, totally futuristic, with soaring granite columns and etched glass sconces. There was a cloud mural on the high ceiling and a vast mural of Manhattan on the north wall. The Cloud, as it was known, also boasted a humidor, a barbershop, a stock ticker, and for relief, the biggest men's room in Manhattan. It was business lunch only, and suffice it to say, women were not welcome.

But it was the perfect spot for Trippe to outline his own New Deal. Trippe offered to buy $40 million of J-75 engines, 120 in total, enough to power thirty jets, whether they be Douglas's or Boeing's. This totally upended the way planes were made. The frame always came first. Trippe didn't care. That was the old way, and that was why there were so many anemic planes that couldn't fly as fast as they should. Trippe was laying down a bet, a huge bet, that he could get someone, i.e., Rentschler, to turn the process upside down; and that he could get someone else, that someone being either Donald Douglas or Bill Allen, to build him a plane for Fred Rentschler's superengines.

Maybe it was the Cloud Club, or maybe Trippe had just worn him down. Rentschler finally said yes. Trippe wouldn't get his engines until 1959, but get them he would. It was the last big decision Rentschler would ever make. In April 1956, he died unexpectedly at his winter home in Boca Raton, Florida. It turned out that he had been concealing a serious illness for several years, something that the all-knowing Trippe may or may not have known. Not that Trippe should have felt guilty about hounding Rentschler to his grave; Trippe would have expected the same treatment had their positions been reversed. Men were only the messengers. The airplane was the message. The airplane always came first.

Once Trippe had Rentschler's word on the engines, he went back to Seattle to see Allen with his fait accompli. Allen, however, refused to be moved. His 707 was even more accompli. He simply wasn't going to change it. Back, then, to Santa Monica. This time Trippe didn't need a Cloud Club to close the deal. The engine commitment and huge check would suffice. On the spot, Trippe told Douglas he would buy twenty-five of his DC-8s, equipped with the J-75s. But it wasn't exclusive.

Trippe had to be fastest, but he also had to be first. Consequently, he could not afford to turn his back on Bill Allen, even if Allen had turned his back on Trippe. And so he gave Allen the consolation prize of an order for twenty of the slower 707s. That way he was certain to be the first American carrier to fly the big jet, and to reap the attendant publicity whirlwind of being number one in a 1958 launch. If Trippe preferred the Douglas planes when they arrived the next year, he planned to unload the Boeing planes on his foreign competitors, or even the American Big Four. He assumed he was going to bull the market and force everyone to ditch the turboprops and get on his jet bandwagon. He knew the plane would speak for itself. *Res ipsa loquitur.*

The one bandwagon Trippe did get rolling was that of Donald Doug-las. Soon after Trippe announced his buy, Pat Patterson of United topped him with an order of thirty DC-8s, equipped with the weaker J-57 en-gines with which both the DC-8 and the 707 were originally conceived. Because United wasn't flying across oceans, Patterson wasn't concerned about the extra range the J-75s would give his plane. The reason he pre-ferred the DC-8 to the 707 was because it was bigger—by six seats. Eastern soon followed suit, with a big Douglas order.

Now American's C. R. Smith was in a corner. The train was leaving the station (or the plane the airport), and he hadn't bought a ticket. He liked being bigger, but he liked being first (domestically) even more. Not wanting to seem like a United copycat, Smith went to Bill Allen with his own gambit: I'll buy your 707 if you make it four inches wider. That would make it one inch larger than the DC-8. Like football, jets were a game of inches. Those four inches would enable the 707 to go from its present three-two economy-seat configuration to six abreast, three by three. Although Allen wouldn't budge for Trippe, he changed his no-changes tune and jumped for Smith, giving him a new plane with those extra inches. Smith made it worth his while by ordering thirty 707s, which were designated "Astrojets."

Boeing's new willingness to customize its 707 held great allure in the foreign market, where geographic peculiarities held sway. Qantas, which needed smaller jets for inter-Australian flights and bigger ones for its European and American routes, was Boeing's first overseas account, soon followed by Air France. However, Bill Allen's biggest bragging rights came when the Eisenhower White House ordered three 707s to become the first jet *Air Force Ones*. Eisenhower may have been spurred on by jet envy. Much had been made about Russia's premier Nikita Khrushchev being the first world leader to fly a jet. That the jet was the Tupolev 104, which would have an even dicier safety record than Britain's de Havil-land Comet, was beside the point. As with Sputnik, Russia did it *first*. As Juan Trippe knew, first was best. Bragging rights were all-important in the tech race. Consequently, Eisenhower joined the jet landslide and contributed to its inevitability. As for Douglas and Boeing, the jet race began as a near-dead heat. A tally of orders at the close of 1956 showed Boeing had 141 to Douglas's 123. In the end, Boeing's first did prove to be best. Douglas was never able to catch up, and the 707, not the DC-8, became the poster plane for the new jet age.

Amid all the jet jockeying among the Skycoons, something very big was missing. The elephant in the room was not in the room. In this tiny ultra-elite club of pioneers battling for control of the skies during the key developmental decade in the history of aviation, where, oh where, was the mad scientist, the pilot of pilots of the group who should have been the pacesetter in this race of the titans? Howard Hughes was arguably the fastest rich man on earth and undoubtedly the most eccentric. Where was he? And where was Hughes's TWA, the only American airline capable of supplanting Pan Am as the colossus of the skies? TWA was "bi"—that is, it had a huge international presence—that made Trippe fear it, and a huge domestic presence that made the rest of the Big Four fear it as well. Because of Hughes, who was not only an aeronautical genius but also a movie mogul, playboy, and billionaire industrialist/ philanthropist, TWA was capable of generating more publicity, more headlines, than all its rivals combined.

Hughes was so outrageous that he could have been a figment of Igor Cassini's imagination. Who cared what Juan Trippe was doing in the Cloud Club when the public's interest could be piqued by what Hughes was doing in the clouds with everyone from Jean Harlow to Katharine Hepburn? Because of Hughes's huge Hollywood presence, TWA was known as the "Airline of the Stars," and it had a lock on the glamour/ celebrity factor that sold papers and tickets as well. The Ivy Skycoons, like Trippe and Rentschler, had the pedigree but not the filigree. They weren't social at all, not enough for Cholly Knickerbocker and certainly not for Hedda and Louella. Legends like Rickenbacker, or big bosses like Smith and Patterson, were all too rough-hewn to be part of any "set." Most significant, they were all working far too hard to have time to socialize in a major way that would have generated column interest. But Hughes, the ultimate antisocialite, was pure column catnip. Plus, he loved to fly, and fly faster than anyone else. So where is he in this saga?

Hughes was actually trying to live up to all the expectations that he would be the Lenin of the jet revolution. As usual, he had his own way. Rather than get caught in the Trippe-provoked contest between Boeing and Douglas, Hughes's solution was "neither." Instead, in 1956, he approached a third manufacturer, the San Diego–based Convair, a division of the mighty conglomerate General Dynamics, most famous for its Atlas missiles, and placed his chips, $400 million worth, ordering sixty-three Convair 880s. A few seats smaller than the 707 and the DC-8, the Convair had speed, a top of 615 miles per hour. That would make it the world's fastest jet, for the world's fastest man. The plane fit Hughes's self-image.

What it didn't fit were the expectations of Hughes's Wall Street financiers. Despite possessing seemingly all the riches on earth, even Howard Hughes was at the mercy of the moneymen. Just as Juan Trippe was funding his jet venture through the grand insurance companies, so was Hughes. The seemingly slowest, most deliberate men on earth, the actuarial types who ran Metropolitan Life, the Prudential, and the Equitable, were the fiscal horsepower behind the most mercurial.

THE AVIATOR. Howard Hughes—Hollywood tycoon, record-breaking pilot, and founder of TWA—in his saner days, 1936.

Putting this insurance financing together were three grand investment banking houses: Dillon, Read; Lehman Brothers; and Lazard Frères. These were Juan Trippe people, Cloud Club men, who had no patience for the endless and unfathomable shenanigans of Howard Hughes. No sooner had Hughes made his offer to Convair than the insurers and the bankers made up their mind: TWA could stay; Howard Hughes had to go. They wanted a new boss at the airline. Otherwise, TWA would be grounded for the jet age's inaugural ball, and missing that party meant the end of the game. What followed was a multiyear, coast-versus-coast battle royal between the most vicious attack-dog lawyers of Hollywood and Wall Street.

If the fiduciaries thought Hughes was crazy in the late fifties, they had no idea of the sideshow his life would become. No one in America had ever squandered more promise. Born in 1905 in Humble, Texas, Hughes was the fortunate son of the inventor of the most crucial tool in the oil boom that would create so many of the country's greatest fortunes. That "drill bit," the cutting device central to digging the holes from whence oil might gush, became the key to a fortune bigger than those of the oil wildcatters who did the drilling. The heir to Hughes Tool Company was a born scientist. At eleven, he invented the first radio transmitter in Houston. The next year, he created a motorized bicycle. At fourteen, he flew his first plane. In the two years before he was nineteen, in 1924, both his parents died, leaving him as Texas's prime poor little rich boy.

Hughes immediately dropped out of the Rice Institute, the MIT of the South-Southwest, and married the "boss's daughter," Ella Botts Rice, an heiress whose family had endowed the school. Baker Botts was Houston's leading law firm. Although Hughes could rule Texas, he wasn't interested. He took Ella straight to his fantasy destination, Hollywood. There he discovered he wasn't interested in Ella, either. They divorced in 1929. At six-three and lankily, darkly handsome, Hughes didn't need a Gary Cooper to play him; he looked like a star himself. But the loner was content with, actually intent on, remaining offscreen. Shortly after the split with Ella, the second film that Hughes produced, the silent comedy *Two Arabian Knights,* won the first Oscar for best director.

Hughes's classic was 1930's *Hell's Angels,* at $3.8 million of his inheritance, the most expensive, yet one of the best, films of its time. Starring a teenage Jean Harlow, whom Hughes discovered, as the love interest of competing World War I flying aces, *Hell's* was considered the first big action film. Hughes himself directed and flew in the flying sequences, still considered among the most thrilling ever put on screen. The film was a blockbuster and secured Hughes's place at Hollywood's high table. He followed this with another classic, *Scarface,* though he got more press from his romances than his filmmaking.

One of his most high-profile obsessions was with the Oscar-winning sisters Olivia de Havilland and Joan Fontaine. The first cousin of the sisters' Tokyo-based patent-lawyer father was Sir Geoffrey de Havilland, a sane English take on Howard Hughes. De Havilland had begun his career as a car mechanic before starting the company that produced the unmatched Mosquito fighter plane, before his legend was marred by his ill-fated Comet jet. However, in the thirties, when Hughes was pursuing his cousins, the name was air magic. Some might read a skyborne component into Hughes's quest for the two stars, but the aphrodisiac here, as with Katharine Hepburn, was more likely celebrity than aviation.

Yet even more than for his women, Howard Hughes was famous for his planes and his own high-altitude achievements. In 1937, he flew coast-to-coast, Los Angeles to Newark nonstop, in his self-designed H-1 racer in a mere seven and a half hours. The next year he circumnavigated the globe, stopping in exotic places like Moscow, Omsk, and Yakutsk, in under four days. He worked closely with Lockheed in designing the Constellation, the powerful four-propeller carrier with the distinctive three-fin tail that became the most popular plane to take across the Atlantic from its 1945 debut until the advent of the jets in the late fifties. It was the flagship of TWA's deluxe New York–Paris "champagne" flight, as well as Pan Am's workhorse for its round-the-world service.

In 1944, before its commercial debut, Hughes flew the Constellation across the country in under seven hours, for a new record. He had just bought TWA, and like Trippe, he knew the value of publicity. This speedcapade got him the cover of *Life*. The Constellation would become Eisenhower's first *Air Force One* and would win Hughes the Congressional Gold Medal for distinguished service to American aviation. Hughes was too busy designing brassieres for Jane Russell, and other Hollywood diversions, to be bothered to go to Washington for the ceremony. Insulted, the White House sent him the medal by ground mail.

TWA, before Hughes bought it, had stood for Transcontinental & Western Airlines. Its founder, Jack Frye, had been a Hollywood stunt pilot, a member of an aerial troupe called the Thirteen Black Cats. He then started an air service shuttling movie stars and their mistresses to secret desert hideaways, a clandestine operation that appealed to the undercover lover Hughes. Hughes bought in to Frye's company and, wanting to out-Trippe Pan Am in the postwar period, renamed it Trans World Airlines and began competing for a big slice of Pan Am's foreign pie. Hughes fired Frye in 1947. He would hire and fire four more TWA chief executives in the next decade, contributing to Wall Street's anxiety over the company's stability.

Trippe was privately horrified by Hughes, not so much for his "amoral" lifestyle as for his very real competitive threat. Hughes wanted the world, the whole world, as much as Trippe did. The proprietary Trippe thought he already owned it and that Hughes's desires were simply out of line. Acting on this theory, Trippe leaned on one of his old Ivy boys in Washington to put Howard Hughes in his place. Trippe's chosen instrument here was Republican senator Owen Brewster of Maine, a *Mayflower* descendant and Harvard Law graduate who had been elected governor in 1924 with the support of the Ku Klux Klan, which operated as openly and brazenly in nativist Maine as it did in Dixie.

An archenemy of Roosevelt and the New Deal and an archadmirer of Senator Joseph McCarthy, Brewster was Trippe's main Washington apologist, the senator who carried the ball for the argument that Pan Am was America's "chosen instrument" in international air competition. The idea here was that one airline, and only one, backed by America's full faith and credit, could compete with the nationalized foreign carriers, backed by their countries' massive resources. Hughes might divide the Yank effort, whereby the foreigners might conquer. Attack dog Brewster was unleashed on Hughes. Trippe had convinced Brewster that the richest man in America was actually un-American.

Brewster was the chairman of the Aviation Committee of the Interstate Commerce Commission. In 1947, he held Senate hearings investigating Hughes's receipt of a fortune in defense funds for fiascos like the failed giant transport, the *Spruce Goose,* which flew only once. Hughes, according to Brewster, had cheated the American government for upward of $40 million. However, what Brewster, publicly described by high-placed critics as Trippe's "stooge" and "errand boy," was actually angling for was to use the hearings as a cudgel to force Hughes to sell TWA to Trippe and ensure Pan Am's perpetual dominance.

On the eve of the hearings, with Hughes hoping to forestall them, Trippe and Hughes did meet—top-secretly, of course—for the only time in their parallel lives. Maybe, Hughes thought, he might just buy Pan Am. The summit conference was held in Palm Springs, near where Hughes had rented a compound for the occasion in the high desert. Trippe was alone, per Hughes's rules, while Hughes was accompanied by his notorious right hand Noah Dietrich. Trippe was not there to sell, only buy, and at bazaar prices.

Trippe made Hughes what the aviator regarded as an insulting buy-out offer, and only for TWA's international routes, which was all Trippe ever wanted. Hughes, deeply ashamed that he had wasted a second talking with Trippe, and more paranoid than before that these futile talks would leak, insisted on flying the Pan Am chief personally to the Mexican border, where Trippe was to instruct his own pilot and plane to meet them. Trippe was lucky that Hughes didn't push him out over the Mojave Desert.

The Brewster hearings thus began. They were to Howard Hughes what the McCarthy hearings were to the Hollywood Ten: a witch hunt. But at this point, before he really went off the deep end, Hughes was still a cool daredevil air hero, not some brainy socialist with a typewriter. The public was on his side. So was Congress. A Brewster-backed bill that would have forced a merger of all American international carriers (others beside TWA were stirring to fly the seas) into a Pan Am–dominated "community company" drew screams of un-American-ness, of stifling the essence of capitalism, which was competition. Not only did both houses overwhelmingly reject the measure, but Hughes pulled himself out of his paralytic funk to wreak revenge on Owen Brewster.

When Hughes took his seat before Brewster's Senate committee, he seemed to be channeling James Stewart in *Mr. Smith Goes to Washington*. Hughes took a heartland Texan's aw-shucks attitude toward his success and a no-way response to charges of ripping off the country, *his* country. "I worked pretty hard for what money I have, and I didn't make it from airplanes," Hughes said. "In my transactions with the government, I have made no profit whatsoever." Hughes basically accused Brewster of trying to blackmail him, revealing the senator's offer to call off these hearings if he "merged" TWA into Pan Am on the terms and under the thumb of Juan Trippe. Furthermore, Hughes cited, chapter and verse, very specific occasions of Brewster's accepting Pan Am's free tickets and other largesse, including his being a virtual boarder at Washington's "Casa Trippe," Pan Am's palatial D.C. lobbying headquarters on F Street.

With a patently untrue eye-popping declaration, "Juan Trippe is a man not interested in making money," Owen Brewster basically wrote his own epitaph. But Hughes insisted on dancing on Brewster's political grave. When Brewster ran for reelection in 1952, Hughes threw all his immense resources behind the governor of Maine, Frederick Payne, convincing him to challenge Brewster in the Republican primary. The Payne campaign tarred Brewster with the Klan, with McCarthy, with his shakedown of Hughes. It was a rare defeat for an incumbent senator in a primary, but Payne pulled it off. Without Hughes, six years later, Payne lost to Edmund Muskie. The dethroned Brewster devoted the rest of his life to Christian Science, while Hughes devoted the rest of the fifties to going mano a mano with Juan Trippe in their battle for dominance of the international skies.

Hughes almost pulled it off. He was a great judge of talent, and not just the distaff celluloid variety. In his powerful aviation technology firm Hughes Aircraft, he raided Detroit's Ford Motors to hire its management wizard Tex Thornton, who put Hughes on the cutting edge of missile defense and made him billions more. However, Hughes's eccentricities got in the way of profits. When he insisted on the firm building its new research center next to his desert compound and starlet retreat in Las Vegas rather than on its Culver City, California, campus, an era of bad feelings began, which ended with Thornton's exit and even more nervous agitation in fiscal circles.

Once Wall Street decided Hughes must go, TWA's jet future was frozen. His hands tied with legal tape, Howard Hughes couldn't go to war with Trippe or anyone else. His reign over TWA was over, though he would not be given the final court-sanctioned boot until 1961. Meanwhile, Juan Trippe reigned supreme as Zeus of the Air, launching his first New York–to–Paris 707 right on schedule in 1958. Few Atlantic journeys ever received so much publicity, except perhaps those of Lindbergh and the *Titanic*.

Technically, Trippe wasn't first, but in the colloquialism attributed to Confederate general Nathan Bedford Forrest, Trippe was "firstest with the mostest." Firstest with the leastest was perennial also-ran Sir Geoffrey de Havilland, who already wore the "first Atlantic jet" crown and had developed a new and improved—and supposedly safer—version of the Comet, the Comet IV, which made its first scheduled commercial flight between London and New York on October 4, beating Pan Am "across the pond," as the Brits would say. Alas, what might have been a cause for celebration turned out to be a cold supper of humble pie when a major strike by British transport workers shut down London's Heathrow Airport for weeks and stole all De Havilland's thunder. What good is a safe plane if it can't take off? The unkindest of all cuts came late in the year when BOAC threw in the Brit-pride towel and placed a huge 707 order with Boeing.

On October 16, Trippe presided over a grand ceremony at Hangar 10 of Washington National Airport, where First Lady Mamie Eisenhower christened Trippe's first 707, the *Clipper America,* with a bottle of, not champagne, God forbid, but water blended from each of the seven seas. Trippe, in his address, noted proudly that Mamie was the fourth White House dowager to launch a Clipper, a tradition that had included Lou Hoover, Eleanor Roosevelt, and First Daughter Margaret Truman.

Trippe's encomium to his creation was eloquent. The 707, he said, "speaks for the clearest and simplest characteristics of all things American. It is swift. It is large. It is efficient. It is imaginative." What he didn't mention was that it was about to get even swifter. Boeing's Bill Allen had relented at last and agreed to refit the bulk of the Pan Am 707 order with Fred Rentschler's more powerful J-75s. Trippe couldn't resist counting his goodies, the "2,300,000 citizen-travelers crossing the Atlantic" that year, and boasting that this jet alone, not to mention his coming third-of-a-billion-dollar fleet of forty-nine more "will carry across the Atlantic, each and every year, as many passengers as a ship as large as the Queen Mary." The air messiah saw the 707 was a great bird of peace, the great jet hope:

> How can it fail to smash and shatter the petty provincialism and narrow nationalism . . . making of this world a tragic mosaic of hostility and hate? How can this fabulous new force in the sky fail to serve the hope of the world and the peace of the world?

No oration before an Eisenhower crowd could be without a major dig at the Soviet Union, and a plug for Pan Am as more than just a flying money machine, but, most important, as a bulwark against Communism:

> Aeroflot, the Soviet Civil Airline, has expanded, during the last two years, into sixteen new countries . . . Aeroflot, this direct agent of the Soviet Government, assures a form of communist economic penetration wherever it reaches. It is thus the stern labor of Americans— freely striving, in a free economy—to match the initiative and the resources so massively commandeered by the Soviet state . . . In this sense, this new *Clipper America* is more than a technical triumph for civilian convenience. It is a test of America's capacity to work for its own survival.

Once out of Eisenhower earshot, however, civilian convenience morphed into a Madison Avenue–slaked consumer fantasy that became the theme of the 707 rollout. Trippe's objective was to make a trip to Europe an American birthright, and the 707 America's new dream machine. He wanted to be Henry Ford of the Air. Before the official first commercial flight two weeks hence, Trippe himself flew on the *Clipper America* from Baltimore to Brussels with thirty of the country's most influential journalists and editors, then packed the *Clipper* with more than a hundred lesser pressmen for a bon vivant's whirlwind tour of France, just to show them how seductive this new lifestyle was going to be.

It was champagne and caviar all the way for the Yank reporters. They arrived at Le Bourget Airport early in the morning and took a catnap at their deluxe Champs-Élysées hotel before hitting *les grands boulevards*. The night brought them to the Lido, the greatest of all the Paris night clubs, with its topless Bluebelles. There was no rest whatsoever for the *Clipper America*. No sooner had it deposited the American journalists at Le Bourget than it packed in a full load of European journalists to fly to New York for a little tit for tat. While the Americans were beginning their champagne journey, the Euros, billeted at the Waldorf Astoria, were drinking Jack Daniel's and eating Omaha steaks at Pen and Pencil. No Lido for them but, rather, the Overseas Press Club, the Stock Exchange, the United Nations, and the Circle Line.

Back in France the next morning, the American press group was taken to Épernay, in Champagne, for a liquid lunch at the Taittinger vineyards, followed by a bit of social redemption touring the Cathedral at Reims, then more decadence at the châteaux of two more legendary bubbly producers, Veuve Clicquot and Charles Heidsieck. Juan Trippe obviously had concluded that the way to the heart of the press was through its liver. Returning to Paris, the group was taken to the government *palais* at the Quai d'Orsay. There the journalists met with the French foreign minister Couve de Murville for aperitifs before still more champagne and a lavish dinner on a chartered yacht that plied the Seine. Next morning, the hungover press was flown home to the reality of their typewriters and the looming deadline that was the quid pro quo for the gratis revelry. Like ships in the night at Idlewild, the Yanks passed their European counterparts, who were trekking to the comforts of the homeward-bound 707 that never slept.

The "official" maiden voyage of the *Clipper America* on October 28 came as something of an anticlimax. It was bad enough that it first had to stop to refuel in Gander, Newfoundland. Then a thick fall fog over

France further delayed the 707 by ninety-five minutes, making the jet seem not all that much faster than TWA's Super-Constellations, which made the journey in eleven hours. Howard Hughes, if he was conscious, was probably gloating that the only big names on the *Clipper* were the actress Greer Garson and the foot magnate Dr. William Scholl. His TWA was still "Airline of the Stars," jet or no jet.

Juan Trippe began referring to Pan Am not as the self-aggrandizing "chosen instrument" but as the humble "instrument of the people." Trippe didn't need Hollywood. He had what he needed, Washington and Wall Street. Now all he had to do was to fill the seats of his fifty 707s. Juan Trippe didn't care about stars. He cared about tourists. The people who would become the Jet Set were already going to Europe. They were already in place, in the right place, in Paris, Rome, St. Moritz, Saint-Tropez. Juan Trippe's challenge, and that of his competitors, was not so much to convey the rich and famous but to use the image of the rich and famous to create their own jet set, a jet set of real people, a jet set of citizen-travelers.

5

The Profiler

J UAN TRIPPE'S CAMPAIGN TO DEMOCRATIZE THE JET SET WAS EVIDENT FROM PAN
Am's very first commercial flight on October 28, 1958. He bestilled
his public relations minions from making too much of having on board
the Oscar-winning Greer Garson. Trippe regarded her as English, as opposed to American, and didn't see her as that newsworthy a "get." The
flight's only other celebrity, Dr. Scholl, the man whose bunion pads and
corn plasters adorned the aching feet of countless tourists, might have
made for amusing copy. However, Trippe decided to forgo it, allowing
Scholl and the other far less known tycoons in first class, which Pan Am
called "deluxe," to enjoy their low visibility. Instead, he put the emphasis
on the back cabin, the big one, and focused on the rank-and-file citizen-
travelers, who, he hoped, would inspire a whole new generation of jet
fliers.

No one on that first flight got more coverage, including her picture
in *Look*, than Billie Miller, a New York secretary who had managed to
travel the world on her annual two-week vacations. "I believe there
should be aboard an ordinary workaday person," she described herself,

FLY ME. Early Pan Am 707 ad, 1960. Eschewing clever copy, the airline relied on the new 707 and the vaunted Pan Am logo to speak for themselves.

"the sort that in these wonderful travel days is being seen more frequently on the international flights." Music to Trippe's ears. Then there were the Noble Hopkinses and their four young children from Garrettsville, Ohio, who won the trip in a contest sponsored by Kellogg's cornflakes. Mr. Hopkins was a school bus driver. None of them had ever been on a train, much less a plane. It was proof that Pan Am made anything possible.

William Eck, of Arlington, Virginia, was the first person to reserve a flight on the 707, the first day Pan Am announced it, three years before in 1955. His alacrity provided a note of caution about planning too far in advance: Mr. Eck missed the flight because he had died. But Pan Am made sure his widow was on board. Other featured voyagers were seventeen-year-old Karl Johansen, from Valhalla, New York, who had saved $2,000 for the trip by working at odd jobs since he was twelve, without telling his parents. He stayed in Europe two days and flew back, so as not to miss high school. The most jet-agey passenger was Mrs. Clive Runnels, from tycoons-only Hobe Sound, Florida, an I-Like-Ike, deluxe-cabin, dowager member of the Republican National Finance

Committee who never got off the *Clipper,* setting a record as the first commercial passenger to take the maiden flight in both directions.

Most of the rest of the passengers on the *Clipper America* tended to be either old flyboys who had been aboard Pan Am's premier transatlantic flight twenty years before, twenty-six endless hours to Lisbon, or frequent fliers who loved going to Europe and loved even more the idea of getting there twice as fast. They were "tourists," but not the grotesque polyester-leisure-suited hordes unleashed by Trippe when he introduced truly mass tourism with his behemoth 747 in 1971. Trippe's 1958 tourists may have been a cut below St. Anthony's Hall, but they were squarely in the upper middle class. The ticket prices said it all. Deluxe was $1,010 round-trip, economy $490 (the same as for the prop planes, so as to promote the new jet), but still a perquisite of the prosperous. The only way a bus driver was going to get to Europe was to win a cornflakes contest. The future 747 tidal wave was mass tourism at much lower prices ($200 round-trip), which reflected the economy of scale. At its inception, the 707 was elite no matter where you sat.

Taking a page from Woody Guthrie, Juan Trippe's theme song for the 707 could have been "This Plane Is Your Plane." This plane was made for you and me, that was the message. And what if you bought the message and you bought a ticket? Then what? It was estimated that about 20 percent of all travelers to Europe went in a group. There were those American Express tours, and Thomas Cook tours, and all kinds of package tours to Europe, similar to the ill-fated one of the Atlanta Art Association. But to the majority of Americans, tours were somehow un-American, at least in terms of American enterprise, ingenuity, and exploration. We were the land of Lewis and Clark, of Daniel Boone. A package tour, to many, was one big Donner Party, an insult to free will and a disaster waiting to happen. The adventure was being on your own. Yet it never hurt to have a guidebook just to get your bearings.

Enter Temple Hornaday Fielding. Actually, Temple Hornaday Fielding had already entered, publishing his first *Fielding's Travel Guide to Europe* in 1948, in the eleven-hour era of the Constellation flights, although most of his readers tended to be first-cabin habitués of the *Queen*

Mary or the *France*. As was Fielding. Both he and his wife, in shades of Sinatra, were secretly terrified of flying. Not that fear stopped him from being the advertising face for the new jets of SAS (Scandinavian Airlines System). When Fielding spoke, travelers listened. He was the *Good Housekeeping* seal for luxury in mobility. This was one pathfinder who would never rest on his laurels or his research. He was a one-man *Michelin Guide,* always testing, always current.

But *Michelin* was a staccato, wordless, star-ratings guide only to France, while Fielding was a garrulous, Menckenesque wit who took on the entire continent. "Watch your step at Orly (Airport)," he warned his readers. "The flooring is as slippery as a Marseilles gigolo." So clever, so nasty, so acute, and so totally self-confident were his critiques that, rather than being a means to the end of Europe, the Fielding *Guide* became an end in itself, in that readers traveled to see Fielding's Europe, and only Fielding's. The man defined the continent, Europe as the grab bag to savor the treasures that Fielding, and only Fielding, was able to unearth. By the advent of the jets, the Fielding *Guide* had grown to nine hundred pages, weighed over two pounds, and sold nearly a hundred thousand copies a year at $4.95 each.

There were a lot of words, and they were the last word. Until Temple Fielding changed his mind. This naturally kept the airlines, the hotels, the restaurants, the emporia, all on their toes. The German word for "guide" is *führer,* as in Hitler. Fielding was a führer of pleasure, an autocrat of self-indulgence, and a pied piper for American sybarites in search of the very best of the Old World. President John F. Kennedy, who, along with Jackie, did more to create the mass mystique of Europe than even Juan Trippe, carried only four books on his 707 *Air Force One:* the Bible, *Webster's Dictionary,* a congressional directory, and *Fielding's Guide.* It was the ultimate compliment from the ultimate "Guidester," as Fielding called his acolytes. He carefully avoided the word "tourist," which, to him, had near-Communist connotations, of the herd, of the extirpation of choice and free will and free enterprise. Travelers, voyagers, pilgrims, explorers, pioneers, anything that smacked of luxurious self-determination and self-indulgence, were all fine. But to call a Guidester a tourist would be the unkindest cut of all.

"We shoot for the snob reader," Fielding freely admitted. Fielding, six feet tall, with jet-black dyed and slicked-back hair and lacquered nails, dressed in ascots and bespoke mohair suits by Brioni of Rome, looked the part of a European *boulevardier* or, to some, an aging Via Veneto gigolo. He was anything but that. He was a Princeton man, an army man, an OSS man. He saw himself as one of the Juan Trippe Ivy elect. But Fielding was dealing with a new kind of snob. His readers weren't cultural snobs; they were food and lodging snobs, and Fielding, who detested sightseeing, was just their man, their voice. These people collected memories of staying at the Ritz and eating at the Tour d'Argent like art lovers might collect memories of seeing the *Mona Lisa* at the Louvre. Fielding told these forerunners of "foodies" and "roomies" precisely where to eat and sleep, and gave them bragging rights for sharing the same good taste. Fielding himself barely mentioned the Louvre. He hated shopping as much as he hated museums and cathedrals, but he knew his readers liked to shop, so he left that section of the guide to his wife, Nancy, a former literary agent.

TEMPLE OF GASTRONOMY. Preeminent travel critic Temple Fielding, hamming it up with unmelancholy Danes in Copenhagen on his fiftieth birthday, 1963.

The Jet Age reign and regime of Temple Fielding, alongside that of Juan Trippe, was a product of the evolution of the Grand Tour. The Tour, which originated in the late 1600s with post-Etonian English gents visiting the Renaissance Continent with both a guide, or cicerone, and a physician. The idea was to visit the great ruins, like the Forum and the Colosseum in Rome, and the great works of art, in palaces like the Uffizi and the Louvre. There were no real restaurants then to go to, so the travelers had no choice but to dwell on the culture. The art of living was secondary, though any visit to the court of Louis XIV was bound to give a tourist some fancy ideas. Nonetheless, what gave the English upper class its snob cachet was its cultural superiority derived from this peripatetic education, even more than its lands and wealth. Knowledge (then, at least) was power.

The nineteenth-century advent of steamships and steam railways opened the continent, if not to the rube masses, at least to a wider swath of the populace. The first Cook's Tour took place in 1841, though it had nothing to do with either culture or pleasure. Thomas Cook was a Derbyshire teetotaler who was a devotee of, and a proselytizer for, the temperance movement. When he organized a railway trip for 540 nondrinkers from the city of Leicester to a sobriety rally eleven miles away, the travel agency was born. Although he went bankrupt with the temperance people, Cook hit pay dirt by switching to the would-be Midlands culturati. His first big triumph was transporting Englishmen, in the thousands, across the Channel to the 1867 Paris World's Fair.

Cook followed this with tours to post–Civil War America, where the still-bloody battlefields were the hottest tourist ticket until his company made another fortune taking voyagers to the Pyramids and up the Nile. American Express, originally a shipping company part owned by Wells Fargo stage lines, entered the tour business when J. P. Fargo took his own Grand Tour to Europe and couldn't get cash anywhere outside the major capitals. He invented the traveler's check, and American Express became the giant of the trip business.

Around the same time as the Cook's tours were starting, the first guidebooks began to appear. The undisputed leader was the Leipzig firm of Karl Baedeker, whose name became synonymous with travel books, which were translated into many languages. However, the Baedekers were very Germanic, very scholarly, and no fun at all. The idea of describing a hotel or restaurant with the respect accorded Notre Dame or the Pantheon would have been considered both radical and frivolous. Leave that to the French, whose red *Guide Michelin* began to appear at the turn of the century with the rise of the autocar.

The *Michelins* were originally far more concerned with where a driver could fill his tank than his stomach. It was a basic list of gas stations and garages along the French roads. Only in the decadent, gastronomic thirties did *Michelin* introduce its three-star restaurant rating system. And it was only for France, the presumption being that nowhere else in Europe had good food. After World War II, Temple Fielding found a continent full of bargain pleasures that was completely uncharted. He had the guidebook field all to himself, and he ran for a touchdown.

In addition to being America's reigning oracular epicure, Fielding was also a ladies' man, and not necessarily his wife's. Just as the Grand Tour of the eighteenth century was designed for gentlemen, so was Fielding's twentieth-century version. His was a man's world. His wife was always with him, but as he was paying the American Express bills, her duty was to do her shopping and avert her eyes. Fielding liked to drink and carouse and whore around. The *Guide* had a substantial "nightlife" section, but because these were the high-prudery Eisenhower years, Fielding cloaked the whores in euphemistic innuendo, of which he was a master. To wit, a typical passage, this one on the top bordello in Madrid:

> For men only, Casablanca is still the best, in spite of its recent flood
> of hog mannered U.S. drugstore-cowboys who make me ashamed to
> be an American. Stage show of 20 performers; 2 Latin bands with
> some of the best and loudest Caribbean music on the Peninsula. It's
> the hangout of Spanish painters, sculptors, writers, gents occupied in

the arts and gents interested in pursuing the arts. Huge 4oz. drinks cost roughly $2.50. Go around 12:30 AM. Hostesses galore, both at the balcony bar and at the downstairs tables . . . Open all year, except Holy Week.

Fielding went on to rhapsodize about the Spanish "hostesses" in print as "the most chic, most beautiful, most mannerly group of casual companions to be found anywhere . . . Disease is almost unknown . . . Many make successful marriages." He felt it necessary to issue his own apologia for his fifties double-standard hypocrisies, cloaking it in cross-cultural anthropology. One of his most important travel tips—actually, an edict—was to leave the wife at the hotel, shaming her into even *considering* doing the town with Big Daddy:

> It is not only bad taste but downright stupidity to take ladies of your family to establishments in this special category. This isn't Paris or New York, where slumming can be done on a casual basis by anybody; the Spaniards have an ironclad code of manners and behavior in this direction, and they look upon the occasional American girl who, through ignorance or curiosity, pops up in one of these places as a silly, brainless busybody who combines all of the legendary crassness and pushiness of the least attractive type of U.S. female. They despise both her and the man who permits it.

How Fielding so blatantly and sexistly justified prostitution in his "family" book is a sign of his times, yet even after feminism asserted itself in the sixties, he remained the bestselling travel writer of all time. Perhaps the wives wanted to know the best restaurants so badly that they forgave Fielding and their spouses their boys-will-be-boys antics.

One main difference between Temple Fielding and Igor Cassini was that Fielding didn't "chase strawberries," as the saying went, shorthand for the status quest of the fashionable people who flitted from Ascot to Henley to Longchamp to Gstaad to Capri to Mykonos. He didn't need a top table at Princess Grace's Red Cross Ball in Monaco or to be on the list for Stavros Niarchos's Christmas gala in St. Moritz. That kind of event snobbery held about as much interest for Fielding as the sales at Lanvin. Nonetheless, he was the most finicky man on earth about knowing the right suite at Monaco's Hôtel de Paris or St. Moritz's Badrutt's Palace Hotel.

What went on in the ballrooms below simply bored him, just as it would his target reader, whom he described as "the banker in the small town who is a big shot, has security and respect in his community, and to whom Europe is a jungle." Fielding's fifties Babbitt may have never looked at a Cholly Knickerbocker column. But his Main Street wife probably did, and she probably dreamed of getting mentioned in it one day. To cater to him, Fielding told him where he could go for a "nightcap" while his missus recuperated from her shopping spree. To cater to her, Fielding let her know where the stars ate and slept, but he left it to Cassini to keep her current on whom they ate and slept *with*.

Temple Fielding trafficked in incendiary stereotypes, fortunately for him, in an age before political correctness. He was an ethno-racial profiler long before the term came into existence. His was a White Man's Burden view of the world. For example, he marveled at how "clean and industrious" Spaniards in Spain were, compared to his experience of "lassitude and filth in the Indian-peasant segments of Mexico and South America." Here's his take in the *Guide* on Southern Italians: "The ubiquitous Sig. Doe of this latitude is squat, with broad face and beetle brow. He is ignorant, superstitious, disinterested in government, touched only superficially by civilization. He is a primitive man . . ."

Admitting that "some of us . . . tend to categorize a nation of 47 million good people as 'wops' (taken from *guappo,* a Neapolitan greeting)," Fielding then shows what a broad cosmopolite he is by using more stereotypes to combat his others: "To think of the typical Italian as the arm-waving comedian of a Class-B motion picture is as ridiculous and insulting as to think of you and me—typical Americans—as the fat, crass, back-slapping Babbitt who lights 2-foot cigars with $20 bills and scars every table top in sight with his cowboy boots." Somehow the public ate this up, because he was reflecting the prejudices of his country-club readers, albeit with verbal panache that sugarcoated the bitter pill of racism. This was the "comfort" travel writing that Fielding's perpetual bestsellers were made of. Europe, to him, was a big Bronx Zoo of luxury suites, groaning tables, accommodating prostitutes, jolly peasants, jack-booted Nazis. He was a cultural anthropologist who could demystify a Europe that, to most Americans, was as intimidating as a Lost Continent. The genius of Temple Fielding was his ability to transform his basic xenophobia into his art and his fortune, charting, for other xenophobes, a wide world that could not be denied.

Temple Fielding was born in 1913 in the Bronx, in a thirty-two-room house adjacent to the Zoo, where his maternal grandfather, William Temple Hornaday, was the distinguished director. After a privileged adolescence, the teenager had a rude awakening in 1929 when his father lost everything in the Crash and had to be supported by the retired grandfather's pension. Young Temple, who had been taken twice to Europe as a child on the great liners, was abashed by his fall from grace. He tried to keep up a facade by going to deb parties, where he met his dream girl on the skyscraper roof garden of the Hotel Pierre. Too bad that he couldn't afford the two dollars to take her out for a post-ball supper. That dream got away. Dispirited, in 1930, he dropped out of his Connecticut prep school, near where his family lived in Stamford, and began taking odd jobs, including one as the manager of a beach club, where the seeds were planted for the high standards he set for the concierges of his future life.

The two ubiquitous East Coast questions Fielding couldn't stand were "Where did you prep?" and "Where did you go to college?" Determined to have a good answer to the latter, Fielding went back to Stamford High School at age twenty-one and applied himself so diligently that Princeton accepted him and gave him a scholarship. Fielding's version of Princeton was anything but *This Side of Paradise*. It was more like This Side of Bankruptcy. As an older student and scholarship boy, Fielding was out of the eating-club loop and expected to wait tables to help defray his tuition. Too ashamed to do that, he decided to hustle cash by conjuring up a host of enterprises, starting a student lottery, selling rah-

rah-raccoon coats, anything to make a buck. He kept up collegiate appearances by writing for the student paper and leading the marching band as a baton twirler. He somehow found time to study, graduating cum laude in 1939 and going off to war.

In 1941, at Fort Bragg, North Carolina, as a second lieutenant in the army, he got his chance to write his own Baedeker, "Guide to the Field Artillery Replacement Training Center." The assignment was handed to him by General Edwin "Speedy" Parker, who had unsuccessfully assigned three other officers, including the chaplain, to create a manual that made sense of the sprawling new 550-building complex in the Carolina sandhills. The tone of the camp guide was a forerunner of that of the Europe guide; only the accommodations would change. Fielding was full of tips, most seemingly obvious but helpful nonetheless. He warned recruits of weekly inspections, "Tip: Get ready the night before. You'll save yourself and your sergeant a mess of headaches." Or Fielding on haircuts: "Each regiment has its own barbershop, staffed by civilians. It's good and it's cheap. Don't think that you look like a monkey after your first G.I. trim. Short hair is an Army custom."

Catching the writer's bug that had run in his family, Fielding began doing more general-interest magazine articles and finally found another dream girl. Her name was Nancy Parker, and she was one of the first female literary agents in New York. Although short on credits, Fielding charmed Parker into signing him as a client. Two months later, he charmed her into marrying him. Shortly after their honeymoon, Fielding was dispatched overseas. After spending time in Algeria and Italy, the new OSS took advantage of Fielding's undergraduate training in psychology to turn him into a propaganda expert. His focus was on the Balkans, doing black ops that almost got him killed but ultimately rewarded him with a decoration that honored him with arranging the voluntary surrenders of over thirty thousand enemy troops. It was an award he proudly displayed but, true to his spy code, refused ever to elaborate upon.

Back in New York after the war, Fielding resumed his magazine efforts, with little success. Realizing how hard it was to earn a pittance, much less a living, from freelance writing, he got a job with an advertising agency representing Canadian Club whiskey. He discovered his own market niche in the area of travel. They were doing a "European" campaign, but Fielding was convinced they were clueless about what the real Europe looked like. He talked them into sending him abroad to create something more authentic, with actual continental backgrounds.

In preparation for this 1946 trip, Fielding went looking for a guidebook that told him where to eat and sleep while overseas. He couldn't find one. Wandering through the aisles at Scribner's, Fielding, who had gotten to know Europe somewhat during the war, could find no guide that looked at the continent as a whole and none that went into any detail about the legendary lodging and dining shrines that Fielding had admired on his travels, or even where to find a noninfested bed and non-moldy board along the way. When he complained to his wife, she saw not inconvenience but a golden opportunity. Write your own book, she exhorted him, and she promised she could sell it.

What Fielding came up with for Canadian Club were a series of advertisements recounting whiskey-fueled adventures, which turned out to be ironic misadventures. Typical was his ill-fated effort to go sponge diving in Greece with a local aquatic champion named Nick (what else?). "I dived so deep for an Aegean sponge that the champ had to dive for *me*." It was the male whiskey answer to those "I Dreamed I Was Marie Antoinette in My Maidenform Bra" ads of the era. High adventure, danger, genuine locales, wit, and booze to top it off. Plus a plug for TWA that provided Fielding with free Constellation tickets. "As I left to make my TWA plane connection, I told Nick I'd never dive for a sponge again in anything deeper than a bathtub." The storyboard concluded, "As travel-starved Americans again go wandering, they tell of being offered Canadian Club in 87 lands."

That phrase "travel-starved Americans" kept resonating with Fielding long after he penned it. He traversed Europe over five months and filled countless notebooks with the logistics of his journeys. He returned to New York, delivered the series to Canadian Club, and repaired to P. J. Clarke's bar on Third Avenue, scene of Billy Wilder's recent 1945 hit movie *The Lost Weekend,* and wrote most of his first *Guide.* It took him nine months. Nancy Fielding sold it in one, to the newly founded William Sloane Associates, whose owner was a true blue, or rather orange, Princeton man, Class of '29, eager to lend a helping hand to another literary tiger.

The first *Guide* was a slender 250 pages and a cheap $2, but it filled a glaring need for travelers seduced by the ad-blitz campaigns of Juan Trippe and Howard Hughes to get thyselves overseas. The book took off, and after three successful annual editions, its success enabled the Fieldings to take off as well. They and their young son, Dodge, moved first to Denmark, a destination in the early *Guides* that Fielding proclaimed his favorite in the whole world. Copenhagen's famed amusement park, Tivoli Gardens, was a forerunner to Disneyland; clean, wholesome, and perfect, it became a must for Americans on their postwar grand tours. Here was Fielding's pitch, in tiny part:

"*Don't miss it!* Of all the 90-odd foreign lands I've ever visited, Denmark is the closest thing to a 3-ring circus—and closest, too, to my travel heart . . . Don't take your *Hamlet* too seriously—because if there's a single melancholy Dane left, I haven't met him . . . They're the Pucks of Scandinavia, the Bob Hopes of Europe . . . And cleanliness is a national fetish. Even the United States looks soiled and grimy by comparison. Cockroaches? Bedbugs? Silverfish? Lice? I'll buy you a *snaps* for every one you find in your hotel or restaurant in Denmark."

Cleanliness was godliness to germophobic Americans, who seized on Fielding's pitch. Cool Denmark thus became a hot spot. Fielding was doing even more for the country's image than Danny Kaye would in his smash 1952 MGM musical *Hans Christian Andersen.* A tourism study concluded that over half the American visitors to Denmark were Guidesters who had traveled there because Fielding told them to. Flattered by the attention and fattened in the coffers, the Danish government gave him its highest order of merit, making him a "Knight of the Royal Order of the Danish Flag." With the knighthood came a house, a maid, and an annual stipend. It was a lottery-level largesse the Fieldings couldn't refuse. In 1951, they moved from New York to their new, free house in Hornbaek, thirty miles from Copenhagen, located on the silver strand known as the Danish Riviera.

When they arrived at the airport, they were greeted by a motorcade led by the prime minister. The house was a stunning Nordic modern log cabin set in a deep forest. Outside, an American flag was flying; inside, a pitcher of martinis was waiting. The maid was in uniform, waiting to serve the succulent rib roast she had made. It was perfect, too perfect. The Fieldings loved the country, but they hated feeling like freeloaders. In under six months, they had decided to flee and move to Majorca, the idyllic Mediterranean isle a hundred miles off Barcelona, before it was discovered by heat-seeking Northern European package tourists. They renovated a villa in Formentor, a dramatic cape at the northern tip of the island.

The Villa Fielding, though it had only one guest room, was the Platonic ideal of the European grand hotel that would have earned Fielding's highest accolades. The bar had 116 varieties of liquor. There were six uniformed servants and a larder with gastro-exotica that would have shamed Zabar's: albacore tuna from Oregon, Scotch-grouse pâté, pheasant in Burgundy jelly, Norwegian kippers, Skippy peanut butter. The luxury and service were European, but the comfort and convenience were purely American. The medicine cabinet was a virtual corner drugstore, overflowing with Alka-Seltzer, Band-Aids, Bufferin, insect repellent, a Fahrenheit thermometer. Despite the sea breezes, there was frigid air-conditioning. A black Cadillac convertible, flying both American and Danish flags, was the house car. To ensure that stateside visitors were as at home as they would be in a Holiday Inn, there was a ready supply of filtered ice water, big American-style coffee cups, and no language problem whatsoever. Despite their endless travels, neither Temple nor Nancy Fielding could speak Spanish or, for that matter, any other foreign language. Americans liked that about Fielding. That was why they bought his books. For all his Princeton-ness, he was still something of a babe in the European woods. His struggles were their struggles. He was just like *them*.

And every year, there were more and more of them. In 1958, even before the jets took off, Fielding was in awe of how many people were going to Europe and, of course, buying his *Guide.* "If the Russian bear and the Wall Street bear behave, and if Abdullah Doe in the Middle East can keep his fez on, 1958 will be the dizziest, busiest merry-go-round in European travel history," he exulted, careful to temper his exuberance with a dollop of geopolitical caution. Seven hundred thousand were expected to hit the road or, rather, the sea and the air, in roughly equal numbers, and a good 20 percent of those were Guidesters. The shorthand for the guide, *Fielding's Europe,* was more than just a title. He seemed to own the continent.

In staking that claim, Temple Fielding was the beneficiary of a huge assist from Harry Truman and Dwight Eisenhower, who were the best travel agents Europe ever had. It started with the Marshall Plan, officially the European Recovery Program, which traced its genesis to a 1947 commencement speech at Harvard by General and Army Chief of Staff turned Secretary of State George C. Marshall. A Euro-stimulus plan to pour vast sums of money into war-ravaged Western Europe, it aimed to restore capitalism as the bulwark that would prevent Communism, the bête noire of the postwar period, from taking over.

Many Republicans, then as now, were opposed to any handouts, especially to "foreigners." One Ohio congressman publicly fretted that the stimulus funds would end up in the silk pockets of the old aristocracy, who would squander it, as they had done for generations, at the casinos in Monte Carlo and Baden-Baden. "The United States of America pays and pays and pays while the royalty of the Old World plays and plays and plays." Eventually, however, the Truman Democrats carried the day, and in 1948, they enacted the plan.

One of the compromises made to get the law passed was setting up a tourism program. Many lawmakers lacked confidence that the ravaged, disorganized European countries would effectively use the relief funds to rebuild their industries and economies and thereby be able to afford American exports. But these same lawmakers had immense confidence that American travelers could spend a fortune visiting Europe and thereby replenish the continent's coffers in their pursuit of what Europe had and we didn't: culture and pedigreed luxury, the latter being the raison d'être of the Fielding *Guide*. As one conservative paper, the *Indianapolis Star,* editorialized, "We might as well soak up a little old world culture for our dollars."

Congress created the Economic Cooperation Administration (ECA) to administer the Marshall Plan. An ECA subdivision, the Travel Development Section (TDS), would fund new hotels, subsidize and bolster ship companies and airlines, and restore Europe's hospitality infrastructure to make the Old World safe for, and alluring to, Guidesters. The stimulus behind this stimulus was none other than Juan Trippe's "stooge" and Howard Hughes's nemesis, Maine senator Owen Brewster, before Hughes drove him out of Washington in 1951. Trippe was not only licking his chops at all the Americans he could pack onto his new prop planes, and his jets to come, but licking them even more at the thought of all the beds he could fill in his planned lodging chain, InterContinental Hotels.

Although Brewster had failed to make Pan Am the U.S.'s "chosen instrument," Trippe knew his friend the senator would generate other flying favors and hoped Brewster would also get him the consolation prize of Marshall Plan stimulus financing to help build his hotels. To facilitate Trippe's goals, Brewster got appointed as headman of the TDS one of his Maine constituents, a post–World War I émigré French aristocrat named Theo Pozzy, who had built a new fortune in food canning and electronics in the Pine Tree State. During World War II, Pozzy ran the Plaza Athénée in Paris, the sister hotel of the nearby George V, as a luxe barracks for American officers.

Trippe was under no illusions that tourism in Europe would ever return to the elegance and decadence of the thirties, even if Igor Cassini might chronicle in his column pockets of such resurgence in the Swiss Alps and the French Riviera. That was the era of the Lost Generation, and it was lost forever, remembered mostly in the works of Hemingway, Fitzgerald, and Noël Coward, now as anachronistic as Pan Am's luxurious flying boats. Trippe was way beyond aristocrats, intellectuals, and artsy expatriates by now. He wanted the masses. Aside from pursuit of monopoly, his biggest project after the war was to convince the International Air Transport Association (IATA) into letting him divide his formerly one-class (first) planes into two sections. Trippe's proposed name for the back of the plane was "tourist." Trippe's efforts had begun back in the late forties, before "tourist" became a pejorative word, an insult to adventurers. When the jets were launched in 1958, Trippe would change the class appellation to "economy."

What sounded like an obvious, democratic no-brainer proved to be a labor of Hercules. Trippe himself ranked the creation of tourist class as one of the three seminal events in aviation, behind only the flight of Lindbergh and the creation of the jet. IATA, formed in 1944 and dominated by the nationalized foreign carriers BOAC and Air France, feared Trippe almost as much as Europe had feared Hitler. As state monopolies freed from the imperatives of competition (as Trippe had wanted to be), they had to act as a bloc to prevent him from running the show. They liked keeping prices high. High prices meant high standards. So what, that they were catering to their national elites? That's what Europe was, then as it always had been, in the air as on the post-feudal ground, a society based on the class system.

After years of trying to negotiate with IATA, Trippe called its bluff. He announced he was doing tourist without IATA approval. He bet that no foreign country would suspend Pan Am's landing rights for being the renegade, because that would cost them millions, billions, of American tourist dollars. He bet correctly. In May 1952, Pan Am's DC-6, the *Betsy Ross*, left Idlewild bound for Paris with eighty-seven passengers, most cramped into new seats in the back of the plane, an area that normally carried only fifty-four. The "tourists" got no champagne, no liquor at all, and no fancy meal, only sandwiches and Cokes. But they got the same eleven-hour flight, and they got Paris, for a round-trip fare of $550, compared to the $1,040 the champagne drinkers up front were paying. The tourists had to be plenty well heeled to afford the $550, but they didn't have to be moguls. Indians, not chiefs, but from a good tribe, they, too, were now the target Fielding readers. In the long run, Trippe's class system would lead to mass tourism, with legions of backpackers that would have caused fastidious Fielding conniptions. But in the fifties, Trippe simply expanded that well-heeled demographic. The moral of the story is that you didn't have to be rich to help make Temple Fielding rich. Fielding owed Juan Trippe, big-time.

Fielding also owed Theo Pozzy, who was as fastidious a hotel critic as Fielding was. Without Pozzy constantly hectoring the French hotel industry to raise its standards to American levels, Fielding would have had hardly any hotels in France to which he could give his blessing. And if France was bad, the rest of Europe, with the exception of Switzerland, was far, far worse. These "American standards," which seemed to revolve around modernity and cleanliness, were best encapsulated by the gleaming new Memphis-based motel chain Holiday Inn, started in 1952, whose advertising slogan was "The Best Surprise Is No Surprise." If there is something incongruous about the Holiday Inn telling the Ritz how to run its show, that was because American money talked very loudly. The American love of cars had grown into a love affair with motels. You want American dollars? Give them American suburban comforts, give them what Holiday Inn does: private baths, double beds, ice water, air-conditioning, deep coffee cups, and above all, no tipping.

Most Americans had no idea how to deal with all this service, the maids, valets, porters, concierges, maître d's, all seemingly with palms out, any more than they knew what to do with the bidets that were often the only item of plumbing in a French hotel room. Nothing seemed to confuse Americans more than whom to tip and how much, and that confusion translated into more sales for Fielding, whose annual *Guide* spelled out in minute and painstaking detail exactly what to tip whom in each country.

Pozzy's fiat-like "suggestions" to cater to the Yankee dollar caused immediate revulsion, and almost a revolution, in the French tourism industry. But just as Vichy capitulated to the Germans, there were plenty of French hospitality people who were more than willing to kowtow to the Americans. One thorny problem arose when some Paris hoteliers, bending over backward to cater to "American standards," began refusing to accommodate African-American tourists, just as Holiday Inns in the

South might "reserve the right to refuse service to anyone," as the sign in every Dixie motel read, shorthand for "no blacks." In the country of "égalité," this was way over the line, and the French intellectual journals made a huge issue of it. Only because there were so few African-American tourists in Europe in the fifties did this brushfire not become a conflagration.

The Franco-American hospitality wars had begun with an insult. In 1949, Pozzy, prodded by his patron Brewster, who was prodded by Trippe, leaned on Paris to drop its visa requirement for Americans. A lot of French leaders were loath to do this. They feared that Mormon missionaries or American blacks or just plain American radical beatniks could get into the country and stir up trouble over French imperialism in Africa and Southeast Asia. Pozzy, preaching dollar diplomacy, won the day. But then America refused to grant reciprocity. In the view of nativist Americans, France was full of French Communists who might come to America and subvert the American Way. So No Way on no visas. The French were appalled. They started to resent Americans telling them how to run their hotels and their restaurants and how to tip. And the ice water? Sacre bleu! The French called it Coca-Cola-nization, and they weren't going to be subjugated to America's new imperialism. It was Freedom Fries in reverse.

For Temple Fielding, the French nationalistic backlash was grist for his mill, one more tempest in his teapot that made for piquant copy:

> Generally speaking French hotels are either very fine or very poor . . .
> In Paris and the big cities, you'll find plenty of both extremes. In the Provinces, however, your "average" hostelry is likely to be a dank, musty fleabag, vintage of 1893, with a hot and cold running proprietor complete with seedy vest and toothpick . . . French provincial hotels . . . are the dowdiest and least beguiling regional inns of any European land.
>
> Don't forget *always* to check every item on every bill. The chiseling of many French hotels is disgraceful; big, fat "mistakes" in favor of the house are as common as dandelions.

Don't expect a private bath; don't look for any kind of shower;
don't be surprised if you shave in tepid water . . . The plumbing is
tattered, tired, odious—and usually five city blocks from your room.

About the only virtue Fielding could find in French hotels below the
government's "deluxe" category was that gentlemen could bring *filles de
joie* upstairs for short visits without reprisal. "Unlike Spain, there's no
law against inviting an unaccompanied lady to your hotel room. You
won't be stopped by the elevator man; he'll probably beam his blessings."

His *Guide*'s leering randiness must have been hard for his supposedly
liberated professional wife, Nancy, to take. Fielding clearly left his all-
American family values at home in Majorca when he took off for his
annual five-month one-man road show to update the *Guide*, trolling or
retrolling through 300 hotels, 350 restaurants, and 150 nightclubs.
Aside from his moral compass, he didn't leave much else back at Villa
Fielding. He traveled like a seventeeth-century grand tourist, with every
appurtenance minus the doctor. In the days before excess baggage
charges, Fielding toted, in a bulging raffia palm basket and a commodi-
ous Spanish leather satchel, all the comforts of home, ranging from a
portable phonograph to play his Frank Sinatra albums; Tribuno (American) vermouth, to make the martinis that few European bartenders
could master to his satisfaction; an ice bucket, to chill his drinks; a big
bag of Planter's peanuts, to munch with the martinis; Manhattan cocktail mix, for variety; a bottle of maraschino cherries, to top the Manhat-
tans; and a bottle of Fernet Branca bitters, for hangovers induced by this
traveling bar.

Beyond the alcohol, Fielding packed tiny American cigars; a Bible,
perhaps for atonement; a yodeling Swiss alarm clock; three pairs of
glasses; lots of toothbrushes; sleeping pills; and instant decaf coffee to
wash down his ritual morning breakfast of a ham sandwich, slathered
with the French's mustard that he brought along. "I'm so sick of croissants, I'd rather eat my shoes," he explained to a reporter. He also lugged
a stationery store full of notebooks and pens.

Despite his goal of trying to negotiate the continent mostly by rail and by ferry, Fielding sometimes had no choice but to take a dreaded airplane. To ward off the evil spirits, he wore more good-luck charms than a Margaret Mead island shaman. A *Time* cover profile enumerated the following: "his World War II dog tags, a St. Christopher medal, a brass taxi whistle from Cartier, a gold medal that was presented to him by Pope Pius XII, still another that was a gift from Haile Selassie, a gold-plated English penny and a charm in the shape of a naked lady." "I'm not afraid of flying," he told the magazine, "but these things are what keep the wings on the airplane." He also lugged, or had porters lug for him, two vast suitcases filled with tuxedos, silk pajamas, lounging robes, seal-skin slippers, those Brioni suits, a vicuna and cashmere topcoat (his re-search trips were always in the cold off-season), and thirty-five Swiss linen handkerchiefs embroidered with his signature, a potent leave-behind souvenir for those "research" *filles de joie.*

Fielding's research drill was always the same. For hotels, he'd have his local chauffeur wait outside in the hired Rolls, while he'd enter the estab-lishment, his *Guide* proudly in hand as his calling card, introduce him-self at the reception desk, and ask for a tour of the premises. Inside the variety of rooms and suites he'd ask to inspect, he'd plop down on the beds, run his fingers over window- and doorsills to check for dust, put his ear to the wall to check for noise from the next room, survey the decor, and turn on the shower, if there was one, to check the water pres-sure, sometimes soaking his Brioni suit in the process. His job done, he'd retreat to his hired car and have the chauffeur drive out of sight and park. Then Fielding would spend the next half hour scribbling observations, puns, and other *mal mots* apropos of this last investigation that, when he returned to Majorca, he would decipher and transcribe for the next year's *Guide.*

For restaurants, booking under an alias (usually "Mr. Parker"), Field-ing would often consume several lunches and dinners each day, some-times in the company of local acquaintances, sampling—of necessity, sparingly—his four high-fat, artery-clogging, pre-Pritikin test dishes: eggs Benedict; *coquilles* St. Jacques; *vol au vent,* the puff pastry filled with a creamy ragout of meat or fish; and bouillabaisse, when he was near enough to the Mediterranean to get it. He took his notes during the re-past, under the tablecloth, in a notebook disguised as a cigarette case.

As for nightclubs, the gent did protest a bit too much that this hands-on research was forced labor. He claimed to compress all his re-search for each city's after-hours section into a single-night bar-crawl debauch. He feigned an attitude of "it's a dirty job, but someone's gotta do it." Still, his descriptions of the low-rent fleshpots were often more inspired than those of the gilded grand hotels. Here he is on a club called Bikini, his favorite spot on Hamburg's high road of low sex, the Reeper-bahn (Rope Street):

> Bikini has a telephone on every table, which will ring furiously as soon as the hostesses spot you . . . In the center, a small elevated stage slides out over the dance floor; one of the performances I saw was a wrestling match between two naked and determined gals—in 12 inches of slimy, gooey mud! Adjoining is a bar room, where patrons calmly sip their schnapps, discuss the economic intricacies of the Saar, and casually glance at the sexy, privately produced movies which flash on the screen every 20 minutes or so.

Fielding's gusto for the male-only part of his *Guide* may have come from the fact that, aside from the art and antiquities—which Fielding wasn't interested in—what made Europe different for him, at least in the Eisenhower fifties, was the wide-open sex. America had great hotels, such as the Waldorf, the Plaza, the Palmer House, the Mark Hopkins. America had great restaurants, such as Le Pavillon, 21, the Pump Room, Ernie's, Trader Vic's. What America didn't have was a Reeperbahn, a Pi-galle, a Soho, red-light districts with legal prostitution and high-end sex clubs like the above-described Bikini. They were what Fielding liked, and his target Main Street bank president readers seemed to like them as well.

But the bankers couldn't tell their depositors back home in Middle-town what they were *really* doing on their summer vacations. They needed bragging rights, trophy beds at the Savoy, trophy meals at Maxim's, plus some photos at Versailles and the Pantheon. What Fielding understood best of all was the insecurity of the American plutocrat. In the midfifties, he had a new brainstorm. He not only would tell the banker where to go, he would, in effect, go there with him. He announced his manifesto in a major press release in 1957:

> Nancy and I are so tired of watching snooty European headwaiters treat Americans like country cousins that at last we've decided to do something about it. During 11 years of roaming for our European Travel Guides we've squirmed in silent agony dozens of times as these snobbish ex-busboys have pushed around clean-cut, well-mannered US guests like cattle.
>
> At home, these travelers are often so important that places like 21, the Colony, and the Pump Room break their backs to roll out the red carpet for them.
>
> But across the Atlantic it's different. To the average maître d'hotel, the president of a steel company is just another American tourist off the street, to be patronized, herded behind a pillar, and ignored.

Fielding's solution to this gastronomic lèse-majesté was to create the Temple Fielding Epicure Club, which he asserted was a "nonprofit foundation," ostensibly to fight discrimination against Yankee plutocrats. For a $15.50 annual membership, a couple would get a fancy passport-like membership card and twenty vouchers that would be flashed to an imperious restaurateur. Then, as if a cross had been shown to a vampire, Monsieur Arrogant would be reduced to Mr. Obsequious. The couple would be shown to an A table, complimentary champagne would be poured, and a trophy meal would be at hand.

Fielding assembled twenty of Europe's most esteemed dining temples to join his foundation, an Igor Cassini list of the best of the best, the snootiest of the snooty: Tour d'Agent and Maxim's in Paris; Mirabelle and Le Caprice in London; Hostaria dell'Orso in Rome; Giannino in Milan; the Jockey Club and Horcher in Madrid; and a dozen more.

Horcher, as an example of exclusivity, was Hitler's favorite restaurant in Berlin, which relocated to Madrid after the war with no hard feelings. Thomas Edison ate there, and Charlie Chaplin still did. It had become as much of a Madrid institution as the Prado. Fielding was offering more than food; he was retailing history.

What was in it for the restaurants? Guidester customers, and lots of them. Every table in Europe dreamed of having the Fielding imprimatur. The membership fee paid for the free champagne. Otherwise, the restaurants charged full fare for their food, though what a bargain it was at, Fielding noted, $10 to $15 a meal in Paris, and "the sunny side of $5.00," as Fielding put it, everywhere else. He insisted that he was getting no kickbacks, no commissions, no profit on his dining club, though the unspoken value was publicity, endless publicity, that sold even more *Guides*.

Although Ernest Hemingway and John F. Kennedy were both big fans, Temple Fielding was generally detested by intellectuals and social critics on both sides of the Atlantic. He was widely criticized for taking the adventure and certainly the culture out of travel and replacing it with conspicuous, despicable consumption. His champagne-swilling, suite-dwelling, whore-chasing steel-company president became the model for the Ugly American, or at least the Ugly Rich American. That unfortunate moniker, which came from the title of a 1958 novel set in a fictional Vietnamish Southeast Asian country, was quickly appropriated by the press to describe all boorish Americans abroad, from American Express's penny-pinching package tourists to Fielding's high-rolling gastrotourists.

Fielding may well have been the most envied travel writer of all time. As such, he was bound to create a backlash, and he did, in the meek persona of a New York backroom lawyer named Arthur Frommer, who chose to stake out the opposite, cheap end of the travel spectrum. It could be said that Arthur Frommer was born at a discount, in Jefferson City, Missouri, in 1930. There his father worked in a low-priced pants factory named Oberman's. He grew up during the Depression, hawking newspapers on corners and dressing in wholesale pants from Oberman's.

He learned from the earliest age exactly what things cost, and never to pay full price. In 1944, the Frommers moved to New York. A dedicated student, Arthur made Phi Beta Kappa at NYU and went on to Yale Law School. But Frommer's Ivy League was as different from Fielding's as his future guidebooks would be.

Like Fielding, Frommer got his guidebook start in the army. After Yale, he was drafted and, in 1954, was sent to Germany to the Army's intelligence school at Oberammergau. It was brainy grunt work compared to Fielding's glamorous OSS (Oh So Social, as it was known), but it sufficed to get Frommer to Europe his first time. Oberammergau was known for its anti-Semitic, post-Nazi ambience, so Frommer escaped every weekend to visit somewhere different—the Alps, Munich, Salzburg, Innsbruck, Venice, and his favorite, Paris. He never used any guide on his travels, especially the ritzy Fielding's, priced way out of his league. He found he didn't need one; he did fine on his own.

Amazed at how much he could do and see on his meager private's salary, Frommer decided he wanted to share his adventures in budgeteering. So, while stationed in Germany, now Berlin, he wrote a little book, more a pamphlet, of ninety pages called *The G.I.'s Guide to Traveling in Europe.* In addition to outlining cheap boarding and cafés, he had sec tions on free air force flights and other government handouts. He was hoping that the army newspaper *Stars and Stripes* would publish his opus as a service document, akin to the way Fielding's guide to Fort Bragg got into print.

Stars and Stripes said no. Frommer, undaunted, decided to self-publish. He found a printing press in Berlin that ran off copies, which, using his boyhood newsstand experiences, Frommer got distributed on every corner of Berlin that sold *Stars and Stripes*. When he was shipped home, he left his little guide as a message in a bottle to his fellow Cold War soldiers. Back in New York, he got a cable telling him the *G.I.'s Guide* had sold out. He was flattered, but the success didn't change his life. Why should it? He had just gotten a job at one of New York's most prestigious law firms, Paul, Weiss, in 1950 the first major Wall Street firm to move uptown to Park Avenue.

The firm had the biggest entertainment practice in the city, and its chief rainmaker was distinguished former judge Simon Rifkind, who also made the firm Gotham's leader in pro bono cases. This was the firm that proudly boasted the city's first major female partner, the wife of Supreme Court justice Abe Fortas. It had the first black associate in William T. Coleman, Jr., future secretary of transportation, and it soon would have Adlai Stevenson as head partner in its Chicago office. Arthur Frommer may have been wearing wholesale pants, but whatever his attire, at Paul, Weiss, he was dressed for success.

For all the promise of his legal future, the short, boyish, bookish Frommer couldn't get the writing bug out of his head. On his first Paul, Weiss summer vacation, he flew back to Europe, tourist class, and began researching a guide that would do for civilians what he had done for GIs. The book, then still a gleam in his eye, would be called *Europe on 5 Dollars a Day*. It took two summers of sleeping around before he had enough material to fill a book, which, once again, he ended up self-publishing. And once again, his book caught on and sold out at the newsstands, proof that while money talked, saving money could speak just as loudly.

For all its initial grassroots success, *5 Dollars* remained a newsstand novelty item and no threat whatever to Fielding. Frommer was the gnat on the hide of the Fielding elephant. For its first seven years, *5 Dollars* was a summer hobby for Frommer, who toiled as a litigator at Paul, Weiss on cases like defending *Lady Chatterley's Lover* against the U.S. Post Office on obscenity charges. In 1962, when Frommer divined that he was not going to become an august Paul, Weiss partner, he decided to give up his day job. Assisted by his wife, an English actress whose stage name was Hope Arthur, he started living on his writing. Had he become a partner, with all its attendant prestige, he probably would have taken his place in the pantheon of Manhattan lawyers rather than searching for cheap pizza at the real Pantheon in Rome.

Frommer's timing couldn't have been better. He was blessed by the sixties' changing demographic, as the baby boomers came of college age and travel age. Waiting for them at the nation's airports were the new big jets, ever-lower fares, and a proliferation of even cheaper charter flights designed to cater to student wanderlust. Not only were these collegiate Odysseuses generally too strapped for funds to purchase a Fielding *Guide,* much less follow its recommendations, they also tended to be rebelling against the "capitalist pigs" Fielding was writing for, whose trough might well be shared by the parents at whose authority the kids were chafing.

The fat-cat haters and the Fielding haters could unite in admiration of Frommer for offering a more "authentic" travel experience, roughing it among the "real Europeans," as opposed to Fielding's hermetically sealed universe of toadying bellmen and busboys. One of Frommer's signature pieces of advice was "Never ask for a private bath." A shared bathroom was one of Fielding's worst nightmares. The only "real Europeans" that Fielding seemed to brush up against were prostitutes. That his most inspired writing was about this velvet underbelly of his otherwise too perfect beau monde seemed to make the case for Frommer better than he could himself.

After all, Frommer did not write that much more about the sights and the culture of Europe than Fielding did, other than to tell his readers what day they could get in to the Bargello or the Neue Pinakothek for free, or where to find the very lowest-priced souvlaki stand at the base of the Parthenon. Aside from the students, who turned to Frommer's guiding light out of economic necessity, many of the adult voyagers who bought his books were as obsessive about *saving* money as Fielding's Guidesters were about spending it. These people were hunting for big-game trophy bargains the same way the Guidesters were collecting trophy blowouts. To them, cheapness was a virtue, savings a triumph. It was reverse ostentation, showing off for the folks back at home what a great deal you had found. The very concept of Europe on five bucks a day was the stuff game shows were made of: Who could be the biggest Scrooge? Unfortunately, a compulsive tightwad could be every bit as ugly an American as the compulsive show-off.

The liberal Stevenson Democrat Frommer was, if anything, much less adventurous than the conservative Eisenhower Republican Fielding, who admitted that he had gotten too addicted to creature comforts to start searching out B and B's. Frommer didn't like to get out of his own comfort zone, which was Western Europe. He avoided Eastern Europe, where he admitted a paranoia that his army intelligence background could get him waylaid. Surprisingly, for such a budgeteer, he was far more interested in getting rich than Fielding, and far more entrepreneurial, starting a package-tour company, even building Arthur Frommer Hotels in Amsterdam and Copenhagen. He would eventually divide and conquer Europe not with one massive Fielding-esque tome but with individual guides to countries and, eventually, cities. For Fielding, Europe was forever one continent and one *Guide;* while Frommer, like the Fodor guides, founded in Paris in 1949, followed the Baedeker model of a separate book for every nation and, soon, every capital.

One of the first of the latter was *Surprising Amsterdam,* surprising to many by being paid for by KLM, the Dutch airline. Although travel writers weren't generally held to the same journalistic, no-conflicts standards of, say, a Walter Lippmann or Joseph Alsop, who covered global diplomacy, Temple Fielding, for one, took great pride in trumpeting in the front of every edition of his *Guide,* that he had never in his life taken a penny in any kind of kickback or buy-in. "This book is 100% independent and 100% clean. In its making we stick to one inflexible rule *always*: no commissions, rake-offs, cuts, kickbacks, or outside compensation in any form—from *anybody* . . . We're proud to say that we've always been faithful to our principles as working reporters—and we're going to stay that way."

Fielding insisted on being above reproach, no ads, no favors, and he was known for cutting hotel pals as quickly as he embraced them, if he found dust on a lintel or a bidet with a weak spray. Evidence of his incorruptibility was that, by 1958, he had incurred twenty-one major libel suits and lost only one, to a Brussels taxi concern that he labeled as "the biggest crooks and racketeers in Europe." That bit of hyperbole cost him $3,800, which was chump change compared to the $1.5 million the cab company was seeking. He also kept a scrupulous accounting of his tax-deductible travel expenses—the $15,000 in 1958 would balloon to $60,000 in 1968 and to nearly $200,000 by 1980. In the booming eighties of the big-money Reagan presidency, even Arthur Frommer had to throw in the budget towel and kill the dollar amount on his covers, fearing it would scare readers away. Starting in the Reagan years, nothing on earth could match the inflation of the price of travel, which was dizzying at the Frommer end but astronomical at that of Fielding. The room at the Ritz in Paris that may have seemed out of reach at $25 a night in 1965 was out of this world at $300 a night in 1985. The worst was yet to come, and it keeps on coming. As we look back in envy, the era of the 707 has proved to be the biggest bargain of the twentieth century.

6

Heavenly Host

A S THE NEW JETS, ALONG WITH THE NEW ADMINISTRATION, USHERED IN THE great travel boom of the early sixties, a war of sorts erupted for the hearts and minds and value systems of this next generation of travelers. The information rivals in this conflict, Fielding and Frommer, were both American, differently rooted but similar in terms of education and ambition. On the other hand, the hotels and restaurants—which constituted the bulk of the information Fielding and Frommer were conveying— represented a much more clear-cut clash of opposites, between cultures, values, and continents. Here was a genuine war of the worlds, between Europe and America, between Old and New. Two warriors stood out: Frenchman Claude Terrail, who owned Paris's La Tour d'Argent, was the most famous restaurateur in the world; American Conrad Hilton, who owned the Waldorf Astoria, the Plaza, and many other temples of sleep, was the most famous hotelier. Both were tall and handsome and rich and wildly successful. Interestingly for competing archetypes, the success of one had nothing to do with the failure of the other.

Theirs was a spiritual and symbolic rivalry fought not by them but

by the Old World versus New World adherents of the opposing philoso-
phies the two men so colorfully stood for. While Fielding and Frommer
never even met, Terrail and Hilton ran in the same fast Jet Set world.
Both men married in to the Hollywood flashocracy, Terrail to Barbara
Warner, daughter of Warner Bros. movie mogul Jack Warner, Hilton to
movie star Zsa Zsa Gabor. Neither union lasted; both men were compulsive Casanovas with boldface conquests. But their styles couldn't have
been more opposite. Terrail was a clubby polo player; Hilton was an
open-range cowboy. While Terrail was the quintessence of bespoke-
tailored, hand-kissing, multilingual European sophistication, Hilton
embodied the rolled-up-shirtsleeves can-do true grit of the American
West. What the opposites did have in common was their enormous success. Theirs was a brotherhood of achievement; they had the highest regard for each other, and each other's position at the pinnacle of his "art."
Nonetheless, the "battle" of their lifestyles really defined all the issues of
the jet age.

The battlefield in this case was France, the number one European
target of Americans, by a long way. France was central to over half of all
American itineraries to Europe. No other country came close. Over
40 percent of France's tourism revenues came from Americans. Seeing a
huge market for his unique package of expensive modernity and comforts, Conrad Hilton was planning not one but two major hotels in
Paris, one at the airport, the Orly Hilton, and another in the shadow of
the Eiffel Tower, the Paris Hilton.

Claude Terrail, on the other hand, wasn't planning to open a branch
of La Tour d'Argent in Beverly Hills. Instead, he was holding his hal-
lowed ground in the Tour's aerie overlooking Notre Dame, the Seine,
and the glorious spires and rooftops of Paris, the most iconic view in the
world, old or new. The Tour had only one rival in its exalted class: Maxim's, the Paris shrine of art nouveau. Both restaurants had the ultimate
rating of three *Michelin* stars, and both had more stars at their tables
than there were in the heavens. Both had imperial, intimidating black-
tie service, stupendous wine cellars filled with the noblest vintages, and
kitchens as grand as those of the storied ocean liners, such as the *Nor-*

mandie, serving complex dishes composed of luxury ingredients—foie gras, truffles, caviar, lobster, prime beef, baby veal—and elaborate, often flambéed desserts, prepared tableside with great panache.

But it was the view that was Claude Terrail's trump. Nothing on earth could match it, and it gave him his bargaining power. He would gladly serve Hilton's guests, but he would serve them, as his devoted Hollywood client Frank Sinatra would say, "my way," which was the way his forbears had served hungry travelers, pilgrims, and all manner of tourists for the past three centuries. Hilton stood for the American and the new; Terrail for European tradition. A major culture clash was brewing that would end up transforming both continents.

The greatest ally Terrail (or any French traditionalist) could hope for was the new first lady, Jacqueline Bouvier Kennedy. Jackie's French surname was misleading; she was at most an eighth French, long ago and far away. But she embraced the culture as if she were Marie Antoinette. She had become a brave defender of an alien faith, holding firm against the demands of everyone from the Marshall Planners to Juan Trippe to Temple Fielding that France "modernize" itself to accommodate, aid, and abet the jet-fueled rise of American tourism. No running ice water for Jackie Kennedy, only Evian, Vittel, Perrier, Mouton-Rothschild, Dom Pérignon.

France had plenty of avaricious businessmen in the hospitality trade who were more than willing to sell Paris down the Seine for Marshall Plan handouts and block bookings from American Express. To that end, France was building its own versions of Hiltons: chains like Sofitel and Le Méridien, both financed by Air France. Jackie K was flying in the face of modernity, which in those days had the epic horsepower of Pratt & Whitney. Still, the irresistible force of the American way was meeting the immovable force of Jackie, who had to mind her White House etiquette to avoid provoking a McCarthyite backlash. She enlisted Igor Cassini's brother, Oleg, to be her "beard" designer, knocking off the French couturiers Jackie loved but whom her husband had ordered her to eschew because he didn't want her seeming sartorially unpatriotic or, in his words, "too Frenchy."

Similarly, in redecorating the White House in an ultra-French mode, Jackie's "front" interior decorator was Dorothy May "Sister" Parish, a very American socialite blue blood whose grandfather was Edith Wharton's doctor. But the real work was done by Stéphane Boudin, the preeminent Paris designer and the man who could be said to have "Frenchified" the White House, turning it into what lots of chauvinistic wags ridiculed as "La Maison Blanche." Boudin was also responsible for the Fifth Avenue diamond salon of Harry Winston, whose Hope Diamond Jackie arranged to have Winston lend to France to be exhibited at the Louvre, in exchange for which the Louvre lent "Whistler's Mother" to a grieving Atlanta to commemorate the Air France crash that killed so many of its art patrons.

As for the cuisine at the White House, Jackie refused to have some executive chef from Howard Johnson's dishing up patriotic meat loaf. Instead, she hijacked the Frenchman René Verdon from the Carlyle Hotel, the Kennedy clan's New York pied-à-terre, whose haute cuisine extravagances Jackie knew firsthand from room service. She brought Verdon to Washington in 1961, the same year Julia Child's *Mastering the Art of French Cooking* was published. Having a Frenchman as the Kennedys' head chef did more for Child than any book tour and led to her television show, which would enable America to "eat like the Kennedys."

Jackie Kennedy may have seemed like a one-woman French connection, but she was simply the latest edition of a mystique that went back to such early chief executive Francophiles as Thomas Jefferson and James Monroe. Monroe's presidency had been preceded by a stint as minister to France. That had gotten him as French-hooked as Jackie's junior year abroad had gotten her, but in Monroe's case, it almost bankrupted him through his obsessive "Frenchification" of the original White House with his own funds.

You didn't have to be an ambassador or a president to embrace France. During the Roaring Twenties, when America was mired in Prohibition, Paris was the place to be, and for trust-fund babies and others too big to fail in the 1929 Crash, Paris was even more fun in the thirties. After the war, the City of Light may have become a soot-caked black beauty, in dire need of sandblasting, but it was also the best bargain in the world. The writers poured in: Irwin Shaw, James Baldwin, William Styron, James Jones, plus all the rich post-Ivy preppies like George Plimpton and his *Paris Review* crowd. These writers paid for their cafés and croissants by filling the pages of the super-glossy magazines *Holiday* and *Esquire* with seductive dispatches from the European front. Many of their magazine pieces were in-depth accounts of the conspicuous consumption of Igor Cassini's Jet Set, living the high life at the places Temple Fielding was raving about in his guide. Fabulous photographs by the likes of Slim Aarons captured all the revelry and turned it into a fantasy goal for the readers back home who couldn't wait for Juan Trippe to cut his rates even more.

The biggest pre-Kennedy event of the fifties that primed the future pump for jet travel to Europe, especially France, was the fairy-tale wedding of Grace Kelly of Hollywood and Philadelphia to Prince Rainier of Monaco. In what may have been the most publicized nuptials in the history of publicity, Igor Cassini and sixteen hundred other reporters descended on the tiny Riviera principality, smaller than Central Park, most often described by them as "Graustarkian." (Graustark was a famous fictional kingdom created by the author George Barr McCutcheon in a series of bestselling romantic novels in the 1920s.) Fiction may have been the operative word for a romance that mirrored the plot of Kelly's final film, *The Swan,* released by MGM on the same day as her wedding. In the movie, a Graustarkian princess, played by Kelly, falls for a glamorous commoner, played by *Gigi*'s Louis Jourdan. In real life, the genders were reversed. The match was made by Aristotle Onassis, who essentially owned this Graustark on the Med, controlling its casino, its Sporting Club, its Hôtel de Paris.

Onassis, afraid of losing the return on his investment, concluded that Monaco needed more tourism and, hence, more publicity. He played an Aegean Cupid and created the paradigm that historian Daniel Boorstin described as a "pseudo-event." Nobody did publicity like Onassis. He created a feeding frenzy, a tidal wave unmatched until he married Jackie Kennedy. But the question that nagged the public was what love had to do with it. The whole affair was just too orchestrated, what with the MGM movie tie-in and the radio broadcast of the wedding sponsored by Peter Pan brassieres.

Europe's *real* royalty did not attend; they gave the Grimaldi "pseudo-dynasty" the bum's rush. The closest thing to a king who showed up was an ex, Farouk of Egypt, recently deposed by Nasser, who was spending his exile at the gambling tables of Monaco's famed casino. Randolph Churchill, son of Winston, was there because his ailing papa loved Onassis's hospitality, as did a decrepit Somerset Maugham. But even Randolph was turned off. "I didn't come here to meet vulgar people like the Kellys," he snapped to one gossip.

President Eisenhower didn't send anyone from Washington. That might have seemed too legitimate. Instead, he dispatched as his unofficial envoy his frequent golfing partner Conrad Hilton, whose presence stirred up hope among the tourist-starved locals that he might be scouting for a site for a Monte Carlo Hilton. No such luck. "We never build in resorts or small towns," he said, deflating all expectations. Claude Terrail was the rare celebrity who was not invited. Onassis, who controlled the guest list, was a Maxim's loyalist and decided to exclude the competition.

Even minus the star power, the crowd in Monaco was vast. Televised everywhere, the event got the world talking about Europe as a place where dreams (manufactured though they might be) could come true, even if the most satisfied of all the dreamers turned out to be Onassis. The French mystique had never abated, from the Lost Generation to the Beat Generation and now the jet-enabled baby boomers. France was ever the most favored nation.

England may have been the mother country, but maybe that was why it seemed less foreign, less glamorous, as well as, sadly, too wrecked by the war to match the fantasy that was France. All those killer fogs, all those crippling strikes, all that bad food and warm beer and the pubs that closed at nine. It was all too stiff-upper-lip, and you needed to be as indomitable as Winston Churchill to have the blood, sweat, and tears to endure it. Even Winston Churchill couldn't take it, having fallen prey to

Onassis's unctuous Riviera yacht seductions. It would take the Beatles and the Rolling Stones to make London hot, and that wasn't until 1964.

Italy, by contrast, had everything: ruins, art, style, sun, plus Elizabeth Taylor and Richard Burton making *Cleopatra*. The country provided some of the most unforgettable iconography of the Jet Set era, especially Fellini's *La Dolce Vita,* whose title, more than any other, defined the entire epoch. Who could forget the image of Swedish bombshell Anita Ekberg and Italian god Marcello Mastroianni cavorting in Rome's Trevi Fountain? And offscreen, who could forget the paparazzi images of that other Italian god, Fiat chief Gianni Agnelli, the handsomest man in all big business, with his trademark Rolex worn outside the cuff of his Brooks Brothers button-down? When it came to the Beautiful People, nothing could touch the land of the Caesars. But Italy's infrastructure was a wreck, no one spoke English, and all in all, the country was just too challenging, at least for independent travelers without local connections.

France had as fabulous an image as Italy. Furthermore, that image was unsullied by any negative associations with poor immigrants, like the shanty Irish or the *paisan* Italians or the peddler Jews. There had been no massive French migration, no foie gras famine to escape from. There were no "Little Frances" in the United States, except maybe dreamy New Orleans and ritzy Beverly Hills, the sister city of Cannes. Indeed, aside from the primitive plumbing, what was not to love about *La Belle France*? The people, that's what. So said the great profiler Temple Fielding, who warned his Guidesters:

> As long as the newcomer doesn't arrive with starry eyes, expecting the inhabitants to greet him with the beaming smile and mighty handclasp of the Dane, the Spaniard, the Hollander, the Norwegian, he should enjoy his sojourn. It is important that he remember the basic axiom that the French not only dislike all foreigners, but most other French people as well. This national suspicion of The Stranger, whether from Borneo or the next village, is as deeply inbred as their cynicism, their worldliness, or their appreciation of fine wines.

The image transmitted to America was that the French were arrogant, supercilious, and venal, holding out their palms for undeserved gratuities. Plus, there were lots of *Communists* in France, over 30 percent of the electorate. This was too close to Moscow, too close for comfort. It made America nervous. Forget the friendship of the Marquis de Lafayette. Forget the Statue of Liberty. Forget Maurice Chevalier. The country's image was not helped by President Charles de Gaulle, a giant hero-general whose self-regard and France-regard were at least as megalomaniacal as that of Napoleon.

That America had saved France from the Germans seemed forgotten as De Gaulle, in 1966, pulled France out of NATO and ordered NATO troops out of their French headquarters in Fontainebleau. At the same time, he began getting chummy with Khrushchev. He saw Russia as part of Europe, and sought a détente, which caused lots of anxiety in America. On the other hand, De Gaulle saw Britain not as part of Europe but as a tool of Washington, and he constantly vetoed British efforts to join the Common Market. He also began developing his own nuclear weapons.

De Gaulle didn't want his once imperial, still-imperious nation to be dependent upon America, nor for defense and not for tourism. He was proud of his bidets, his shared baths, his traditions of personal service, and the fat tips that service richly deserved. Let Conrad take his Hilton and . . . The view was that De Gaulle had a lot of gall, and that view was not confined to Temple Fielding. Even the internationalist senator from Arkansas, J. William Fulbright, who created the program that sent thousands of Fulbright Scholars across the globe, specifically to France, went on the record telling his countrymen to "spare themselves the debauchery and sophisticated pocket picking of Paris." Small wonder that JFK was worried about his wife seeming "too Frenchy."

No one could have been more Frenchy than Claude Terrail, whose haute cuisine, even Jackie and Jack Kennedy would have been quick to admit, put White House fare to shame. In the 707 era, the main reason people came to France was the food, and nobody did food better than Terrail's Tour d'Argent, the most expensive, most exclusive, most breathtaking restaurant in the world. It got the highest rating from Fielding, number one in his *Guide,* and the highest rating from *Michelin,* three stars for the cooking, five crossed knife and forks for the ambience. America and France had their differences, but on this, the twain could meet. And you could dine there for all of $15.

In 1959, the first full year of the jets, when tensions over French snootery were high and the Tour was the pinnacle of snoot, Fielding bestowed the ultimate Cold War rave that it gave "far more gracious reception and attention to American clientele than at Maxim's or at any other big-league restaurant in the capital." Julia Child noted on her first visit to the Tour, "The restaurant was excellent in every way, except that it was so pricey that every guest was American." This might have been music to the rip-off-attuned ears of Arthur Frommer. To Conrad Hilton, however, American patronage was the extreme compliment, notwithstanding that the campfire tastes of Hilton never would have tolerated the Tour's signature dish, *canard au sang,* the "bloody duck" whose sauce came from innards crushed in the Tour's Torquemada-ish silver duck press. To Claude Terrail, it was an acknowledgment that he had pulled off his high-wire balancing act, running the most classic, recherché, and arrogant of all French restaurants and still packing in those Damn Yankees. Even Walt Disney, creator of Donald Duck—at the Tour an endangered species—loved the place.

Claude Terrail was born, in 1918, to be a host. Although he never ran a hotel, his father was a major hotelier, having built Paris's first great modern hotel, the George V. When it opened in 1928, at the height of the Roaring Twenties, the deco paradise was instantly embraced for its revolutionary modernity—elevators, air-conditioning, every room with a private bath—by the stars of Hollywood. It remained the go-to lodgings of the film industry into the jet age. This grand hotel was where Claude Terrail grew up, a French male version of the New York Plaza's fictional Eloise. While André Terrail, Claude's father, was building the George V, Conrad Hilton had bought and was running his first hotel in Cisco, Texas. It was a whorehouse, or what the French would call an *hôtel de rendezvous,* where rooms were let by the hour, not the night. Then again, Conrad Hilton would later buy the Plaza, as if to get even.

Hilton and Terrail certainly didn't *start* even. Claude Terrail was born with a silver spoon, as well as a silver room key, in his mouth. In addition to the George V, his father owned the nearby St. Regis, as classical as the V was radical, as well as several other hotels in Paris and on the Calais coast, despite its chill and its fogs, the pre-airplane summer playground of rich Parisians. His resort flagship was the Royal Picardy in Le

MASTER OF HIS DOMAIN. Claude Terrail, at the top of the gastronomic world at his restaurant, La Tour d'Argent, 1958.

Touquet, which was Hiltonesque, the first French lodging with more than five hundred rooms and an Olympic swimming pool with a wave-making machine. With a phone in every room and a mini-golf course, it was advertised as the largest and most luxurious hotel in Europe.

While Claude Terrail's father was a hotel kingpin, his mother, Augusta, was restaurant royalty. Her father, Claudius Burdel, had owned the Café Anglais on the Boulevard des Italiens, which was to nineteenth-century Paris café society what Oscar Wilde's beloved Café Royal in Piccadilly was to London's. The Café Anglais's Adolphe Dugléré was arguably the first modern celebrity chef. Having cooked first and privately for the Rothschilds, he made the Anglais a dining shrine by creating such famous rich, buttery, creamy dishes as Pommes Anna, Potage Germiny, Sole Dugléré, and Tournedos Rossini, for which the *Barber of Seville* composer dubbed Dugléré "the Mozart of the kitchen."

While Duglére died in 1884, the Café Anglais continued to reign until it became a victim of the rise of Maxim's and closed in 1913. Maxim's had started in 1893 as an Italian ice cream parlor, but a dramatic art nouveau redo in 1899 made it the hot spot for tourists to the 1900 World's Fair, for which the Eiffel Tower was built. With its murals of naked nymphs cavorting on the walls and its famed courtesans, such as La Belle Otero, cavorting at the tables and on the dance floor with the crowned heads of Europe, Maxim's fused elements of the bordello with those of the restaurant. The hybrid was a huge smash and was immortalized as the setting of Franz Lehár's 1905 operetta, *The Merry Widow*. André Terrail knew he could never take on Maxim's. No one could. He decided to start fresh and keep his distance, on the Left Bank, buying out a small hotel-restaurant on the Quai de la Tournelle, across from Notre Dame, and stocking it with the vintage bottles of the Café Anglais's vaunted wine cellar.

The name, La Tour d'Argent, was far grander than the place. The hotel building was nineteenth-century, recent vintage compared to the mythology of its predecessor namesake, an inn called the Silver Tower founded on the spot in 1562. It served traveling royalty dishes like roasted swan, omelets with rooster testicles, and nineteen preparations of artichokes. The Silver Tower stories may all have been fabrications of André Terrail's showmanly press kit. The hotel he bought was totally modest, nothing like his George V. But as always, his plans were wildly ambitious. André Terrail closed the hotel part and brought Duglére's recipes to the ground-floor restaurant, plus the creation of his father-in-law, Burdel, the bloody duck, prepared tableside with *beaucoup de panache,* then the brilliant theatrical touch of giving each duck eater a numbered certificate as a treasured souvenir of the whole food show.

The liveried waiters would play food professors, explaining to the customers how the ducks were raised, in the prime fowl country of Challans, in the French Southwest, and how they were killed, by asphyxiation, so that all the blood would be retained and it could be squeezed out in the press and flambéed with the duck meat to showmanlike succulence. Duck number 328 had been served to the Duke of Windsor, later

King Edward VII, at the Café Anglais back in 1890. The first king to get numbered at the Tour was Spain's Alfonso XIII, number 40,132, in 1914. Little Claude Terrail, who had grown up in family quarters above the restaurant, watched Franklin D. Roosevelt, then governor of New York, devour number 112,151 in 1929. Although the dish had been selling in the tens of thousands, a luxury precursor of the hamburger tally McDonald's would flaunt under its golden arches, the whole duck thing was too much for Claude. He vowed not to follow his father into the hospitality trade. He wanted to become an actor.

Terrail had been ambivalent about the power of food. His first lesson in this regard had come when, dispatched to a French boarding school at an early age, he was given a huge foie gras by his father to present to his headmaster/priest as a Christmas gift. Nine-year-old Claude was appalled. You gave a priest a *Bible* or something lasting, he thought, not something to *eat*. His fears of expulsion were unfounded; the schoolmaster adored the foie gras and gave Claude a big hug of thanks. Still, he was conflicted about killing geese and ducks, less so about playing cowboys and Indians and shooting arrows at the George V doorman from the Terrails' new apartment next to the hotel.

Claude's thespian ambitions came from a teenage crush he developed on actress/singer Jeanette MacDonald, resplendent as the queen of Sylvania in the 1929 talkie smash *The Love Parade,* opposite Maurice Chevalier. MacDonald, pursued by suitors from two continents, took up residence at the George V, and Claude's teen fantasy was to join her love parade. Alas, his indignant father prevented Claude from finding out her room number. He shipped his son off across the Channel to an English boarding school for a year, hoping the rain and fog would cool his son's rising sap. It did not. What the British exile did accomplish was to give Claude a deep appreciation of his father's kitchen and that of his country. His nickname of "Froggy" bothered him less than his breakfasts of cold porridge and his lunches of boiled haddock and potatoes. The highlight of his stay was when his father, who knew the queen's French chef, took him to Buckingham Palace to visit the royal kitchen.

To separate Claude from the malign temptations of his celebrity-filled hotel, André Terrail shipped his son abroad once more. This time the exile was to regal Vienna, to study diplomacy (it was preferable to drama) at the Hapsburg-founded Theresian Academy, where Europe's future Metternichs were made, if not born. Diplomacy turned out to be perfect training for running a restaurant of massive egos, as the Tour would prove to be. But Claude was unwilling to go back to Paris to apprentice in the Tour d'Argent, as his father wished. He got his first real job, as attaché to the Egyptian ambassador in Bucharest. That, however, was the beginning and end of his diplomatic career. André Terrail had no more patience with his son's wild oats. He decreed that Claude would be following in his footsteps at the Tour. That was it. Claude was summoned home to Paris.

Dutiful French son, Claude accepted his destiny. In the midthirties, he began wearing his father's trademark buttonhole carnation, helping to greet such rich Depression-proof Americans as John D. Rockefeller, William Randolph Hearst, and Charlie Chaplin. André's best American friend was Bobby Lehman of Lehman Brothers, who helped provide the financing that got Juan Trippe's Pan Am circling the globe. Claude's first brainstorm was to convert the Tour's roof into a summer garden and begin serving *en plein air*. It was the first time that the place had taken advantage of its view, so spectacular that the "duck on the roof" experience was written up in *The New York Herald,* the first salvo in what would become a perpetual fusillade of great publicity. That a lot of dishes may have gotten cold en route up the six flights from the kitchen to the roof was beside the point. The view was the thing. A new kitchen on the same level would not come until years later.

In 1939, with war looming, Claude, who had learned to fly, joined the French air force. But the air ministry kept him grounded in a desk job where his main task was getting tables for officers, politicians, and other VIPs at the Tour, which had been duking it out with Maxim's for nearly three decades as the hardest reservation in the city. That all ended with Paris's quick capitulation to the Nazis in June 1940. Then stationed in Lyons, Claude got an emergency leave to fly to Paris, where he managed to brick up a false wall in the Tour's wine cellar behind which he secreted his finest bottles, only hours before one of Göring's lieutenants came to requisition the whole stock of rare 1868s. The Tour regretted that they had all been consumed, and the Germans, unable to find them, bought the lie.

The German high command, self-styled gastronomes who had targeted the Tour as a trophy destination, never figured out the ruse. Although the restaurant was about to close because all its staff had traded their servers' uniforms for military ones, the Germans insisted that it reopen, but only for them, as a sort of officers' club. Claude obliged them, though insisting that he keep a small public dining room open for his aging French regulars, those too old to have fled the Nazis. This move was not about cuisine but about intelligence. The little room became a nest of spies, one of the best sources of information in Paris about the moves of its despised occupiers. The Tour treated the Germans as tourists of the dumbest stripe. This was the one and only time Claude Terrail admitted to the "Frenchy" tactics—padding bills, disguising spoiled food with heavy sauces, putting the cheapest wine in the most expensive used bottles and recorking them—that he and his fellow hosts were accused of foisting on armies of American visitors in the postwar decades. The suckering of Nazis, he declared proudly, was not a vice but a point of honor.

Claude Terrail did not confine his wartime exploits to the Tour. His work in liberating Alsace-Lorraine and capturing Hitler's fortress at Berchtesgaden won him a Croix de Guerre. But he could never escape his connection to the restaurant. He was tapped to have the Tour cater a "Big Four" victory dinner in Berlin for Allied generals Eisenhower, Montgomery, Koenig, and Zhukov. Given the destruction of everything, the logistical challenges of this movable feast were daunting, but Terrail, flyboy that he was, commandeered some troop transports and used them as flying Fauchons (the Paris gourmet emporium) to bring in the goodies.

The meal was such a success that Eisenhower, who no one would have guessed was a foodie, became a friend and a lifetime devotee of the Tour. It was during his first meal at the restaurant, in 1951, that he decided to run for president. At the end of the repast, Ike gave the Terrails a toast that proved the general of generals had unexpected wit as well as taste: "Gentlemen, you have given me a fine demonstration of your capabilities and know-how. I hope that I shall never again have the occasion to show you mine."

In 1947, André Terrail, then sixty-seven and ailing, formally handed over the restaurant to his son, whose first publicity coup as *patron* was to win the contract from Air France to cater its first transatlantic Paris–New York service on Lockheed Constellations. The Waldorf Astoria, about to be acquired by Conrad Hilton, secured catering rights for the eastward journey. For his first menu, Terrail served a lot of cold food, foie gras, smoked salmon, jambon de Bayonne, a cheese board, all surrounding the hot entrée of *canard à l'orange*. It was as close as he could get to his trademark *canard au sang*. Air France wouldn't allow the duck press and the flambéing up in the air.

Up in the air is where Claude took the Tour, moving its main dining room permanently to the roof and glassing it in. He cut a deal with the city of Paris to give him a special light switch that illuminated the gargoyles and flying buttresses of Notre Dame on his command. Every male customer told his significant other that the illumination was arranged specially for *her;* it became the signature romantic gesture in this capital of romance.

Terrail's second great publicity coup was getting to host Prince Phillip and Princess Elizabeth of England on the first night of their Paris honeymoon in 1948. When he lit up Notre Dame for the future queen of England, he was illuminating his restaurant for the whole world to see. Nor did Terrail overlook his kitchen, which had been rated slightly below that of Maxim's, though the two were considered social equals. Hiring new chefs, he won the Tour its third *Michelin* star in 1951, establishing it as one of the top ten sites on earth for a food pilgrimage, not to mention the unmatched thrill of seeing stars. The widely held assumption that when the view went up, the food quality went down, was dramatically rebutted. No one could ever now accuse the Tour of being a grande luxe tourist trap. This was serious gastronomy.

At the same time as the Tour's postwar renaissance, Maxim's was beginning to show its age. While being a divine relic was a great part of its appeal, Maxim's seemed dark and claustrophobic compared to the glittering Tour. The orchestra, the dancing, the bordello ambience all seemed old-fashioned to the new generation of airline travelers. Besides, most of this new generation couldn't get a table at Maxim's, which was much smaller than the Tour and had a totally dismissive attitude toward "tourists."

The Tour, on the other hand, was always tourist-friendly. Business was business, and Claude Terrail welcomed anyone who dressed properly and could pay his tabs. That warm welcome won the hearts of insecure Americans and made Terrail a rich man. Snobby Maxim's had its stalwarts, like Onassis and a host of aging royals who refused to live anywhere but in the past. While the food at both places was equally rich and creamy ancien régime cuisine, somehow the Tour seemed both more relaxed and cutting-edge compared to its chief competitor.

That third *Michelin* star made a genuine star out of Claude Terrail. He began hanging out with his celebrity clients, particularly the great ladies' men: Porfirio Rubirosa; Aly Khan; Paul-Louis Weiller, the art-collecting industrialist-philanthropist-sportsman who was the main money that got Air France off the ground (his father backed the Wright Brothers), and who got Terrail the airline's catering contract; Denniston Slater, the Manhattan aristo-playboy who owned the Fanny Farmer candy colossus; Jorge Guinle, the Brazilian fellow polo player and proprietor of the Copacabana Palace Hotel, the setting for Fred and Ginger's debut film, *Flying Down to Rio;* Franz Burda, the Munich-based German press lord; and Bob Taplinger, powerful head of publicity of Warner Bros., who was a one-man clearinghouse for Hollywood starlets and, as such, indispensible to world-class Lotharios.

Every one of these men was a frequent Igor Cassini column item. Igor himself, as well as brother Oleg, became part of Terrail's inner circle, in Paris and abroad, especially now that Tour-catered Air France had daily flights to America on which Claude could ride for free. Claude's very best friend from Hollywood was Orson Welles, who hosted him on his first trip to the coast. His best friend on Wall Street was the Soviet Georgian banker Serge Semenenko, who financed many of the Hollywood studios. Semenenko, who liked taking Claude with him on food tours of France, always traversed Europe in one Cadillac limousine with an empty one following behind. When Claude asked Semenenko why the backup car, the moneyman told him it was there to take Claude back to Paris in case they ever disagreed over what restaurant to go to.

While the Maxim's crowd of titled aristocrats may have dismissed Claude as a bourgeois restaurant man, a glorified version of the help, Claude was never offended by their arrogance. He was having too much fun, living higher than any European prince. To entertain his fellow playboys and to lay the groundwork for future conquests, Claude Terrail constructed Paris's coolest bachelor pad two floors below the Tour's dining aerie. In addition to the best food and wine in Paris, served by an Italian valet, there was a screening room, a billiards room, a shooting gallery with bulletproof walls, a huge stuffed-toy collection, and two miniature electric grand prix racetracks, one for cars, another for horses, that the otherwise somber J. Paul Getty like to play with for hours on end when he normally would be counting his millions. All of Terrail's food, fun, and games, to say nothing of his sporty Beau Brummel élan, were catnip not only to Bob Taplinger's starlets but to the superstars as well.

On that first trip to the coast with Orson Welles in 1950, Terrail was overwhelmed by the pulchritude but underserved by all the starlets who kissed him good night at ten, saying they had to be fresh for their early-morning calls at the studio. There was only one girl, a shy blonde who said she was content never to be on the big screen, that she was doing fine just modeling, and was happy to stay up all night. Claude seized the situation and did the town with her, taking her to the Chasen's-Ciro's-Mocambo circuit and on to Las Vegas.

It was swell but not serious, and Terrail quickly forgot the girl's name. Two years later, he was back in L.A. and regretting his forgetfulness. He thanked his lucky stars, and *comme le monde est petit,* rediscovered her at a party given by his friend, Romanian director Jean Negulesco.

Negulesco was surprised that Terrail knew "his future star." Star? Terrail
was confused. He'd assumed she wasn't interested in all that. Negulesco
laughed. This "discovery" of his—and apparently of Claude's—was on
tap to be in the upcoming *How to Marry a Millionaire* and a lot else. She
was Marilyn Monroe.

And she wasn't the only one. Terrail had a serious and secret affair
with Ava Gardner, secret because of fear of violent retaliation from her
estranged husband and his prime star client, Frank Sinatra. It all began
one night in Paris, when Ava called the restaurant saying she was fam-
ished and wanted to get a table. It was midnight. The kitchen was closed.
But a perfect host never can refuse a guest, certainly not a perfectly beautiful, famous guest like Ava Gardner. So he had her come to the Tour,
where he thought he could satisfy her with smoked salmon, pâté, great
cold stuff like he served on Air France. No dice, Ava said, I want a big,
sizzling steak. Terrail's never-confessed failing was that he had learned
everything in life except how to cook. Now he had to try. Gardner pronounced his effort the worst steak she had ever eaten. She went to bed
with him anyhow, and a long, turbulent affair that spanned the globe
ensued.

More risky frisky business ensued with Jayne Mansfield, whom Terrail met at Castel, which reigned with Regine's as the most exclusive of
Paris nightclubs. Terrail had an obvious weakness for Hollywood blondes,
and to this end, he pursued Mansfield to the Cannes Film Festival. There
he met another violence-prone estranged husband, this one Mickey
Hargitay, the strongman and former Mr. Universe who surprised the
couple at the Carlton Hotel. He smelled a rat, or at least a ratatouille.
And the ex was a serious publicity seeker, far more desperate for a column mention than even press hound Terrail. Frank Sinatra might have
gotten his Mafia goons to take care of Terrail; Hargitay would do it himself. He cornered Terrail at the Carlton Bar, asking him to step outside.
Taking heed of a lesson learned from Orson Welles, that an American
never hits a sitting man, Terrail white-knuckled his barstool until a frustrated Hargitay gave up and left. End of Mansfield affair.

Aside from actresses, Terrail made a lot of time with heiresses. One of his most passionate flings was with Lorelle Hearst, the Dallas-born starlet and now ex-wife of William Randolph Hearst, Jr., whose prior affair with Igor Cassini got him the Cholly Knickerbocker column. Lorelle, who kept her Hearst column after her divorce from the chief's son, was a Jet Setter who seemed faster and more ubiquitous than any jet. She had become the best friend of the Duke of Windsor and always seemed to be in Europe, at the right time and at the right events. She was the perfect playmate for Terrail, who enjoyed taking her on hunting trips to his friends' ancestral castles, which were invariably less grand than Lorelle's ex-father-in-law's pile at San Simeon. There, Claude once brokered a rapprochement between old man Hearst and Orson Welles, who had taken his life, if not his name, in vain in *Citizen Kane.*

After a lot of close calls, in 1955, Claude Terrail decided to get married, almost as if to please his father, who had just passed away. The highly status-conscious André Terrail would have loved for his son to marry royalty. That he did, though not the Versailles-type royalty André might have had in mind. He married Hollywood royalty, Barbara Warner, the soigné Sarah Lawrence–educated daughter of Jack, who lived in a Tara-style *Gone with the Wind* mansion that might have impressed the Sun King. At his first dinner chez his future father-in-law, in the stellar company of Gary Cooper, John Wayne, and Errol Flynn, Terrail was served a giant grilled T-bone and a baked potato. Attached to the plate was an engraved card that read, "This is Steer Number 123 from my own ranch." Jack Warner, who had begun his business career soling shoes, had a vaudeville sense of humor and was poking fun at the Tour and its numbered ducks.

The marriage barely survived the arrival of the jet planes and was over by 1960, having produced one daughter, Anne-Jacqueline. Those jets made it easy for Claude to make his gâteau at the Tour and eat it in Beverly Hills, as well as to commute between Malibu and Warner's Villa Aujourd'hui in Cap d'Antibes, which put high-roller Jack in easy betting distance from Onassis's casino in Monte Carlo. Terrail was so grateful to be part of this new Jet Set that he made friends in Santa Monica with jetmeister Donald Douglas, whom he called "Monsieur DC-8," and

Howard Hughes, who was the only guest he'd allow in the Tour wearing jeans and sneakers.

But his more usual crowd was the Darryl Zanuck A-list polo set, which included him in their notorious all-night high-stakes croquet matches in Palm Springs. The Terrails's best friends were other bicontinental French-speaking couples, Kirk and Anne Douglas and Gregory and Veronique Peck. Barbara Warner had her father's sense of humor. When Anne-Jacqueline was born at the American Hospital in Neuilly, Barbara announced to her husband that the precocious baby was already talking. What was her first word? an amazed Claude asked. "Maxim's," Barbara taunted him.

Barbara did more than taunt when she began an affair with Raymond le Sénéchal, the pianist at the Elephant Blanc nightclub and long time accompanist of playboy-crooner Sacha Distel, whose smash record "La Belle Vie" became an even bigger smash as Tony Bennett's "The Good Life." Distel was the lover of Brigitte Bardot at the time of his pianist's transgressions with Madame Terrail, giving Igor Cassini endless grist for his gossip mill. One bit of grist that almost closed the mill was Claude Terrail's assertion that Jack Warner and his Hollywood goon squad were preparing to kidnap his daughter, Anne-Jacqueline, who was living with him while her mother played.

As was his ability, Jack Warner brought immense pressure on the Hearst papers to clear his name. Cassini jumped to it, warning Claude that there would be a bloody-duck boycott by Hollywood if he didn't bite his tongue. "Certainly I retain, in spite of these painful experiences, all my affection for my American clientele," Claude retreated in the Cholly column. Within a year, the divorce was finalized and everyone had kissed and made up, as Cassini reported in a column about a Manhattan cocktail party for polo pals Terrail and Rubirosa. Honoring the two studs was a Jet Set all-star lineup of Serge Semenenko, Oleg Cassini, Jack Lemmon, Pat DiCicco (ex-husband of Gloria Vanderbilt), NBC head Robert Sarnoff, Opel heir Gunter Sachs (future husband of Brigitte Bardot), and front and center, Jack Warner, as proof that duck conquers all.

As Barbara's jibe indicated, the rivalry between the two temples of the Tour and Maxim's was intense. But Claude's high-profile romances, his high-profile marriage, and his high-profile friends made him a major star, the first restaurateur to achieve this level of celebrity, and his ability to put a face, his well-known face, on the Tour gave him a big publicity edge over Maxim's. The Vaudables, the family who owned Maxim's, simply could not match the glamour of the Terrails. Even in the New York cradle of publicity, Henri Soulé, owner of its chief celebrity temple, Le Pavillon, was a dumpy, untelegenic autocrat. He may have instilled fear, but he lacked charisma.

What Soulé and the Vaudables did offer, power-snobbery, was precisely what the sixties critics of French inhospitality were complaining about. Terrail may have been the snobbiest of the lot, but one never felt it. When asked what was the best table in the house, Terrail would reply, "Wherever you sit, mademoiselle," followed by a deft kiss of the hand. Retro-aristo places like Maxim's drove the sixties radical-communard-Frommer types crazy, but miraculously, the Tour was able to escape their wrath. It had become as essential to Paris as Notre Dame, something that had to be experienced once in a lifetime. Terrail was simply someone whom no one could ever dislike. He might have been the stuff of parody, but his charm and style made him critic-proof. The Tour's china may have been Limoges, but its owner was pure Teflon.

7

As American as Ice Water

I F CLAUDE TERRAIL'S IMAGE WAS THE PARISIAN PRINCE OF SOPHISTICATION, CONRAD Hilton's was the Beverly Hillbilly. However, that wasn't a bad thing in Eisenhower America, where up-from-nothing success was the hallmark of Yankee ingenuity. Hilton's remarkable achievement in becoming the king of the hotel world was the apotheosis of the American Dream. Until John and Jackie Kennedy squeaked into the White House, sophistication of a Terrailian order was looked upon with great suspicion by most Americans, to whom all things foreign were presumed subversive, if not Communist.

Besides, Conrad Hilton wasn't the hayseed he appeared to be. That was part of his own subversiveness. He was as educated as he was motivated. He had been an officer in World War I in Europe. He had seen the world, dined and danced at Maxim's. He was an intimate of Presidents Truman and Eisenhower, heads of state around the world who wanted his hotels, as well as the wizards of Wall Street, the City, the Bourse, who financed his hospitality juggernaut. In Los Angeles, he was close to fellow westerner Gary Cooper, but also to German temptress Marlene Dietrich.

He has been portrayed as a rich hick from the sticks for having married Zsa Zsa Gabor. But Gabor was no cheap floozy. She was one of the goddesses of her generation. Before time turned her into a caricature, almost any man would have fallen prey to her. The most urbane actor in Hollywood, George Sanders, certainly did; he married her after Hilton. The world's greatest playboy, Porfirio Rubirosa, certainly did; the only thing that kept him from a trip to the altar was the siren call of Barbara Hutton's billions. Then Hilton's son Nick topped Daddy by wedding the ultimate Hollywood trophy, Elizabeth Taylor. At a time when men were judged by the distaff company they kept, the Hiltons could hold their own with anyone in the Jet Set. Perhaps what made Conrad Hilton seem like a rube, a country bumpkin, an innocent abroad and at home, was his deep Catholicism. Going to church, as he devoutly did, didn't get you in to Cholly Knickerbocker. Hilton often quoted the Bible, but he also cited Boswell's *Life of Samuel Johnson:* "There is nothing which has yet been contrived by man by which so much happiness is produced as by a good tavern or inn."

ON THEIR TOES. Hotel magnate Conrad Hilton with his new daughter-in-law Elizabeth Taylor, 1951.

One of the greatest businessmen of all time, Conrad Hilton had a life that was better than a Horatio Alger story, a primer on how to succeed in business by trying and trying and trying. He was born in 1887 in what was then the arid mountainous wild of the New Mexico Territory, one of eight children of a plucky immigrant family. His father, Augustus Halvorson Hilton, had journeyed from Norway and settled in a territorial hamlet called San Antonio, midway between Albuquerque and El Paso in the valley of the Rio Grande. Conrad Hilton may have inherited his unerring instinct for prime locations from his father, a powerful six-footer with a handlebar mustache who became the big man of his small town. That hamlet grew rich as a depot for the nearby coal mines and cattle and sheep ranches. As the owner of San Antonio's one general store, he was Mr. Big. He was known to the Spanish-speaking locals as El Coronel, or the Colonel. Conrad's mother called him Gus.

Mary Laufersweiler, of German stock, had smitten her future spouse as the May Queen in Fort Dodge, Iowa, where Gus Hilton first alighted on coming to America. To her prosperous merchant father, however, Gus Hilton showed too little promise, and Fort Dodge offered too little opportunity for him to prove himself. So south by southwest he went, surviving an Apache ambush that killed four fellow travelers, until he decided to stake his claim in the middle of nowhere and carve out a career as what was called a trafficker and trader, of beaver pelts. He saw plenty of opportunity for success if he could manage to avoid being scalped. Eventually, he did well enough to reseek Mary's hand, and this time her father gave in. Gus returned to Fort Dodge and, after a honeymoon in New Orleans, brought his bride to the Wild West.

The worst part of pioneer life for the new Mrs. Hilton was not the Apaches but the absence of a Catholic church. In Iowa, she had never missed a daily mass. To fill that void, a circuit-riding Belgian missionary would visit San Antonio. When the padre couldn't get to the Hiltons, the Hiltons went to the padre, wherever he was in the mountains or desert, in a buckboard wagon. The cultured Mary Hilton taught Conrad and his siblings to play the piano and to speak French to the prelate and Spanish to almost everyone else. Every summer, she would pack the kids onto the Santa Fe railway and take the long journey back to Fort Dodge.

Conrad loved the Pullman sleepers, whose modernity and cleanliness would become the hallmarks of his hotels. The Pullmans' electric lights, running water, and elaborate bathrooms were a magic ride into the future.

By 1904, Gus Hilton had become a rich man, selling his investment in local coal mines for over $100,000. To celebrate what today would be multimillionaire status, he took the family by Pullman to the St. Louis Exposition. They stayed in a fancy hotel, Conrad's first such experience, called the Inside Inn, owned by the Hilton of his times, E. M. Statler, whose Statler chain Conrad Hilton would acquire in 1954. After the World's Fair trip, the newly rich Hiltons left the desert for the ocean, moving to the breezy luxury of Long Beach, California. Conrad's sisters were sent back east to a Catholic finishing school; he was being prepared to attend Dartmouth, where he would major in economics and acquire eastern polish. Unfortunately, a stock market crash in 1907 made the Hiltons poor once again and sent them packing back to New Mexico, shattering Conrad Hilton's boyhood dreams of Ivy.

Searching for a way to recoup his fortune, Gus had the brainstorm of turning his rambling adobe home in San Antonio—which, luckily, he had not sold—into what would become the first Hilton hotel. The location was perfect, across from the new train depot. Mary was a great cook. He'd put her in the kitchen. And Conrad and his brother, Carl, would be the bellhops. Gus hung out the shingle. The room rate was two dollars a day, full board. Conrad hated his new job, meeting every train, schlepping heavy trunks, running all over town to do errands for guests, always hustling. Then one man gave him a five-dollar tip that changed his mind and his life. Before, the biggest tip he'd ever gotten was a nickel. Five dollars was winning the lottery.

Lottery or not, Mary Hilton insisted that Conrad get an education, and not just in life. She enrolled him in the fledgling New Mexico School of Mines in nearby Socorro, where he could board with a Norwegian cousin, Olaf Bursum, and come home every weekend to bellhop. Conrad credits all the math courses he took at the little three-building campus with making him an accounting wizard, a bottom-line skill he considered the cornerstone of his hotel triumphs.

The campus life at Sorocco was a far cry from that of Hanover, New Hampshire, but it did exist. Conrad learned to play tennis, to drink (with all the get-rich-quick types, there were lots of bars), and to dance, at a circuit of balls held in the various area haciendas of rich ranchers. He enjoyed the Texas (or New Mexican) two-step, but his favorite for formal occasions was the Varsoviana, a waltz-mazurka fusion Polish import that Conrad always used as the first dance to commemorate the opening of any new Hilton around the world.

By 1911, Conrad had graduated and New Mexico was about to become the forty-seventh state. Cousin Olaf, who had become the sheriff in Socorro and a rising Republican power broker, arranged to get Conrad elected to the first state legislature. Moving to the capital, Santa Fe, Conrad Hilton overnight became a player and, at twenty-four, one of the new state's most eligible bachelors. He became the toast of the cosmopolitan Palace Hotel, where he learned all the "eastern" dances the Ivy League boys were doing in New York at the Plaza. The dances all had animal names, the fox-trot, the bunny hop, the camel walk, the chicken scratch. He also picked up the neo–Jazz Age slang: Beat it. Sure. Nutty. Classy. Get your goat.

Conrad had calling cards printed, an advertisement for himself to the ladies of the desert. There was nothing shy about this young man on the make: "Conrad Nicholson Hilton. Heart Broker. Beware of Fakes, as I Am the Original 'Honey Boy.' Love, Kisses and Up-to-Date Hugs a Specialty." It may have lacked the suave subtlety of a Claude Terrail, but it played in Santa Fe. At the inaugural ball for the state's first governor, held at the Palace, Conrad danced his way into the heart of New Mexico's dream girl, the classiest belle of the entire Southwest. She was Jouett Adair Fall, the daughter of Judge Albert Bacon Fall, whose campaign to be New Mexico's first senator Conrad helped spearhead.

That campaign, which Fall handily won, marked Conrad Hilton's loss of innocence. There, and in the legislature, he saw firsthand how corrupt politics were. No one was more corrupt than Conrad's almost-father-in-law. Senator Fall would slime his way ever upward into Warren Harding's cabinet as the secretary of the interior who presided over the Teapot Dome oil lease bribery scandal, for which he would go on to prison and infamy. After his one disillusioning term in the legislature, Conrad left Santa Fe and came home to San Antonio and father Gus with a plan to start a chain, not of hotels but of banks. Just as he sold his father on the idea, however, World War I broke out. Though at thirty, Conrad was almost over the hill for fighting, he boarded the train to San Francisco and enrolled at officer candidate school at the Presidio. His co-bellhop brother, Carl, had just finished Annapolis. Patriotism ran in the family.

The lieutenant-in-training was awed by San Francisco. It was his first visit to a real metropolis. He had his eyes on the women and his mind on the banks, but his imagination was stirred by the grand hotels, the Palace on Market Street and the Fairmont on Nob Hill, the Bay City having completed its earthquake retrofit under Julia Morgan, the architect who would design Hearst Castle. Everywhere Conrad Hilton went during the war, he noticed the hotels. In Boston, he was taken to the new Copley Plaza and a Harvard-Yale ball that put the dances in Santa Fe to shame. In New York, from where he shipped out to Europe, he was intimidated by the scale of the city but mesmerized by the Plaza. And in Paris, he focused not on the smallish Ritz (under a hundred rooms) but on the Continental (nearly four hundred rooms) two blocks away, the largest hotel in the city, which Juan Trippe later would acquire and convert into his Paris InterContinental, to compete with Hilton. To Conrad Hilton, size always mattered.

Hilton wasn't about to go back to the ranch after he'd seen Paris, and Gus didn't expect him to. In fact, he wanted his son to go even farther, to Capetown, since Gus's new scheme was to get into the South African mohair business. Alas, Gus Hilton was killed in an accident in his new Model T, which skidded on ice into a ditch on New Year's Eve, 1918. Conrad Hilton had no choice but to muster out and come home to New Mexico.

Conrad returned to what seemed a wasteland. All of Gus Hilton's big plans had died with him. The hotel had closed. There was nobody left to run the general store. Conrad's mother was never one to hold him by the apron strings. Her advice to him, which he never stopped telling people, was "If you want to launch big ships, you have to go where the water is deep." Conrad soon learned that the deep water in those parts was deep in the ground, deep in the heart of Texas. In the early twenties Texas was on the verge of an oil boom that would have a huge and permanent effect on the state's development and on its larger-than-life character. Conrad was planning not to drill but to start his chain of banks in the Lone Star State, providing all the prospectors with a place to store their new wealth.

Regarding the $40,000 inheritance from his father as a grubstake, Conrad set off first for Wichita Falls, Texas, to buy his first bank. But no one there, or anywhere else in oil country, was willing to sell him one. He couldn't even find a hotel room to sleep in. The boom was that great. He was mightily impressed by the oilmen, every one a likely millionaire in big boots and fancy clothes, and by the retinue of gamblers, hookers, promoters, and sideshow of ambition that followed in their wake. It was in Cisco, Texas, striking out in trying to find a bank or a bed to sleep in, where Conrad Hilton had his moment of conversion, à la St. Paul en route to Damascus. Forget the bank, he decided. He'd use his legacy to buy a hotel.

The only beds in booming Cisco were at a flophouse called the Mobley, which rented them by the hour, with a maximum stay of eight; the rooms were turned over three times a day. Conrad Hilton didn't care who was sleeping in those beds, prospectors or prostitutes. He just liked the volume, and he used his School of Mines training to calculate the prospective profits. In a few days, he closed a deal to buy the Mobley for $40,000. He got the hotel but not a bed. The no-vacancy sign remained on. Conrad Hilton ended up sleeping in a hard chair in the office of what would become the foundation of the Roman Empire of innkeeping. He sent the following telegram to his beloved mother, his rock and redeemer: "Frontier found. Water deep down here. Launched first ship in Cisco." The Western Union man read the dispatch literally. A ship in landlocked Cisco? He thought Hilton was insane.

So did a lot of other people for a long time. Hilton set out to renovate the Mobley in a way that would presage the way he would run his Hiltons to come. First of all, realizing that his "profit was in beds," he closed the sprawling ground-floor dining room and converted the space into more bedrooms. He also added a newsstand, a tobacco shop, and a gift store. He gave pep talks to the surly staff and pumped them up, comparing them to the American Expeditionary Forces (AEF) he had just proudly served in Europe. He also promised them raises and long-term jobs, as long as "Cisco spelled Mobley" to travelers.

The problem with his formula was that relatively few travelers were coming to Cisco. Conrad began looking for better locations with more traffic. Learning of two such Texas properties with wasted space, he bought these seedy hotels for a song. He cleaned them up and made them profitable. Then he sold all three of his properties, plowing his capital into the from-scratch fifteen-story beaux arts high-rise private-bathed Dallas Hilton, known as the "million-dollar hotel" because of its cost, much of which came from a local financier named Harry Siegel. It was the first time Conrad Hilton had done business with a Jew, and it was the beginning of many equally beautiful cross-religious friendships. The ecumenical nature of his financing led to a lifetime of deep-pockets charitable support of the just-founded National Council of Christians and Jews.

In 1925, the same year the Dallas Hilton opened, Conrad Hilton closed the book on his bachelor life and married Mary Barron, by whom he was smitten during one mass at his Catholic church. Mary, from Owensboro, Kentucky, was visiting Dallas cousins. As soon as the Hilton became profitable, Conrad beat a path to Kentucky and popped the question. They split their honeymoon between country and city, Lake Louise in Canada and Chicago. You could take Conrad out of his Hilton, but you couldn't take the Hilton out of Conrad. When he saw the Chicago construction site for the Stevens, slated to become the largest hotel in the world, the honeymoon was over and the calculations began. Like every other hotel he saw and coveted, the Stevens one day would be his.

Having survived the Depression by the skin of his teeth (his marriage did not; after having three sons, Nick, Barron, and Eric, the Hiltons divorced in 1934), Conrad took his first holiday since his honeymoon. It was 1938, and he decided to visit his cousin Joe Hilton, a doctor in Los Angeles who had a beach house in Playa del Rey, south of Santa Monica. The first thing Dr. Joe did when he saw Conrad was to put him in a hospital for a week for exhaustion. Once he was released, Conrad was overwhelmed by the beauty, the climate, and the healing properties of Southern California.

But the workaholic obsessive in him was even more taken with the Town House Hotel on lower Wilshire Boulevard, down the road from Bullocks Wilshire, the incomparable art deco temple of commerce that was the department store of the stars. Aside from the Beverly Hills Hotel, the Town House was the place to stay in L.A., and the only place to stay if proximity to the Hollywood studios was the object, which it usually was. Back then, the Beverly Hills was a resort getaway, far from the action. The Beverly Wilshire was an apartment house and not even in the running. The Town House meant business. As did Conrad Hilton, who made one of his famous snap decisions that he would move to the sunny, beachy California of his briefly rich childhood. Besides, as one of America's highest-profile eligible bachelors, Conrad could see that Hollywood, the fertile crescent of available pulchritude, was everything to a dancing fool like himself that Texas was not.

The Town House wasn't for sale. Wanting to buy something to be his beachhead, Hilton found an opportunity up in San Francisco in the Sir Francis Drake on Union Square, one of the many grand hotels around the country that still had not recovered from the 1929 Crash and its endless aftermath. As such, it was a great deal: built at a cost of $5 million, bought by Hilton for $275,000 cash. Opened in 1928 at the height of the boom, the Drake flaunted the miracle of ice water on tap, radios in every room, an indoor mini-golf course, and special windows that supposedly admitted "healthful" ultraviolet rays, a real selling point in that gray and foggy city.

Hilton celebrated his big-time acquisition by buying a hilltop Spanish-style estate adjacent to the Bel Air Country Club. It was the platonic ideal of the mission architecture he grew up with in New Mexico. Here he could pursue his new passion for golf, and his old passion for women. He didn't have to hand out cards now. Distaff Los Angeles knew precisely who he was and greeted him with open limbs. Among the women he went out with were sugar heiress Kay Spreckels, who would marry Clark Gable, and Texas-born Ann Miller, she of the million-dollar legs, with whom he loved to dance and reminisce about his adventures in the Southwest. Miller's father was the lawyer for outlaws like Clyde Barrow and Baby Face Nelson who robbed the western banks that Hilton had dreamed of starting. He was always nostalgic for his cowboy roots.

Conrad Hilton wasn't the only hotel kingpin in Los Angeles. Far grander was Arnold Kirkeby, whose empire of trophies made Hilton look like a cheap motor-court operator, and whose Bel Air mansion, which would become the setting for the television smash *The Beverly Hillbillies,* made Hilton's new Bel Air hacienda look like a hillbilly shack. The awesome Kirkeby collection included New York's Sherry-Netherland, Gotham, Hampshire House, and Warwick; Chicago's Drake and Blackstone; Havana's Nacional: and in Los Angeles, the Beverly Wilshire Apartments, and the one that Hilton wanted, the Town House. He never would have had a chance were it not for Pearl Harbor.

The Japanese invasion had freaked out the entire West Coast, including Arnold Kirkeby. California went on high alert, assuming it would be next. There were constant air raid drills, night blackouts, and armored convoys up and down Wilshire Boulevard. The beaches were empty. The Town House was empty. Los Angeles had turned into a ghost town, a hotelier's nightmare. Arnold Kirkeby wanted out. Hilton wanted in. The soldier in him wasn't afraid of another Japanese invasion, because he believed that America would win. He offered Kirkeby $800,000 for the

Town House, valued as at least a $3 million property. It was a classic Hilton steal. Hilton improved it with what he called "a few dainties," tennis courts, sand from Santa Monica to beachify the pool, his beloved running ice water. Then he made a deal with the government to billet its top brass at his new property, and presto, without a single tourist, the Town House was full, and Hilton was hailed as a genius. He was embraced as an equal by Kirkeby, who would die during the jet age's hotel boom in 1962, in one of the cluster of 707 crashes.

The ego rush of landing the Town House propelled Conrad Hilton straight into the arms of an even bigger trophy, Sari "Zsa Zsa" Gabor. Gabor, an international-beauty-pageant winner, had two equally gorgeous sisters and a hat-designing mother who had big designs for her glamorous daughters. Wags called the family "the Gold Diggers of 1942." Dig they must, and dig they did. Gabor had just arrived in Hollywood from Europe and a divorce from a prominent Turkish diplomat she had met in Switzerland, where she attended a top boarding school. At twenty-four, she already had been crowned Miss Hungary and was a rising opera star.

Hollywood was at Gabor's feet, and as the new kid in town, she was invited everywhere, as was the new kid Hilton. He met her at a party and immediately brought her out to El Paso, home of the El Paso Hilton—and his mother. Despite her Jewish roots, despite her failed marriage, Zsa Zsa was given the thumbs-up by Mama Hilton. Miss Hungary sang, and danced, and *thought*. Despite Mary Hilton's devout Catholicism, she was willing to overlook Zsa Zsa's no-no divorce. After all, Conrad, too, had his own no-no divorce. Love, and the trademark Hilton optimism, would conquer all. They married in 1942.

For once in Conrad Hilton's life, his boundless faith in himself failed him. His fatal mistake was in trying to manage his wife the same way he managed his hotels. Gabor might have been a Hilton now by law, but in no way else. Zsa Zsa was as wasteful as Conrad was frugal, and Beverly Hills was a dangerous place for someone with no economic boundaries. To Zsa Zsa, there was no such thing as a budget. But what troubled Conrad more than his wife's extravagances was his gnawing guilt that,

HUNGARIAN RHAPSODY. Zsa Zsa Gabor, ex-wife of Conrad Hilton, free-spending and high-flying at Heathrow Airport, London, 1968.

having been denied communion because of their divorces, they were both, in the eyes of the Church, living in sin. Zsa Zsa dutifully attended mass with Conrad every Sunday at Beverly Hills's Good Shepherd Catholic Church, but when all the other celebrities, such as Frank Sinatra, rose and went up to the altar to receive Holy Communion, the Hiltons had to stay kneeling in their pew. Depriving a Hilton of his sacraments was akin to depriving a Hilton guest of his ice water. After having a daughter, Francesca, Conrad and Zsa Zsa would end their infatuation in divorce court in 1946.

There was also a complicating jealousy factor with Conrad's first-born, Nick (Conrad Nicholson Hilton, Jr.), who was a heavily hormonal seventeen when his father married Zsa Zsa. The six-foot-tall, rangy, handsome heir to the Hilton fortune had his father's looks but not his drive. The apple of Conrad's eye, Nick was spoiled, totally lacking the hunger that had driven his father to his pinnacle. Conrad wanted Nick to succeed him and had sent him to the École Hôtelière de Lausanne, the Swiss West Point of hospitality. Expelled after six months, Nick was delighted to return to Los Angeles, where he drank, gambled, and did drugs, including heroin, and notoriously began a long affair with his stepmother after his father divorced her.

The Oedipus business had started when a teenage Nick, ogling Zsa Zsa in a semipublic display of affection with Conrad, asked what he had to do to get a kiss like that. Conrad, western-barroom-style, knocked his impudent son across the room. Nick was also playing with the fastest crowd in Hollywood. His best friend was the outwardly dashing but terribly troubled Peter Lawford, who would arrange the introduction to Elizabeth Taylor after Nick spotted her at the Mocambo nightclub.

Realizing it was better to sublimate his passions by pursuing hotels rather than women, Conrad Hilton, chastened by the Zsa Zsa debacle, went on an amazing run of "dowager" conquests. These weren't rich widows but great old properties that had seen better days. Hilton could get them for a relative song. First came the Big Bertha that was the giant Stevens in Chicago, followed by its far fancier neighbor, the legendary Palmer House. In Washington, D.C., he bagged the Mayflower, known as "Washington's Second Best Address" because Truman stayed there while the White House was being renovated. In New York, Hilton acquired the Roosevelt, the Plaza, and his proudest big buy, the Waldorf Astoria.

At which point Washington came calling, asking Conrad to become the Marshall Plan's hospitality point man, bringing his Hilton hotels to Europeans as a form of foreign aid that would end up giving back more to America in profits than America gave to Europe in help. In 1949, Hilton obliged Washington by going on a grand tour of Europe's grand hotels, his first visit since World War I. He was shocked by how tarnished the grandeur had become.

England was particularly poignant. The great houses like Claridge's and the Savoy were victims not of German bombs but of English neglect. There had been no new linen for years. The windows were caked with the grime of war. The plumbing was primitive and barely worked. Price controls stifled the profit motive. The only good thing Hilton found was the courtly service.

France was slightly better. The main problem he noted was the scarcity of soap, a deficiency that he had noted after World War I. *Plus ça change* . . . The local and venal black market provided better food and bedclothes than the nonmarket of England. But Paris hadn't seen a new hotel go up in over thirty years. To Hilton, tradition was just a way to put a positive spin on everything having been lost. Germany had nothing left, and Italy not much more. All Hilton saw was endless opportunity for an American innovator.

It was unclear which got more front-page publicity, Conrad's 1949 acquisition of the world's most beautiful hotel, the Waldorf, or Nicky's 1950 acquisition, by marriage, of the world's most beautiful woman, Elizabeth Taylor. Taylor, only seventeen to Nick's twenty-three, was having her own troubles, chafing at the constraints of her starry indentured servitude to MGM. She had two possible modes of escape: going to college or getting married. She hated to study, so that left Nick, who seemed like just the ticket out of her bind. The moment they met, the gossips went wild, nastily intimating that this was as much about money as it was about love. Louella Parsons quoted the ostensibly virgin teen goddess vowing, "Nothing comes off until the ring goes on." The diamonds quickly arrived, and 1950's wedding of the year was scheduled by MGM to coincide with the release of *Father of the Bride,* just as it would coordinate *To Catch a Thief* with the royal nuptials in Monaco in 1956.

With the frenzy of a Chinese Theatre premiere, 3,000 fans mobbed the street outside the Good Shepherd Church to get a glimpse of some of the 600 celebrities inside, a Who's Who of showbiz that included Astaire and Rogers, the Gene Kellys, the Bing Crosbys, the William Powells, the Dick Powells, and, to protect his investment, Louis B. Mayer, actually crying for joy in a front pew. Zsa Zsa Gabor was conspicuous in her absence. The newlyweds drove up the coast in Nick's Mercedes convertible to begin their honeymoon at the Carmel Country Club, where humorist Art Buchwald happened to be vacationing. On what was supposed to be his big night with the queen of the world, Nick was found by Buchwald alone and drunk in the bar, which he seemed to inhabit for the lovebirds' three-day stay.

The pair then took a train to Chicago to stay at Hilton's Palmer House, then to New York and Hilton's Waldorf, before catching the *Queen Mary* to Europe. Conrad's wedding gift to Elizabeth was a big block of Hilton shares. It didn't seem romantic, but to Conrad Hilton, the gift was his supreme expression of love. On the *Queen*, Nick gambled away $100,000 in the ship's casino while Elizabeth found solace playing canasta with the Duke and Duchess of Windsor, the second most famous couple aboard that crossing. With Nick's mounting inebriation and wagering losses, things that began ugly eventually turned violent, as the newlyweds turned the *Queen* into a floating boxing ring.

The fights continued at André Terrail's George V, which, because of its long Hollywood connections and its rare-in-Europe air-conditioning, was the young Hiltons' Paris headquarters. There PR dynamo Elsa Maxwell took them in tow, giving a major bash for them at Maxim's, graced by Orson Welles, Maurice Chevalier, and every crowned or turbaned head in the city. Nick Hilton was unimpressed. He chewed gum the entire evening. Next stop was a private villa on the Via Appia Antica in Rome, where Elizabeth escaped Nick by hiding out with director Mervyn LeRoy, who was at Cinecittà studios directing the sword-and-sandals megamovie *Quo Vadis*. To help restore Elizabeth's sanity, LeRoy put her in the film as an uncredited extra, playing a Christian martyr at the Colosseum. Elizabeth embraced it as typecasting. Nick was typically furious. When Elizabeth vanished from the villa, he trashed the entire place. The bill was sent to Daddy.

Then came the Riviera and the bridal suite of the Carlton Hotel in Cannes, where La Taylor seemingly drew more press than the entire recent Cannes Film Festival. Nick escaped to the casino but was angrier at Elizabeth for her diamond purchases at Van Cleef on the Croisette than at his even more extravagant wagering losses. He saw their future as a replay of his father's marriage to Zsa Zsa, minus the sex, plus even more shopping sprees, if possible. To try to make up for his wife's bruises, Nick bought her a poodle called Banco.

After three months of European sparring, the Hiltons moved to a large and lavish bungalow at the Bel Air Hotel, which was opened in 1946 by one of Conrad's former Texas partners, Joseph Drown. Alas, all the room service on earth couldn't save the union. The pair separated in December 1950. The dream marriage had lasted all of six months, making the Conrad/Zsa Zsa match seem like high fidelity. Elizabeth fled to New York, this time to escape the shame of it all, seeking the solace of buddy Montgomery Clift. She checked in to the Hilton-owned Plaza, assuming she would be comped. She assumed too much. On checkout she received a bill for $2,500, informed that she was no longer part of the Hilton family. She called Clift over to help her smash everything in the suite. Together they stuffed a linen store's worth of towels into her luggage. The Hilton Corporation sent her an even bigger bill for the damage and the theft. In the bitter end, when the divorce was granted in early 1951 on grounds of mental cruelty, Elizabeth asked for nothing except to keep her jewelry and her Hilton stock. Her taste in men was debatable, but she knew a great investment when she saw it.

Hilton father and son rebounded from their marital woes in similar fashion. They both went out with actresses, though not double-dating. Conrad squired around Jeanne Crain, Hope Hampton, and the French bombshell Denise Darcel, revisiting his weakness for foreign-accented sultriness. Nick went the bombshell route as well, courting the likes of Mamie Van Doren and Joan Collins. Nick also went mano a mano with Howard Hughes for the favors of Terry Moore.

Conrad was still convinced that Nick could play out this wild-oats phase and be made into a hotelman. He took the boy on a second honeymoon to Europe, visiting potential sites for his Marshall Plan–inspired chain of luxury fortresses of American capitalism against the omnipresent Communist threat. Unfortunately, Nick was much more interested in partying than in innkeeping. Conrad had to plot his European invasion all by himself. The Marshall Plan expired in 1952, without providing the bonanza of easy financing that Hilton had expected. Instead, he had to go from country to country looking for money. Nonetheless, the Hilton name was magic, synonymous with success, American-style, and Conrad found himself in the enviable position of having to turn away foreign investors.

Hilton's first project on the continent was in Madrid, where the developers of what would be the city's first high-rise modern hotel had run out of money. Taking over and renaming the edifice the Castellana Hilton, after himself and the broad new boulevard it overlooked, Hilton chartered two TWA Constellations from his friend (and Nick's amorous rival) Howard Hughes, full of show people for the 1953 grand opening.

The paint hadn't dried, the elevators were broken, and the air-conditioning sputtered on and off, but publicity conquered all. The most famous of the stars was Gary Cooper, synergizing the Spanish premiere of *High Noon* with his buddy's hotel premiere. So awed were Madrileños by the presence of Cooper that fan calls short-circuited the Hilton switchboard, knocking out phone service along with everything else. Mary Martin was there, serenading the opening-night crowd with "My Heart Belongs to Daddy," as the spotlight fell on Conrad, who had led off the festivities by sweeping Jinx Falkenburg onto the floor for his trademark Varsoviana. Swimming champion and cover girl Falkenburg was one of America's media stars. Her top-rated radio interview show with her husband, Tex McCrary (*Tex and Jinx*), was broadcast every weekday morning from Peacock Alley at Hilton's Waldorf Astoria. Tex and Jinx—who happened to have been born in Spain and was perfect for this launch—led the campaign to get Hilton golf mate General Eisenhower to run for president. Synergy was Conrad's motto, even though he didn't have a clue what the word meant. Hilton's one overreach was to dress all the Castellana's service staff in clichéd peasant costumes that looked as if they had come from the MGM wardrobe closet rather than the fields of Segovia. After a public outcry, Hilton redressed all the bellmen and waiters in tuxedos.

Two years later, in 1955, Hilton was doing the same Varsoviana, this time at the Istanbul Hilton, the first of his global hotels to have been built from scratch, his preferred approach. Hilton was lured to the Bosphorus by a lavish financing venture between the Turkish government and the Marshall Plan that provided a sultan's ransom to Hilton to erect and manage a monument to himself. The Castellana Hilton had been a dry run that convinced Hilton the more American his hotels could be from the ground up, the better. Although he made something of a show of employing local architects and craftsmen, these efforts were akin to Ivy League colleges' efforts at "geographical distribution"; they were tokens that revealed Hilton's lack of esteem. Bearing a rather déjà vu resemblance to Conrad's 1953 Beverly Hilton, the Istanbul Hilton was a glaring symbol of American architectural imperialism and a harbinger of all the Hiltons to come. Yes, there were the acres of wall-to-wall carpets made by the famous weavers of Konya, but to have imported American synthetic rugs to the land of the magic carpet would have been beyond the beyond. That the Turkish carpets were cheaper probably made the decision for bottom-line Hilton.

Aside from the flooring, the boxy eleven-story white concrete slab of uniform modernity was as fifties American as a suburban split-level. On a verdant site that formerly was the Armenian cemetery near the contemporary business hub of Taksim Square, there were American-style green lawns that created a very country-club feel. Glimpses of the swimming pool and tennis courts tantalized with American leisure, not Oriental culture. The entry pavilion was a shopping mall dominated by the glass-walled offices of Pan Am and American Express. A traveling Dorothy from *The Wizard of Oz* might not be in Kansas anymore, but she would be hard-pressed to know she was in Istanbul. Praised by critics as reminiscent of Le Corbusier, this Hilton was designed by Gordon Bunshaft, the principal of the esteemed firm of Skidmore, Owings & Merrill, responsible for such fifties masterpieces as Park Avenue's Lever House. There was a Turkish architect as well, but he was a deeply silent partner.

Only inside the hotel and in the more expensive rooms did a traveler realize he was at a mystical crossroads of history. The view of the Bosphorus and the opposite, exotic shore of Asia was the thing. But the exotica was safely distanced behind a capitalist curtain of air-conditioning and coffee-shop burgers and milkshakes and antiseptic imported Danish-modern furniture that was the same in every room.

Those cookie-cutter guest rooms, sixteen by twenty feet, were equipped with telephones and radios (Turkey didn't have television yet) and could have been the inspiration for the *Leave It to Beaver* set. In one continental touch that invariably stymied American visitors, the marble bathrooms were all equipped with bidets. The more salient feature of the bathrooms were the three sink spigots that would become the trademark (and the curse) of Conrad Hilton: one for hot water, one for cold water, and one for ice water, an ingenious invention credited to E. M. Statler, whose chain Hilton would acquire the following year, making Conrad's company the biggest hospitality concern on earth.

The ice water was the item that got Europe's goat, the "let them eat cake" symbol, though the continent was divided on whether to trash it or gulp it. That same year, the Terminus Hotel in Dijon, France, made an homage to Hilton by installing a system where red and chilled white vin de Bourgogne were piped into guest rooms. It was both an advertising gimmick and a French slap in Hilton's face. Drink wine, not water, was the message.

Hilton was oblivious to it. The Istanbul Hilton was a major event, and the third-world Turks, obviously needier than the French, welcomed the American presence of Conrad Hilton the way the Philippines welcomed General MacArthur when he made good on his promise, "I shall return." For the kickoff, Hilton had arrived in Istanbul with 113 celebrities on two chartered Douglas DC-6s, this time from Pan Am, which had the lobby concession at the hotel. Repeats from Madrid included Jinx Falkenburg and Leo Carrillo. New Hiltonites included Carol Channing, Irene Dunne, Merle Oberon, Sonja Henie, and ex-girlfriend Ann Miller.

The mayor of Istanbul gave Conrad Hilton the key to the city, and the festivities, worthy of a MacArthurian conquering hero, began. In place of bullfighting, there were whirling dervishes, military parades, cruises on the Bosphorus, private tours of the Topkapi Palace, which would be the centerpiece of the Jules Dassin–directed 1967 *Topkapi,* a wanderlust-inducing thriller about a jewel heist that was filmed in part on the palatial grounds of the Istanbul Hilton, where the protagonists planned their caper. The hotel's modern image against an ancient setting, its invocation of Jet Set wealth against third-world poverty, was the publicity gift that would keep on giving. In the first year after the hotel's opening, Turkish tourism shot up 60 percent, and much of the credit went to Hilton and his ballyhoo.

The Turkish and coming European embrace of Hilton wasn't about Conrad's money. The Marshall Plan was pretty much a bait-and-switch operation where American millions for European hotels were concerned.

What the Europeans ended up getting was not the money but Conrad Hilton, who took *their* money in return for his unique American genius. In Madrid, in Istanbul, in Athens, in Paris, in London, and everywhere he planted the Hilton flag, the local investors put up all the money to build the hotels. For a huge piece of the profits, usually a third, Hilton would lend his name and his management. Thus the Euros were not working for the Yankee dollar; Hilton was working for the Euro dollar, making out like a Texas bandit, a Pretty Boy Conrad, who was not only looting the treasuries of the continent but turning the Old World into a simulacrum of midcentury America: Scarsdale on the Bosphorus, or the Seine, or the Thames. The outrage was that, with Hilton, as with McDonald's decades later, Europe wasn't Europe anymore.

In the Cold War, the Istanbul Hilton (and each Hilton to come) was as much a political statement as an architectural one. Hiltons weren't merely places to sleep. More important, they were a kind of NORAD with rooms, a seductive line of defense against totalitarianism. As Hilton told the crowd in his Istanbul inaugural address:

> We view our international hotel ties as a firsthand laboratory where men of Turkey . . . may inspect America and its ways at their leisure . . . We mean these hotels, too, as a challenge . . . to the way of life preached by the Communist world. Each hotel spells out friendship between nations, which is an alien word in the vocabulary of the Iron Curtain. The Marxian philosophy with its politically convenient dialectic has a way of reducing friends to slaves. To help fight that kind of thinking and that kind of living we are setting up our hotels of Hilton International across the world.

The ebbing of the Hilton tidal wave that seemed as if it would deluge the world began at what may have been its high-water mark and moment of greatest overreach, in 1958, the same year as the triumphal debut of the 707. That period saw the dual openings of the Habana Hilton, just as Castro was threatening to take over the island, and the

Berlin Hilton, just as Khrushchev was threatening to cut off the divided city from the West.

In keeping with Conrad Hilton's policy of "déjà vu all over again," the Habana Hilton, a 30-story, 550-room, $44 million extravaganza, was designed by modernist Welton Becket, the architect of the Beverly Hilton, as well as the Capitol Records turntable-shaped tower in Hollywood. It was muscled into existence by dictator Fulgencio Batista and funded by the rich pension fund of the Cuban Catering Workers' Union. With its Trader Vic's, its casino, supper club, and wall-to-wall showgirls, it was a perfect symbol of capitalist excess and a sitting duck for Fidel Castro, whose revolutionary agents had been responsible for a series of killings, kidnappings, and bombings that the Hilton-Batista publicity machine had managed to play down as a low-risk universal urban vacation hazard.

The threats of sabotage did necessitate the presence of more than a hundred armed policemen creating a *cordon sanitaire* around the skyscraper, jutting upward like the sorest of thumbs above Havana's colonial elegance. The state of siege scared away most of Hilton's Hollywood regulars, but Hilton was undeterred, arriving with his latest romantic interest, the Peruvian Gladys Zender, who had been crowned 1957's Miss Universe at the Long Beach Hilton's grand ballroom. The eighteen-year-old was the first Latina to win the crown and was considered the perfect date for the Cuban festivities. Conrad's celebration was short-lived. After seizing power in early 1959, Castro made the Hilton his personal headquarters before nationalizing it, closing its emblem-of-evil casino, and renaming it the Hotel Habana Libre. How the mighty had fallen.

Echoing his new man in Havana, Nikita Khrushchev was making similar bellicose promises of "we will bury you" that November when Hilton chartered two more Pan Am planes to ferry his stars to the grand opening of the more intimate (14 stories, 350 rooms, $6.5 million) Berlin Hilton, still another modern blockhouse, overlooking the city's famed zoo. Just two weeks before the kickoff, Khrushchev had issued his "Berlin Ultimatum," giving the Allies six months to remove all troops from West Berlin. Conrad Hilton's Wild West response to the Eastern threat was "if Berlin did not already have a Hilton, I would have to start building one now."

The junket got off to an inauspicious start when the Pan Am Clipper bearing Hilton and his special guest, the wife of Supreme Court Chief Justice Earl Warren, developed engine troubles over Nova Scotia and had to return to Idlewild. The defective plane was a turboprop DC-7, not a 707. If it had been the latter, the bad press would have been greatly magnified. But Juan Trippe didn't have enough jets yet to give one to his biggest booster, even though Trippe and Hilton had worked out a cooperative advertising campaign cross-pollinating the jet and the blockhouse: "Introducing Germany's Newest Hotel . . . Designed for the Jet Age." The ads made the point that Hilton's Berlin blockbuster was as "up to the minute" as Trippe's jet spaceship.

While Trippe's cousin by marriage über-diplomat David Bruce, now ambassador to Germany, was front and center at the gala, Trippe and Hilton never became close. Was it because Trippe wanted to out-Hilton Hilton with his own chain of InterContinental Hotels? Was there an undercurrent of competition beneath their shared anti-Communism? Or was it because Hilton's shoot-from-the-hip western candor was so alien to Trippe's closed and clubby Ivy style? If Conrad Hilton had only realized his mother's plan for him to go to Dartmouth, the two titans might have been best friends forever.

Side by side with Ambassador Bruce at the Hilton was the charismatic Berlin mayor (and future German chancellor) Willy Brandt. The opening came during Berlin's traditional winter ball season, a remnant of a decadent imperial past that Conrad Hilton resurrected just to shove it in Khrushchev's peasant maw. All the guests were required to dress in medieval pageant costumes as knights and maidens of the realm. The supermodern ballroom was decorated like a fairy-tale castle, with a few Hiltonian touches, such as a coat-of-arms pennant bearing the logo "Trink Coca-Cola." Unlike the quick demise of the Habana Hilton, the Berlin Hilton successfully called Khrushchev's bluff and fulfilled Conrad's mission to "show the countries most exposed to communism the other side of the coin."

Temple Fielding, the grand arbiter of success in this regard, ranked the Berlin Hilton the top hotel in the city, a worthy successor to the prewar laurel worn by the Hotel Adlon, next to the Brandenburg Gate. "Despite our lack of enthusiasm for one or two other Hiltons abroad, here is *the* hotel for any discriminating visitor to this city," Fielding gushed. He also recommended Guidesters hie themselves to the Hilton roof and its El Panorama supper club "with dinner-dancing every night, a tropical bar, and a historically significant view—the bright lights of the Free City in one direction and the gloom of darkened East Berlin in the other."

Conrad Hilton liked to say that each of his foreign hotels was "a little America." A little Beverly Hills would have been more to the point. Just as Claude Terrail gave gourmets a slightly Disneyfied version of haute cuisine, Conrad Hilton was providing his own Disneyfied version of haute hospitality. If an American wanted to experience Europe in the most luxurious, least challenging, and most sanitized fashion, his best approach would be to eat at the Tour and sleep at the Hilton. The two ostensible rivals were in truth opposite sides of the same coin, the Yankee silver dollar.

The Guidester would have to wait until 1965, when the Paris Hilton finally opened, to kill the two great birds in the same great city. He could warm to the task by enjoying the Hilton experience in Berlin in 1958, in Amsterdam in 1962, and in Athens and Rome and London in the HH (Hilton Hotels) banner year of 1963, by which point the Vietnam situation had so antagonized the world toward America that the ice water had taken on a different kind of chill, and Hilton was becoming a dirty word, connoting fat-cat imperialism and warmongering. By the same token, the phrase "Jet Set" was beginning to lose its soaring mystique and was taking on unexpected negative connotations of its own.

8

Blind Ambitions

IGOR CASSINI WAS TORN BETWEEN MADISON AVENUE AND PENNSYLVANIA AVENUE. By 1961, the one avenue where he was not interested in traveling was his long-trodden beat as the most powerful social columnist in America. He was sick of lapdogging around to Conrad Hilton's grand openings and promoting his ice water, sick of chronicling the celebrities who were eating Claude Terrail's duck, sick of being the reflector of other people's glory, sick of being a lot less rich than the people he was writing about. Igor was happily married now to Charlene Wrightsman. They had a new son to raise. Igor was feeling the pressure of being a family man, of having a serious career.

And well he should. Charlene was one of the most attractive, most eligible girls in the world, a supercatch that Igor, little Igor, had landed. He had to live up to this trophy, and he was trying hard to be a good husband and a good father, not only to his new boy, Alex, but to Charlene's first son, Dana, and to his daughter by Darrah, Marina. Amazingly, for all the action in his life, Igor seemed to be embracing stability. The allures notwithstanding, being Cholly Knickerbocker somehow lacked the gravity that Igor was craving. Madison Avenue, on the other hand, had the weight, and it had the gold. Martial, the public relations agency founded by Igor and Oleg in 1955, had just kept on growing.

With John F. Kennedy in the White House and Igor having secured for his ex-Hollywood costumer brother the "by appointment to her majesty" plum as Jackie's official dress designer, Oleg Cassini had managed to become Martial's own client, up there in a stellar roster of accounts that included Harry Winston, Lanvin, Gianni Agnelli and his family's Fiat, and the national tourist boards of both Brazil and Mexico. Igor Cassini found himself in the position to consider chucking the column and becoming the man in the gray flannel suit.

Gray flannel, however, was too subdued and understated for Igor Cassini, who was dressed to the hilt by Park Avenue's A. Sulka, also a Martial client. That was where the Pennsylvania Avenue alternative came into play. Rather than being the social tool that he currently was, writing as Cholly Knickerbocker, or the corporate tool that Martial was enabling him to become, the Kennedy ascension stirred him to reconsider his original lifetime ambition: to be a diplomat in the grand tradition of his noble Russian grandfather, the tsar's ambassador to Venice, to Beijing, to Washington. Power politics were his bloodline. He read with envy the prestige D.C. columns, Joe Alsop's "Matter of Fact," Drew Pearson's "Washington Merry-Go-Round." That was print diplomacy. That was what a Cassini should be doing, not recounting Conrad Hilton's numbingly standardized routine of doing the Texas two-step at the Cairo Hilton.

Igor Cassini's in-laws, the Wrightsmans, lived next door to the Kennedy compound in Palm Beach. Aside from his aversion to touch football, Igor was practically family with the Irish dynasty. Igor got girls for Joe Kennedy. He chased girls with Jack Kennedy. He had made Jackie Kennedy famous, the first pressman ever to notice her, anointing her as "Deb of the Year." No one who hadn't been to Harvard with JFK could have had better access. Igor wanted to take advantage of it, wanted to serve his adopted country. He was swept up in the anti-Communist fervor of the times, just as much as Conrad Hilton and Juan Trippe. Or

BROTHERS OF CAMELOT. Igor Cassini and Bobby Kennedy, before Bobby indicted him, 1962.

even more. His aristocratic Russian family had been dispossessed by the Communists. He had more than ideology, more than patriotism. He had a grudge. He was just waiting for the right moment.

Wanting to escape the gilded straitjacket of being Cholly Knickerbocker's ghost—or *negre,* the demeaning French term for ghostwriter—Igor Cassini found his golden opportunity through one of his favorite subjects and best friends, Porfirio Rubirosa, the legendary, small (five-eight), but fearless Dominican polo-playing lothario who had married both of the world's reigning heiresses, Doris Duke and Barbara Hutton. Even before the Boeing 707 took to the skies, Rubirosa had become the globe-trotting role model for all aspiring Jet Setters. Other than the Kennedys, no subject provided Cassini with more column inches, appropriate for a man whose own immense "column" (of reputedly over a dozen inches) occasioned the renaming, by haughty restaurant maîtres d'hotel, of the *poivrier,* or pepper mill, the "Rubirosa."

The sexual dynamo's big break had come from the first of his five marriages, to Flor de Oro, daughter of the brutal billionaire Dominican Republic dictator Rafael "El Jefe" Trujillo, with whom Rubirosa stayed close even after his divorce from Flor. Trujillo had made "Rubi" the Dominican envoy to Paris, the scene of Rubirosa's initial forays into world society. Back in Santo Domingo, the capital, Trujillo made his country a citadel of Franco-esque Spanish fascism in the azure Caribbean seas, now threatening to turn Russian Red. When Castro took over the Habana Hilton in 1959, he also seized the Cuban gambling empire of the American Mafia. Igor Cassini instantly envisioned the Dominican Republic's capital Santo Domingo as the reborn Havana, the ultimate Jet Set playground, and one that would be totally pro-American.

To that end, the moment Castro took power, Cassini, using favorite son-in-law Rubirosa as his advance man, charmed Trujillo into hiring Martial to do public relations for the country. Cassini easily won the account, but this was one client he could not brag about. Trujillo may have been a scourge against Communism, but he was hardly a poster boy for democracy. Ridiculed sub rosa by his fearful populace as "Chapitas," or Bottlecaps, because of the way he festooned himself with round, shiny medals, the dictator similarly festooned his entire nation with his motto, "Dios y Trujillo" (God and Trujillo). No Hollywood star was ever as megalomaniacal. No Roman emperor was as bloodthirsty. As a career military man who seized power at age thirty-eight in 1930, he quickly suppressed his mother's mulatto background and then embarked on a vicious campaign of ethnic cleansing against Dominicans with "Haitian blood," the largely black descendants of the once enslaved denizens of the island. His genocidal body count was thought to be as high as 50,000 people.

Trujillo didn't confine his death wishes to blacks. God help his opponents. He did his best to murder his enemy, President Rómulo Betancourt of Venezuela, a failed effort that would get his country expelled from the Organization of American States (OAS) in 1960. He was already in the Washington, D.C., doghouse for his successful 1956 ordered murder in a New York subway station of Jesús Galíndez, a Columbia University lecturer and brainy, credible critic of the Trujillo reign of terror. Because of Trujillo's being blacklisted and because of his dreadful press, Cassini set up a Bahamas subsidiary, Inter-American Public Relations, with his and Martial's name nowhere on the masthead, to do the job.

Still, Trujillo was a "get" Cassini was thrilled to have gotten. So what that it might take a mésalliance between dictators and crime bosses to make the world safer for democracy? It was better than Khrushchev. If Cassini could bridge Hollywood and Washington, as he did by running interference (and beautiful starlets) between the Rat Pack and the White House, why not also create a spur to Little Italy? Wasn't that just what Sinatra was trying to do for his beloved and feared godfather figure, Chicago capo Sam Giancana? Giancana was the brawn behind the Cuban gambling empire that had been masterminded by the Mob's finance wizard Meyer Lansky. But Sinatra's bridge to gangland was too obvious, too inflammatory. Everybody knew Sinatra had the Mafia taint. Igor Cassini, conversely, was beholden to no one. With his impeccable social links to JFK and Rubirosa, Cassini saw himself as the next Dean Acheson or John Foster Dulles. Forget Cholly Knickerbocker. Think Metternich!

Great PR man that he was intent on being, Cassini immediately began cogitating how to play up the virtues of his new client. On the positive side of the Trujillo ledger, if such can be said to have existed, El Jefe's desire to "whiten" his country had made it a haven before, during, and after World War II for European Jews, as well as many other displaced Europeans. Trujillo therefore was toutable by Cassini as a "friend of Israel" to Kennedy liberals, while redneck Dixiecrat Strom Thurmond Southerners could not so secretly admire his muscular racism. In any event, for all his evil, Trujillo was way preferable to Castro in post-McCarthy America, especially if the casinos got rolling. Hot hands made for short memories.

Trujillo had two polo-playing playboy sons, very much in the mold of their brother-in-law and style mentor, Rubirosa. Star fixtures for years in the Cholly Knickerbocker column, the "dictator's boys" were the toast of Paris. The brothers were named Ramfis and Rhadames, after characters in *Aida,* and they lived in pharoahonic splendor that provided Cassini tons of copy. Ramfis had cut a swath in Hollywood, dating Zsa Zsa Gabor after her divorce from Conrad Hilton, as well as Kim Novak and lots of other starlets. His generosity toward these women was unmatched. His gifts to Gabor of a Mercedes and a chinchilla coat, reported gleefully in Cassini's column, prompted Congressman Wayne Hays of Ohio, who would have his own front-page sex scandal in the seventies, to denounce Gabor as "the most expensive courtesan since Madame Pompadour."

The Hays broadside was also dutifully reported in Cholly, as was Mother Jolie Gabor's defense of her golden girl: "What should a man send a girl like my daughter? Flowers?" Ramfis shared Gabor's favors with Rubirosa, in between his brother-in-law's big-bucks marriages to Duke and Hutton. Again Cassini was all over it, selling reams of newspapers. After his Hollywood idyll, Ramfis had spent a long time getting electroshock therapy. Rhadames, no slouch in the starlet sweepstakes, hit his peak when he stole away Darryl Zanuck's mistress Bella Darvi. Rhadames also was famous for trashing more five-star hotel rooms than Keith Moon of the Who. Wild and crazy guys, yes, but good clean fun compared to Daddy's death squads.

After a year of little success bringing either positive publicity or gambling interests to his still-blacklisted, secret-client country, Igor Cassini finally got the chance he'd been waiting for. The moment of diplomatic opportunity took place on a Palm Beach golf course, where Cassini was duffing with Joe Kennedy and the CIA head Allen Dulles, brother of Eisenhower's secretary of state. Cassini contrived to bring up the mounting possibility, gleaned both from Rubirosa and from his own work for the country, that the Dominican Republic was ripe for a Castro-style uprising. He expressed his opinion that JFK would be wiser to fortify a right-wing regime than to risk it being replaced by a left-wing Comintern.

While Joe Kennedy was more interested in the size of Rubirosa's member and its gilded peregrinations, Dulles, all business, sparked to Cassini's gambit and expertise and galvanized Joe into leaning on son Jack to take action, which he did. In April 1961, just after the CIA's disastrously botched invasion of Cuba at the Bay of Pigs, the president dispatched Cassini as a top-secret envoy to the Dominican Republic to sound out Trujillo himself about improving U.S./Dominican relations, both public and private. A measure of the seriousness of the Cassini mission was the company he was to keep. JFK chose as Cassini's partner one of America's most respected big-time diplomats, Robert Murphy, a former ambassador to Belgium and Japan and, most recently, Eisenhower's undersecretary of state for political affairs.

A superpro like Murphy was needed because there were a lot of affairs to improve. At first Cassini and Murphy's mission appeared to be a success. They had productive meetings with the generalissimo and his puppet president, Joaquín Balaguer, so productive that Cassini later wrote he had visions of himself as the ambassador to the Dominican Republic, not to mention the millions he would make in pieces of the action at the new casinos he assumed he would do the PR for.

But the best-laid plans of Cassini and Kennedy went even more astray than had the Bay of Pigs. In late May 1961, barely a month after their meeting, Trujillo, en route in his turquoise Cadillac to visit his mistress, was ambushed in a military coup d'état. He went down shooting, riddled with over two dozens bullets fired by a team of hit men assembled by a general who happened to be married to Trujillo's sister. Alas, the coup turned out to be less bang than whimper, a Caribbean Keystone Kops farce that concluded with the general and his co-conspirators being imprisoned and tortured under orders of *fils* Ramfis, who assumed his father's power, albeit behind the facade of frontman Balaguer.

When Trujillo was killed, Ramfis and Rhadames had been in Paris, living their typical high life with their brother-in-law, Rubirosa, all playing on the same world-class polo team. When they got the news, they paid $27,000 to Air France to charter a 707 to bring them back to their country, where they quickly took control and the would-be plotters lost their nerve. Igor Cassini was never concerned that death might stop the Trujillos. The night of the coup, the first person called by CIA chief Allen Dulles was his golfing partner Cassini, who he believed knew more about the island than any other American. Cassini told Dulles to rest easy. The Dominican Republic would be business as usual. Nothing would change except for the better.

Rubirosa redonned his old diplomat hat and became the official spokesman for this new version of the ancien régime. Giving him a forum in the Hearst papers was none other than Igor Cassini, who adored putting aside his Cholly Knickerbocker chores for this vastly more august Joseph Alsop routine. If the Dominican coup was Keystone Kops revolution, this was Keystone Kops journalism, Rubirosa playing statesman and Cassini playing pundit. Rubirosa assured Cassini, hence the world, that the political prisoners would soon be freed, the dictatorship was over, and American-style democracy was nearly at hand.

It was the baldest display of insincere public relations imaginable, but it was enough to allow Cassini to transcend Trujillo's death and secure for Martial a fat new secret three-year contract between the new Dominican regime and his shell corporation Inter American to continue working for the banana republic. The fee was $120,000 for the first year, a hefty sum in 1961, with annual increases, plus a big bonus as soon as the Americans and the Dominicans resumed diplomatic relations.

Rubirosa, who allegedly got a finder's fee for getting Cassini this contract, cut his own deal with Ramfis—who had effectively assumed his father's dictatorship—that would net Rubi a cool $250,000 the moment Washington removed the country from the OAS blacklist. That cleansing seemed like a fait accompli now that Trujillo, the despot who had ordered all the hits, had been hit. The Trujillo Hit Parade seemed finally to be over. To cement the deal, Rubirosa's shuttle diplomacy took him on several Kennedy–Rat Pack yacht trips, one to the Riviera, another off the New England coast.

Even Fidel Castro found the Rubi-Frankie-Camelot triangle a bit much and denounced it on his radio broadcasts. Despite Cassini's efforts to whitewash Ramfis, other investigative journalists began filing reports of Trujillo Junior's reign of terror against his father's assassins: hair-raising tales of torture that made waterboarding look like a day at the beach. There were eyelid slashings, genital electroshock, all sorts of truth serums, and as the pièce de résistance, a delicious blanquette served to one of the starving imprisoned suspects who, at the height of his satiety, was informed that its chief ingredient was the entrails of his son. The suspected assassin was reported to have died of a heart attack on the spot. Then there were rumors that Ramfis not only led his own satanic cult but possessed a private freezer stuffed with the decapitated heads of the lovers of his unfaithful mistresses, a kind of cold-storage trophy case. The presumptions of evil were harder and harder for Cassini to dispel.

Ramfis must have felt the heat. In November 1961, in the dead of night, Ramfis and his entourage flew back to Europe on another leased Air France 707, filled to the gills with millions of dollars, plus jewelry, art, and stock certificates worth tens of millions more. He was given sanctuary in Madrid by fellow dictator Francisco Franco and resumed his playboy high life, blithely conceding that he never was cut out for politics. In January 1962, the Trujillo puppet, Balaguer, was overthrown by still another general, Rodriguez Echeverria, but the illusion of change was enough for the OAS to finally lift its sanctions.

Now Cassini and Rubirosa should have been able to really cash in, but their deals were with the Trujillos, not the new government, which repudiated everything the Trujillos had done. So the diplomatic windfall the two men expected never came to pass. Rubirosa, who needed the money, was beyond furious at Ramfis and his Trujillo in-laws. He had played the diplomat for them, and now he was made to look like their fool. Retreating to Paris with his polo ponies and his Ferraris and his new young wife, Odile, for once neither a star nor an heiress, Rubirosa, now in his fifties, never spoke to the Trujillos, nor played polo with them, ever again. Cassini, who was too much of a comedian to mind playing the fool, was more upset that his chance to elevate his status turned out to be a pipe dream. What he didn't realize was that the pipe dream would become the nightmare of his existence within a year.

The route to Pennsylvania Avenue having been closed off, Igor Cassini focused on Madison Avenue as never before. If he couldn't be a big diplomat, he had to become a big businessman. Even though Igor's father-in-law, C. B. Wrightsman, had a fortune valued at over $100 million, there was no guarantee that Igor's wife, Charlene, would get one cent. Hadn't old C.B., as mean and nasty as an Okie cattle rustler, disinherited Charlene's older sister for eloping with the scoundrel Freddie McEvoy? Igor was a scoundrel, too, in a different way, and he never felt secure with C.B. Actually, he never felt secure anywhere, given his displaced family's past. And what journalist really felt secure? Even though he was earning more than his chief gossip rival, Walter Winchell, at this point, Igor felt the imperative to diversify, to get into business, real business.

Hence he set out to make Martial the undisputed publicity top shop in all the media. Martial was necessary but not sufficient for Igor's dreams of corporate grandeur. Cassini had another big plan in the works: to get into the global franchise business, using a vehicle that had never been franchised, the new French version of the nightclub known as the discotheque. Igor wanted to become an after-hours Conrad Hilton. In late 1961, right after the Trujillo sons fled the Dominican Republic, Igor, determined to recoup his Caribbean losses, founded Le Club, a snobby, doorman-rejecting-everyone, French-style discotheque that aimed to ape the wild success of two Parisian temples of pop-music-paced revelry, Régine and Castel. These clubs mixed old guard with new wave, tycoons with noblemen with movie stars—in short, the Jet Set as Igor Cassini wrote about it.

For the New York take on the Paris model, Igor, with Oleg's design help, found an old photographer's studio off Sutton Place near the East River, decorated it in the taxidermic style of a baronial, high-ceilinged Austrian hunting lodge, and mounted a discreet "Members Only" plaque on the front door. The formula was El Morocco, Manhattan café society's premier supper club, but without a coat and tie, and everyone doing the twist to Chubby Checker. Igor quickly enrolled 600 members for a space that could hold only 200, an instant guarantee of scarcity-based exclusivity. The roster included Kennedys, Vanderbilts, the Duke of Bedford, the Maharaja of Jaipur, actor Rex Harrison, producer Sam Spiegel, lyricist Alan Jay Lerner, writer George Plimpton—the same people who danced at Régine and Castel, Claude Terrail's Tour d'Argent people, Igor Cassini's Jet Set people. Le Club was *their* club.

The brothers had done a successful dry run at this kind of Europeanization of American leisure several years before, when they launched an exclusive Swiss-style ski resort in Sugarbush, Vermont. Igor had introduced the place in his column as "El Morocco on the Rocks." Why, he asked, go to Gstaad or St. Moritz when Sugarbush was a five-hour drive,

much closer than the eight-hour jet to Zurich, and minus all those alpine roads? So they built it, and They came: the Kennedys, the Agnellis,
those party-animal Greeks. This effort to Alpinize and glamorize the traditionally subdued, low-key Vermont winter sports experience was such
a hit that the Cassinis were emboldened to try to reinvent New York's
midnight-hour experience. They saw themselves as the Pied Pipers of the
leisure class dressed by Oleg and immortalized by Igor.

Like Conrad Hilton's chain of hotels, the Cassini ventures were financed with someone else's money. Igor's chief backer for Le Club was
the man who provided the hardwood for the elegant dance floor that the
power couples of the time, from Ari Onassis and Maria Callas to Eddie
Fisher and Elizabeth Taylor, were twisting and frugging and Watusi-ing
on. But this floor man was strictly a penthouse dweller. Known as America's floor king, he was the chairman of the Tennessee-based E. L. Bruce
Company, the Rolls-Royce of hardwood. His factories may have been in
the rural South, but his fast-lane life took him all over the world in the
highest style. His name was Eddie Gilbert, and he was by far the most
glamorous businessman in the country, a glamour created in part by Igor
Casssini, who coined for the thirty-nine-year-old Gilbert the name "Boy
Wonder of Wall Street," just as he had coined the name "Jet Set" for
Gilbert's crowd.

Eddie Gilbert was fascinating to the public because of his bold and
acrobatic maneuvers, not only in corporate takeovers but also in social
climbing. His remarkable success in both arenas made him one of the
rare Jews in the upper reaches of the Jet Set; he was also the most colorful
high financier in the business pages. Gilbert was living proof of the new
mobility, both geographical and social, engendered by the jets. Fast and
easy travel was opening up the world and breaking down once rigid class
barriers. The old WASP establishment was beginning to crumble, replaced by a far less stratified and more permeable society defined by
flash, glamour, and publicity. Instead of the Knickerbocker, always the
most exclusive men's club in New York, Le Club became the place everyone who was anyone wanted to join. All his energy and his wiles notwithstanding, Eddie Gilbert could not have gotten where he was without

the promotional skills of Igor Cassini. Thanks to Igor's efforts, Eddie Gilbert became *the* case study on how to rise to the top of the new 707-fueled social order.

Cassini's Martial had a very fat contract to do E. L. Bruce's corporate public relations. But people, certainly the Cholly Knickerbocker people, didn't think of floors when they thought of Eddie Gilbert. They thought of his lifestyle, which was probably unmatched among *Fortune* tycoons, and was certainly unequaled among men in their thirties, other than hereditary princes like the Aga Khan. Eddie Gilbert had palatial residences on Fifth Avenue, in Palm Beach, in Cap Martin on the Côte d'Azur. Although he was tiny (five-five), with receding hair, and evoked a bantam Jewish boxer, Eddie saw himself as his rich parents saw him, as a prince of the realm. All his trappings were princely even if he didn't look the part.

With his perfect wife, he collected the best French art and antiques and was a major patron of Broadway and the Metropolitan Opera. An Ivy Leaguer, a millionaire by inheritance, and a multimillionaire by his own efforts, the best-dressed Gilbert, while of Jewish origins, was "club-bable" enough to socialize with Wall Street lions like John Loeb and André Meyer and global moguls like Aristotle Onassis and Stavros Niarchos. He was an after-hours high roller as well, a fixture at the casino in Monte Carlo and the money behind not only Le Club but also John Aspinall's Clermont Club in Berkeley Square, London's entry in the Jet Set nightlife sweepstakes. In short, Eddie Gilbert was a man after Igor Cassini's heart.

Gilbert and the Cassinis were close. Geographically, Gilbert's Fifth Avenue apartment was only a block away from the adjacent Sixty-first Street townhouse offices of Igor and Oleg. The brothers themselves were almost Siamese in connection. They'd joke in Italian, fight in French, and tell secrets in Russian. Igor created a legend for Eddie Gilbert; Oleg created a look. Oleg dressed Gilbert's wife, Rhoda, transforming her into another sleek, swanlike Jackie Kennedy clone (in Camelot America, there could never be too many Jackies). Once Oleg completed Rhoda's makeover, Igor would enshrine her on his best-dressed list. That was how the Cassini tag team worked. At their frequent multiple-martini lunches at the Colony, which was the Cassini commissary, Igor would hang on Eddie Gilbert's every word, especially when it came to money. Igor loved big business, and Eddie was a trophy for him, not to mention a source of stock tips in the go-go years before insider trading acquired its own high profile as Wall Street's prime "capital" offense.

Edward M. Ginsberg was born in Flushing, Queens, in 1922, to a Lithuanian immigrant father and a Hungarian immigrant mother. The family was in the lumber business and became rich in the twenties building boom. Their company, Empire Millwork, provided enough upward mobility for them to change their name to Gilbert and buy a waterfront mansion in the privileged enclave of Manhasset, Long Island, fittingly the inspiration for *Gatsby*'s East Egg.

The Gilberts later sent Eddie to be a boarder at the exclusive and then partly residential Horace Mann School in Riverdale, where his best pal and classmate was the unlikely preppy Jack Kerouac, long before he hit the road. Jack did Eddie's essays; Eddie did Jack's math. Eddie's only teenage setback was being rejected by Harvard. While Jack Kerouac went on to Columbia on a football scholarship, of all things, Eddie settled on Cornell as his Ivy fallback. In 1940, after two years of discontent over not being at Harvard, Eddie decided he would rather give his life for Uncle Sam than give his all for Cornell. He dropped out, joined the army, and saw the world.

After serving throughout Europe, Eddie came home to work for Daddy in the New York office. He met Igor in 1948, just as Cassini was beginning to make his mark as the new Cholly Knickerbocker. Eddie became a regular at all Igor's haunts, the Stork, El Morocco, the Colony, and gave him good copy by carrying on a high-profile courtship with tennis star "Gorgeous Gussie" Moran. The Santa Monica–born, movie star–pretty Moran was the first sex symbol of her sport, less famous for her volley than for her trademark lace panties.

Quickly making his mark as a "player," Eddie became a disciple, and soon rival, of that player of players, Huntington Hartford, Harvard man and A&P heir. Hartford, who dated more actresses and models than

Howard Hughes—from whom he tried to buy RKO Pictures—was an important role model for Eddie as the archetypal preppy playboy. Eventually, however, Eddie settled down into a married lifestyle befitting the young prince who had taken the reins of his father's empire of wood. At a country-club dance in Westchester, Eddie had met a willowy eighteen-year-old goddess from Central Park West named Rhoda Weintraub, who could have been the mold for Herman Wouk's bestseller about a Jewish princess, *Marjorie Morningstar*. Rhoda looked the part to be the princess to Eddie's prince. But she didn't sound the part. She had a grating Bronx accent that bespoke her parents' climb out of that borough. No problem for Eddie, who found Rhoda a vocal coach, adorned her with baubles from Martial client Harry Winston, and then married her on the St. Regis Roof in October 1951. Eddie and Rhoda moved to 817 Fifth Avenue, in the heart of Cassini-land, and he began his social climb of the Manhattan Alps.

Eddie soon realized that to get to the summit, he needed a lot more millions. That was when he discovered the underperforming Memphis-based E. L. Bruce Company, which was as Old South–hidebound as the servant-shined plantation-house hardwood floors it manufactured. Like a Yankee stealth raiding party during the Civil War, Eddie began secretly acquiring Bruce shares until, in March 1958, he had cornered the market in Bruce stock. Market corners were rare; Commodore Vanderbilt had done three of them during his rise in the post–Civil War era. J. P. Morgan and E. H. Harriman had achieved their own corners in the Northern Pacific manipulations of 1901. Eddie quite fancied the swashbuckling image of this tradition. Just as the Rebels in Memphis were no match for their Yankee invaders, the modern Memphians were no match for Commodore Gilbert, to whom they surrendered and, on October 26, 1958, made chairman of the Bruce board of directors.

Two days later, on October 28, Pan Am made the first scheduled commercial flight of its 707 *Clipper America* from New York to Paris. Eddie Gilbert's appearance on the front page of many of the country's newspapers for his fiscal tour de force was virtually simultaneous with Pan Am/Boeing's cover stories for their technological tour de force. His financial status secure, Eddie set out to fuse the two phenomena into a *social* tour de force: not just random mentions in Igor Cassini's column but a permanent place in the Jet Set pantheon. To accomplish this, he set out to become a benefactor of the arts, beginning (with Igor's aid, of course) by helping to fund Italian composer Gian Carlo Menotti's new Spoleto Festival, as well as other high-profile cultural events.

In the midst of his social climb, Eddie's E. L. Bruce became a prime corporate client of Martial. Most of the publicity, though, was given not to the stick-in-the-mud Tennesseans but to the jet-setting Gilberts, who seriously began to dominate the columns after 1960, when they acquired both a second New York residence, a Tudor minicastle on East Seventieth Street to accommodate even grander parties; and the twenty-room Villa Zamir, perched on a Riviera cliff, which *The Saturday Evening Post,* with Gilbert clearly in their moralizing gunsights, described as a "motel for the jet set, where Edward had to be introduced to his own guests." The *Post* described the villa in Fitzgeraldian terms: "it was open house every day with a jazz band for luncheon dancing at the (Olympic) pool and an orchestra at night."

Other drooling profiles, placed by Igor, described Eddie as a wild and crazy host. "Let's all go bowling!" he might declare after lunch, and have his fleet of limos ferry fifty guests to Monte Carlo's four-lane bowling alley. After nocturnal events, Eddie was said to caravan his partiers down the road to Le Pirate, the most exclusive nightclub on the Riviera, the favorite of Onassis and the Golden Greeks, and pick up a check in the thousands of dollars. Temple Fielding had eviscerated Le Pirate as the biggest clip joint on the Mediterranean, but people like Onassis and Gilbert were oblivious to reviews. The more they paid, the better the place. Le Pirate's money-machine gimmick was that it was a French version of a Greek taverna, with the guests following Hellenic traditions by smashing all the dinnerware in an ouzo-retsina frenzy, at Olympian tabs. It was Eddie Gilbert's honor to finance such Jet Set orgies. Gatsby never lived as large, and Eddie loved the continual comparisons.

But Gatsby didn't have Eddie's *culture*. He didn't support the Met or

Spoleto. His West Egg walls weren't hung with Rembrandts, Canalettos, Monets, Bouchers, Sisleys. Eddie became one of the top clients of the Wildensteins, the premier art dealers. Aside from culture, Gatsby wasn't anywhere as *connected* as Eddie to the rich and famous. Eddie was a gambler of the highest order, winning and losing half a million dollars a night at the Monte Carlo Casino, playing with Onassis, King Farouk, Aly Khan. He could mix high and low, WASP and Jew, *Burke's Peerage, Almanach de Gotha,* Social Register, the post office's most wanted. There was a New Society being made, and Eddie was key in creating it. He was the embodiment of the Jet Set, so much so that he began a clandestine affair with Turid Holtan, a Norwegian Pan Am stewardess whom he met on one of his constant transatlantic jet crossings. Although he had transformed Rhoda into a Jewish Jackie, Eddie was ready to fly on.

But to play like Eddie, you had to pay like Croesus. Money was the common denominator. Rhoda would want a fortune; therefore Eddie would have to make another. That was why he courted the biggest names in finance, in hopes that they might underwrite his Wall Street ambitions. He won over John Loeb of the powerful investment firm Loeb, Rhoades by donating $100,000 to Loeb's alma mater (and Eddie's one crushed dream), Harvard. He courted André Meyer of that other great banking house Lazard Frères by wining, dining, and arting the eminence into agreeing to be his "rabbi" on a new deal that he hoped would enshrine him in *Fortune* and get him a chair at Harvard Business School.

This deal to end all deals was for Eddie's E. L. Bruce to acquire Celotex Corporation, the building insulation giant based in Chicago and listed on the New York Stock Exchange. Celotex was much bigger than Bruce but not too big for Eddie to covet. With the help of André Meyer and the Kennedy bull market, Eddie knew he could be Jonah and swallow the whale. He was so confident of success that he began acquiring Celotex shares personally and on margin, rather than through E. L. Bruce. Going through Bruce would have been cumbersome and time-consuming, with directors' meetings, SEC filings, and the like. Eddie wanted to do a stealth blitzkrieg-style takeover, selling his shares to Bruce when the deal was done. He was totally confident the surging stock market would enable him to do it his way.

Certain that the deal would set him free, Eddie chose this moment to break the bad news to Rhoda about the Pan Am stewardess and moved to Nevada for a quickie divorce, or what Cholly Knickerbocker, from Maury Paul days, would call a "Reno-vation." Eddie was actually based in Carson City, and he took full advantage of the new jet age, flying back and forth from there to Chicago and New York within the same twenty-four hours so as not to violate the six-weeks-consecutive-residence requirement to qualify for his Nevada split.

But then the Kennedy bull turned bear, and as the Celotex stock began dropping, Eddie's margin requirements began to rise. He borrowed from everyone, from Swiss bankers to Italian gangsters, but the market kept going down. Eventually, he had no choice but to invade the Bruce treasury, writing checks of $2 million to pay nonexistent bills to dummy corporations in order to cover his personal margin calls. Even though Eddie had art and real estate that would satisfy the amount easily, those assets were anything but liquid. Besides, he loved his paintings too much to sell them, and to put his mansions on the market would have been a disastrous PR move. So the high roller committed what amounted to grand larceny, praying to the god of chance that the bear would become a bull again in time to cover his tracks.

Instead, what Eddie got was the infamous Blue Monday, May 28, 1962, the century's second-worst day on the New York Stock Exchange after 1929's Black Tuesday. He had to rush back to New York, abandoning his Nevada divorce to save his skin. He thought he could also abandon his Celotex takeover bid and return the money to Bruce by selling his Celotex shares to a rival company called Ruberoid. But when that deal fell through, Eddie saw his choice between jail and Brazil, the one relatively civilized country that had no extradition treaty with America.

Eddie went into a huddle with his parents, who encouraged their son to fly away. Then he huddled with Turid Holtan, who gave him back her eight-carat Harry Winston engagement ring to sell, then live on the proceeds, supplementing his suitcase filled with $8,000 in hundreds. It would go a long way in Brazil's third-world economy, where a room at the top-banana Copacabana Palace Hotel cost under five dollars a night. Turid was a fly girl. Rio was just nine 707 hours away. It was a no-brainer for her, just as it was for Eddie's confidant Igor Cassini. Go, Igor said, fly away. So off Eddie went, in the century's highest-profile flight from justice, an escape that captured the public's imagination and made it surreally glamorous beyond belief to be a Wall Street fugitive. In short, it was a great PR move, orchestrated by the great PR man Igor Cassini, who soon would be fighting the law to save himself. Igor and Eddie, two of the prime poster boys of the Jet Set, were about to become poster boys on the criminal list of the U.S. Department of Justice, America's Most Glamorous transformed into America's Most Wanted. No reversal of fortune could have been more dramatic.

9

Flight Risks

WHEN IGOR CASSINI COUNSELED EDDIE GILBERT TO GO TO RIO, IGOR HAD every intention of using his publicity wizardry and formidable connections to bring his client back to America legally unscathed. Given Gilbert's fiscal malefactions, the case would be a huge challenge, but Igor loved challenges. After the frustration of his diplomatic ambitions in the Trujillo affair, he wanted to prove his and Martial's preeminence in publicity as never before. He also had ulterior motives, in that his planned tour de force would serve two of his Martial clients and not just one. The second client was the Brazilian national tourist board. Igor saw Eddie's great escape as a wonderful way to promote Rio as the most romantic, newly accessible city in the Jet Set world.

The Rio where Eddie Gilbert landed in June 1962 already had the potential to become the South American version of the Côte d'Azur, its continuing mystique aided immeasurably by the 1933 Astaire/Rogers classic *Flying Down to Rio,* which was actually shot mostly in Santa Monica. More recently, Rio had been re-romanticized by another film, Marcel Camus's *Black Orpheus,* a global hit set during the *Carnaval* bacchanal.

FLYING DOWN TO RIO. Eddie Gilbert, Wall Street mogul turned Jet Set fugitive in Brazil, 1962.

Now that Pan Am had cut a multistop twenty-hour ordeal into a non-stop eight-hour sky party, increasing numbers of jet travelers were seriously considering Rio, none more than international female socialites of a certain age who wanted to partake of the rejuvenation magic offered by the grand master of plastic surgery, Dr. Ivo Pitanguy. If the aviation century had a premier fantasy destination, Igor believed Rio was it. He promised the Brazilian government that he would bring down more and more North Americans. Eddie Gilbert would be Igor's inadvertent advance man.

For all its alluring images of physical beauty, sex, and samba, Rio had another reputation (obviously glossed over by Igor) as a louche, anything-goes haven for financial scoundrels. America's "Big Three" defalcators of the current bull market were all living high and free in Rio. The first among these superswindlers was Ben Jack Cage, the "Texas Tornado," a backslapping hustler who had conned $5 million out of trusting members of Lone Star labor unions in an insurance scam. Then there was another "boy wonder" like Eddie, this one Earl Belle of Pittsburgh, who had bilked three old-line banks out of $1 million in watered stocks. The third scoundrel triumvir waiting to greet Eddie was Lowell Birrell, the son of an Indiana Presbyterian minister. Birrell was a blue-chip Wall Street securities lawyer who had used his technical genius to loot and ruin companies through sophisticated stock maneuvers. Now Fast Eddie was about to join this dubious club, while Igor began to transform the reality of a flight from justice into the fantasy of a flight to paradise.

Eddie initially settled in Ipanema, which the song "The Girl from Ipanema" would put on the map when it became the world's number one hit in 1964. Two years before that, it was just another suburb, and Eddie found a small hotel across from the stunning broad strand. As he walked the golden sands barefoot, in his Gatsby-esque white linen suit, he saw the international papers plastered with his photograph. They all talked about the $2 million he had stolen and taken to Rio. All the money was gone, gone in vain to pay margin calls. Eddie bristled, despaired, that they had gotten it so wrong. He bought sunglasses, a hat, a nondescript windbreaker. Back at his hotel, he got his first local call. It was none other than Earl Belle, one fleeing boy wonder to another.

Eddie met Belle at a sidewalk café. They recognized each other from the papers. Four years before in 1958, Belle had been front-page, too. He told Eddie how great Rio was, how safe he felt, especially since he had taken a Brazilian wife and had two Brazilian children, which by law prevented deportation even if the extradition treaty ever got passed. Belle had also gotten rich again here on Brazilian sugar, which was in high demand now that Castro's sugar supply was embargoed. Life was beautiful.

The next day, Eddie met again with Belle, this time accompanied by Ben Jack Cage, a large, scary man in the Sydney Greenstreet mode. They asked Eddie for $25,000 in protection money, which they claimed would go to certain corrupt Brazilian authorities to ensure Eddie's safety. They didn't want to believe $8,000 was all Eddie had. Eddie didn't mention the Harry Winston diamond. Somehow he convinced the crooks that he was telling them the truth. Belle stopped calling. Theirs was one fraternity that Eddie would not be joining, to Igor's vast relief. That guilt by association would have been the worst press possible.

Instead, Igor began getting Eddie great press, although deftly managing to stay out of the spotlight as the ringmaster of what would immediately become a media circus. Now that the word was out that Eddie Gilbert was in Rio, the whole world began calling. The attention was the perfect antidepressant for Eddie, who had an insatiable gluttony for publicity. Accordingly, when Igor arranged for *Life*'s Miami bureau chief to offer him a Kennedy-sized spread, Eddie couldn't say no—not that Igor would have let him. The layout would be a class act: Eddie would be photographed by the august Cornell Capa and essayed by Jack Kerouac, whom *Life* would be paying handsomely to profile his old prep-school classmate. *Life*, after *Reader's Digest*, was the highest-circulation magazine in the country. It was in its prime, huge in stature, huge in size. It was the ideal forum for Eddie to resume his glory and plead his case.

And so it went. The article was entitled "Case of Eddie Gilbert Versus Himself." Capa shot Eddie alone, a man in black walking the white sands of Copacabana Beach, with Rio's iconic mountain on the shore, the Sugar Loaf, looming over the wall of white art deco high-rise apartments on some of the most fabled beachfront property on earth. Kerouac, who saw himself as "a New England athlete boy" lost and adrift in a sea of Ivy Jews, lauded Eddie as the most "fantastic wit" among the "incunabular Milton Berles" of Horace Mann. The great writer viewed Eddie's Wall Street maneuvers as a giant caper, a "last fantastic joke to tear the funny guys of Horace Mann apart for once and for all."

The *Life* editors recounted all of Eddie's fiscal triumphs, his good deeds supporting Korean and Italian orphans, his donations to Harvard. There were pictures of his properties, the East Side Tudor castle, the Villa Zamir—which *Life* noted was bigger and more expensive than Joe Kennedy's nearby rented Riviera estate—and pictures of Eddie at the Monte Carlo casino with Helmut Newton blondes a head taller than he. It was an ad for Eddie Gilbert. He couldn't have dreamed of bigger, better coverage. It was also an ad for Pan Am, something that Temple Fielding might have concocted in his own Madison Avenue days. It made people want to fly down to Rio. It pleased, mightily, the Brazilian tourist board. It made Igor Cassini proud.

Via Igor's relentless efforts, even bigger coverage soon materialized in the person of Charles Kuralt, who came to Rio to produce a CBS TV *Eye-witness Reports* special on Eddie. "Refuge in Rio" aired in late July 1962, a month after the *Life* layout. The distinguished correspondent Charles Collingwood played host, introducing Eddie as "an American financier who, after some confusion in his accounts, recently found asylum in Brazil." In order to have Eddie on the air, the normally tough Colling-wood was playing softball, letting Eddie speak his piece: "I want to prove to everyone, as well as to myself, that what I did was not a criminal act. I want to remake my life, my career . . . I want to repay everybody that I owe money to, that lost money in this horrible catastrophe."

Igor Cassini had worked his PR magic on his friend the CBS network boss, William Paley, to run the special. Chafing at the constraints of being a behind-the-scenes manipulator, this time an emboldened Igor took to the small screen with Collingwood to limn Eddie's high life, of course without disclosing that Gilbert was one of his biggest clients. On the special, Igor was in exalted company, the company he had wanted to keep before his dreams of Kennedy diplomacy were shattered in the Trujillo fiasco.

Following Igor on the small screen was none other than Robert Kennedy. The attorney general was interviewed by Roger Mudd about the proposed treaty that could lead to the extradition of Eddie, if Brazilian courts judged it to be retroactive, which sounded very ex post facto and un-American. Attorney General Bobby seemed skeptical about ever getting Eddie back, especially if his fiscal wrongs on Wall Street weren't seen as crimes in the much wilder world of finance in Brazil, a country that had rewarded Cage, Belle, and Birrell with new successes.

Bobby Kennedy turned out to be the worst adversary Eddie Gilbert, and soon Igor Cassini, would ever have. Bobby had become a changed man, his own man, after the devastating stroke that had befallen Joseph Kennedy in December 1961, just after Ramfis Trujillo had fled the Dominican Republic. After the stroke, the all-powerful paterfamilias lost all of his influence. He couldn't walk. He couldn't speak. And for once he couldn't control his son Bobby, who, as the attorney general suddenly imbued with a new puritanism, became America's Holy Roller.

No sooner was his father silenced than RFK ended his brother's obsessive friendship with Frank Sinatra, ostensibly because of his ties to Sam Giancana and to the Mob. Many have speculated that Bobby's "purification" drive may have been a reaction to his own impure lust for his brother's (and Sinatra's) consort Marilyn Monroe, particularly in light of her mysterious death in the summer of 1962. In Bobby's mind, the whole Jet Set—Cassini, Gilbert, Rubirosa, the whole damned lot—was tarred with the same glamour-is-evil brush, and without his father to restrain him, he considered going after any of them if one ever crossed the line. Eddie Gilbert had crossed it big-time. On television, a subdued Kennedy was simply underplaying his hand.

The TV special came across as another massive advertisement for Eddie Gilbert and for the glories of Rio. But Igor didn't want Eddie to seem so seduced by Rio that he was going native there. Although it was in fact the case, Cassini could not afford to let his client seem like a fugitive from justice. On the special, Eddie therefore carefully refused to apply the "f-word" to himself. As he told Charles Kuralt, "Well, Charlie . . . I came here basically to solve some serious personal problems . . . and I felt that if I stayed in New York I wouldn't be given the chance . . . to have the peace and quiet . . . I wouldn't have a minute's peace." The image of Rio as think tank, ashram, spa for high rollers who may have rolled too high couldn't have been more seductive.

Rio was an appealing place for Eddie's friends and colleagues to come spend time with him. One caller who had ridden the wave of high times with Eddie's largesse was London gambling king John Aspinall, who, on Eddie's hot tips, had invested heavily in E. L. Bruce stock. Now that the stock had cratered, Aspinall had his own margin calls, of hundreds of thousands of dollars, to contend with. Aspinall wasn't liquid. Everything he owned was tied up in his Berkeley Square Clermont Club, which would soon house Annabel's, the private *Burke's Peerage*–populated disco that opened in 1963 and was inspired by the Gilbert/Cassini Le Club. But Aspinall was a gambler who took the long view. He stuck by Eddie and jetted to see him with a suitcase of cash for his friend raised from his Brit aristo circle. He sincerely believed Eddie would rise again.

As much as Eddie appreciated the money, the visit he savored the most was that of his fiancée, Turid, who took a leave of absence from Pan Am and used her stewardess's deep discount to fly to Rio several times. Some of her visits coincided with those of Arnold Bauman, the high-powered attorney whom Eddie's father had hired to bring his boy back to him in Sulka linens, not prison stripes. In a longer version of the Washington, D.C., shuttle, Bauman kept bringing SEC and Justice Department officials down to Rio to negotiate a plea deal with Eddie, who had begun playing the Brazilian stock market with the great results that had accrued to his fellow capitalists in exile. He took a penthouse apartment, hired a Cadillac and a chauffeur, began to entertain. He even partied with soccer god Pelé and with visiting literary god John Dos Passos, who was interested in constructing an *à clef* novel about Eddie.

With his wife and son to attend to, Igor Cassini had been making an uncharacteristic commitment to being a family man and limiting his jetting about. He stayed out of Rio during Eddie's residence. Nonetheless, Eddie initiated a telephone and mail dialogue between his publicist and both Pelé and "Girl from Ipanema" composer Antonio Carlos Jobim in which the Brazilians would hire Martial to raise their profile in America. It wasn't quite the Villa Zamir, with feijoada instead of bouillabaisse, but for the moment, Eddie wasn't homesick.

Bauman finally worked out a deal, and on October 28, 1962, Eddie Gilbert jetted back to New York. Dozens of reporters were waiting at Idlewild. But the federal marshals greeted him first, boarding the plane and taking him into custody. A caravan of cars transported him directly to Manhattan's federal courthouse, where, with Bauman by his side and his father behind him, Eddie pleaded not guilty to a fifteen-count indictment that included wire and mail fraud and filing false SEC reports. He was released on $15,000 bail, posted by Harry, who added another $10,000 to the bail amount for further charges filed by the New York district attorney's office for twelve counts of grand larceny. Then Eddie went home with Daddy.

Given the high crimes he was charged with, the low bail was a quid pro quo for Eddie's *voluntary* return to face American justice. He had made over $100,000 in his fewer than five months in Rio. He was still a wizard. He could have stayed in Carioca splendor, and America never could have touched him. But he wanted to come home, and thanks in large part to Igor's mythmaking, Eddie Gilbert got exactly what he wanted. It would be five long years of freedom and high living before Eddie Gilbert would stand trial on those twenty-seven charges, proof of the kind of time and justice his money could buy.

Meanwhile, Eddie basked in the front-page splendor of every paper in New York, with Igor Cassini beaming in the wings at his handiwork. The prodigal son was being received like a favorite son. The press described Eddie Gilbert not as an accused felon but as "the playboy-financier." All the reports made prominent note of his deep Rio suntan. He was here to face the music, but the main music in his head was the disco siren call of Le Club. Eddie couldn't make quite the grand entrances he used to before his flight. His chauffeured Rollses were gone, his Seventieth Street Tudor castle foreclosed, his Fifth Avenue apartment abandoned by the abandoned Rhoda, who refused to speak to Eddie and tried to keep their children from him. He still was crazy for Turid, but he couldn't give her a wedding date without a divorce decree in hand. The Riviera was off-limits; his bail agreement forbade him to leave the New York metropolitan area. So at thirty-nine, Eddie moved back in with his parents, who now lived in a spectacular duplex aerie in the Carlyle Hotel.

The Carlyle wasn't a bad place to hole up and get restarted, which Eddie, with his father's help, immediately did, creating a new hardwood wholesale operation called the Northerlin Company. Soon he was back in the game, with offices on Madison and Fifty-seventh Street. The little wizard, the "floor man," proved his touch by turning an instant profit. In three years, the company would have sales of $10 million. Even without Dos Passos, who passed on the project, a major publisher gave Eddie an advance to write a book about himself and enlisted a top *New York Times* business writer to be his ghost. Eddie Gilbert, pure adrenaline and pure confidence, sincerely believed he would eventually beat the rap that he was a crook.

But within weeks of Eddie's return in the fall of 1962, the spotlight unexpectedly shifted to Igor Cassini as the man with the crook rap to beat. The man who called Igor on the carpet was a young reporter from *The Saturday Evening Post* named Peter Maas, who would go on to fame for writing *The Valachi Papers, Serpico,* and other true-crime books. That most wholesome of American magazines, famous for its Norman Rockwell covers, had fallen on the hard times occasioned by losing its audience to television and more sophisticated, more sensational journals. The *Post,* desperate to survive, decided to fight fire with fire by basically publishing a new exposé in every issue. Igor Cassini had been selected to be the flavor of the week in the upcoming January 19, 1963, publication.

Initially, Maas's brief was to nail Cassini for conflict of interest, that is, writing in his column about his PR firm's clients. But because gossip columns were not expected to have the highest of journalistic standards, Maas's exposé wasn't going to be particularly shocking. Things changed when the Trujillo connection came into Maas's purview by way of a canceled check made out to Martial by the Dominican government when Trujillo was alive and dictating. Until then, no one outside the White House had known of the Joe Kennedy–initiated Cassini-Murphy mission, and not even the White House knew the extent of Cassini's contractual labors for the Trujillo regime. Just as Cassini wanted to go to Washington, so did Maas. Now he had a government scandal to work with, and he went to work as hard as he could.

The best thing Maas had to work with was the appearance that Igor Cassini, confidant of the president, was a "foreign agent" under the Foreign Agents Registration Act (FARA). The idea of foreign agents sounded more menacing than it was. It wasn't cloak and dagger at all. The legal definition included any lobbyist, American or foreign, working in America for a foreign government. FARA required them to register with the Justice Department and disclose their earnings and other activities that might have an impact on national security. Japan and Russia had the most agents registered under FARA. Japan had a world war to apologize for; Russia had a Cold War it was fighting, even in America. The country with the third largest number of agents was the Dominican Republic. Obviously, because the Trujillos had been so bad, the Dominicans needed all the lobbying they could get. But the law was that all such agents had to register, and the big reveal was that Igor Cassini had never done so and thus had broken the law, giving Bobby Kennedy a chance for another major Jet Setter.

In 1938, on the eve of World War II, Congress had enacted FARA. The obvious idea was to smoke out Axis spies, and since war's end in 1945, there had been only nine convictions under the act for failure to register. The act was pretty much an anachronism until the Trujillos became a cause célèbre. In 1959, Alexander Guterma, a Siberian-born Wall Street financial wheeler-dealer in the Eddie Gilbert mode, was sentenced to two years in jail and a $10,000 fine for failing to register under FARA. Guterma, who was closely involved with two of the bad boys from Brazil, Earle Belle and Ben Jack Cage, had made a fortune in commissions buying American airtime for Trujillo to tout the glories of the Dominican Republic. But he didn't register, and to prison he went.

The successful Guterma prosecution revitalized FARA and became a sort of flypaper for catching lobbyists who worked sub rosa for Central American and Carribean strongmen. Igor had registered as an agent for Mexico and Brazil, even for Cuba, when Battista had given him a brief commission before Castro took over, but not for the Dominican Republic. The aspiring diplomat in him knew that playing with Trujillo was playing with fire, and he wanted to keep the connection under wraps to protect Martial's reputation and his own.

Igor Cassini may have wanted to be famous, but not like this. Maas's profile marked the first time in Cassini's charmed life that he would ever be scrutinized in depth by the press, *his* press. The hunter had become the game, the reporter the subject, and all America would soon want to know just who this secret agent really was. Maas's long-anticipated article hit the stands in the second week of 1963. For once, the increasingly irrelevant, anemic *Saturday Evening Post* sold out. Entitled "Boswell of the Jet Set," the article opened by turning a raised eyebrow on Igor's own definition of this exclusive new class of high fliers: "people who live fast, move fast, know the latest thing and do the unusual and the unorthodox."

"Unorthodox," Maas riposted, "is a mild word for some of Igor Cassini's activities, which might surprise the millions of readers who savor Cholly Knickerbocker's tidbits about the jet set. The strange relationship between Cholly Knickerbocker and the Martial public relations firm . . . alone is enough to justify some angry questions from anyone who believes in a free and independent American press." Maas's material supporting such enraged inquiry over Igor's conflict of interest was extremely underwhelming, consisting mostly of mentions of sightings at balls and resorts of the owners of companies that Martial represented.

For Lanvin, a Martial client, Maas enumerated the products Igor had mentioned in one of his many Igor (not Cholly)-bylined magazine articles: "Lanvin Salon, Arpège, My Sin, Crescendo and Spanish Geranium." It was hardly a smoking gun. If Lanvin didn't smoke enough, Maas served up the currently incendiary Eddie Gilbert, noting the countless Cholly features on Rhoda, and trying to serve up something sinister in the fact that Gilbert was one of the main investors of Le Club, which Igor constantly plugged in his column. It was old-fashioned logrolling, but there was nothing illegal about it, no worse than if *Vogue* did an editorial photo spread on a big advertiser like Chanel or Dior.

Maas's only truly big scoop was that Igor had been working, for pay, for Trujillo as far back as 1959, not just starting with his 1961 Joe Kennedy–inspired diplomatic mission. Igor, who had met with Maas for the article to prove he had nothing to hide, made his one mistake by denying it. "When I saw Cassini in his office at Martial," Maas reported, "he said Rubirosa had tried 'once or twice' to get him to take the Dominican account but that he had refused. Other than that he denied he had any dealings with the Dominican Republic or Trujillo before 1961."

That was Igor's equivalent of Bill Clinton's "I did not have sexual relations with that woman, Ms. Lewinsky." Maas presented a statement from a disgruntled ex-Martial exec that Igor had been on the dictator's payroll since '59. Igor had fired him, the man claimed, when he balked at any association with Trujillo. Maas waded through a morass of shell corporations to find the links to Inter-American Public Relations, the contractor with Trujillo, which had been incorporated in Nassau, the

Bahamas, but had its home office in Rio. Its president was João de Rezende, a gossip columnist who fancied himself the Igor Cassini of Rio and had written at length about Eddie Gilbert when he was residing there. Maas discovered that Cassini had attended Rezende's wedding.

These were ties that bound but were bound to frustrate and deceive a less dogged sleuth. Maas kept searching and finally tracked down the man who paid Inter-American's Rio bills, a seventy-five-year-old lawyer named Paul Englander who worked in an apartment across the street from Martial whose lessor was Oleg Cassini. The Sherlockian Maas tracked down Englander, who admitted he had signed the contract with Trujillo, acknowledging that Igor "just tossed it my way," then boasted that he had done "a damn good public-relations job for them." Maas ascertained that Englander, like Cassini, had not registered as a foreign agent, then confronted him with the fact. He reported Englander's irate response: "You're not acting like a reporter; you're more like a private detective or a member of the FBI or worse." To Maas, the attack was the highest form of flattery.

Almost as a counterpoint to the Maas screed, the February issue of *Esquire,* which was on-stand in January simultaneously with the *Post,* featured a huge laudatory profile entitled "The Brothers Cassini: Oleg and Igor. The Clothes and the Column, Making the Best of Nearly All Possible Worlds." The author was Brock Brower, a recent Rhodes Scholar and one of the rising stars of the Tom Wolfe–led New Journalism. Brower made the brothers look like the coolest guys on earth. He was blasé about Igor's secret mission to Trujillo. "It very closely resembled diplomacy," Brower wrote, "and wasn't that Count Cassini's old family trade? Wasn't that Ghighi's original ambition?" Brower gave Igor the floor to explain himself, which he did: "Trujillo has such a reputation for having paid everybody that anybody who ever went there was supposedly paid off. I was not among the lucky ones." Again, it was a denial that Igor never believed would come back to haunt him.

Esquire was much more likely to be read by John Kennedy's New Frontier brain trust of government lieutenants than the unhip *Saturday Evening Post.* That had to be what Igor was praying for, that the good

Esquire word would get back to Washington and influence Bobby Kennedy to call off his Justice Department attack dogs. Igor knew those dogs were on the hunt because no sooner had Maas's piece come out than Charles Wrightsman began giving him and Charlene the silent treatment and stopped inviting them to his Palm Beach events, often attended by Jack and Jackie Kennedy. Joe Kennedy had been Igor's main champion. But with Joe totally incapacitated by his December 1961 stroke, Igor didn't have an in-house Kennedy to plead his case. In that same cruel December, he had also lost his greatest adviser of all, his mother, to a heart attack at age seventy-nine. He was in extended mourning and very much at sea. "Maman" would have known exactly how to finesse this Dominican embarrassment.

With the two huge profiles on the country's newsstands, Igor Cassini became prime gossip overnight. A month later, at the end of February, he became front-page news. As it turned out, even in the White House, the *Post* trumped *Esquire*. Square beat hip, Norman Rockwell beat George Lois. Bobby Kennedy, purer than ever and intolerant of his brother's predilection for guys and dolls, for Hollywood and Vegas and Hoboken, was pushed over the edge by Maas's story. RFK formally declared war on the Jet Set when he got a Washington grand jury to indict Igor on four counts, including conspiracy with Englander, of violating the 1938 Foreign Agent Law. Igor faced a possible fine of $40,000 and, far worse, twenty years in prison if found guilty.

Igor quickly got on the phone and retained Louis Nizer, the country's top gun. Nizer was the author of *My Life in Court,* the bestselling lawyer memoir of all time. Nobody could beat Louis Nizer. So nobody could beat Igor Cassini. Or could they? Nizer quickly brought Igor to court in Washington and had him plead not guilty on all counts. Igor repeatedly insisted he had never been an actual agent for the Dominican Republic, certainly not under the law as written. But per the indictment, his companies had been paid over $200,000 by *someone* and would have made over $300,000 more had the Trujillos remained in power and honored their commitments. That was a huge fortune, and not just to *Saturday Evening Post* readers. It looked rotten, as rotten as Eddie Gilbert's self-help "borrowing" of the $2 million from his company. Looks aside, expert insiders felt it was a weak case under a weak law. It was a long way from an indictment to a conviction, and nobody had a bigger wall of defense than Igor with Nizer as his mouthpiece, with Wrightsman, Dulles, even JFK, as his presumed allies, and with the government itself involved in dispatching him on his diplomatic mission to Trujillo in 1961.

Nizer went directly to cut a deal with RFK and his deputy attorney general, Nicholas Katzenbach. With all the problems in the country and the world, from civil rights to Vietnam wrongs, why are you pursuing such a Mickey Mouse case? Nizer pressed them. Katzenbach tried to placate him with logic, that Justice needed a test case under the foreign lobbyists' registration act, but Bobby cut to the chase. "Ghighi has not come clean with me," he snapped to Nizer. "Your client is a son-of-a-bitch blackmailer." It was then that Nizer realized Igor's phones were being tapped. During one conversation with Nizer, Igor had lashed out at Bobby by threatening to use the power of Cholly against him. "That self-righteous bastard," Igor had fulminated. "I know the redhead he's sleeping with."

Igor was convinced that Oleg's lines were being tapped as well. Despite Igor's troubles, Oleg was still a Kennedy darling. That tight-knit clan couldn't seem to grasp that the Cassini brothers were even tighter than they were. The Kennedy sisters—Pat Lawford, Eunice Shriver, Jean Smith—were foolishly indiscreet about Bobby's vendetta against Igor. "Bobby's going to put him in jail," they'd joke with Oleg about how fire-and-brimstone Puritan their Catholic brother had become. Ever protective Oleg would immediately call from Hyannisport, Palm Beach, the White House, wherever he was, and blurt out the news to Igor, begging him to throw himself on Bobby's mercy. What mercy? Igor would laugh. He was one stubborn, proud Russian count who made it a point to stand up for his honor, even if he knew that the law was on Bobby's side.

Igor determined that he would subscribe to the John Paul Jones school of "I have not yet begun to fight." First, however, he went to Hearst and did the gentlemanly thing of offering to resign his Cholly Knickerbocker column. As he put it in his memoirs, "For a social arbiter, part of whose job was to reveal the peccadilloes of the privileged, to be caught with my own pants down was death." He counted on the Hearsts to refuse his offer in a gentlemanly fashion and give him a vote of confidence. He had eighteen years of service, fifty syndicated papers, twenty million readers. He was like blood with the Hearsts. He assumed they would stand by him forever. His assumptions were pure hubris. The Hearsts granted him an indefinite leave of absence with no writing and no pay. Igor fingered Randolph Hearst as the one who did him in. The father of future terrorist-fugitive Patty Hearst treated the indictment as if it were a conviction. His employer's cautious response was the handwriting on the wall.

The finger, pointed at Igor, writ even larger at Martial, where the clients began resigning in droves. Igor's indictment was the opposite of the public relations they had signed on for, especially with the mounting broadsides against his endless conflicts of interest. Only Gianni Agnelli stayed the course. Igor also stepped down as president of Le Club. Overnight, the social arbiter became untouchable. One day at La Caravelle, the Kennedy canteen in Manhattan, Igor was having a power lunch with another aristo-PR man, Count Rudi Crespi. They couldn't believe the way the beautiful people, yesterday their dearest friends, were crossing the room to avoid them. Then they looked behind them. At an adjacent banquette was the Duchess of Argyll, whose kinky sexual escapades, emerging in her divorce, would give the Profumo Scandal a run for its money as Britain's Disgrace of the Year in 1963. Igor blamed his being avoided on the proximity of the duchess, though in time he was able to clear a room all by himself.

Petty treachery turned to grave tragedy in April, when Igor's fall hit home. Charlene, now thirty-five, had been depressed long before Bobby Kennedy turned on her husband. That her father had put Igor on his "no fly" social zone following the *Post* article had only added to her sense of desperation, a sense that ran in her family. Her mother, Irene, had drunk herself to death, deeply depressed because C. B. Wrightsman gave her barely a penny despite being worth a fortune; everything went to his new Jayne. Igor had to support "Big" Irene, and he was the one who had to break down her door to discover her dead body. C.B. had disinherited older daughter "Little Irene" and was not much more generous with her sister, Charlene. He had recently upped her monthly "allowance" from $500 to $1,000, hardly heiress money.

The Jet Set Cassinis were running on empty, prompting Charlene on March 31, 1963, to write a Dear John letter to her former suitor and close friend and neighbor. "Dear Mr. President," she began, questioning whether the chief fully realized "the repercussions of Ghighi's indictment. Brushing aside the personal embarrassment it has caused our family—it has completely ruined us financially . . . just at a moment when there are staggering lawyer's bills to meet. My father hasn't made a gesture to help us, and if it were not for Oli who lent money, Ghighi couldn't have even afforded a lawyer . . . I tell you this simply because this alone should satisfy Bobby who seems to be hell-bent in punishing Ghighi . . . My husband is not an arch-criminal, and whatever mistakes he may have made they don't warrant the . . . 'full treatment.' " Charlene told Jack, as she referred to him later in her plea, that if he thought it would work, she herself would go and see Bobby.

Charlene never received a response, formal or informal, that April: for her, the cruelest month of her life. To begin with, on April 6, her dear friend and glamorous ski instructor from Sugarbush, Peter Estin, was found dead from an overdose of vodka and sleeping pills in his room at the posh Westbury Hotel on Madison Avenue. The Prague-born Estin, who had degrees from Dartmouth and Harvard and had taught skiing in Chile, seemingly had everything to live for as the booming Vermont resort's director of skiing. The same age as Charlene, he had been with her at Sugarbush when she broke her leg several seasons before. Charlene, great at golf, horses, the slopes, treated the leg cavalierly, dancing on her crutches. The leg never healed correctly. In 1962, changing a lightbulb on a stool, as in a Polish joke, she fell and broke her nose. She also suffered a concussion and began taking painkillers and sleeping pills for severe headaches.

Those headaches prevented her from attending Peter Estin's Boston funeral, as well as that of Burt Rupp, an old boyfriend and the husband of a Chrysler heiress who, a few months before, had taken his own life with the same vodka-pill combination. C. B. Wrightsman had seen his daughter (but not Igor) a few days before and, not liking what he saw, insisted she check in to a clinic. Charlene was insulted, and Igor backed her up, letting her simply cool out at their Fifth Avenue apartment (he still worked in his Sixty-first Street townhouse) while he flew to Boston on the plane of George Skakel, Ethel Kennedy's brother, to attend the Estin rites. Even with Bobby threatening to destroy his life, Igor was like family to the Kennedys and their satellites—a bad brother, perhaps, but family nonetheless.

On April 8, Igor returned from Boston and tried to get Charlene out of the apartment to go to an Academy Awards party for Charlie Allen, the head of Allen & Company, the investment house behind Columbia Pictures. Charlene begged off, preferring to enjoy Hollywood vicariously by watching the Oscars on television. So Igor left Charlene with her fourteen-year-old stepdaughter, Marina, and their nine-year-old son Alex's Polish nanny, assuming she was in good hands, to watch Columbia's *Lawrence of Arabia* dominate the proceedings.

No sooner had Igor left for the Allen fete than Charlene asked Marina to pick up a prescription for her down Madison at Zitomer's pharmacy, druggist to the rich and famous. The prescription was for Tuinal, a powerful barbiturate. Once Marina returned, Charlene left her and the nanny. While Gregory Peck gave his acceptance speech for *To Kill a Mockingbird,* Charlene went into the master bathroom, swallowed all thirty of the pills, and never woke again. Igor arrived home in black tie just as an ambulance was rushing his wife to Lenox Hill Hospital, where her stomach was pumped and other emergency measures were taken. To no avail.

Society Suicide. It would have been the perfect thing for Igor to cover in wrenching detail were it not about himself, and if he had somewhere to write. But he didn't. He was that most alienated of creatures, a columnist without a column. Charlene's funeral at the Frank Campbell Funeral Chapel on Madison, undertaker to the East Side elite, was sparsely attended, in great contrast to the overflowing ceremony for

Igor's mother at the Russian Orthodox church a little over a year before. Of Charlene's family, only sister Irene showed up. C.B. and Jayne attended a mass for her, then jetted back to Palm Beach.

Oleg was there. Oleg was always there, plus a few odd Russian aristocrat/fellow PR men like Serge Obolensky, who represented Conrad Hilton, and Vava Adlerberg, who had taken over Igor's account for Harry Winston. When Charlene's will was read, the estate of the daughter of one of the richest men in America amounted to a paltry $100,000, not counting some jewelry, which she bequeathed to her sister. Igor got the rest, including sole responsibility for Alex. He had joint custody of Marina with her mother, Darrah.

Igor had nothing left but to fight, to win back his honor and, more important to this eminently practical man, his career. Accordingly, he shipped Marina off to prep school at Oldfields, her mother's alma mater, and took little Alex out of Buckley and flew him to enroll as a boarder at the Ecole Nouvelle in Lausanne, near Igor's own childhood playing fields. He rented out the Fifth Avenue apartment, took his two dogs and his tennis racket, and crashed at Oleg's new palace near Gramercy Park, which had been assembled stone by stone from its original Dutch Renaissance incarnation by a Wells Fargo heir. There were suits of armor, stuffed animals, and equestrian collectibles everywhere. It wasn't New York. It was Europe. And the Old World was precisely what Igor needed, to get away from the constant and ruthless hounding of a very modern press whose style he helped create, and of a government that he'd recently had dreams of serving in high style. How indeed the mighty had fallen.

Igor was retrenching because he was planning on waging a Hundred Years' War, if need be, with Louis Nizer, against the despot who was Bobby Kennedy. His biggest problem was that he couldn't afford a hundred-day war. Louis Nizer's rates were the highest in the land, and he didn't do criminal cases on contingency. Igor's hope was that Oleg would continue to foot his legal bills. Unfortunately, Oleg, thanks to his inside track with the Kennedys, knew precisely how much Bobby wanted his brother's scalp. Nizer had outlined a long, complex, and expensive technical defense that he convinced Igor would carry the day. Oleg was terrified of Bobby's passionate vendetta. No legal technicalities, he believed, would withstand the wrath of RFK.

Jack Kennedy had mentioned to Oleg that Bobby might settle for a nolo contendere plea. It wasn't an admission of guilt, but it wasn't not guilty, not by a long shot. Jack told Oleg it might satisfy Bobby's need to inflict shame on Igor. Igor didn't like the idea of trusting Bobby *not* to send him away for twenty years. Nizer went to see JFK at the White House, where the president gave Nizer "my word" that Igor "wouldn't be punished." Armed with the JFK off-the-record guarantee, on October 8, a little over a month before the assassination in Dallas, both Igor and Paul Englander pleaded nolo contendere to the government's charges.

On January 9, 1964, JFK was gone but his promise was kept. Igor was fined $10,000 and placed on six months' probation. Englander got the same sentence. The real guilty verdict had come back in late October 1963 from the Hearst Corporation after the nolo plea. Igor's suspension was declared over. He was formally fired, his place taken over by a busty, sassy Texan named Aileen Mehle, whose "Suzy" column in the *New York Mirror* had long been nipping unsuccessfully at Cholly Knickerbocker's heels. A countess Mehle was not. Subtle she was not. She was from El Paso, Conrad Hilton's tombstone territory. Her idea of fun was to start a feud with Hilton's Zsa Zsa by cattily nicknaming her Miss Chicken Paprika of 1914.

The timing was uncanny. Just as the brash, uncultured Texan Lyndon Johnson was replacing the suave John Kennedy in the White House, a similarly brash, uncultured Texan was replacing the suave count Igor Cassini in the House of Hearst. It seemed there were barbarians at all the gates. Suzy wasn't exactly Arthur Frommer to Cassini's Temple Fielding, because she was covering the same ritzy beat that Cassini had. But she was tourist class, not deluxe. Although she tracked the Jet Set, she was a complete outsider, nose pressed up against the crystal, sneaking a peek through the first-class curtain. There would never be another genuine article like Igor Cassini.

It was rotten luck that Eddie Gilbert was also saddled with his own legal nightmare. Igor knew Eddie, always the gambler, would have backed him whatever the odds. But Igor, himself a gambler, was betting on Eddie's resurrection. He better come back, Igor declared to himself. There were lots of things they could do together. Igor still had Le Club, and he still wanted to franchise it. And he had an idea, a big idea, for a magazine called *Status*. Columns were so fifties. Look at *Esquire*. Look at *Playboy*. Magazines were hot. *Status* would be the hottest. Igor was only forty-seven. He had the ultimate Rolodex.

The Rolodex cards, however, were changing, and faster than Igor realized. The crashes of Eddie Gilbert and Igor Cassini were even more damaging to the Jet Set than the cluster of 707 crashes was to the jet. Here were two of the standard-bearers of the new supercharged world of glamour, and both were terribly tarnished. The veil of the Jet Set had been lifted, and what was behind it was a darkness the public never expected. It wasn't that these emperors had no clothes; they had dirty clothes. And their falls from grace were nearly simultaneous with the death of President Kennedy, the ultimate symbol of the Jet Set.

The bloodstains on Jackie Kennedy's pink Chanel suit in Dallas said it all; that it was a Chanel suit and not an Oleg Cassini suit said something as well. The order was changing. The fantasy of the perfect upper class had been exploded. Camelot had been destroyed. A new medievalism of violence, discord, and civil unrest seemed to be descending. America's postwar boom, which had evolved from Eisenhower wholesomeness to Kennedy sophistication, was about to be upended by another war, in Vietnam. Still, leisure remained a fact of life, and people needed to escape, now more than ever. But the tone was different, and the fliers were different. Just as Frommer was beginning to compete with Fielding, the Jet Set of the rich was about to face a showdown with the jet set of the masses. Juan Trippe understood this more than anyone else. A month after Igor's sentencing, he and Boeing began to develop plans for a new mass jet that would become the 747.

10

007 and the 707

"ON THE WAY THE PAPER BAG WAS ON MY KNEE / MAN, I HAD A DREADFUL flight." "Back in the USSR," the Beatles' 1968 "Communist" parody of the Beach Boys' "California Girls," was musical proof that the Fab Four were anything but chauvinist apologists for their long-struggling national airline, which barely had more charm than Aeroflot. If Juan Trippe listened to the Beatles, he would have been amused by their song. Without listening, he was delighted by what was then the publicity coup of the year, when the Beatles selected Pan Am over BOAC to fly to New York in February 1964 to make their first appearance on *The Ed Sullivan Show*, a five-song set that shook the world.

Thus was launched the so-called British Invasion of pop culture: in music, with the Rolling Stones, the Who, the Kinks and many more who overturned the whole Top 40 sound; in fashion, with Mary Quant's miniskirt; in modeling, with Twiggy and Jean Shrimpton and David Bailey calling the shots; and in nightlife, with Annabel's mixing peerage and steerage in a radical new way. Overnight, that *Ed Sullivan* night, the postwar miasma of England, which had always seemed so foggyish and

A HARD DAY'S FLIGHT. The Beatles board a Pan Am 707 for their first visit to America and *The Ed Sullivan Show*, 1964.

fogeyish, was pierced by the sunlight of the new baby boom generation, finally old enough to book Juan Trippe's tourist fares. England was impossibly glamorous and happening and foreign, yet so close. The 707 could take them there in under six hours, far less than a hard day's night.

The Beatles were an even bigger "coup" for Juan Trippe than Winston Churchill had been in 1961 when the Old Lion chose Pan Am to fly him to New York. Fail Britannia! Churchill's defection to a Yank carrier was almost as sad a day for England as the Battle of Yorktown. What an entourage he took with him on the 707 Clipper *Fair Wind:* his doctor, two nurses, his personal secretary, and an inspector from Scotland Yard. The airborne feast Trippe had Maxim's lay out for the most famous of all Englishmen was something out of *Tom Jones:* prosciutto, salmon, caviar, terrapin soup, lobster thermidor, Dover sole, Himalayan partridge with wild rice, prime rib, Stilton, tarte Maxim. Trippe insisted the 707 stock some extras especially for Churchill, such as Colman's dry mustard, spicy horseradish, Tiptree jam, and crumpets, plus eight bottles of Lafite Rothschild '52, a fifth of Bisquit cognac, another fifth of Rémy Martin, a bottle of Greek ouzo (a taste acquired from his new friend Onassis), and a box of Romeo y Julieta cigars. No skies were ever this friendly again.

The Beatles were infinitely less demanding. Innocents abroad, they were thrilled just to be on a 707. Their days of Stilton and cigars were ahead of them. American youth was badly in need of heroes. The all-powerful baby boom generation, coming of teen age, had a huge obsession deficit to fill. Their "king" Elvis Presley had abdicated following being drafted into the army, then had been sucked into the Hollywood maw, making unwatchable movies. Just three months before, in November, their new king John F. Kennedy had been assassinated. The Beatles and their fellow young Brits couldn't have emerged at a better time from the gloom of England to dispel the gloom of America and fill the lacunae of icons. However, the one Brit icon who did more for Juan Trippe and the other Skycoons of the jet age wasn't a young Brit at all. He was a throwback to Churchill, whom Trippe had bowed before and cosseted as the great connoisseur. He wasn't Carnaby Street; he was Savile Row, Pall Mall, Buckingham Palace, Blenheim, Eton. If God couldn't save the queen, this man would do it. Somebody had to do it. Postwar Britain had lagged far behind France in a slough of despond, of rationing and deprivation. Its glamour was in its history, its imperial past, on which the sun was rapidly setting.

The savior here was a true Brit of the old school, a stereotype that Temple Fielding would have embraced and would have extolled. He was a man after Temple Fielding's heart. If Temple Fielding had written novels, he might have created him. This Brit, the rugged face who launched a thousand jets and a million Guidesters, was James Bond. Starting in 1962 with *Dr. No,* the James Bond film series rolled out one blockbuster after another, year after year, and every movie ticket was a potential airline ticket. The films were, in essence, supertravelogues, with sex, suspense, violence, gadgets, and the most conspicuous consumption ever put on screen. Double oh seven, all by his cunning self, got more people wanting to visit England than Henry Higgins and Eliza Doolittle in *My Fair Lady.* The shot of the Pan Am 707 roaring in to a perfect landing in *Dr. No* was a masterful piece of product placement that could have been engineered by Juan Trippe, even though it wasn't. It was just part of the zeitgeist; Trippe's airline had entered the subconscious as a shorthand for elegant escapism. The image was saying, "James Bond has arrived—by jet, by Jove, by Pan Am."

Although it was the films that were James Bond's gift that kept on giving to the travel industry, the sleek, slick hyperkinetic image of the Jet Set spy all started with the word. The author who created James Bond was very much a British version of Temple Fielding. Ian Fleming was a highborn spy, an epicure, a womanizer, and a true and literate wit. He loved

ON HER MAJESTY'S SECRET SERVICE. Sean Connery as James Bond, in a *Dr. No* publicity shot with distaff co-stars Eunice Gayson, Zena Marshall, and Ursula Andress, 1962.

good martinis, shaken, not stirred; he loved bad ladies of the evening, the morning, whenever he could get them. He lived in an island compound in Jamaica, just as Fielding lived in his island compound in Majorca. They dined at the same gourmet restaurants, slept in the same luxury hotels. Ian Fleming would have loved to be a travel writer, a *rich* travel writer like Temple Fielding. But Fleming's older brother had beaten him to it. Peter Fleming was the top travel writer in England. And there weren't any other openings. So Ian Fleming, late in his game of life, went the novelist route and succeeded beyond anyone's wildest dreams. Temple Fielding used the facts to make people want to travel, to see the world, the world at its best. Ian Fleming did the same job, but he did it with fantasy.

Ian Fleming was born in 1908, five years before Temple Fielding and even higher on the social scale, in the heart of Mayfair, London's poshest precinct. His father was a member of Parliament for Henley, home of the

Regatta, and an heir to a Scottish banking fortune. The father, a major and a hero of the Great War, was killed by Germans on the Western Front in 1917. His huge estate was so tied up in trusts that Ian was tantalized but never got an inheritance. Even before he became a writer, for whom penury is a frequent occupational hazard, he was obsessed with money and would remain so for his entire life. Never a good student, Ian flunked out of Eton and went to Sandhurst, which he left in a cloud of shame after contracting gonorrhea.

Ian was perpetually in the shadow of his golden-boy brother, Peter, a star at Eton and Oxford, a celebrated adventure author (*One's Company*), the husband of movie star Celia Johnson (*Brief Encounter*), and a World War II hero and OBE winner. Peter had Bond's brand of "right stuff," which Ian, inspired by Peter's exploits, could only fabricate on the page. Ian was also inspired by such pre-Bondian bon vivant Brit-lit lone-wolf characters as Bulldog Drummond and Simon Templar, also known as "The Saint," because of his initials. Templar was the creation of the writer Leslie Charteris, who had the same last name as Fleming's wife, Ann Charteris. They weren't related. Leslie Charteris was a half-British, half-Singaporean Chinese named Charles Yin who chose his pseudonym because of its elegant ring. Roger Moore, who would later play James Bond, made his name by playing the Saint on British television in the early sixties.

Leslie Charteris would make Simon Templar a household name, the James Bond of the 1930s. He had moved to Hollywood, where the dashing George Sanders, future husband of Zsa Zsa Gabor after Conrad Hilton, would be the star of a series of *Saint* films. Meanwhile, Ian Fleming was dawdling through life, failing as a Reuters foreign correspondent and forced to take boring financial jobs, first in a bank, then a brokerage, which he despised. Even during World War II, when he went to work for British Naval Intelligence, he was stuck behind a desk in Whitehall while brother Peter was in the field, doing his derring-do in Norway, Greece, and Southeast Asia, and Temple Fielding was liberating the Balkans. In short, Ian Fleming was much more Walter Mitty than James Bond.

The only place where he was a firsthand, first-rank swashbuckler was in the bedroom. A confirmed bachelor, he carved out a specialty in sado-masochism. That was his bond, as it were, with Ann Charteris, whom he met at Le Touquet at the swimming pool of the Royal Picardy Hotel, owned by the father of Claude Terrail, proprietor of Fleming's favorite Paris restaurant. The Picardy's avant-garde wave-making machine was the kind of high-tech gimmick that would inspire Ian's Bondian gadget-itis. Married to Lord O'Neill, from one of the realm's oldest clans, Ann may have been high-class, but as Elvis sang, that was just a lie. She liked it down and dirty and painful. She and Ian embarked on a long and bloody affair. She liked being whipped, tied up, flayed with bulrushes. As with James Bond, cruelty was the aphrodisiac.

When Lord O'Neill was killed during the war in North Africa, Ann wanted to marry Ian, taking the ache to the altar. But Ian, not the mar-rying kind, turned her down. Instead, Ann married Lord Rothermere, the press baron who owned the *Daily Mail*. Conjugality notwithstand-ing, both Ann and Ian remained addicted to their pain game. Playing a James Bond lothario, Ian followed Ann and her press lord around the world, staying in all the Fielding-choice hotels and arranging secret as-signations under Rothermere's nose. The danger was almost as exciting as the hurt. Eventually, the lord got wise. Ann became pregnant with a child the lord knew was not his. He settled a fortune to be rid of Ann in 1951. That fortune was an even bigger aphrodisiac to Ian than the bul-rushes. At last he could become a writer. At age forty-four in 1952, the playboy finally took the vows. Armed with Ann's money, he also took the plunge to realize his fantasy of becoming a writer.

Fleming's one big overseas wartime trip had been to a naval confer-ence in Jamaica. Instantly hooked on the tropical paradise, he had bought some cheap property in 1945 and built a house called Golden-eye, after the code name of one of his sabotage operations based in Gi-braltar. Unlike Fielding's Majorca compound, Goldeneye was anything but plush. It had no hot running water, no glass panes in the windows, no air-conditioning. Conrad Hilton would have had it condemned. But the British in Jamaica were hardy types who didn't need American luxu-ries. Ian Fleming quickly joined Noël Coward as one of the island's two leading hosts. After the war, not yet married, the always cash-strapped Fleming had to take another boring desk job, this one on the business end of the newspaper chain that owned the London *Sunday Times.* The post's main allure was that it allowed Fleming a long holiday in Jamaica two months a year, January and February. In those months Goldeneye became an "A" social destination.

Once Fleming married heiress Rothermere, he was able to quit his day job, and the "A" became an "A Plus." Errol Flynn was a regular guest, as were Elizabeth Taylor, Katharine Hepburn, the Wrightsmans, the Paleys, the Kennedys, all the people Igor Cassini was writing about in Cholly Knickerbocker. Amid all the partying, Fleming somehow found two months to knock out his first James Bond book, *Casino Royale.* He had a hard time getting it published and did so only because Peter Fleming leaned on his own house, Jonathan Cape, to do his brother a favor. The book came out in 1953; it surprised its publisher and everyone else by taking off. Dreary Britain was ripe for Fleming's revisionist fantasy that the country was a power in the world, that it still mattered. It was also ready for the sex and the travel. It was pure wish fulfillment, plus a kick in the groin. Thus began the series.

From the beginning, Fleming had his eye on Hollywood, leaning on every American who drank his shaken martinis at Goldeneye to lead him to some influential movie producer who could put James Bond up on the big screen. Hollywood was typically, totally unimpressed. The only screen that had any interest was the small screen of television, then an outcast medium and hardly what Fleming was aspiring to. In 1954, William Paley, who liked to vacation in Jamaica at the Round Hill resort in Montego Bay, had his CBS give Fleming a very unprincely $1,000 fee to adapt *Casino Royale* for a one-hour episode of its series *Climax!* Fleming's dreams of Cary Grant embodying James Bond evaporated into the reality of B-actor Barry Nelson playing an Americanized cardsharp "Jimmy" Bond. The villain, Le Chiffre, was played by Peter Lorre, who had to sell a reluctant Nelson, who never read the book, on doing the show.

Putting aside his celluloid dreams, Fleming kept writing, one new book every year, if only to distract himself from his meal-ticket wife and howling new son. After their first baby was stillborn, Ann had tried again and succeeded, though she needed a cesarean to deliver the boy, Caspar. Following the surgery, her body was seriously scarred, which turned off her fastidious spouse. Apparently, the only blemishes that could arouse him were the ones he inflicted. Now that Ann was a mother, the sex and the violence petered out.

Writing all day, punctuated by endless martinis and an eighty-cigarette-a-day addiction, Ian began having affairs—lots of them. His favorite new mistress was Blanche Blackwell, the reigning queen of the island, who was said to be the inspiration for Pussy Galore in 1959's *Goldfinger*. Born Blanche Lindo, the darkly mysterious beauty came from a long line of Portuguese Sephardic Jews who had fled the Inquisition for the Caribbean and great riches as colonial merchant-planters. Ian would later arrange a *Dr. No* production assistant job for Blanche's son, Chris Blackwell, who later in the sixties would discover Bob Marley and become a great reggae-rock impresario.

All through the fifties, the books kept coming. They also kept getting nastier. Fleming's S&M avocation was increasingly dominating his new vocation. One English reviewer in the high-toned *New Statesman* denounced *Dr. No* when it was published in 1958 with the headline "Sex, Snobbery and Sadism." The reviewer elaborated on those three elements that were "all unhealthy, all thoroughly English: the sadism of a schoolboy bully, the mechanical, two-dimensional sex-longings of a frustrated adolescent, and the crude, snob-cravings of a suburban adult." Because the reviewer was English and inculcated with the prejudices of empire, he may not have noticed a fourth damnable "-ism," racism. Fleming and Fielding were blood brothers of the stereotype. Almost all of Fleming's villains and heavies were sinister Asians, neo-Nazis, or fanatic Communists. The white man's burden was heavy indeed for James Bond, but its heft was what created the suspense.

All of the above apparently appealed to Hugh Hefner, who in 1959 began serializing the Bond novels in his magazine. Hefner would later describe a Bond movie as "*Playboy* with a Gun." Fleming also appealed to John F. Kennedy, through whom Fleming got the biggest boost of his career, one that finally propelled him to his own ultimate fantasy, the silver screen of Hollywood. In March 1961, *Life* published a big article entitled "The President's Voracious Reading Habits."

The article concluded with an Igor Cassini–style list of JFK's ten favorite books. The president preferred nonfiction biographies, of Lincoln, John Quincy Adams, John C. Calhoun. But there were two thrillers on the list, John Buchan's *Montrose* and Fleming's *From Russia with Love*, ranking ninth, ahead of Stendhal's *The Red and the Black*. Signet, which published Fleming in paperback, took the *Life* plug to the bank, creating an ad campaign that featured a solitary light on in a nocturnal White House. The grammatically clunky caption was "You can bet on it he's reading one of these Ian Fleming thrillers." Fleming, instantly recognizable with his trademark cigarette holder and bow tie, became an unexpected celebrity, a face of Britain that Americans began to recognize.

Kennedy had met Fleming in Washington soon after he became president. JFK's interest in Cuba and the Caribbean was bottomless, and who was better placed to fill him in on Caribbean intrigues than Britain's man in Jamaica, Ian Fleming. The same obsession with tropical Communism that would soon lead JFK to dispatch Igor Cassini to try to broker an entente with Trujillo had the president hanging on Fleming's every word, most of which were slurred by gin and, in the cold light of day, never would have made it into his next novel. The author pitched JFK some crazy Bondian schemes, such as emasculating Castro by cutting off his beard, and dropping millions of dollar bills onto Cuba to drive the people wild with capitalism. Then again, not long afterward, the CIA actually tried to assassinate Castro with exploding cigars, so the agency's truth was stranger than Fleming's fiction, if not inspired by it.

The *Life* piece got Fleming invited back to the White House. But he was about as unimpressed by Washington as Hollywood had been by him. He didn't care about the White House. He'd done that. He wanted Hollywood, more than ever. And now he got his chance. Before *Life*, the Bond books had sold well but not spectacularly. Overnight, they began selling in the millions. And overnight, Hollywood was ready to make a Bond movie. Well, not actually Hollywood itself.

The moguls in Los Angeles still had their doubts. Bond was too English, too Etonian, they thought, for American audiences to relate to. To them English meant effete, snobby, witty: in short, David Niven in *Around the World in 80 Days*. David Niven was great, but they couldn't feature him killing people. Cary Grant wasn't the killer type, either. George Sanders was too old. The bottom line was that the moguls couldn't see John Wayne as James Bond. That was the kind of star they were looking for. Picking up on Fleming's unvarnished penchant for S&M, the moguls also thought the Fleming books were too kinky for American viewers.

So it would take two American producers living in exile in London to take a relatively recherché British series of books and turn it into the biggest blockbuster series of movies that America, and the world, had ever seen. At first blush, these men were completely alien to the Coward-Fleming Jamaica-London axis that was the heady stuff from which Igor Cassini concocted the Jet Set. The two exiled Hollywood wannabe moguls, Harry Saltzman and Albert Broccoli, respectively a Montreal Jew

BONDSMEN. Film producers Harry Saltzman (left) and Cubby Broccoli (right) flank author Ian Fleming, 1963.

and a New York Italian, were much more the stuff of *Expresso Bongo,* a 1958 musical about desperate entertainment hustlers in London's Soho red light/showbiz quarter.

Ironically, *Expresso Bongo* would become a *Rocky Horror*–like cult hit that was the inspiration for both Brian Epstein, who would manage the Beatles, and Andrew Loog Oldham, who would manage the Rolling Stones, to choose the heretofore obscure career of pop talent manager. But the star of the film, a deliciously sleazy Laurence Harvey, managed to make something very sexy out of the amoral operator he was playing, a man who would lie, cheat, even stab *himself* in the back to close a deal. Out of the bowels of Soho were thus forged the highs of the sixties.

The writer of *Expresso Bongo,* a Cockney Jew named Wolf Mankowitz, would introduce the two then-downmarket American producers, each of whom possessed elements of his Laurence Harvey character. In return for that introduction, Mankowitz was hired to write the screenplay for *Dr. No,* about which he was so ashamed and pessimistic that he took his name off of it. Mankowitz's origins in London's poor and teeming East End were the opposite end of the spectrum from Ian Fleming's in Mayfair, but without this nexus of opposites, the mighty Bond-Beatles-British quality of the Jet Set might have been only a Temple Fielding aside about meals at Mirabelle and nights at the Savoy.

In 1961, in the midst of the *Life*/Kennedy-inspired Bond feeding frenzy, Harry Saltzman had optioned the rights to the Fleming series for a then-fat $50,000, for only six months. Then again, Saltzman was a born risk-taker. As a teenager, he had run away from his poor Montreal family and joined not Her Majesty's Secret Service but the circus, in order to see the world. During World War II, he fought for the Canadians in France; he ended up in Paris, married a Romanian refugee, and became a talent scout. However, the French film industry was slow to revive. Just before Brigitte Bardot gave French cinema its shot of adrenaline in 1956, Saltzman threw in the towel and crossed the Channel. Using British government subsidies, he quickly mounted his first production, *The Iron Petticoat,* a *Ninotchka* knockoff that had the distinction of being the only Bob Hope film that ever failed at the box office, even with Katharine Hepburn as the female lead.

Saltzman learned a lesson to avoid comedies and turned to serious fare, teaming up with the king of the Angry Young Man set, playwright John Osborne, to produce acclaimed film versions of Osborne's *Look Back in Anger* and *The Entertainer,* as well as the social-realist classic *Saturday Night and Sunday Morning.* For all the brilliant reviews, none of these films made Saltzman much money. They were too arty, too angry. He needed to find something commercial, and when he read *Goldfinger* in 1961, Harry Saltzman had his eureka moment and bet the house on optioning Bond.

When the six months were about to expire and Saltzman was about to lose that house, he turned in despair to his pal Mankowitz, who came up with the idea of teaming Saltzman with Albert Broccoli, who was just coming off a huge flop in *The Trials of Oscar Wilde,* starring Peter Finch and James Mason, its failure occasioned by American censors forbidding any advertising because of the film's homosexual subject matter. Mankowitz had been hired to write a script for Broccoli's company Warwick Films, which *Wilde* had just put into bankruptcy. He knew Broccoli had for years had the hots for James Bond and would at this point be motivated by sheer desperation.

What had cooled Broccoli off in the past was that his senior partner at Warwick, Irving Allen, had mortally insulted Ian Fleming at a 1957 dinner at Les Ambassadeurs, a private dining-gambling club on Park Lane that was the precursor of the John Aspinall–Mark Birley midsixties extravaganza of the Clermont and Annabel's on Berkeley Square. The Polish-born Allen, a master deal-maker who knew how to work the Marshall Plan, the IRS, and England's Inland Revenue, had made more than two dozen films in England in the fifties.

Ostensibly, Allen, an Oscar winner, knew whereof he spoke. What he said to Fleming was that his books were hopeless as cinematic source material. In fact, Allen decreed, they weren't even "good enough for television." So much for Broccoli's hopes of acquiring Bond. But now that

Broccoli had split from Allen after the *Wilde* debacle, Mankowitz knew that Broccoli would love another shot at Bond, but that he dare not go to Fleming himself, because no matter how many martinis the author had downed, there was no way he would forget the slight from Broccoli's partner.

Saltzman and Broccoli had almost nothing in common except a burning desire for solvency. When they met in a Mayfair office, Saltzman was offended by Broccoli's chutzpah in telling him he wanted to buy out his option and at a big discount, given that the clock had run down. However, because Saltzman was an arty indie foreign producer who had logged no time in Hollywood, he viewed Broccoli, who had cut his teeth (or fangs) in Los Angeles as a relative insider. That was the only reason Saltzman didn't walk out on him and cool his heels in Berkeley Square. Biting his tongue, Saltzman suggested a 50/50 partnership. Saltzman owned the option; Broccoli's task was to find the money to exercise it and make the film. Broccoli grudgingly took the deal.

The new partners soon took a Pan Am jet to New York, not Hollywood, which had its doubts about Bond. In Manhattan, Broccoli knew a junior executive at United Artists, less risk-averse than the Hollywood studios, who was a huge Ian Fleming fan. But this was no ordinary junior exec. This man's uncle was the head of the company. Walking in with a connection, Broccoli and Saltzman walked away with a commitment for $1 million to make *Dr. No,* which would become the inaugural film of the Bond series and the first of nine Bond movies Broccoli and Saltzman would produce together before splitting up. *Dr. No* was hardly big-budget. *Lawrence of Arabia,* which had just wrapped, cost $13 million. Still, it was a deal. James Bond was going on-screen, and Ian Fleming couldn't have been happier. The snob to end all snobs was finally getting his dearest wish: to go Hollywood.

Fleming was so thrilled about his movie deal that he dismissed rumors that Broccoli was a gangster. So what? Wasn't that what James Bond did, deal with gangsters, albeit on a global scale? Besides, the equation of "Italian" with "gangster" was an unfortunate and ubiquitous prejudice. It would take the new jets and mass tourism to show Ameri-

cans the true style and elegance that was Italy, and to replace the stereo-
type of Al Capone and Lucky Luciano with that of Gianni Agnelli and
Marcello Mastroianni. The problem for Albert Broccoli was that the
Lucky Luciano part was hitting awfully close to home.

That home was originally Calabria, and part of the Broccoli myth
was that the cruciferous vegetable famously despised by George Bush
was named after his family. Amusing but untrue. The word "broccoli"
has Dutch origins, referring to a hybrid of kale and cabbage, and lots of
Italians, of many names dating back to the Etruscans, grew it. The American Broccolis, who washed up in Little Italy in the mass immigrations
at the turn of the twentieth century, had fled the tenements of Mulberry
Street for a small farm on Long Island, where they grew, among other
produce, broccoli.

Albert Romolo Broccoli, born in 1909, was given the nickname
"Cubby," an Italian contraction of the name Abie Kabibble, a famous
Jewish comic-strip character in a series called *Abie the Agent* for whom
young Broccoli was supposed to be a dead ringer. Talk about stereotypes!
Basically, what the nickname was saying was that Albert Broccoli may
have sounded like a vegetable, but he looked like a Jew.

What was uncanny was that the cousin who gave Broccoli his nickname was Pasquale "Pat" DiCicco, who became the first powerful Italian
talent agent in Hollywood and who helped cousin Cubby get a job as a
Hollywood agent in 1934. Pat was sleek and handsome; Cubby was not.
Other than his name, there was nothing externally Italian about DiCicco,
who looked like a more rugged version of James Stewart. Not far below
Pat's glossy surface, however, were far darker undercurrents. Despite his
outward charm and courtly manners, DiCicco was known and feared in
Hollywood as the not so secret agent of Lucky Luciano, who made one
of his many illicit fortunes being the top drug supplier to the emerging
movie colony. Thus the stereotype that what goes around, comes around.

DiCicco made his mark quickly in Hollywood, marrying movie star
Thelma Todd. Before tying the knot with her, he had introduced her to
Luciano, who had his own affair with Todd before ceding her to his col-
league. Gangsters, like everyone else in America, were mad about stars,

and DiCicco made the capos' dreams come true. He would also play matchmaker between mobster Bugsy Siegel and actress Virginia Hill. Thelma Todd owned a successful roadhouse on the ocean in Pacific Palisades that Luciano coveted. Unable to get DiCicco to make her an offer she could not refuse, Luciano was frustrated. Thelma Todd ended up dead in her car, in one of Hollywood's most notorious unsolved mysteries. The case was ruled a suicide by carbon monoxide poisoning; few believed it.

No rumors stopped DiCicco, who became best friends with Howard Hughes and Cary Grant and made world headlines only slightly smaller than Pearl Harbor in 1941 by marrying the seventeen-year-old heiress Gloria Vanderbilt. Cubby Broccoli struggled along in his cousin's shadow, selling jewelry in Beverly Hills and running a Christmas-tree lot during the holiday season. DiCicco eventually rescued Cubby from obscurity and found him a post as an assistant on *The Outlaw*, aiding Howard Hughes in designing Jane Russell's famous "twin bullet" uplift brassiere. Hughes came to like and depend on his young assistant. Broccoli was by Hughes's side for his Washington, D.C., showdown with Juan Trippe's stooge Senator Ralph Owen Brewster, designed to put Hughes out of competition with Trippe. It was Broccoli who led the discovery that Hughes's suite at the Carlton Hotel in Washington had been bugged, an invasion of privacy that made Hughes paranoid for the rest of his life.

As Hughes drifted further away from movies and into madness, Broccoli found his grail as an agent for Charles Feldman's Famous Artists Agency. Feldman would later switch to producing and, in 1967, have a huge disaster trying to challenge his former underling's James Bond triumph by acquiring the rights to the one Fleming book Saltzman and Broccoli could not get, *Casino Royale*. Notwithstanding a blockbuster cast, including David Niven (to whom the studios had said a vehement no to being Bond); Ursula Andress, whose bikini had gone a long way toward making *Dr. No* a hit; plus comic geniuses Peter Sellers and Woody Allen, *Casino*, a would-be farce, was a huge gamble that lost. Starting with *Dr. No*, Saltzman and Broccoli had crafted a winning formula that tolerated no deviations, even by geniuses.

The key to their formula was de-Etonizing James Bond by casting the least Etonian actor in all the British Isles, Sean Connery, a former lifeguard and Mr. Universe runner-up whose ham-hock forearms sported the tattoos "Mum and Dad" and "Scotland Forever." The producers' two top choices, Patrick McGoohan and James Fox, had turned them down on moral scruples over Fleming's prurient sex and violence. Broccoli had vetoed Fleming's choice of the rising Roger Moore as too clean-cut, only to return to him after Connery quit the series. Broccoli's buddy Cary Grant, who had attended all three of Broccoli's weddings, felt at almost sixty that he was way too old for all the shenanigans.

Searching high and low for his secret agent, Broccoli had spotted Connery, standing out like two sore thumbs, in the Disney leprechaun fantasy *Darby O'Gill and the Little People*. He showed the film to his new wife, Dana, who concurred that the rugged man who, not too long before, had danced in the chorus of *South Pacific* in the West End should be given the license to kill. Ian Fleming initially felt that Connery was all wrong, though after the film was a hit, he decided he was all right. The film's director, Terence Young, an aristocratic old Harrovian wartime tank commander, and a gourmet after Temple Fleming's heart, also balked at the thuggish Connery. When the producers held firm, Young took Connery on a Fielding-esque eating tour of London's fanciest restaurants, so that Connery's Bond would present some aura of verisimilitude when he ordered vintage wines, caviar, and foie gras instead of the actor's preferred fish and chips and toad in the hole. While some observers felt that Connery wasn't acting but rather channeling Terence Young, the Pygmalionizaton worked so well that Connery would star in seven Bond films and become the standard by which all future Bonds will be judged.

With endless production problems, *Dr. No* was anything but a surefire hit. To begin with, there was a terrible script. The basic story in Fleming's book had British intelligence dispatching 007 to Jamaica to investigate the murder of their station chief and to aid the CIA in finding out who was using radio signals to disrupt American rocket launches from Florida's Cape Canaveral. The villain in both cases was the evil

Eurasian Dr. No. The producers wanted to revoke Wolf Mankowitz's license to write when his first draft turned *Dr. No* into a monkey. Mankowitz and his cowriter, Richard Maibaum (the top gun of the Warwick Productions writing crew), had found Fleming's villain such a racist anti-Chinese caricature that they created a whole new antagonist who kept a little rhesus monkey named Dr. No as a pet on his shoulder.

The producers hit the roof and insisted on the caricature. Fleming tried to get his pal Noël Coward to play the bad doctor, but Coward had about as much confidence in the enterprise as Mankowitz and begged off. Mankowitz may have taken his name off *No,* but he took a credit later on *Casino Royale* that turned out to be a debit nearly ending his screen career. Before he went anonymous, Mankowitz did the producers the great favor of introducing them to his *Expresso Bongo* composer Monty Norman, who wrote the twangy Bond theme that became the trademark of the series.

As with the theme, a lot of what would make the film a classic happened by serendipity, not design. Ursula Andress, who may have done more for the bikini than any other woman in history, had to be spray-tanned to Caribbeanize her alpine-white skin, while her Swiss German accent was so ponderous that it had to be dubbed to give it a softer sex appeal. While there was some location shooting in Fleming's Jamaica, Dr. No's lair and other interiors were re-created in England's Pinewood Studios, where most of the early Bond films would be shot. For all the glamour it was intended to convey, *Dr. No* was very much a low-budget film, in which the beauty of the Caribbean exteriors just managed to transcend the cheesiness of the Pinewood sets, where, for example, Dr. No's giant aquarium was nothing but a blown-up goldfish bowl.

Such was the magic of filmmaking that the glamour won out. Because of its exotic locales, its elegant hero, its glossy sex, its sports cars, its shaken martinis, its bespoke suits, and its global-dominance-minded villain, *Dr. No* became the first and arguably the quintessential Jet Set movie. Not that the critics were bowled over when the film came out in England in the fall of 1962 and in America in the spring of 1963. *Time* derided the film as "silly," calling Connery a "great big hairy marshmallow." *The New York Times* concurred about the film's frivolity. Famously fuddy-duddy critic Bosley Crowther saw the effort as "nonsense escapist bunk," unleashing a volley of box-office-killing blurbs: "wickedly exaggerated," "patently contrived," and "not to be believed." Then he sheepishly admitted that *Dr. No* was "lively and amusing," conceding the formidable entertainment value of Connery's showdown with a tarantula and Andress's show-off with her bikini.

Worried that American audiences would not cotton to what their chief executive described as a "Limey truck driver," United Artists had initially hedged its bets in America, opening the film not in the New York and Los Angeles temples of cinema but in Southern drive-ins, where the hicks would be fooled into buying tickets. But given Bosley Crowther's influential guilty-pleasure review as well as a lot of raves around the rest of the country, UA was shamed into a wide release, which grossed big numbers, twenty times the budget. As usual, as the Hollywood truism went, nobody knew nothin'.

The next year's *From Russia with Love* doubled the budget to $2 million and quadrupled the gross. Ian Fleming, who died in 1964 at fifty-six of a long-feared drink-and-smoke-induced heart attack, never got to see the $3 million *Goldfinger,* released later that year, which grossed $125 million and produced the bestselling toy of the year, a British racing-green model Aston Martin DB5. The release of *Goldfinger,* coinciding with the release of *Meet the Beatles,* turned London into the hottest Jet Set location on earth. For all their newfound success, Saltzman and Broccoli still were far from the toasts of the booming American film colony in London, one of the world's most glamorous collections of high livers and high rollers. The more serious Saltzman was considered something of an aging schlepper. Broccoli had more affectations, such as his racehorses, and his DiCicco-underworld connections gave him as much mystique as the Bond box office. But they were no more than two faces in a very glittering crowd. It was this London-based but international community that was, more than any other, the defining microcosm of the society of glittering global nomads that the new jet planes had wrought.

11

Swinging London

I N THE FIFTIES, SOME AMERICANS IN FILM CAME TO LONDON MAINLY BECAUSE IT WAS cheap, there were subsidies, and making it there was easier than in Hollywood. Now the top dogs of Hollywood were coming to London as a first choice, not a last resort. All the hot new stars were here: Michael Caine, Albert Finney, Alan Bates, David Hemmings, Vanessa and Lynn Redgrave, Julie Christie. The 707 and the DC-8 had made Europe in general, and London in particular, easily accessible as a place to shoot and, suddenly, triggered by the explosions of Bond and the Beatles, the place to be. It was too bad that Igor Cassini had just lost his column in disgrace. The scene in London would have given him years of great copy.

The Jet Set emperor of the London film world—in fact, the world film world—was Sam Spiegel. Spiegel was so grand, he wouldn't even consider doing James Bond. Long before *Dr. No* was a gleam in the golden eye of Saltzman and Broccoli, Spiegel, who saw everything before anyone else, had dismissed the manuscript as "nonsense. I don't make pictures like that." The pictures Spiegel made were grand and serious pictures, the grandest of all time. He won three best picture Oscars, for

On the Waterfront, The Bridge on the River Kwai, and *Lawrence of Arabia.* Artistically, if not commercially, 007 was less than zero compared to these.

Sam Spiegel, who was in his age-defying sixties in the youth-obsessed sixties, had an energy unconstrained by generation. He was the prototype of the Boeing Jet Setter. Born in Poland, he had lived everywhere, was at home everywhere, Vienna, Jerusalem, Berlin, Paris, London, New York, Hollywood. He

AQABA! Uber-producer Sam Spiegel (right) on the *Lawrence of Arabia* set in Jordan with director David Lean, 1962.

was fluent in six languages. His yacht, the *Malahne,* was an even hotter invite than the rival pleasure crafts of Onassis and Niarchos. Because Spiegel was truly Hollywood's last tycoon, he hosted the biggest stars of all, who were catnip to the biggest aristocrats and the biggest politicians. The *Malahne* was a floating Igor Cassini column.

For all the glory of his films, his friends, his homes on Park Avenue, in London, and on the Riviera, his impressionist art collection, his globe-trotting epicurianism worthy of both Fielding and Fleming, Sam Spiegel was nonetheless affectionately known as the greatest con man in a business of con men. If Sam Spiegel was born to be Jet Set, it was because he was basically born on the run. He had started life in Galicia, a part of Poland that was something of a fertile crescent for Hollywood moguls. Mayer, Goldwyn, Fox, Zukor, and the Warner brothers all came from the same province, one that had a terrible reputation for its conniving peasants, a reputation that Spiegel always tried to avoid, claiming he was born in elegant Vienna. By his late teens, he had fled Galicia for that city of the waltz, then went on to Palestine as part of a Zionist youth movement. There he found and married a rich girl, had a child, and after five years, in the wake of some shady business dealings, completely abandoned them and fled to America.

Once Spiegel arrived in San Francisco, things quickly got shadier. Pretending to be an Egyptian government agent scouting royal investment opportunities, Spiegel was arrested by federal agents on charges of immigration fraud. He was convicted and spent nine months in a San Francisco jail. When he got out in 1930, he was deported. He ended up in Berlin at the height of its decadent *Blue Angel* period. There he finagled a job working as a publicist for the German releases of Carl Laemmle's Universal Studios. His first big project, *All Quiet on the Western Front,* bombed—literally. The Nazi brownshirts ignited explosives at the theater, with shouts of "Judenfilm." Universal pulled all its product from Germany, and Spiegel was out of one more job.

Undaunted, he made his way to London, stopping in Paris to stay— most likely on the house—at André Terrail's George V, where he made movie connections with Fritz Lang and Buster Keaton. In London, Spiegel got a room at the Mount Royal Hotel, near Marble Arch, where he made one of his greatest contacts, with a just-starting young film editor named David Lean. Spiegel was jailed three times in Britain for assorted frauds and eventually deported to France, which in turn deported him to Mexico for trying to cheat the casino at Deauville. Slithering across the porous border at Tijuana, Sam Spiegel, who, as a multiple deportee, was persona non grata in the United States, changed his name to S. P. Eagle and found his way to Hollywood, where he knew he belonged.

Intent on becoming a Hollywood producer, Spiegel arrived in Los Angeles in 1939 as part of the huge wave of European creative émigrés, a fleeing, incredibly brilliant Art Set that included Billy Wilder, Thomas Mann, Igor Stravinsky, Aldous Huxley, and Bertolt Brecht. Spiegel's chief apologist was the superagent of the day, Paul Kohner, himself an earlier German émigré who was married to Lupita Tovar, a south-of-the-border Katharine Hepburn whom Spiegel had befriended during his exile in Mexico City. But even Kohner got sick of the complaints he was getting over Spiegel's endless bounced checks. Spiegel somehow connived to rent a fancy home in Beverly Hills that was known as "Boys' Town" for its all-night gin rummy games and hot and cold running hookers. A dedicated enthusiast for what would be a hallmark of the Jet Set male set—hiring expensive prostitutes—Spiegel once told Harold Pinter, "The secret of happiness is whores." Billy Wilder often fantasized about a magic mattress that, *apres l'amour,* would fold up into a card table and make the woman disappear. Why did the Jet Set become such a hive of misogny? Because to the Set's male players, women were nothing more than decorative pawns in a game of kings. Until Jackie Kennedy took charge of its culture and Mary Wells Lawrence started writing its airplane ads, women were viewed as either fashion objects on Igor Cassini's best-dressed lists, sex objects on Temple Fielding's best-brothel lists, or wealth objects on *Town & Country's* most eligible lists.

Spiegel's uncanny ability to track down Hollywood's most beautiful starlet-harlots gave him a reputation that was a badge of honor in a business of Bad Boys. It led to a friendship with Paul Kohner's rival power agent, Charles Feldman, who helped Spiegel mount his first American production, *Tales of Manhattan,* released in 1942. *Tales* was about a set of tails, a bespoke tuxedo that brought severe misfortune to all who wore it. It brought great fortune to Spiegel, though, because it was an anthology film that allowed him, with Feldman's aid, to assemble a huge cast of stars—Rita Hayworth, Ginger Rogers, Henry Fonda, Charles Boyer, Edward G. Robinson, W. C. Fields, and many more—to whom Spiegel endeared himself.

By giving short and profitable work to half the town, Spiegel instantly made himself a job creator and part of the showbiz inner circle. Even though it took him four more years to get his next project off the ground, he began giving legendary New Year's Eve parties for all the stars he was meeting, fetes that were the everybody-goes-there precursor of the superexclusive Swifty Lazar and *Vanity Fair* Oscar parties decades hence. True to form, Spiegel often stiffed the catering companies, though there was always another starstruck aspirant who would fall for his star bait. Meanwhile, the starlets kept on coming, some to be discovered, some to earn some pin money, such as a very young Marilyn Monroe, who became one of Spiegel's top drawing cards.

In 1951, Spiegel turned fifty and, at an age when most producers were either finished or famous, he had his first smash, with *The African Queen*. *Queen* was a pure Jet Set movie, pre-jet, filmed on location in Africa with the headline cast of Humphrey Bogart and Katharine Hepburn, the headline director John Huston, and the headline screenwriter Peter Viertel, who had lost his last wife, supermodel Bettina, to Aly Khan and was now married to Deborah Kerr. Producer Spiegel was too terrified of the snakes and bugs to spend time on location; he kept track of things by long-distance phone from Europe's casinos. Once the Oscars started coming, the Immigration and Naturalization Service forgave him his past transgressions, and S. P. Eagle became *the* Sam Spiegel, the mysterious man of movies. The next year, the success of *Queen* spawned another African pre–Jet Set epic, *Mogambo,* starring Clark Gable, Grace Kelly, and Ava Gardner, not to mention an offscreen Frank Sinatra, who, armed with Harry Winston jewels, chased Gardner to Africa to try to put their marriage back on track and keep her out of the clutches of Gable. The public was riveted by these African romances, which did more for inciting lust and wanderlust than any issue of *National Geographic*.

By the time Saltzman and Broccoli had managed to get *Dr. No* off the ground and still could not get a good table at Mirabelle unless Ian Fleming took them there, Spiegel was wallowing in so much *Lawrence of Arabia* Oscar gold that Fleming's grandly rapacious villain Auric Goldfinger would have been wild with envy. Hugh Hefner would have been wild with envy over Spiegel's sex life. The producer was on his third marriage. When he had begun to make a name for himself, his first wife had emerged from Israel and tracked him to Beverly Hills, where she nailed him for child support. His second wife, a twenty-year-old six-foot-tall Texas model-starlet, slashed all of his bespoke Savile Row suits and his Picasso paintings when she divorced him. Next up was another gorgeous model, this one from Virginia, with whom he enjoyed an open marriage, he with his entourage of call girls, she with her entourage of married tycoons, including William Paley and Jock Whitney. Tit for tat, Spiegel would also make plays for the wives of famous men, such as *mesdames* Henry Fonda, Harold Pinter, Aga Khan. When his wife ran off with Omar Sharif, Spiegel would attempt the same with Anouk Aimée. The name-dropping was as deafening as the smashed dishes.

The sixties may have been the decade of sexual revolution, but Sam Spiegel had been revolting since the time of Trotsky and Lenin. His domestic arrangements would have been conventional only by the standards of a Turkish sultan. Hugh Hefner, by comparison, was a homebody. Even though this was the jet age and he would have his own DC-9 by the end of the sixties, "Hef," as he was known, was a lot like Frank Sinatra in trying to replicate all the comforts of home, in his case the Chicago Playboy Mansion, everywhere he went.

By the midsixties, Hefner had built a Playboy Club next to the new Hilton on London's Park Lane, overlooking Hyde Park. The hotel and the club were the twin towers of the era's American cultural imperialism. Hilton and *Playboy* were deeply fascinating to the English, who were far more intrigued by sleeping and partying in the New World mode than by doing the same at their twin towers of tradition, Claridge's (or the Savoy) and Annabel's. The lines waiting to get into the Hilton's 007 Bar, a slick Hollywood-American homage to a vanished British colonial muscularity, were longer than those to come a block away at the Hard Rock Café, another landmark of America's colonization of its former colonizer.

Neither Hefner nor Hilton before him spent much time at their hot properties. Hilton had good reason to stay out of town. The 30-story, 500-room behemoth London Hilton, which opened in April 1963 as the tallest structure in proudly low-rise historic London, was considered by far the ugliest Hilton in the whole international chain. Its size overshadowed the dome of St. Paul's, the clock tower of Parliament, and the spires of Westminster Abbey, all visible from the Hilton's hideous glass-walled rooftop restaurant. It stood out like the sorest of thumbs, casting its modern Yankee shadow over discreet Mayfair. Buckingham Palace was only blocks away. Here was Conrad Hilton, looking down on the queen. Hilton was more than happy to give the credit for the hotel to its English moneybags developer-financier Charles Clore.

A Spiegelesque self-made early corporate raider and property king-pin, Clore was born poor, Russian, and Jewish. He had fled the pogroms for London, where he had gotten his start in the rag trade. An art collector like Spiegel, Clore had amassed the world's largest collection of Turners. Like Spiegel, he craved class, and he craved trophies. What better a trophy than one of London's famous hotels? He tried to buy the Grosvenor House but was rebuffed. Then he tried a hostile takeover of the group that owned the Savoy, Claridge's, and the Berkeley. The Old Guard was even more hostile to Clore than he was to them. Again his takeover failed. So one nouveau riche turned to another. Clore told Hilton, Give me your name, and I'll build a hotel with it. It was unclear whom London resented more, Clore or Hilton, the Jew or the cowboy. But Clore was around to take the heat—not that he cared. He was used to being despised by the threatened English upper classes and the bitter lower ones. The Yiddish-speaking philanthropist may have been lampooned as "Santa Clore," but he was secure knowing that he gave as good as he got.

In the end, the James Bond movie memorabilia, the Conrad Hilton ice water, and the New York–style skyscraper views conquered all. The "Little America" that had sprouted up on Park Lane turned into a Little Las Vegas two years later with the construction of the equally garish Playboy Club. In the case of *Playboy,* Hefner didn't need an English fall guy like Charles Clore to deflect the domestic snobbery. He had his own American fall guy in his number two man, Victor Lownes, paradigm of the wannabe Jet Setter, a man who bought the Igor Cassini myth and gave it a Chicago spin. Reminiscent of Eddie Gilbert minus the crime, Lownes was a spoiled rich boy who wanted to live like James Bond.

Famous for his definition of a playboy—"someone who is getting more sex than you are"—Victor Lownes probably got more sex in real life than James Bond did in film *and* fiction. Lownes, born in 1928 in Buffalo to a prominent (if not Charles Clore–ish) building contractor,

BUNNY HOP. *Playboy* London chief Victor Lownes training British Bunnies, 1965.

grew up on a Florida estate with servants and chefs. After accidentally killing a friend with a rifle he didn't realize was loaded, Lownes was sent off for supposed discipline to the New Mexico Military Institute where Conrad Hilton had briefly stopped on his abortive educational journey to Dartmouth and where Conrad's playboy-in-the-making son Nicky was one of Lownes's classmates. The two rich kids hit it off, getting drunk on tequila Nicky smuggled in from his father's nearby El Paso Hilton.

Despite the booze, Lownes was a top student and went on to the University of Chicago. He got married almost as soon as he matriculated, to a pretty and wealthy, plantation-born Southern girl who had been runner-up in the Miss Arkansas contest. Settling in to a Chicago version of *The Man in the Gray Flannel Suit* postwar surburban country-club dream, Lownes took a job as an advertising manager for *Dog World* magazine. He soon switched to the family business, an alarm company called Silent Watchman. By 1953, only in his midtwenties and without even having read an Ian Fleming novel to give him a role model, Lownes had a midlife crisis and, Sam Spiegel–style, walked away from his wife, his two children, and all convention.

Lownes rented a loft in downtown Chicago and began hanging

around the jazz clubs, where he met Hugh Hefner. Hefner, also fleeing his wife and kids, had just launched *Playboy*, with its famous Marilyn Monroe calendar nude that called the world's attention to the fledgling publication. Hefner used the handsome Lownes as a male model in aspirational fashion spreads. In one typical feature, Lownes posed as a corporate executive flying to meetings in his private plane, foreshadowing the private Learjets of the *Fortune* 500. The two men had so much in common that Hefner, in 1955, convinced Lownes to work for him as *Playboy*'s promotions director, mobilizing student reps on college campuses and ferrying Playmates around the country to increase circulation and convince advertisers that this was no sleazy porn sheet but the cool, liberal, and liberated voice of a new generation.

One advertiser that succumbed to his spiel was the Gaslight Clubs, members-only "key" clubs that featured bosomy cocktail waitresses corseted into Gay '90s costumes. Lownes turned that Gay '90s corset into the even more constricting and more revealing bunny uniform, and the concept of the Playboy Club was born. Neither Lownes nor Hefner knew anything about food service, but Lownes had a friend who did: Arnie Morton, whose family members were major Chicago restaurateurs. Arnie's father, Morton C. Morton, had invented the "Mortoni," a mixture of gin, vermouth, and a pickled onion. Shaken or stirred, the minimalist snob Ian Fleming would not have approved, but to Chicago, the Mortoni was the height of sophistication. Lownes, Morton, and Hefner became partners, and in 1960, the Playboy Club of Chicago opened and became as instant a cultural phenomenon as James Bond would be two years later.

By 1963, having opened a string of enormously successful Playboy Clubs in America and infected with jet-age wanderlust, Lownes convinced Hefner to let him take the concept overseas. His first two targets were London and Jamaica. Loaded with *Playboy* development money, Lownes jetted to London and checked in at Conrad Hilton's brand-new hotel tower in Mayfair, which was either the talk of the town or the shame of the city, depending on who was judging it. Lownes immediately noticed a seven-story Hiltonesque apartment house down Park

Lane between the Hilton and the Dorchester. The edifice had a pedigree far grander than that of the derided Hilton. The architect was the Bauhaus master Walter Gropius. Not only one of the great locations in London, it also appealed to Lownes's modern aesthetic, as had the New York Playboy Club, whose building was designed by Edward Durell Stone.

What Lownes knew would make the London Playboy Club the cash cow of the Hefner empire was that it was not merely another T&A emporium but rather one of gaming, Lownes's own Casino Royale. Barely a year after Fidel Castro took power in Cuba and nationalized the capitalist-pig casinos that had been controlled by the American Mafia, England, smelling desperately needed foreign exchange, introduced the 1960 Betting and Gaming Act that saw an explosion of 1,500 legal casinos in England within a few years. Suddenly, all the Meyer Lansky/Sam Giancana–led mobsters whom Igor Cassini had hoped to divert from Cuba to the Dominican Republic seemed to end up in Mayfair. At the Colony Club, for one, movie star George Raft was the celebrity front man for Meyer Lansky, attracting the Hollywood crowd. Victor Lownes coveted that crowd, and he set to work building a better money trap.

While Lownes began negotiating to acquire the Gropius building and convert it from a block of flats to a Bunny hutch, he left the Hilton and moved into a very stately traditional British home on Montpelier Square, in Knightsbridge, hard by Harrods. There he used the *Playboy* cachet, which was then enormous, to begin entertaining the rich and famous, visiting and local. Chez Victor was, in effect, the Playboy Mansion–Europe, and the ease of jet travel created a whole new phenomenon of itinerant celebrity. The same stars might be spotted at dinner at Chasen's one night, at 21 the next, and at a party at Victor Lownes's on the third. The Beatles and the Stones were there, as were Warren Beatty, Frank Sinatra, Telly Savalas, Laurence Harvey, and Tom Jones, most lured by the catnip of the perfumed and microskirted horde of Playmate and Bunny aspirants. The mood was very "What's new, pussycat?," which had become Beatty's trademark greeting and was the title of a hit movie written by Woody Allen, who was featured in a huge *Playboy* spread on the film with the topless dancers of Paris's notorious Crazy

Horse Saloon. Allen, too, joined the scene at Lownes's. "Normal" women were rare, unless one considered Judy Garland a normal woman.

Victor Lownes reigned as one of the century's masters of publicity manipulation. He began a massive Bunny hunt across England. When he found his first six, he flew them to the Chicago Playboy Club for training, labeling the group "Bunnies from Britain," to evoke the patriotic wartime "Bundles for Britain" campaign. Sex sold, and Lownes knew how to walk that high wire over the straits of prurience. He also connived to get the archbishop of Canterbury into the act. Someone had sent the prelate an invitation to join the Playboy Club at a discount rate, and he wrote a letter to the London *Times* expressing his displeasure at the notion, which meant more front-page publicity for Lownes.

The Playboy Club finally opened in June 1966, at the height of "Swinging London." On only his second trip to Europe, Hefner was greeted by an entourage of thirty-two Bunnies at Heathrow waving American flags, which incited a protest from the American embassy that Old Glory was being sexualized as well as commercialized. Again more headlines for Lownes. Opening-night guests were a Jet Set Who's Who, including Rex Harrison, Roman Polanski, Ringo Starr, Tony Curtis, Rudolf Nuryev, Jean-Paul Belmondo, Lee Radziwill, and a bunch of British royals led by the Marquis of Tavistock, one of the few blue bloods who still had millions to gamble away.

When Sean Connery showed up a few months later, Victor Lownes knew he had hit the jackpot as London's premier host. Lownes couldn't get enough of England. He would later go mano a mano with his boss, Hefner, over the affections of an English goddess named Marilyn Cole who would be the magazine's first "full frontal" Playmate. Before that, Lownes would make his own full-frontal assault on the British Establishment, the Ian Fleming crowd, when he decided to take over the Clermont Club, London's ne plus ultra gambling den. Playboy was flash; Clermont was class, all the way to Windsor Castle. The showdown brought into high relief the dramatic contrast between the new American aspirational jet set, who could admit an ambitious *bourgeois gentilhomme* like Victor Lownes, and the crusty, stratified, exclusionary

European Jet Set, who would rather fall on their ancient swords than admit a promising newcomer. It was the Old World versus the New, Bond before Connery versus Bond after Connery, fighting it out for the occupancy of the dance floor of Annabel's.

The two old boys taken on by the new kid on Park Lane were John Aspinall and Mark Birley, proprietors, respectively, of the gaming club and the dancing club that comprised the two-headed hydra of intimidating snobbism in the center of London's garden of aristocracy, Berkeley Square. The snobbier of the two, Birley encapsulated the conflicts of the jet age through an exchange he had with a BOAC air hostess. He was seated in first class, of course, smoking a Havana cigar. The hostess asked if he would mind putting it out, because the smell was wafting back into the plane and disturbing the denizens of economy. He politely refused, noting that if he weren't complaining about the smell "back there"—

as he referred to the section that dare not speak its name—why should "they" complain about the smell "up here."

Aspinall was by far the more eccentric of these two arbiters of exclusivity. A child of empire, John Victor Aspinall was born in the midst of his mother's social climb in 1926 in India, where his putative father was a doctor in the British colonial army. He later learned that he and the good doctor had no biological link. His mother had been trading up, having an affair with a

MAMA SAID. Nightclub impresario John Aspinall goes to London court with his mother on illegal gambling charges, 1958.

general, and John was the result. After divorcing the doctor, Mrs. Aspinall was sailing back to England when she met a shipmate who happened to be a baronet, Sir George Osborne. She soon married him, and John was to the manor adopted. His stepfather sent him to Rugby, from which he was expelled, and then to Jesus College, Oxford, where he boasted that he never attended a single lecture and from which he dropped out, skipping exams to go to the races at Ascot.

From an early age, the stylish blond Peter O'Toole–ish John Aspinall loved to gamble, and he soon turned his hobby into his profession. This was the fifties, before the Gaming Act made gambling legal. But Aspinall knew how the British upper classes loved games of chance, and he became the Nathan Detroit of Debrett's, running the biggest floating crap game in London. In Aspinall's case, the craps were replaced by "chemmy," Brit for baccarat chemin de fer, which happened to be the favorite game of Ian Fleming and his alter ego, James Bond. The entire plot of *Casino Royale* centers around a game of chemmy between Bond and SMERSH villain Le Chiffre.

Some say the addiction known as "le vice Anglais" refers to a schoolboy S&M fantasy of being disciplinarily whipped; others say it is gambling. Aspinall managed to combine the two, renting hotel rooms for his upper-class acquaintances to squander their fortunes before Inland Revenue could take them away. He got his original guest list from a friend he met at the track, Bernard van Cutsem, who was the queen's racehorse trainer. Van Cutsem knew all the aristocrats, and he knew their weaknesses, which he shared with Aspinall. That knowledge came to be power. Summoning his guests to his peripatetic gambling tables with engraved invitations from Smythson's of Bond Street, Aspinall knew precisely how to cater to upper-class needs. Like Sam Spiegel in his Hollywood "Boys' Town," Aspinall always provided the finest champagne and provisions from Fortnum & Mason, often served by delectable tarts who were there to accommodate the gamblers in any way possible.

Big money changed hands, and a lot of it went into the hands of Aspinall. At one of his enchanted evenings, Lord Derby was said to have lost 300,000 pounds, a major fortune in those postwar depressed times.

Aspinall took the money to pursue his other grand passion, wild animals. He was less passionate about women, though he did take several wives, starting in 1956 with top model Jane Hastings. They moved to a fine home on Eaton Square, where Aspinall transformed the gardens into his own little game preserve for a young tiger, two Himalayan bears, and a rhesus monkey. In 1957, Aspinall bought a Palladian mansion near Canterbury, called Howletts, where he created his own large and free-range zoo. Cages were anathema to him, for both his wildlife and his wild life.

In the next year, one of Aspinall's chemmy games was busted. His spirited defense led to the passage of the 1960 Gaming Act, which all of England knew as "Aspinall's Law." This new legislation, which spurred the English gold rush in casinos, led to his renovating one of London's grandest Georgian houses into the Clermont Club, at 44 Berkeley Square. Not everyone in Aspinall's orbit was an aristocrat. Gambling was a Mob sport, and "Aspers," as his friends called him, of necessity had to deal with such British gangsters as the Kray twins and their mentor, Billy Hill, a Jack the Ripper–inspired killer who left his trademark "V" carved into the faces of his (V)ictims. Hill was reputed to have formed an unholy alliance with Aspinall to create specially marked packs of cards that a plant at the table could read and help fleece the swells out of millions, a portion of the loot going to the shakedown specialist Hill.

Among the first wave of the early-sixties fleecees of the Clermont were five dukes, five marquesses, twenty earls, and two cabinet ministers. New York's Eddie Gilbert conveniently helped finance the enterprise, just as he had financed Igor Cassini's Le Club, which in turn inspired Aspinall to create a version of Le Club in the Clermont's unused basement. That was when Aspinall turned to his pal Mark Birley, who was at loose ends and needed something to do. The imposing six-foot-five bespoke-suited Marcus Lecky Oswald Hornby Birley, who even had his socks custom-tailored, was almost the same age as Aspinall but much more effete.

Mark Birley came by his aestheticism as naturally as Aspinall had come by his social climbing; his father, Sir Oswald Birley, was one of

England's premier portrait painters. Everyone from Winston Churchill on down had sat for him. Birley's Irish mother was also an artist, as well as an eccentric who created gourmet dishes like lobster thermidor to feed to her flowers. Mark's sister, Maxime, crossed the Channel as a young woman to model and design couture for Elsa Schiaparelli in Paris and to marry into the aristocratic de la Falaise clan. Maxime's brother-in-law had been the third husband of Gloria Swanson. Mark Birley thus grew up with that classic pre–Jet Set mix of artists, stars, tycoons, and aristocrats.

After leaving Oxford, Birley had tried his hand at American commerce, working as an adman at the London office of J. Walter Thompson, and French luxury, opening an Hermès boutique in the Burlington Arcade. He found both experiences too foreign for his hard-core Englishness. Birley's chief asset was his unequaled social network, through his own family, through his education at Eton and one year at Oxford (like Aspinall, he quit), and through his marriage to Lady Annabel Vane-Tempest-Stewart, the daughter of the Eighth Marquess of Londonderry, whose famous palace, Londonderry House on Park Lane, was demolished to make way for the London Hilton and its imitators, other American modern, totally un-English lodgings, on that prime location. Birley decided to name his new nightclub, below the Clermont, after his wife and consecrate it as a proudly British refuge against Hiltonism and Playboyism and all the other *vices américains*.

While the Clermont's key backer was Eddie Gilbert, the money behind Annabel's was that of Birley's dear friend the fiscal buccaneer Jimmy Goldsmith, who swept Annabel Birley onto the dance floor on opening night and into a flagrant affair that would cuckold Mark Birley for the world to see. If Birley lost his wife to Goldsmith, he nearly lost his son Robin to John Aspinall when one of Aspinall's beloved tigers mauled the boy beyond recognition and permanently disfigured the handsome heir. And the whole Clermont-Annabel's set was implicated in the unsolved mystery of one of the charter members, Lord Lucan, who disappeared after killing his maid, mistaking her for his cheating wife. Both Aspinall and Birley were suspected of helping him hide in Africa, though nothing was ever proved.

Annabel's annual membership fee was the same five guineas as that of the Playboy Clubs, but for that equivalent of fourteen dollars, instead of getting a tacky Vegas filled with pneumatic Bunnies and wall-to-wall Sinatra, the Annabel's member got an English country house filled with posh and porcelain debutantes twisting (but never shouting) to the Beatles. While the typical Playboy Club member (unless he was a star) probably could not pass Mark Birley's fierce scrutiny and get into Annabel's, most of the *Playboy* people couldn't have been any more disturbed by that exclusion than they were about sitting "back there" in Juan Trippe's 707s.

By 1972, Aspinall was in financial trouble. He was forced into a fire sale. For a little over half a million pounds, *Playboy*, spearheaded by Victor Lownes, acquired the Clermont Club, that most English of trophies. The Broccolization of Bond, James Bond, was finally complete.

12

Coffee, Tea, or Me?

JAMES BOND WAS, IN FEMINIST-SPEAK, A MALE CHAUVINIST PIG, BUT IT TOOK QUITE a while—until the late sixties, in fact—for that appellation to speak its name. Until then, Bond was, pure and simple, *the* male role model for the Jet Setter. For all its glamour, the advent of the jet age gave American women a lot to be angry about. The notion of the Jet Set was invented by and populated with a cadre of high-flying Bondian playboys who, in the view of early feminists, were wallowing in a sexist pigsty. The opening up of Europe exposed traveling American men to a continent of pliable women far beyond their previously chaste marriage-oriented fantasies of Eisenhower-era prom queens. As per the folklore of the times, European women were the Asians of the sixties, docile, obedient, adoring. The myth was easy to sell, and the dollar's rate of exchange proved to be a remarkable aphrodisiac. Furthermore, if a voyager's irresistible Yankee masculinity somehow failed to spark an offshore romance, he always had the fallback of turning to Temple Fielding's "nightlife" section.

That Fielding-reader wives were not grievously offended by the author's pay-to-play suggestions was a sign of the misogynistic times. Betty Friedan's heretical *The Feminine Mystique,* which called into question such suburban-housewife docility and bad-boy toleration, was not published until 1963, five years after the new jets had been enabling American men to sate their satyriasis in the compliant Old World. The National Organization for Women (NOW) was not founded until 1966. Before that, the only thing even resembling a feminist manifesto to which women could turn was a translation of Simone de Beauvoir's 1949 *The Second Sex,* which was banned by the Vatican and sold a minute fraction of the copies of Fielding's annual *Guide* or any of the Bond series.

Although the early jet age seems like a stone age for women's liberation, the seeds of change were being planted in this period by a number of jet-setting influential international woman innovators: the advertising whirlwind Mary Wells Lawrence, the iconoclastic designer Mary Quant, the nightclub impresario Régine. These were the pre-feminists, businesswomen all, who were making big marks in the men's world they lived in.

FLY GIRLS. Pan Am's stewardess training class, Miami, 1968.

Although they were all, in varying degrees, dependent upon men and played to often offensive male fantasies in order to accomplish their ambitions in the testosterone jungle, their vast successes were a warning shot across the bow of male dominion, a harbinger of the change that was coming sooner than the playboys of the Jet Set might have guessed.

However, the prevailing stereotype before Betty Friedan's tome hit the stands was that, sexually, jet-age Europe was a satisfaction-guaranteed sure thing, a continent of conquests. Every American could be his own James Bond. On the other hand, not every American woman could be, nor wanted to be, a Pussy Galore. The concept was as anathematic to one gender as it was fantastic to the other, setting the stage for what would become in the seventies a violent feminist backlash. Never had women been more objectified. And no women of the era were considered more covetable sex objects than jet airline stewardesses, who were basically Hefnerian Bunnies and Playmates with wings, centerfold creatures who had ascended, quite literally, to a higher plane. One of the biggest bestsellers of the Jet Set era was 1967's *Coffee, Tea or Me?*, a concocted erotic memoir of two swinging stewardesses that was actually written by a man, Donald Bain, whose day job was as a publicist for Pan Am. Although no airline was specified, the book was unmatched product placement for all of them.

In the category of Jet Set entertainment, *Coffee* was the direct descendant of the French farce *Boeing-Boeing,* a play by Marc Camoletti, which premiered in Paris in December 1960, soon after Air France inaugurated its 707 service across the Atlantic. The comedy is the story of a playboy juggling three air-hostess mistresses, whose life gets terribly complicated when the new jets cut the ladies' flying times in half and double the playboy's troubles. This was one concept that lost nothing in translation. A version opened in London's West End in 1962 and played for seven years, giving the perennial *No Sex Please, We're British* a run for its money. In 1965, Tony Curtis and Jerry Lewis did a movie version, which was a hit for Paramount, albeit not in the stratosphere of the James Bond films, where the suspense seemed to add a je ne sais quoi to the sex, and the sexism.

The one woman whom most feminists would nominate as the rare heroine of the jet age was an adwoman who nonetheless trafficked in the same sexual stereotypes as the men who ruled the times. This was Mary Wells Lawrence, whose most famous of many famous advertisements, for both print and television, was Braniff's "The Air Strip." Here, as the jet flew south from the frigidity of the New York winter to the tropical steam heat of South America, a chorus line of nubile air hostesses performed an ecdysiastic removal of their multilayered Pucci uniforms, from a heavy coat and boots down to a miniskirt and heels. The seduction wasn't subliminal; it was in your face. That was advertising, turning a client's product into an object of desire. Somehow the sex that sold airline tickets seemed sexier when it was concocted by a woman, especially a sexy woman like Mrs. Lawrence, who may have confounded women's libbers by having married the boss at Braniff who gave her the account that she was playing so sexy with.

The Pussy Galore of Madison Avenue started out as a little fraidycat in small-town Ohio. Or, in the word of Helen Gurley Brown—another adwoman (before running *Cosmopolitan*) and putative heroine of the jet age who won the career game playing by male rules—Mary Wells Lawrence had been a "mouseburger." The Brown appellation signified a plain Jane who wasn't Bunny or Playmate or stewardess material. The best strategy for a mouseburger was the time-honored one of trying to find a Mr. Right to take care of her. What *Cosmo* added to the mix was advice on how this housekitten could erotically objectify herself into a sexual tigress and land an even righter Mr. Right. This was not the stuff of feminism.

Lawrence was born Mary Georgene Berg in 1928 in steelville Youngstown, Ohio, of the same heartland German stock that produced fellow Ohio airline moguls Eddie Rickenbacker and Frederick Rentschler. Her father was a traveling salesman of furniture; her mother was a buyer for a local department store. Teen Mary, whom everyone called Bunny, got her first taste of freedom and the sophistication for which she would become synonymous when her mother got her involved as a child actress in the Youngstown Playhouse. Her desire to act led to her escaping Youngstown's blast furnaces for the bohemia of New York's Hell's Kitchen to study under Sanford Meisner at the Neighborhood Playhouse School of the Theatre.

Mary Wells Lawrence later credited her year of learning Method acting as an invaluable boot camp for Madison Avenue, where every campaign was akin to mounting a Broadway show. However, Meisner didn't think she was ready for Broadway and sent her back to the Midwest, where she enrolled in the theater department of Carnegie Tech in Pittsburgh. Bunny Berg was cute, blond, and collegiate, but hardly a bombshell. So she did the mouseburger thing, ensnaring an engagement ring from Bert Wells, a handsome big man on campus headed for a big industrial design career. If she couldn't make it in New York on her own, she would ride there on his coattails. To build a nest egg for their eventual move to Manhattan, the mouseburger dropped out of Carnegie Tech and moved back to the family home in Youngstown, taking a lowly job writing ad copy for the department store where her mother worked. Her assignment was promoting sales in the store's bargain basement.

Eventually, Bunny and Bert got married and moved to New York, leading the same kind of conventional fifties gray-flannel-coupled urban existence that had driven Chicago adman Victor Lownes out of the arms of his wife and into the arms of Hugh Hefner. Like Lownes, Bunny Wells was soon champing at the Eisenhower bit. While her husband climbed the corporate ladder, getting a top job as art director of Ogilvy & Mather, she took a drudge job in the ad department of Macy's, then managed to score a lowly position in the emerging television department of the huge agency McCann Erickson, in Rockefeller Center, whose motto was "Truth Well Told." Even though the couple's joint income enabled them to live high on the hog on Sutton Place, the best place in Bunny's mind was no place in America. She divorced Bert Wells and took a slow boat to Europe, hoping to get an advertising job there.

The agencies in Europe then were too small to take on foreign talent. After a year abroad, Bunny Wells mouseburgered up once again, coming home and remarrying Wells and adopting two children, reaffirming her faith in an American Dream that had already bored her out of the country. She also took another job, this one at the hottest shop on Madison Avenue, Doyle Dane Bernbach. If McCann's motto was "Truth Well Told," Doyle Dane's should have been "The Awful Truth." In the sixties, Doyle Dane would become famous for bringing irony into a wasteland of earnestness with its "Think Small" Volkswagen and "We Try Harder" Avis campaigns. In 1959, when Wells was starting there as a copywriter and the 707s had just started flying, the firm landed the account of the French tourism authority, which wanted to inspire people to visit the French provinces and not just Paris. Paris was enough for Madison Avenue, who saw no virtues in the countryside that they couldn't find better on the left bank. In those days, Provence and the Loire Valley weren't considered magic; they were considered the deep sticks. Every other big agency turned France down, and every copywriter at Doyle Dane found excuses to avoid the job. So Bunny Wells, whom Bill Bernbach insisted on upgrading to the more serious Mary, got it by default. If Wells couldn't work *in* France, she could work *on* France. She was thrilled by the challenge.

Treating herself to an extended research trip from the Ardennes to the Dordogne, Mary Wells asked famed photographer Elliott Erwitt to create a shot of a Frenchman riding his bicycle on a tree-lined road, his tiny son and a huge baguette perched on the jump seat behind him. The ad turned out to be iconic and had the effect of sending thousands of American tourists exploring the paradise beyond Paris. It also made Mary Wells's name. In a business where clients play musical agencies, switching every few seasons, Doyle Dane kept the France account for a full decade, from 1959 to 1969.

This was basically the entire term of the presidency of Charles de Gaulle, who had been terribly concerned about the Hiltonization of French tourism. By luring the travelers away from the Paris Hilton to the country inns and converted châteaux of the beautiful provinces, Mary Wells was re-Frenching the tourist experience and thereby playing to De Gaulle's objectives. Doyle Dane's long campaign became known as "hip Gaullism." It included such ads as one of traditionally costumed Breton women with the warning "Five years from now it won't be the same," scaring travelers into "getting it while they can." Another ad addressed America's fear of French rudeness by painting a smiley face on a map of the country with the caption "There's a big smile on the face of France."

There was an even bigger smile on the face of Mary Wells when she left employeehood at Doyle Dane in 1964 to become a principal at Jack Tinker Associates, where she made waves with the famous Alka-Seltzer ad "Plop, plop, fizz, fizz, oh, what a relief it is" and then got the Braniff account that made her the undisputed Queen of Madison Avenue. Her first connection to what would revolutionize the way airlines sold themselves came in 1964, when two characters came into her office straight out of central casting, one looking like a cowboy and another looking like a movie star. Central casting turned out to be Continental Airlines. The cowboy turned out to be Continental's chairman, Bob Six, the movie star his corporate president, Harding Lawrence. Taking a page from the Juan Trippe "first is best" playbook, Six had made Los Angeles–based Continental the first airline to order the Concorde, the Anglo-French supersonic craft that promised to revolutionize flying even more than the 707 had. The plane was barely a glimmer in its makers' eyes and wouldn't be operating for nearly a decade. But Six wanted bragging rights, and he was looking for an agency to help.

Continental Airlines, best known for its Chicago–Los Angeles route, was a maverick American carrier whose plan for the Concorde was to create a unique and expensive Jet Set corridor between the West Coast and Hawaii. Because Continental wanted to cater to the Los Angeles celebrities who could now vacation in a newly accessible Hawaii, the Pacific-bound Concorde was conceived as "the movie-star route." Continental's kingpin, Bob Six, was a colorful, gun-toting, boot-wearing, horse-riding cowboy who was even more starstruck than Conrad Hilton. There must have been something in the southwestern desert that spawned the careers of both men and gave them a genetic susceptibility to show business. Or maybe it was just opposites attracting. Six was the best friend of John Wayne. He had married Ethel Merman after her Broadway triumph in *Annie Get Your Gun* convinced him she was a gal after his own heart. Merman may have gotten a man with a gun, but she couldn't keep him. Six divorced her and moved on to Audrey Meadows, Jackie Gleason's long-suffering spouse on television's *The Honeymooners*. Her sister Jayne was the wife of urbane television host Steve Allen.

Bob Six, who was six-six, was in reality even less of a cowboy than Hilton. His father was one of America's first plastic surgeons, his mother from a prominent California pioneer family. They lived in Sacramento. The family, with paternal Dutch roots, had one of America's largest collections of Rembrandts. Just as Hilton was prepped for Dartmouth, Six, who was born in 1907, was prepped for Annapolis. But no school could contain the massive Six, who, inspired by Charles Lindbergh, flew biplanes and started his own California air-sightseeing service. When that failed, he shipped off on a tramp steamer to Shanghai for two years, flying planes for the Chinese national airline. In the thirties, he returned to California and linked up with Jack Frye's TWA, which Howard Hughes would take over and vastly expand. In 1934, Six bought an El Paso to Pueblo, Colorado, puddle-jumping airline and built it into Continental, a rising colossus that was using the Concorde purchases as a dramatic public relations ploy.

Harding Lawrence, by far the handsomest man in American business, was a silver fox who was made for not just the cover of *Fortune* but *Esquire* as well. Born in 1920 in Drumwright, Oklahoma, Harding Luther Lawrence grew up in a fundamentalist family that moved to the relative prosperity of East Texas, where his father taught school and was a circuit-riding preacher. Lawrence was studying to become a lawyer when his plans were upended by World War II. Having been a wartime flight instructor, he joined a regional airline in Houston and worked his way through the system until he had become Bob Six's right hand at Continental. Lawrence was the perfect fifties family man, with a wife and three children, the oldest son oddly named State Rights, reflecting his father's Dixiecratic conservatism. That perfection was shattered the moment Lawrence laid eyes on Mary Wells. The erstwhile mouseburger was wearing her new success to very sexy effect, in sixties minis that showed off her million-dollar legs the same way Six and Lawrence planned to show off their billion-dollar Concorde. Their meeting also

AIR FORCE. Madison Avenue advertising czarina Mary Wells and her husband, Braniff Airlines chief Harding Lawrence, with a model of an Alexander Calder–decorated jet, early 1970s.

ended Mary Wells's attempt to renew her own married idyll with her husband. Wells and Lawrence both divorced their spouses and would become Big Business's "fun couple," marrying in 1967.

Lawrence had quickly left Six with his drawing-board "imaginary" Concorde to become president of Braniff, a Dallas regional airline that had been taken over in 1965 by Troy Post, a Texas corporate raider. Lawrence took Wells, his new love/ad guru, along for the ride they were planning for Braniff, now rebranded as Braniff International, from Texas backwater to intercontinental glamour. So confident was Wells in Lawrence's future success that she left Jack Tinker, lured away her cleverest associates, and started Wells, Rich, Greene, which immediately was hailed by the financial press as the "new" Doyle Dane Bernbach. So confident was Lawrence in Wells's abilities that he gave her untried new agency the Braniff account, worth over $6 million in annual billings. In one fell swoop, Wells was a "made" woman, though feminists might have caviled that she was more of an old-fashioned girl. In any event, she became a famous woman. Because of her looks, her style, her sex appeal, and her unconcealed romance with superstud Lawrence, Mary Wells, corporate "hotness" personified, was walking product placement. She was now able to utilize all the acting skills she had learned from Sanford Meisner at the Neighborhood Playhouse to seduce some of the nation's top corporate clients to her new firm.

Sexual politics aside, Mary Wells's work was what mattered, and that work was as radical a change from what had been happening with airline advertising as the new Brit rock of the Beatles and Rolling Stones was from the old Tin Pan Alley pop of Frankie Avalon and Fabian. All the excitement for the new jets had been in the air, not *on* the air, nor on the page. For all the fantasy, the travel, the space technology, Madison Avenue had been woefully short on poetic license until Mary Wells made the scene. The Pan Am ads, created by the behemoth J. Walter Thompson, were as corporate and unimaginative as the establishment tycoons with whom Juan Trippe lunched at the Cloud Club.

"You can meet them in London *tonight*," trumpeted one of the Thompson ads, depicting a stiffly dressed country-club couple fine-dining on starched linen with Big Ben looming in the distance. But maybe you didn't want to meet *them;* maybe you wanted to meet Mick Jagger. However, no one had thought of that yet. Most of the Pan Am ads just showed the big 707 soaring over the clouds and the ocean below. "Now you can fly the world famous Pan Am Jet Clippers across the Pacific and to South America as well as to 9 cities in Europe." Dullsville. The plane, J. Walter Thompson figured, was the money shot. Who needed anything else?

In 1961, Bob Six spiced things up a bit with his suggestive double-entendre Continental campaign, "The proud bird with the golden tail," which later devolved into "We move our tail for you." Mary Wells went way beyond that. While she was still at Jack Tinker, she came up with her first big Braniff ad, "The End of the Plain Plane." But this wasn't mere idle chatter, mere Mad Ave puffery. It signaled a total overhaul of the airline. Harding Lawrence was putting his money where Mary Wells's mouth was. After taking a fact-finding grand tour of all the airports in

North and South America served by Braniff, with its Latin slant, Wells issued her own Warren Commission–style report on the sorry state of airline aesthetics. She described the universal color scheme as "greige" and likened airports to prisoner-of-war camps. Planes, she found, were stuck in a military mind-set, comfort- and beauty-wise.

In retaliation, she had Braniff paint all its planes a rainbow of brilliant colors, from red to yellow to green to turquoise, which made them as exotic as flying saucers. She hired Alexander Girard, a Santa Fe–based Italian-born designer who had won kudos for his vibrant Spanish restaurant La Fonda del Sol in the Time & Life Building on Sixth Avenue, to redesign the interiors of Braniff's planes, first-class lounges, and dinnerware. Then she hired Italian count Emilio Pucci, another color master and the best childhood friend of Igor Cassini, to create new uniforms for the stewardesses, whom she upgraded to the British usage "air hostesses." Pucci's uniforms were the basis of Wells's next campaign, "The Air Strip," which in one sense was a big tease. Pucci had also designed tiny bikinis, which the stewardesses modeled in magazines but never wore on the planes.

Businessmen, thinking they were going to be joining the mile-high club, or at least get a live burlesque show aloft, suddenly began inventing excuses to fly down to South America. The most they got was a flash of betighted thigh. Still, the fix was in, and America's sexist corporate pigs made Braniff "their" airline. The tagline of one popular commercial was a purring voice asking, "Does your wife know you're flying with us?" Soon the Braniff hostesses were being referred to as "Pucci Galores."

If the "Air Strip" campaign created a universe of airborne sex maniacs, another Wells campaign created one of flying shoplifters. This television commercial showed a cute little old lady stuffing all of Girard's silverware, dishes, blankets, and pillows into an infinitely expandable carry sack. The ad ended with the little old lady driving an airport tractor hauling the brilliantly colored 707 behind her home to God knows where. The announcer's tag was "We're glad you like us, but please, let's not get carried away."

And then there was the classic "If you got it, flaunt it" series, which paired very, very odd couples of celebrities, seat by seat, strangers on a plane: Andy Warhol and Sonny Liston; Salvador Dalí and Whitey Ford; Mickey Spillane and Marianne Moore. The line was a lift from the 1968 hit *The Producers,* but homages to pop culture were Mary Wells's forte. Jet-commuting between Lawrence's Dallas headquarters and Wells's Manhattan headquarters, as well as their ranch in Arizona, their Cliffside home in Acapulco, and their villa on the French Riviera, the Lawrences were the only jet business couple who actually lived like the Jet Set. If Igor Cassini had kept his column, he would have made book on them. Notwithstanding their lack of prestige college degrees, they otherwise were precisely his kind of people.

If Igor's brother, Oleg, was considered the fashion designer of the Jet Set by virtue of his exclusive relationship to Jackie Kennedy, once she left the White House in 1963, a new talent emerged from the pop ferment in England who rightfully could be considered the premier designer of the entire jet age. As a woman, she was another of the era's handful of heroines, but like Mary Wells Lawrence, she achieved her heroism by arguably selling out her gender, turning the once staid working girls of all continents into the hottest sex objects the new world had ever seen. The woman was Mary Quant, and her invention was the miniskirt. Wells had come from the cynical world of advertising; Quant came from the even more jaded one of fashion. The real question was whether the mini was an act of revolution or one of enslavement.

Mary Quant was never a mouseburger. Although she didn't come from any privilege whatsoever (her parents were Welsh schoolteachers), she was a born (1928) artist and a born eccentric who had the great luck to link up at sixteen with the love of her life, who also was a born eccentric, yet also born to privilege and to the Mark Birleyish connections that grease the path of social mobility in England more than almost anywhere else. It's good to be the queen, and it's also good to know the queen. Mary Quant met her kinky Galahad at Goldsmiths' College, London's answer to the Rhode Island School of Design. He was Alexander Plunket Greene, an aristo-bohemian cousin of Bertrand Russell and the great-grandson of composer Hubert Parry ("Jerusalem"). His father's best friend from Oxford was Evelyn Waugh.

Young Alexander Plunket Greene, APG to everyone, was never interested in Oxford, only in art. His public school was Bryanston, a sort of pre-hippie Eton, which fed him into Goldsmiths', which fed him into Chelsea, which was London's cutting edge in the fifties. Greene was a six-two jazz-trumpet-playing fusion of Mick Jagger and Paul McCartney before they came on the scene. He dressed in his mother's silk pajamas and in raccoon coats. The minute he spied Mary Quant at Goldsmiths', he was smitten by her chic and by her legs, long perfect legs like those of Mary Wells. Quant flaunted them in super-short skirts and tights that were inspired by her love of ballet. The style was radical indeed for a postwar, tightly rationed gray London still dominated by frumpy women and gents with bowler hats and furled umbrellas. Quant was model-willowy and had her hair bobbed by a young East End stylist named Vidal Sassoon. She was an overnight fashion plate.

Just as Mary Wells and Harding Lawrence became the hot couple of American corporate life, APG and Mary Quant became the hot couple of the rudimentary English fashion scene, cool Britannia long before the fact. They moved in together, which was totally avant-garde. APG bragged how he coiffed Mary's pubic hair into the shape of a heart, then sent naked pictures of him and Mary to all their friends, nudity as tonsorial art. In 1955, they opened their boutique Bazaar on the Kings Road, with cool clothes Quant designed on the ground floor, and cool food APG cooked in the basement. Both the clothes and the food were revelations to a London inured to a grim Blitz mentality. Princess Grace and Prince Rainier were spotted dining there on a trip to London shortly after they were married. *Le tout* London, from the Oliviers to the Churchills to the Krays, followed in their wake. And that was before the music started.

Bazaar was bizarre. That was its great allure in a stratified stiff-upper-lip nation that prized resigned conventionality and tolerated eccentricity only in its upper class. APG was a classic upper-class eccentric, and he was the lure to all his fellow nobs and swells. Debutantes flocked to Bazaar to shop and to work as salesgirls. Their presence was all the validation the enterprise needed, akin to a By Appointment to Her Majesty seal of approval. Among Bazaar's foreign clients were Brigitte Bardot, Audrey Hepburn, and Leslie Caron, while rising photographers like David Bailey would hang around Bazaar to pull "birds." The most famous models of the Jet Set, Twiggy and Jean Shrimpton, were closely identified with Bazaar, while the Stones's first manager, Andrew Loog Oldham, worked for the APGs as a messenger boy before changing the course of rock. One of Quant's best friends was John Lennon, who bought his trademark black leather cap from Bazaar and whose stage fright she helped to conquer.

Huge publicity followed in the stars' and aristocrats' wake. Yet the designs Mary Quant was creating were anything but upper-crust. Instead, they were bubbling up from the street, if not from the Underground. Bazaar was a perfect balance of snob and Mob. Quant wasn't anti-fat; she just expected people who wore her clothes to be thin. Most people in England *were* thin of necessity. There wasn't enough food, and certainly not enough good food, in postwar England to allow people to get fat. Quant often said she had never seen a fat person before her first trip to the United States, where she would license her brand for untold millions. To her, it didn't matter whether the required angularity came from being poor and hungry or being rich and chic or being tyrannized by fashion magazines. Mary Quant would grow rich, though never fat, off thin women.

The style Mary Quant was trading in emphasized comfort and freedom, yet at the same time, it made the wearer a prisoner of male lust. Quant's half-naked appeal to voyeurism could not help but make the wearer feel self-conscious. Still, wasn't showing off the essence of fashion? The idea was to turn men on. The APGs became millionaires on Quant's mini (named after the MINI Cooper) and tights, her white detachable Peter Pan collars, her Jeepers Peepers eye shadow, her Blush Baby rouge, her Starkers foundation, her Pop Sox, her Booby Trap unwired brassieres. Quant went chemical, designing coats and dresses made of PVC, or polyvinyl chloride. The same way Mary Wells used color to spice up gray airplanes for Braniff, Mary Quant used colors to spice up gray postwar British faces and bodies. Even makeup became psychedelic, years before people started tripping.

Quant was nearly as skilled at creating advertising as she was at creating

SHORT CUT. London designer Mary Quant in one of her trademark miniskirts, flaunting her Order of the British Empire medal, 1966.

fashions. She designed the "Crybaby" campaign for her new waterproof mascara that wouldn't run, in tears or in rain. A huge poster of an eye, a tear, and unsmudged mascara became a totem above the Kings Road, a London version of *The Great Gatsby*'s Dr. T. J. Eckleburg optometry poster above the wasteland of Queens. In 1965, Quant joined the British invasion of America, creating a mass-market line for JCPenney. The strange bedfellows proved to be—at least dollar- and poundwise—a match made in the heaven of Wall Street, though women's-liberation skeptics complained that Mini Mary was turning the teens of two continents into jailbait. By 1966, for her contributions to the suddenly booming British economy, Mary Quant was invested by Queen Elizabeth with the Order of the British Empire.

Contrary to expectations, she refrained from wearing her miniskirt to the ceremony. The OBE for the APGs with their PVC was fitting proof that the rebels, and England itself, had come a long way, baby, in the transformational speed that was typical of the jet age.

Across the Channel in France, too, young women were wearing miniskirts, and not always purchased at Bazaar on ferry hops to London. The space-age designer André Courrèges was flashing minis around the same time as Mary Quant, who loved wearing his thigh-high boots with her tiny skirts. Courrèges also did his own PVC line. Yet somehow Mary Quant got all the credit, if only because fashion itself, *any* fashion, seemed such a dramatic departure in dowdy London that it became pressworthy. Once the Beatles emerged, adding to the youthquake started by the APGs, Vidal Sassoon, and the David Bailey photographic school of cool, Paris, barely two hundred miles away, suddenly seemed square and quaint, eclipsed by the British upheaval. France appeared almost unaware of the new youth culture. The "French Elvis," Johnny Hallyday, was actually a Belgian truck driver named Philippe Schmidt. His wife, the "yé-yé" girl Sylvie Vartan, was a pretty blond Bulgarian, but her record sales didn't begin to approach those of Marianne Faithfull or even Annette Funicello. French rock, or whatever it was, did not travel. When Brigitte Bardot did her shopping at Bazaar in London, one knew Paris was in trouble.

Yet one Parisienne did emerge as a beacon for women's success. And she did it without marrying the boss (even Jackie Kennedy did that) or turning women into fetish objects or trading on their (or her) sexuality. Hers was a completely pure success story, based on an uncanny understanding of the needs of the Jet Set. She was an unlikely beacon, but she would soon shine all over the world. This lighthouse of the night was Régine, the Queen of Clubs, who proved that for all the talk of democratization, for all the Pan Am tourist fares, for all the Frommer guides, snobbery and elitism still had a powerful effect. In nightclubs, as in restaurants, Parisian exclusivity proved to be an exportable commodity. Nothing could make a place more *in* than keeping people *out*.

Régine Zylberberg (an easy last name to drop) was precisely the kind of person most Paris maître d's would have given the bum's rush. She was chubby, small, unimposing, a sub-mouseburger in looks and presence. She looked like what she was, a Galician peasant, Sam Spiegel with a red wig. Régine was born in Brussels in 1929 to poor Polish-Jewish émigrés who couldn't even afford to get married. Belgium was the butt of most French ethnic jokes, and the other components of Régine's heritage didn't give her much of a leg up. Nor were her own legs anything like the Wells-Quant gams that might have propelled her—at least by sex appeal—out of her seemingly guaranteed obscurity. Furthermore, she was quickly abandoned: Her mother moved without her to Argentina when she was four.

Her baker-drinker-gambler father took Régine and her brother, Maurice, with him to Paris, where he managed a bistro in the poor, Arab-intensive district of Belleville. Eventually, he vanished as well. Régine spent the war years hiding out in the French countryside, first at a convent, where the Catholic girls tormented her for being Jewish, and then at an old-age home. She would later learn jujitsu to defend herself. It was said that all the lavish parties she threw as an impresario were to make up for the total absence of birthday celebrations in her bereft childhood.

After the war, teen Régine reunited with her brother back in Paris and worked as a maid and as a peddler, hawking brassieres and neckties on street corners. Her big break, in 1953, was getting hired as a hat-check girl at the Whisky à Go-Go, behind the Palais Royal, near where she had been street-selling on the Rue de Rivoli. She didn't stick to the job description for long. Instead, she became the entertainment. Régine had a mouth and she had a voice, which she used to sing Piaf chansons with wild abandon while balancing a champagne glass atop her head. She was also a great dancer and knew how to get a party started, leading the reluctant likes of Aristotle Onassis onto the tiny floor. The customers took to her, and what customers they were. Jean-Paul Belmondo. Alain Delon. Porfirio Rubirosa, the ultimate bon vivant, whom Régine would sit and listen to, drink after drink, until closing time at six A.M., when

Rubirosa drove off to the Bois de Boulogne in his Ferrari. She had iron discipline; she never drank or smoked.

The Whisky à Go-Go owed its origins to a World War II Aryan no-no. During the war, the Germans had shut down Paris's dance halls, which, the Germans feared, were playing black jazz. An alternative club, La Discotheque, opened in 1941, giving Parisians the chance to dance to records. In the austerity after the war, other discotheques proliferated, as it was far cheaper to play records than hire a band. The Whisky à Go-Go was one of these clubs, decorated with a tartan theme and crates of Scotch from floor to ceiling. The name was derived from an Ealing comedy called *Whisky Galore!*, about a little Scottish island that tries to plunder a huge cache of whiskey from a marooned ship. The French title of the film was *Whisky à Go-Go,* the "à go-go" a French idiom for abundance. The Whisky's chief claim to fame, aside from its wild hat check girl, was that it had Paris's first jukebox, with a lot of American early rock on it. Soon Régine was promoted to disc jockey. She proved to be a masterful mixer and was surely the first celebrity DJ who didn't build her reputation on the radio.

By 1958, Régine had charmed enough rich men, in particular one of the Rothschilds, at the Whisky that she got backing to start her own disco, called Régine's, on Rue du Four in the heart of the Quartier Latin. Her first Jet Set client was the dour J. Paul Getty, whom she cajoled into dancing with her. Among her other big names were Sam Spiegel, Zsa Zsa Gabor (Conrad Hilton was long gone), Darryl Zanuck, Salvador Dalí, Brigitte Bardot, Françoise Sagan, Frederic Chandon of the champagne dynasty, fellow Pole Roman Polanski, and Claude Terrail, there every night after he closed the Tour d'Argent. From the day she opened, she hung a "complet" (full) sign at the door, making it impossible to get in unless she knew you. At the beginning, the place was completely empty a lot of nights. But it kept its impossible standards, and in time, a star was born.

Régine did things that no other disco owner did, like serving her clientele a spaghetti dinner at three a.m. and giving all the regulars the most thoughtful gifts. She cultivated the French intelligentsia, like Sagan and Sartre and André Malraux, and invited them to special dinners at her apartment above the disco. Even in Belleville with her father, she always lived above the store. In France, an intellectual clientele provided a unique cachet, proof that Régine's was not just for the mindless rich. She put on special events, like an all-white Jean Harlow night, where all the women wore white satin and the men white tie, a white entrance carpet was rolled out, and white Rollses ferried the guests. Also, Régine was known to have the most sympathetic ear in Paris. Even men like Rubirosa and Onassis could get lonely, and she was always there. A major turning point came in early 1961 when the traveling cast of *West Side Story* visited the club and brought Régine the Chubby Checker recording of Hank Ballard's "The Twist." It never stopped playing. The Jet Set had found its dance.

Meanwhile, her international habitués got busy knocking Régine off. The Cassini brothers loved what they saw, and with Eddie Gilbert's backing, they re-created it in New York as Le Club, carefully not inviting Régine to the opening. Mark Birley, a frequent Channel-hopper when visiting his sister Maxime de la Falaise, a Régine's regular with her daughter, Loulou, and Loulou's boss, Yves St. Laurent, loved what he saw, and *did* welcome Régine to Annabel's. She provided lots of helpful advice to Birley in starting his club. Still, like most of her countrymen, she had no interest at the time in France's historical enemy. Mary Quant notwithstanding, she didn't believe the British were capable of style and taste. Even Régine could make mistakes.

Régine had the elite Paris night all to herself until the latter sixties, when a tough ex–soccer player named Jean Castel opened his own disco a few blocks away from her on the Rue Princesse. Castel managed to pitch his appeal to the children of the rich and famous, the *jeunesse doré,* and because everyone wanted to feel as young as their kids, suddenly, Régine had a rival. In 1968, ceding St. Germain to Castel, she moved to new quarters in Montparnasse, where she called her club New Jimmy'z, Old Jimmy's being one of the dance halls the Nazis shut down (the "Z" at the end was for Zylberberg). Paris wasn't everything anymore. Régine had begun creating an empire, first in Monte Carlo, where her club Maona was named not after something in the South Seas but as an acronym of her top customers Maria (Callas) and Onassis. Soon Rio would follow, then the world.

Success seemed to run in the Zylberberg genes. While Régine was becoming queen of the night, her younger brother, Maurice, was becoming the prince of fashion. Starting in lowly jobs in the Paris *sentier,* or garment district, he rose to become a manufacturer, making the clothes for Pierre Cardin and Yves St. Laurent. The two would fight it out over who was more famous, the brother of Régine or the sister of Maurice. The one thing they could agree on was never to forgive their mother. Once her children had become famous, she returned to France from Argentina, assuming they would take care of her for life. Both refused to see her.

Régine was less successful in her private affairs than in her public ones. Soon after she moved to New Jimmy'z, at age forty, she finally fell in love, a first in a life lived totally on the defensive. The object of her affections was Roger Choukroun, a sensitive, handsome Moroccan Jewish computer engineer a decade her junior whom a *Vogue* editor brought to Régine's new club. Choukron had preferred to go to Castel. Régine's crowd was too famous, too intimidating. He wanted something less pressured. But the editor insisted. Régine dragged Choukroun onto the floor, then sent him right back. "You are a terrible dancer," she passed judgment. "Go sit." His interest piqued by the put-down, like that of the countless wannabe Jet Setters rejected at her door, Choukron began coming back to the club night after night. Although he may not have developed into a disco Fred Astaire, his persistence appealed to Régine, as did his good looks. They were married within the year.

The self-making of Régine, out of whole cloth, was surely an inspiration, a Dale Carnegie course, for sixties feminists. However, there weren't that many of them to be inspired. Feminism was gestating in the mind of the housewife turned magazine writer Betty Friedan. In 1963, the same year her *Feminine Mystique* was published, her fellow Smith College alumna Gloria Steinem worked as a Bunny in the New York Playboy

Club to do an article for *Show* magazine. Steinem's boss was the model-chasing billionaire Huntington Hartford, the quintessential sexist male of the Jet Set. The bottom line of the era was that most women were anything but "liberated." Liberation to them meant wearing a Quant mini or no bra, not so much to move easily and feel free but as a sexy means to achieve the Gurley Brown end of getting a man. Being a stewardess, a Bunny, a Playmate was, like becoming a movie star, a respectable fantasy. Just look at what the secret satyr John F. Kennedy was getting away with in the White House, cavorting with a panoply of females, from innocent interns to jaded celebrities.

When Adlai Stevenson, the Democratic presidential nominee, addressed the 1955 graduating class at Friedan's and Steinem's Smith College, he defended the housewife's worthy task of catering to the needs and whims of the Kennedy-esque archetype he called "Western Man." "Your job," he exhorted the brainy graduates, "is to keep him Western. We will defeat totalitarianism, authoritarian ideas only by better ideas." That was Stevenson's idea of how the Smithies could best use their expensive liberal arts education, by being highbrow geishas to their Ivy League spouses and thereby inspire them to win the Cold War.

The year of Kennedy's assassination, 1963, capped one of the vintage periods of international scandal and mystery that had kicked off with the death of Marilyn Monroe in August 1962. This period, a dark age for women, saw a climax of conduct-unbecoming Jet Set behavior, both decadent and lawless, that came to a sobering halt when JFK was gunned down in Dallas. Before that, the news seemed to be dominated by famous men, fine "Western Men," in Stevenson's phrase, behaving badly, very badly. The public was still feverishly speculating whether the sainted Kennedys killed Marilyn when Eddie Gilbert fled to Rio, shattering the myths of Wall Street probity, and then Igor Cassini plunged from grace to oblivion. In England, that greatest of all global sexcapades, the Profumo Scandal, would also erupt in this time frame, bringing an end to a certain type of English old-boy leadership and casting the revered British aristocracy in the darkest of shadows.

Aside from the Profumo Affair, England had another blockbuster in

1963, a reverse daily double for an embattled peerage. This was the case known as the Argyll Divorce. The action concerned Margaret, the Duchess of Argyll, the beautiful commoner daughter of a Scottish millionaire. Her husband, the Duke of Argyll, alleged that she had committed adultery with a grand total of eighty-eight men, including three royals; two cabinet ministers, one of whom was Duncan Sandys, the son-in-law of Winston Churchill; the German diplomat brother of ex-Nazi Wernher von Braun, the father of rocket science; and the American movie star and ex-husband of Joan Crawford, Douglas Fairbanks, Jr.

In her day, the duchess, born Margaret Whigham, was considered the most beautiful girl in England. When she married the American playboy-golfer Charles Sweeny in 1933, Cole Porter immortalized her in "You're the Top" with the lyric "You're Mussolini, you're Mrs. Sweeny, you're Camembert." The most titillating evidence in this longest (four years) of British divorce trials were the "headless horseman" photos of the duchess performing fellatio and other lewd acts on one of her lovers, cropped at the neck. No one knew or ever found out who had taken the pictures, which were authenticated by the courts. Chief suspect was Sandys, then minister of defense. The Conservative prime minister Harold Macmillan insisted that Sandys be examined by a Harley Street urologist, who concluded that Sandys's pubic hair did not match that in the photos.

Now suspicion fell on Fairbanks, whose handwriting most closely matched the inscription "thinking of you" on one of the Polaroid photos, all taken in the duchess's "party flat" in Mayfair while the poor duke was all alone up at his Inverary Castle in Scotland. Now happily married to an ex-wife of Huntington Hartford, the swashbuckling Fairbanks steadfastly denied the charges. Although the headless man's identity was never fully determined, the duke finally won the case and got his divorce. The presiding judge blasted the duchess as "a highly sexed woman who has ceased to be satisfied with normal sexual activities" and castigated her for her "disgusting sexual activities to gratify a debased sexual appetite." She moved into the Grosvenor House Hotel, kept on partying, and would die penniless.

As Al Jolson had sung, the judge, Lord Denning, who would later that scandalous year of 1963 head a commission on the Profumo case, "ain't seen nothin' yet." The Duchess of Argyll, for all her kinks, was in her fifties when all her perversions were going on. The world was riveted by her name and her fame, but the humiliation of a shameless middle-aged lady could not compare to the wild orgies of the teenage protagonists in the Profumo Affair. The duchess was Old Guard, old hat, and just plain old, but the Profumo girls, who were straight off the floor of Mary Quant's Bazaar, were the faces of a new and swinging London. These weren't debs or heiresses but real girls, poor girls, having real fun and infiltrating the Jet Set.

The whole world was vicariously riveted by these gorgeous English girls, Christine Keeler and Mandy Rice-Davies, who became role models of supersonic upward mobility. These were the girls other girls wanted to be. Most young ladies of the day didn't want to be Mary Wells, because few could write great copy. They didn't hope to be Mary Quant, because few could design great clothes. And they didn't think they'd ever be Régine, because few could match her great outrageous chutzpah. But they could relate to Christine and Mandy the same way they related to the advice Helen Gurley Brown dished out in *Cosmo*. They just had to take Gurley Brown's philosophy of pleasing a man one step further, to its inevitable conclusion. These blooming English roses were a new generation's Horatio Algerettes. Their story could be called *How to Win Friends and Influence People Through Sex*.

The stunning Christine Keeler was often compared to supermodel Jean Shrimpton, minus opportunity. Shrimpton came from a relatively posh background; Keeler grew up in a converted railway carriage. She had a predatory stepfather and had to sleep with a knife under her pillow. She had come to London at fifteen in 1957, worked in a dress shop in Soho, got pregnant by a black American GI, and lost the child. Then she took a job as a stripper at Murray's Cabaret Club, a Soho fleshpot straight out of *Expresso Bongo*. She was amazed that despite her own horror at the havoc pregnancy had wreaked on her body, men were still dying to ogle her. In her world of buffeted helplessness, that objectifica-

THE GIRL CAN'T HELP IT. London call girl Christine Keeler, provocative center of the Profumo scandal that toppled the prime minister, going off to see the judge, 1963.

tion was empowering. Within all the indignity, she found dignity and projected the grand illusion of confidence. At Murray's, Christine met Mandy Rice-Davies, the bubbly blond daughter of a policeman and an occasional model who worked auto shows at Earl's Court. Both girls needed money and would do anything to get it.

Opportunity knocked in the presence of the twin serpents in the Eden that was swinging London: two men, one English, one American, who could connect beautiful girls to powerful men who could make their wildest dreams come true. The Englishman was an osteopath/sociopath named Dr. Stephen Ward. The son of a minister, Ward had worked as a carpet salesman before traveling to Missouri to attend a dubious osteopathy school. While the difference between a chiropractor and an osteopath is hazy, and neither is an accredited MD, Stephen Ward was undisputedly great with his hands. During World War II, Ward had been court-martialed for treating officers for muscle problems without the proper credentials. He was demoted to being a stretcher-bearer in India but, proving brilliant at networking, ended up treating Mahatma Gandhi for a stiff neck and won his friendship.

Back in London after the war, Ward began working at a clinic. One day he got a call from American ambassador Averell Harriman, looking for the best man in London to cure his aching back. Ward volunteered himself, and a celebrity practice was born. Apparently, credentials were irrelevant. The rich and famous loved Ward's results. Harriman referred Winston Churchill, who referred Duncan Sandys, who referred his sexual blood brother, Douglas Fairbanks, Jr. Word got out to Hollywood, and Ava Gardner signed up, as did Mary Martin. But the most eventful of Ward's celebrated patients was Lord William Astor, the hypochondriac son of the legendary Virginian Lady Nancy Astor and now master of Cliveden, one of the stateliest of England's stately homes and locus of the prewar Cliveden Set, an upper-class cadre sympathetic to Hitler. Lord Astor got so addicted to Ward's magic fingers that he gave him a cottage on the Cliveden estate where Ward would spend weekends.

Ward had two other great talents. The first was portraiture. Churchill, an amateur painter himself, declared Ward's genius, and soon Ward was sketching the faces of the same high and mighty whose spines he was manipulating. Among his royal subjects were the Duke of Edinburgh, the Earl of Snowden, the Duke and Duchess of Kent, and Churchill himself. Ward became an even more in-demand portraitist than Mark Birley's famous father, Sir Oswald, and he was very much part of the Birley-Aspinall Clermont set.

Ward's other great talent was finding the prettiest women in London and creating his own harem. He haunted the Soho clubs, such as Murray's, where he discovered Christine and Mandy, and he began inviting them out to Cliveden, where Christine caught Bill Astor's roving eye. Astor was already married to one of England's top models, Bronwen Pugh, but if you were an Astor, there were never enough top models, and Christine was an undiscovered gem.

It was during a pool party at Cliveden in 1961 that Ward made the fatal introduction of Christine to John Profumo, the dashing secretary of state for war in the Macmillan cabinet and the rising star of his Conservative Party. Profumo was married to British movie star Valerie Hobson, but just as one top model wasn't enough for his host, Lord Astor, one cinema celebrity wasn't enough for Profumo. At the same party was Yevgeni Ivanov, an equally dashing naval attaché at London's Soviet embassy who helped Ward get papers to go to Russia to sketch Khrushchev and other Politburo leaders. Ivanov wasn't married to anyone. He was on the prowl. London at that lofty level was very sophisticated. There was nothing untoward about mixing capitalists and Communists, as there would have been in the still-Red-scared United States. Profumo and Ivanov were equally smitten with Christine, and there was the rub.

Enter the American serpent in the garden, Tom Corbally, who was a more ruggedly masculine version of Stephen Ward and who shared overlapping harems. Corbally was arguably the most connected American in the entire Jet Set. He knew all the same power hitters as Ward, and he was more ruthless in that knowledge and in his manipulation of his enviable address book. Furthermore, he was truly the playboy of the Western world. Unlike Ward, who was a "friend" and confidant to his girls, Tom Corbally never met a beautiful woman he didn't sleep with. How could they resist? He looked like Jason Robards, dressed like the Duke of Windsor, and sounded like Johnny Cash minus the twang. His was the voice of America, deep, powerful, certain. A good friend of Ian Fleming, he was later known as "the American James Bond."

Nobody knew what Tom Corbally did. He lived in splendor in Mayfair, near the Duchess of Argyll. He wasn't on the list of eighty-eight, though that didn't mean he shouldn't have been. He had been linked to Doris Duke and Barbara Hutton, among other heiresses. Heiresses loved him, as did call girls. They all did. He just didn't appear on lists or in little black books. He didn't have an office. Some thought he was in advertising, some thought business of the vaguest sort. Everyone just assumed he was a spy. It was a good assumption, though what Tom Corbally was, was a master fixer. He supposedly fixed things for President Roosevelt, who had assigned him as an aide to General MacArthur to report back on the "old soldier" so the president could stay a step ahead. Of course, this, like almost everything about Corbally, was off the record.

On the record, he had been in the Office of Strategic Services (OSS), the precursor of the CIA, at its inception in World War II. In 1956, he had briefly married the tennis champion "Gorgeous" Gussie Moran, she of the shocking lace panties. He had beaten out Eddie Gilbert for her favors but stayed close to Gilbert far longer than he did to his wife. Corbally had come from a line of cloak-and-dagger men. He was born in Newark, New Jersey, in 1921. His grandfather, an Irish potato famine–era immigrant, had been a police inspector who then founded a detective agency. His father worked for the Newark municipality. Naturally, Corbally knew his Hoboken neighbor Frank Sinatra, whose mother, Dolly, was active in local politics.

An early bloomer, Corbally learned to wear a tux, cross the Hudson, and hang out with the debs at the Stork Club starting at age fifteen. He quickly concluded that the world was bifurcated between the girls you slept with and took to the relatively downmarket Copacabana and the girls you kept your hands off, bought orchids for, and took to the august Stork. Corbally was a college man, but not much of one. He attended the Catholic school Seton Hall for two years, until mid-1941, before Pearl Harbor forced America into the war. Itching to fight, he quit school and joined the Royal Canadian Air Force, flying Spitfires over Germany. He went on the ground in Germany after the war to do intelligence work, then he began his secret shuttle diplomacy between New York and Europe.

In New York, he was closely allied to Gotham's master lawyer-fixer, Roy Cohn, the judge's son who became the pet of J. Edgar Hoover and the scourge of American Communism as the terrifying right hand of Senator Joseph McCarthy. In London, Corbally was close to everyone who mattered. The hottest ticket in the empire was to one of his fabled Mayfair sex parties, his flat having become a kind of advance Playboy Club long before Victor Lownes ever got to town. After one of these orgies, Corbally injured his knee. At a subsequent, more decorous event, Stephen Ward noticed Corbally's limp, introduced himself, and went to work. In moments, Corbally's pain had vanished, and a friendship was forged. What they mainly had in common were passions for famous people and striking women, though the two showed their love in very different ways.

Ward had been married once, in 1949, to a fashion model. That union was briefer than Corbally's with Gussie Moran. Ward's wife left him after six weeks. Ward had many other public liaisons with high-profile beauties, usually models, such as one with Eunice Bailey, the top Christian Dior mannequin of the fifties, but the romances were reported to be all show and no go. Ward had Christine Keeler and Mandy Rice-Davies move in to his Wimpole Mews flat soon after they met. He was one of the few men on earth who could be that close to the sex kittens and not give in to lustful thoughts. Meanwhile, Tom Corbally, introduced to the girls by Ward, did everything with them that Ward did not.

While Ward would have liked to Pygmalionize the girls, Corbally preferred to accentuate the negatives and keep them as kinky Eliza Doolittles. He gave them top billing on his orgy list and began stirring the pot of temptation with both Profumo and Ivanov. As a spymaster, Corbally knew the girls could obtain secret pillow talk from Ivanov that Corbally's top Washington contacts surely could utilize. What he wanted them to obtain from Profumo was less clear. Did Washington want to

FETE ACCOMPLI. CIA key man in Europe Tom Corbally (standing center, left) and restaurateur Claude Terrail (standing center, right) partying at Paris nightclub Scheherazade with rich American friends, 1960.

compromise him in some way that could destabilize the Macmillan Conservative government? Who could know? It was always unwise to try to second-guess the inscrutable Tom Corbally.

The plot thickened thanks to the new 707. Two girls from the Ward-Corbally London orgy circuit were also plying their oldest profession in New York, and both had been linked to President Kennedy. The two were Suzy Chang, a Chinese playgirl often seen at the bar at 21; and Mariella Novotny, a Czechoslovakian former Soho stripper, like Christine and Mandy. The Czech stunner had married a Soho underworld character named Hod Dibben who owned the notorious Black Sheep Club, a hangout of the Kray twin gangsters.

Dibben installed his new bride, four decades his junior, in a stately home in Sussex and a stately flat in Eaton Place. Given a long leash by her husband, Novotny loved the new 707s and was soon flying back and forth between London and New York, running an international call-girl ring and attempting to rival that in Paris masterminded by Tom Corbally's close friend, the celebrated sex agent Madame Claude. Mariella's man on the ground in Manhattan was the prominent television producer Harry Alan Towers, whose prestigious British TV movies were partially financed by his friend Huntington Hartford, that insatiable devourer of models. Towers was also a good friend of JFK's brother-in-law Peter Lawford, who was making his own mark on TV as the Thin Man.

Lawford, in turn, was John Kennedy's chief procurer. He reportedly had Chang and Novotny dress as nurses and attend to the president's always ailing back. Whether Kennedy ever enlisted the redoubtable aid of Stephen Ward in this regard is not known but not unlikely, especially since Ward was treating JFK's Rat Pack buddy Frank Sinatra during this period. Sinatra often sent his valet George Jacobs to massage Kennedy; if the chairman had been pleased with Ward's handiwork, he probably would have bestowed him on the president. Not to mention all the fringe benefits of Ward's harem. This was when Mariella Novotny was at the height of her reputation as a sexual hostess. She organized a famous orgy in London that Keeler, Ward, and Corbally all attended, known as the Feast of the Peacocks, where she cooked rare peacock for dinner, then donned a corset and brandished a whip for the just dessert of all the submissives. One of these pain-seekers was the distinguished film director Anthony Asquith (*Pygmalion*), whose father had been prime minister. Under Novotny's orders, Asquith served guests cocktails wearing only a maid's apron and a black leather mask.

Chang and Novotny also worked the Washington, D.C., sex circuit, their assignations arranged by LBJ aide and Mr. Fixit Bobby Baker, the Texas lobbyist. Suffice it to say that J. Edgar Hoover, the ultimate voyeur, was on top of the whole situation. The knowledge of presidential peccadilloes gave Hoover immense power as well as thrills. In March 1961, New York police raided Towers's Fifty-fifth Street apartment and arrested him and Novotny on international white slavery charges that involved as clients seemingly half the diplomats at the United Nations. Novotny absconded and smuggled herself aboard the England-bound *Queen Mary*, where it was far easier to get lost than on Pan Am's Clipper to London. Lawford was able to use his influence to get the charges against Towers dropped.

Chastened by her brush with the law, Mariella Novotny stayed put in London, where she had known both Profumo and Ivanov, all part of the Ward-Corbally movable feast. But both men were too obsessed with Christine Keeler to be distracted by Novotny. J. Edgar Hoover was not amused by the New York sex bust. The New York cops thought they were just doing their job; Hoover wanted to keep the honey trap going, for all the dirt it provided him. With Novotny out of action, Corbally in July 1962 helped dispatch Christine and Mandy to New York for fun and profit and possibly the delectation of the head of the FBI, giving them all the right numbers to call. It was widely rumored that one of their to-do items during the two weeks in the Big Apple was to spend some time with President Kennedy.

Back in London, as the clock ticked down to the Cuban missile crisis that October, and relations between East and West grew increasingly tense, Christine Keeler was in the heat of her own East-West ménage à trois of sexual politics with Profumo and Ivanov. The previous year, she'd had an abortion. She said it was Profumo's child, but it also could have been Ivanov's. Or someone else's, specifically that of Johnny Edgecombe, her jealous Jamaican drug-dealer boyfriend who followed her to Stephen Ward's flat in Wimpole Mews and fired a gun at her. This was the shot heard 'round the world, and its echo broke the scandal wide open.

Despite her involvement with the upper strata, Christine Keeler seemed to feel more at home in the depths. She had a thing for Jamaicans. She had fallen for her marijuana dealer, an ex-con named Lucky Gordon, right after she and Mandy had returned from their glamorous trip to Manhattan. And then she two-timed him with his fellow miscreant Johnny Edgecombe. The two Jamaicans had been involved in a knife fight over her at a Soho club called the All-Nighter. That had scared Christine into breaking with both men, inciting Edgecombe's pistol attack. The shots brought the police to Ward's flat, and Edgecombe was arrested and charged. Both Christine and Mandy were there, and while the shooting might not otherwise have achieved much traction, the combination of a black man, two white goddesses, and the house of the most famous healer in England was the stuff of dreams for tabloid reporters.

The siren call of Fleet Street, with its checkbook journalism, was music to the ears of Christine, who, despite her wealthy call-girl clients, never seemed to have any money. For a thousand pounds, she told her story to the *Sunday Pictorial*. What started out as the tale of an innocent country girl in the big city, torn between the high society of Stephen Ward and the low society of the Jamaicans, quickly stepped up to become a nail-biting saga of international intrigue, wherein Christine embellished herself as a Mata Hari being used by Ivanov to extract secrets about nuclear warheads from Profumo.

Ivanov had never asked for any such thing from Christine. This, to him, was strictly man's work. He had asked his friend Ward to get the warhead information from Profumo, and Ward had shared his conflict over the cloak-and-dagger request with Christine. But now, to make a good story great, she lied and recast herself as the fulcrum of the tale, the woman between. She hated both Ivanov and Profumo for using her without commitment. Now she would have a hooker's revenge and become famous to boot.

The Cuban missile crisis tensions had resulted in the recall of Ivanov to Moscow. John Profumo was left alone in England to face the music. The Americans, with all their connections to the matter, were getting nervous as well. After Christine Keeler's tabloid confessions hit the newsstands, the American ambassador, David Bruce—incidentally, Juan Trippe's cousin by marriage—turned to Tom Corbally, the man who knew everything, for an explanation if not an exegesis. Corbally had previously introduced one of Bruce's Mellon in-laws to Mandy Rice-Davies, whom Mellon had taken to Paris for a wild weekend. They were all in this, very deep. Responding to the ambassador's request, which, notwithstanding his friendship with Profumo, Corbally could not refuse, he arranged a lunch for himself, Ward, and Bruce in the café of Simpson's in Piccadilly, a midrange department store where none of them was likely to be recognized. Wanting to dodge the bullets in what promised to be an endless fusillade, the Nijinsky-like Corbally danced out of harm's way by throwing his ostensible pal Profumo under the double-decker London bus.

Once Corbally, with Ward's aid, had told the ambassador the full and awful truth about the erotic triangle of Profumo, Ivanov, and Keeler, Bruce came clean by passing the information to Harold Macmillan. The Labour Party, smelling blood, called on Profumo to defend himself. In March 1963, the secretary of state for war responded to Labour's summons. Speaking eloquently, as was his wont, on the floor of the House of Commons, he denied everything. He conceded that he had a nodding acquaintance with Christine Keeler through Ward, but nothing more. He declared, fatally, that there was "no impropriety" in their relationship. The prime minister, knowing full well from Ambassador Bruce that Profumo was lying, nonetheless stood behind the prevarications of his minister, a loyalty that would lead to his own downfall.

On June 5, cornered by Labour leaders who by then had been leaked the revelations of the Corbally luncheon, Profumo had to eat his words and resign his post, ending a brilliant career that most Britons had assumed would culminate at 10 Downing Street, not crash and burn in Tom Corbally's bachelor pad. The next day Stephen Ward, Corbally's partner in crime, but not Corbally, was arrested and charged with pandering, living off the immoral earnings of Christine Keeler, Mandy Rice-Davies, and other prostitutes for the last two years. He was refused bail, as a flight risk, and because it was feared he might use his enormous connections to influence witnesses. The court need not have worried. In late July, after Christine, Mandy, and several other admitted working girls testified against him, Ward took an overdose of Nembutal sleeping pills. He was in a coma when the jury returned a guilty verdict, and he died three days later. The king of Jet Set networking was dead. Long live the new king Tom Corbally.

Christine Keeler herself went to jail for perjury in the subsequent trial of her lover Johnny Edgecombe. When she was released, she had a brief fling as a boldfaced name of Swinging London, dating the likes of Victor Lownes and Warren Beatty before going back to her roots, marrying a day laborer and at last becoming a mother. Mandy Rice-Davies ended her friendship with Christine, moved to Munich in 1964 to become a cabaret singer, and in 1966 married a rich Israeli who set her up in her own disco. Mandy's quickly became the Régine's of Tel Aviv.

Harold Macmillan and the Conservatives went down in a bitter defeat as Harold Wilson's Labour Party took over in 1964 and paved the way for a new England dominated no longer by the Clermont Set but by Labour types like the Beatles. Lord Astor, whose Cliveden was where the seeds of the aristocracy's destruction were planted, had a nervous breakdown over losing the curative skills of Stephen Ward. His model wife, Bronwen Pugh, hired a Catholic exorcist to perform a ceremony cleansing Cliveden, and particularly the Ward cottage, of its resident evil. It didn't work. The exorcist had to return and repeat the ceremony a month later when the cottage's next tenant, like Ward, committed suicide. Lord Astor died in 1966, after which his widow vacated the estate and leased it to Stanford for its junior-year-abroad program, a Jet Set version of student aid. The stated goal was to promote better Anglo-American understanding. That may have been what Stephen Ward and Tom Corbally thought they were doing, but it never hurt to try, try again.

By the time Stanford-in-Britain moved in to a presumably exorcised Cliveden, women's studies had become an important part of the curriculum, there and everywhere else. The scandals of the times showed how far women would have to go before the 1968 Virginia Slims "You've come a long way, baby" cigarette campaign would memorialize their dramatic progress. In 1963, most of that progress was ahead of them. Betty Friedan's bestseller, a wake-up call to complacent women, had been an unspoken rebuke to the Jet Set's bad boys, the very men Freidan's readers probably had dreamed of as ideal marriage material.

Gilbert, Cassini, Profumo, the Kennedys—all these enviable men were shown to have feet of clay that all the Gucci shoes in Florence couldn't cover up. The mighty had fallen. Nevertheless, Juan Trippe wasn't worried at all. Even as the Jet Set was being discredited and losing its mystique, Trippe had never believed in relying on the swells in first class for Pan Am's expansion. No, Trippe was much more interested in those ambitious Virginia Slims women and those kids headed for junior year at Cliveden. The Jet Set may have imploded, but where Juan Trippe was concerned, the sky had no limit. His unbounded optimism and his gambler's lust for risk proved to be the hubris that brought the Jet Set era to a close and came close to bringing the entire go-go airline industry to a giant fatal crash.

13

The Tripping Point

"BILL ALLEN TOOK OFF HIS COAT A FEW TIMES" WAS HOW JUAN TRIPPE, IN HIS classically understated style, described the five years of Herculean labors from 1965 to 1970 through which he put Allen, the head of Boeing, in creating the 747.

"It brings sweat to the palms of my hands" was how the equally understated Allen described his reaction to the 747, the biggest plane in commercial aviation history and, for a long while, what seemed to be the biggest disaster, one that threatened to bankrupt the industry.

The deal was made, as it was so often in those glory days of Old Boyism, on *The Wild Goose,* the yacht Allen and Trippe leased from John Wayne for their annual Alaskan salmon fishing trip. Each man loved a dare, and the very idea of the 747 was, like the 707 before it, one of the dares of the century, a dare waiting to happen. "If you build it, I'll buy it," the Yale man Trippe challenged the Harvard man Allen. "If you'll buy it, I'll build it," Allen replied. And they were off, on one of the most dramatic gambles of all time.

The 747 came to be known as Trippe's Folly, a leviathan that would savage the most brilliant reputation in the business of airlines, or even the business of business, rather than becoming its consummation. Actually, for Juan Trippe, the 747 wasn't intended to be his swan song. Trippe didn't sing swan songs; he expected to rule the skies forever. For him, the 747 was simply the next step on the journey from the 707 to the SST, or supersonic transport. Trippe's credo was that bigger was better, but faster was best of all. By 1965, he'd realized that his 707, which had seemed like a rocket at its birth in 1958, was already obsolete, a victim of its own success.

But what success. The 707 had quickly vanquished the ocean liner, consigning it to the dry docks of history. By 1965, 83 percent of all transatlantic travel was on jets, a dominance that was increasing every year, with the airlines' phenomenal growth rate of 15 percent and attendant multiplication of stock prices. Airlines were the technology stocks of the early sixties in what was known as the Kennedy bull market, the one that, when it morphed into a bear in 1962, would maul Eddie Gilbert and send him 707ing down to Rio. But if an investor held on to Pan Am or Boeing, the sky was truly the limit. The Trippe-Allen fishing trip

BIG BUSINESS. William Allen and Juan Trippe board their riskiest joint venture, the massive 747, 1970.

was the tipping point of jet travel, and of the social phenomenon of the jet set, which was set to explode from exclusivity into something all-inclusive. Unfortunately, the combination of arrogance, economics, and social change turned this tipping point into a tripping point, one of the greatest stumbles that big business would ever take.

As a symbol of Trippe's overweening self-confidence, he erected the fifty-nine-story Pan Am Building, widely considered the ugliest, most boastful skyscraper in Manhattan. In 1963, at the height of his game, Trippe moved Pan Am out of New York's most beautiful tower, the Chrysler Building, into fifteen floors of this brutal Walter Gropius–designed blight, which overshadowed the landmarks of Grand Central Station and the graceful New York General Building, and, standing enormously in the center of Park Avenue, ruined the view down Park to lower Manhattan for all time. The building supplied Trippe the superlative he required: the world's largest commercial space. It also had the biggest mortgage—$70 million—of any commercial property in the city's history.

Trippe was of the "If you've got it, flaunt it" school long before Mel Brooks ever coined the phrase or Mary Wells Lawrence turned it into a commercial. The Pan Am Building was most of all a giant commercial for Pan Am. Trippe tried to build thirty-foot-tall letters spelling out Pan Am atop the behemoth, but the city bargained him down to fifteen and, in reaction to this advertisement for himself, would soon pass a law prohibiting such logo-mongering atop Gotham's skyscrapers. Missing his Cloud Club at the Chrysler, Trippe built his own faux-baronial Sky Club on the fifty-seventh floor, but it never quite caught on. That didn't matter, since Trippe preferred walking across Vanderbilt Avenue to his beloved Yale Club. In the context of the Pan Am Building, the Moby Dick–ish 747 made total sense. Trippe was clearly a "size king"; the Pan Am building was his royal castle, and the 747 would be his royal coach.

If the 707 had vanquished the ocean liners, it had also vanquished the rival DC-8. And Trippe did it not by being faster but by being *first*. Douglas still sold many of its jets, yet would always remain in Boeing's shadow; it couldn't wait to create the next generation, so it would never repeat its mistake of following a Boeing lead. Time was getting to be of the essence not only to Donald Douglas but also to Bill Allen, Juan Trippe, and all the other Skycoons. In the 1960s, sixty was *not* the new forty. Sixty was the final countdown. In 1965, Juan Trippe was sixty-five, Bill Allen sixty-six, Donald Douglas seventy-three, and Frederick Rentschler long dead, having made it only to sixty-eight. Eddie Rickenbacker, seventy-four, had just retired as chairman of Eastern. The emperors of the air were thinking obsessively about their Olympian legacies. Hence they were thinking big, imperial, gargantuan. That was how and why the 747 came to pass.

The roots of the 747 were military, as was much of American aviation. In 1964, as if anticipating American involvement in Vietnam, the Pentagon began a competition for a new monster transport jet, the C-5A, that would be twice as big as any existing aircraft. Washington was looking for a plane that ideally could carry 90 tons of cargo and fly 5,000 miles nonstop at 500 miles per hour. The goal was to achieve the lowest ton-per-mile cost for the longest mileage. The winners of this contest were General Electric for the engines and Lockheed for the aircraft. The big loser was Boeing, and a sore loser at that. Boeing hadn't had a hit since the 707. As big a hit as it was, in order to keep Wall Street salivating, the company needed another smash, and it had counted on the C-5A to be the one. When it wasn't, Bill Allen soon began looking for a way to amortize the enormous research costs Boeing had incurred and convert this knowledge into its own supersized new airplane.

Having lost the U.S. Air Force as a customer, Boeing's engineers decided to turn their design into a commercial plane, a plane that had Juan Trippe written all over it. Given their triumph together with the 707, Boeing and Trippe were the natural first couple of the skies, and because he loved to be first, Trippe would have been mortally wounded if Boeing had dared to approach anyone else. However, Trippe was thinking way beyond what Boeing was thinking. An enormous subsonic jetliner was the vision among Boeing's engineers, but speed merchant Trippe was ahead of that. To him, anything subsonic was as antiquated as a Model T. He wanted to go flat out; he wanted supersonic. He wanted it so badly that, in 1963, he had signed an option agreement to buy six Anglo-French Concordes when that plane was little more than the techno-fantasy of Charles de Gaulle.

Sick of the Americanization of France, of Conrad Hilton's running ice water, of Pan Am's economy-class, Frommer-clutching, bad-tipping tourist hordes, De Gaulle was desperate to beat the Americans at *something* modern. That something was supersonic transport. De Gaulle wanted it as much as Trippe did, enough to team up with the hated British, who also were desperate for something to make the world forget all their De Havilland tragedies and false starts. Here was the one big chance for the Old World to beat the New.

Juan Trippe was as patriotic as any American. He didn't want to be a traitor. But he didn't want to be second, either. He couldn't have stood to see BOAC or Air France go faster sooner than Pan Am. He may also have been calling America's bluff. Three days after Trippe signed the option, Najeeb Halaby, the head of the Federal Aviation Administration—who ultimately would succeed Trippe at Pan Am—wrote to President Kennedy with the dire warning that getting beaten by the Concorde and not having a supersonic competitor would cost America 50,000 jobs and $4 billion in lost income, not to mention the humble-pie factor. Furthermore, the Russians were said to be developing their own supersonic, dubbed the "Concordski." No one in Washington wanted to have another Sputnik situation where America was scooped by the sinister high-tech Communists. Kennedy immediately got with the speed program and announced that America would develop its own SST, as the supersonic transport was called here.

The competing European and American supersonic planes represented the values and enormous differences of the two rival cultures. The Concord, as it was originally called before De Gaulle insisted on Frenchifying it with the "e," was a small, expensive, elitist plane, geared to a rich aristocracy or at least a plutocracy, a true Jet Set, the kind of people who danced at Régine's and Annabel's and wanted to get to Le Club in record time and keep on dancing. The SST was designed as a big democratic plane, seating more than two hundred, twice as big as the Concorde. It was also much faster, Mach 3, or three times the speed of sound, compared to the Concorde's Mach 2.2 (the fastest 707 flew at Mach .8, or around 600 miles per hour).

Compared to the European, effete Concorde, the Kennedy SST was going to be a big, macho cowboy plane, one that would appeal to the kick-ass sensibilities of the muscular warmonger elite lampooned in Stanley Kubrick's *Dr. Strangelove*. Nobody on either side of the Atlantic was worrying back then about ecology, or sonic booms, or global warming, or noise, or the ozone layer, or the myriad other deleterious effects that these planes might have on the environment. "Green" referred only to the envy the winner of the speed race could inflict upon the loser. In 1964, early in this game, that loser seemed to be the Concorde. When the Profumo scandal drove the Tories from office, the new Labour government announced British withdrawal from the "Concord" project, which they saw as an airborne manifestation of the upper class so discredited by its call-girl shenanigans. Why give the toffs another toy to misbehave in? was the attitude. But within a few months, that attitude reversed. The new Wilson government discovered that its agreement with France to develop the plane had the force of an international treaty. Walking away would provoke a major incident and incur penalty costs far greater than the program itself. England had no choice but to stay the course, a bitter and costly pill.

It was also a long, endless course. Because the Concorde was projected to take ten years or more before it could begin regular service, the Skycoons of the world all realized they needed another aircraft to meet the seemingly infinitely elastic demand for jet travel. That was when Boeing came up with the 747 and customized it to the megalomania of Juan Trippe. But both Allen and Trippe looked at the 747 as a stopgap measure, a holding plane that would fly until the midseventies, when Boeing's SST, known as the 2707, hopefully would win the supersonic sweepstakes and become the standard-bearer of a new jet age. The 747, from its inception, was an ungainly workhorse. The 2707, in contrast, was a flight of fancy. It was everyone's ego trip.

Nonetheless, the 747 was a major leap beyond the 707. Boeing promised to deliver it to Pan Am by 1969, by which time the ever bullish Trippe had projected that travel demand would have stretched his fleet of 707s beyond capacity. Trippe insisted that it carry double the load of the 707, at least 400 passengers. He even envisioned an all-economy configuration of 500 or more. The Ivy aristocrat was perfectly willing to sell out his class for the greater glory of Pan Am. At one early point, the 747 was going to be a double-decker 660-tourist cattle car, but no engineers could figure out a way to evacuate the craft in case of an emergency, in order to meet FAA rules.

Tripp wanted the 747 to fly a mile or two higher than the 707, which would further minimize turbulence and allow the Pratt & Whitney–powered plane to go a little faster, maybe fifty miles per hour faster, which would cut the travel time between New York and London by half an hour, to a neat six-hour journey. (The SST would take only half that.) He also came up with his own plans for the 747's trademark upper bulge, or "hump."

Because the 747 was to be used as a cargo plane, too, the cockpit was placed above the nose cone, which could be opened to load freight. The cockpit was in that hump. Trippe wanted to use the space behind it to re-create the luxuries of his original Clipper flying boats, with grandiose staterooms for Skull and Bones and Cloud Club types. On this one rare occasion, Trippe's underlings convinced him that he was living in the past and a cocktail lounge was a more promotable utilization of the space.

To build the 747, Boeing built a whole new assembly plant in Everett, thirty miles north of Seattle, which was the largest enclosed space ever constructed, large enough to envelop more than forty football fields. The plant itself cost $200 million; 50,000 people would work to create the plane. The total development cost was over $2 billion. Without Juan Trippe's guaranteed $550 million order for twenty-five 747s, the plane never would have been built. It was high-risk for the high-flying high rollers. Then again, risk was what aviation was all about.

Trippe and Boeing were playing a billion-dollar game of chicken with the other airlines of the world. Both Douglas and Lockheed were developing their own wide-body jets, bigger than the 707 by half but not twice its size, like the 747. Neither of them was as bullish on the passenger market as Trippe. With Trippe in hand, as the Big Man of the business, the risk taker who had won all the chips with the 707, Boeing's Allen was ready to call the bluff of the other airlines. Again he bet correctly. The herd mentality prevailed. What was right for Juan Trippe was right for the world. Within months, all the big airlines had jumped on board. TWA ordered twelve 747s, BOAC six, Air France, Lufthansa, and Japan Air Lines three each. Even the domestic carriers didn't dare avoid going where Juan Trippe did not fear to tread. American, United, and Northwest each ordered three of the jumbos. Bill Allen knew he would recoup his investment.

Few oracles could have guessed how the world would change from the signing of the 747 contract in 1965 until the plane began flying in 1970. The change was as great as the transition from John F. Kennedy to Lyndon B. Johnson and then to Richard M. Nixon. The joy and exuberance and discovery of travel that had characterized the Kennedy years turned out to be fine champagne that had lost its fizz. Watching LBJ struggle into JFK's custom shoes to preside over the Great Society was as discomfiting as watching Aileen Mehle as Suzy Knickerbocker struggle into Igor Cassini's column and report on High Society.

What could Suzy expose that would get attention, the sex lives of Martin Luther King, Jr., and Malcolm X? When the whole world was imploding and exploding, the fun and frolic of the Jet Set seemed archaic, if not irrelevant, even as a mode of escape. The LBJ administration was done in by a combination of warfare and welfare, creating an inflationary spiral that was inimical to the travel boom of the JFK glory years. Inflation, which was at 1.6 percent in 1965, quadrupled to 6.5 percent in 1970. Meanwhile, the Dow, which had risen 86 percent from the 1962 crash that sent Eddie Gilbert fleeing to Rio to an all-time high of 995 in 1966, began falling and plummeted to 669 in 1970.

Following JFK's lead, LBJ refused to raise taxes for his seemingly limitless liberal social programs like Medicare and for the seemingly bottomless conflict in Asia. Chastened by the 1962 stock swoon that became known as the "Kennedy Crash" and chastised for his quote "My father always told me that all businessmen were sons of bitches," JFK had held out an olive branch to Wall Street in the form of tax cuts that LBJ left in place. The absence of revenue, however, left no way out but for the Yankee dollar to become the victim of inflation. Not only was Europe more expensive to get to, since airlines kept raising ticket prices to compensate for the overall decline in passengers, but also, the weaker dollar made Europe more and more expensive for whoever managed to get there. It was all bad news for the approaching 747.

The campus rage at the Vietnam War and urban unrest may have impelled Americans to go to Europe just to get away from home, but with the stock market going down and airfares going up, the 707s began to fly with an increasing number of empty seats. As the 747 got closer and closer to completion, the Everett plant was resembling a modern version of the construction of the great pyramids at Giza, with thousands of workers spread across a vast space, creating giant monuments to the heavens. Even the irrationally exuberant Juan Trippe was starting to sense an occasional sinking feeling that the jumbo could be his own personal Frankenstein monster, his great white whale of a plane with nobody on board.

With this giant specter of failure looming above him, the reality of competition was also staring Trippe in the face. Its Wall Street lenders having effectively banished Howard Hughes from the airline he had built, TWA in 1966 stole the airlines' profitability crown from Pan Am and began carrying more passengers across the Atlantic. The "Hollywood Airline" had gone even more Hollywood by pioneering in-flight movies. Its airborne premiere came in 1961 with *By Love Possessed*, a melodrama starring Lana Turner and Efrem Zimbalist, Jr., on a 707 flight between New York and Los Angeles.

The public loved it. These films, bland as they had to be to avoid offending any market segment, became one of the greatest gimmicks in the history of aviation, right up there with the minibottle cocktails and galley-cooked steak dinners. For once, Trippe wasn't first, and this TWA scoop hurt him grievously. TWA scooped him again in 1962 by creating the first "architectural" terminal at Idlewild Airport, the sci-fi-ish "space hub" designed by the trendy Finnish-American architect Eero Saarinen. And in 1967, with Conrad Hilton nearing eighty, TWA seduced his son Barron into a merger that young Hilton thought would facilitate his family's dreams of owning an airline. As it turned out, the merger facilitated TWA's dreams of owning a hotel chain—one with 42 properties in 28 countries, to be exact—that dwarfed and outclassed Pan Am's heavily South America–weighted InterContinental chain. All of a sudden, the Hollywood Airline was displacing Pan Am as *the* international carrier.

Leading the TWA charge was its new president, Charles Carpenter Tillinghast, Jr., a Vermont Yankee who had never worked for an airline until he was recruited away from Bendix, a Detroit brake-shoe manufacturer. On New Year's Eve 1958, Tillinghast had been stranded in Paris when the prop-driven TWA Constellation he was booked on broke down and no replacement was available. Somehow he got on one of the new Pan Am 707s; it was a revelation. Tillinghast vowed to fly only Pan Am for the rest of his life, until one day in 1961, when he got a call asking if he wanted to be TWA's new president. The caller was Ernest Breech, a former president of Bendix and one of Ford Motor Company's whiz kids with Defense Secretary Robert McNamara. Breech was representing the Hughes trustees and basically browbeat Tillinghast into taking the job. He had just turned fifty and represented a new generation of often Ivy-educated technocrats devoid of roots in the air; they would be replacing the barnstorming Skycoons who had built the business.

Despite his New England roots, Tillinghast had grown up in New York, where his father had been the headmaster of Horace Mann, the fancy alma mater of Eddie Gilbert and Jack Kerouac. A middling student, "Till" went on to Brown, where he was a big man on a small football team, playing center. The English major picked up his academic game and went on to Columbia Law School, then to the august New York firm of Hughes Hubbard & Reed. The Hughes there referred to Charles Evans Hughes, Jr.—son of the Supreme Court chief justice—not Howard. Howard would come into Tillinghast's life later.

In Wall Street circles, Howard Hughes was known as the "spook" of

American capitalism. At TWA, notwithstanding his flying feats as a younger man, he spent more time redesigning overhead bins than he did studying his airline's unbalanced balance sheets. His last president of TWA, Carter Burgess, a former assistant secretary of defense, had been dismissed after eleven months of never having met with his boss. Meanwhile, Tillinghast, who had been hired to run Bendix after doing a stellar job on the legal work, was brought to TWA with one of the biggest golden parachutes in history—to protect him if Hughes rose from the mists, retook TWA, and summarily fired him, as he had done with his last five presidents. Instead, in 1966, Hughes quietly cashed out, selling his TWA shares for $550 million, a sixfold increase in their original value thanks to Tillinghast's brilliant stewardship, proof that you didn't need to fly a plane to run an airline.

In 1968, perhaps seeing the economic handwriting on the wall, Juan Trippe suddenly retired as chairman of Pan Am. He didn't leave the Pan Am Building. He just moved down the hall to a small office, bestowing his famous antique rolltop desk on his designated successor Harold Gray, sixty-two, an Iowa-born company man who had begun his career piloting flying boats across the Pacific and had entered company folklore as the pilot of Pan Am's first transatlantic flight in 1939. In another sign of the times, Gray unceremoniously removed the Trippe rolltop, put it in storage, and installed a modern desk of his own.

In appointing Gray as his successor, Trippe was aware that Gray was battling lymphatic cancer and receiving debilitating radiation treatments. A more obvious choice would have been the healthy Najeeb Halaby, fifty-two, whom Trippe had hired away from the FAA in 1965. Halaby had one of the greatest résumés in aviation. Born in Dallas, he was the son of a Syrian immigrant who sold rugs at Neiman Marcus together with his Southern-belle wife, whose grandfather had been a Confederate war hero. Halaby had graduated from Stanford and Yale Law and had been a much decorated navy jet test pilot in World War II.

After the war, Halaby had joined the State Department and become chief adviser to King Ibn Saud in developing Saudi Arabian Airlines, before being picked by JFK to run the FAA. He was a staunch advocate of the SST. Halaby's biggest problem at Pan Am was that he didn't get along with the old-fashioned Harold Gray. But with Juan Trippe, it was always age before beauty. He remained loyal to his star pilot, cancer or no cancer, and kept Halaby cooling his heels as Pan Am's man in Washington while Gray shepherded the 747 into service. Company insiders have said that the 747 made Gray even sicker than he already was. His illness was compounded by having to fight off a hostile takeover by Charles Bluhdorn's Gulf and Western (Engulf and Devour, per Mel Brooks's *Silent Movie*), a threat that made Trippe emerge from his office and fly back into action. He buttonholed new president Richard Nixon into leaning on Congress to pass legislation preventing such a takeover without approval of the new Civil Aeronautics Board. The bill passed, and it drove Bluhdorn away.

In 1969, an enervated Harold Gary stepped down as chairman (he would die three years later). Trippe at last transferred the reins of power to Halaby, who, appalled by the antimanagement chaos of Trippe's one-man rule, commenced a corporate purge, firing three dozen top managers (and demoting Trippe's son, Charles) and trying to turn Pan Am into a Harvard Business School case study. Juan Trippe himself moved twenty-three stories down to a relative cubbyhole in the Pan Am Building, to stay out of Halaby's and harm's way as the 747 made its debut, never giving voice to his darkest fear that, in this newly recessionary and turbulent climate, his big new bird might end up being the biggest turkey of all time.

On January 15, 1970, following a long Pan Am tradition, First Lady Pat Nixon christened the 747 Clipper *Young America* at Dulles Airport in a ceremony nearly as grand as her husband's inauguration, attended by almost all of Congress and the Supreme Court, as well as many leaders of Wall Street and big businesses around the country. Everyone except Juan Trippe, whose absence spoke volumes. Things got off to an inauspiciously rocky start when Mrs. Nixon pulled a huge gold lever that unleashed a jet spray of red, white, and blue "christening water," which was not the traditional champagne but a combination of food coloring and aviation deicer. When the first lady pushed the lever back to stop the flow, nothing happened. It was like a bad Peter Sellers movie, the toxic patriotic spray that wouldn't end, splashing all over the dignitaries, all ninety gallons of it, until it petered out. The air force band played—and played—"The Stars and Stripes Forever," forever, it seemed. When someone later asked Mrs. Nixon why champagne wasn't used, her curt reply was "Why waste good champagne?"

Najeeb Halaby gave a slightly off-color speech. Rather than Trippely windbagging away about how the 747 would end the Cold War and the Vietnam War and make the world safe for capitalism, he told a salty tale that invoked the ghost of John F. Kennedy's concupiscence, something that the press was still discreetly keeping under wraps in 1970.

> When we were dedicating this airport eight years ago, I recall President Kennedy passing before some of these very attractive stewardesses, and at that moment there was a little controversy in the FAA about whether or not stewardesses should sit on the laps of the pilots in flight. And, the President paused before one of these girls and she said, "Do you know, Mr. President, I think that you ought to instruct Mr. Halaby to put out a new rule—Fly now; play later."

Halaby spoke on a dais below the towering four-hundred-seat 747, which was parked next to a tiny Ford Trimotor. The twelve-passenger all-metal three-engine plane, first built by Henry Ford in 1925 and known as the "Tin Goose," was a utilitarian Model T of the air and enjoyed a nine-year run until the far-advanced Douglas DC-2 toppled Ford as the kingpin of commercial aircraft manufacturing, a warning to all present that even the mighty could fall. The Goose had been flown in its day by the intrepid chairman emeritus Harold Gray, standing behind Halaby on the dais. The Ford cost $55,000, the 747 $23 million. After the speeches, Pat Nixon toured the *Young America,* recalling having taken flying lessons herself as a young woman in Los Angeles in 1937. She marveled at how high the cabin in the hump was off the ground—a full six stories. "You fellows have a seat near heaven," she told the pilots, admiringly puzzling how "anyone can keep track of all these instruments."

A week later, at seven o'clock on a frigid January evening, a whole planeload of jumbo passengers—332 of them—began asking the same question when the same *Young America* had to abort its inaugural commercial departure from Kennedy Airport (Idlewild had been changed to honor the late JFK) to London. The flight was already a half hour late when the pilots, taxiing for takeoff, found a problem with one of the big Pratt & Whitney engines and, preferring shame to flame, steered the mighty ship back to the gate. Buses took the stranded voyagers to a Queens restaurant called the Chelsea Lobster House, as gallows humorists joked that this was probably as close to the London borough of Chelsea as the group was going to get.

What good was all that extra space (economy seats were a whole two inches wider than those on the 707s) in the 20-foot-wide, 8-foot-high cabin that could accommodate Wilt "the Stilt" Chamberlain if the plane couldn't get off the ground? Forget the 747, one of the frustrated fliers jibed the chagrined ground crew. Get us a 748. Pan Am luckily had a backup that *worked*, the *Clipper Victor*, one of the three 747s that Boeing had delivered. Eight hours later, at around two in the morning, the *Victor* managed to get airborne, at just the time the *Young America* was supposed to have landed at Heathrow.

The problems of the 747 had only just begun. By the summer of 1970, Pan Am had taken delivery of its twenty-five jumbos, and none of them seemed to work. There were engine and other mechanical problems that caused a domino-effect cascade of delays, returns, thwarted takeoffs, and emergency landings. Pan Am admitted that 10 percent of its 747 flights had been delayed in some way, but frequent travelers had much higher estimates of malfunctions. Not that it mattered to that many people, as the new planes were flying half empty, not half full. The nation was mired in the quicksand of recession. No one was traveling for fun. Fun was positively un-American in these early Nixon years. The protest anthem of the era summed up the general prospect: It felt as if the country were on the "Eve of Destruction."

The 17 percent annual growth rate that Juan Trippe had assumed in order to justify his decision to buy the 747 had dropped to 4 percent and was still falling. At the same time, the jumbos gave Pan Am nearly 20 percent more seats to fill. The expected groundswell of orders for the 747 never happened. Boeing had to lay off so many workers because of curbed demand that Seattle became a disaster area. Boeing employment plunged from 84,000 in 1968 to 20,000 in 1970. An endlessly photographed billboard near the Boeing plant read "Will the last person leaving Seattle turn off the lights?"

The fact that the economies of Europe were doing even worse than Seattle's, not to mention the continent's civil unrest, served to compound the airlines' problems. Of course, the glories of the Old World were there for the New World to see, but when you were teargassed in front of Notre Dame or trampled in a riot at the Pantheon, the glory of the glories could easily get lost in translation. When Temple Fielding made the cover of *Time* in June 1969, it was estimated that more than two million Americans would be visiting Europe that year, recession and Vietnam be damned. That cover marked the high point of the Jet Set and of the travel boom. The attitude was definitely eat, drink, and be merry, for tomorrow . . . the stock market would crash. Fielding sold 100,000 guides that year, Frommer twice that many. Yet neither of them could entice enough travelers to fill next year's 747s.

The bad situation that greeted the inauguration of 747 service in 1970 got far, far worse with the emergence of a new wild card that Juan Trippe, the ultimate cardplayer, had never seen coming. That wild card the Skycoon missed was the skyjacker. Nothing could chill a ticket sale like the specter of a mad terrorist at 30,000 feet. In December 1969, two weeks before the 747's grand Washington, D.C., christening, a striking twenty-nine-year-old Lebanese schoolteacher and her two handsome consorts boarded a TWA 707 bound for New York at the Athens, Greece, airport. They were dressed like Jet Setters, maybe a little too Jet Set. The three carried identical expensive large leather briefcases.

A suspicious ground crewman called the Greek police, who boarded the plane and inspected the fancy satchels. They hit the mother lode. The three chic voyagers were carrying a commando cache of pistols, hand grenades, and other explosives. They were arrested and discovered to be members of a terrorist cell known as the Popular Front for the Liberation of Palestine (PFLP). Their thwarted plan had been to hijack the 707 to Tunis and blow it up, unless TWA agreed to stop flying to Israel, where the flight had originated. The three were given life sentences by a Greek court. Justice was done, and the jets roared on.

Juan Trippe didn't lose any sleep over this one. Pan Am didn't fly to Israel. Besides, the terrorists literally didn't get off the ground. The other Skycoons shrugged off the threat as well. But six months later, the collective tossing and turning began. This time the PFLP struck gold. Six of them, minus the matching valises, had no trouble boarding in Beirut one of Aristotle Onassis's Olympic Airlines Boeing 727s, bound for Athens, and skyjacking it to Cairo. Their quid pro quo for not blasting the jet and its passengers to oblivion was freedom for the three life-imprisoned terrorists, and for four other jailed PFLP bombers who had tried to blow up the Athens El Al office.

The price was paid and a Greek tragedy averted by blackmail. But it was only a matter of time until it happened again. The PFLP, an offshoot of the Palestine Liberation Organization, had a radical Marxist-Leninist ideology. They were committed to destroying what they called "global imperialism." What could have been more imperially global than the big airlines? Pan Am and its beleaguered fellow imperialists had to face the fact: They shared a terrible new problem that was not going to fade away.

Skyjacking was a jet-age phenomenon. Between 1948 and 1957, there was a grand total of fifteen airline hijackings worldwide, about one annually. Once the jets took off in 1958, in the next decade, that total jumped to forty-eight. Once Castro took over Cuba, the numbers exploded. In January 1969, there were eight hijackings to Havana in a year that saw a total of eighty-two diverted planes. Luckily, on the Cuban runs, there were no fatalities or even injuries. A side trip to Havana was joked about as a booby prize for going to Miami. But then the Palestinians, smarting from their humiliating defeat by Israel in 1967's Six-Day War, changed the game. They got their bright idea from the Cuba hijackings. What they added to the formula was death and destruction. They demonized all of Israel's rich Western allies as the ultimate in capitalist piggery. What could be more symbolic than destroying the jets that were those nations' techo-trophies?

Sunday, September 6, 1970, was the Palestinians' Pearl Harbor. It all began in Amsterdam, where a voluptuous young woman with a Honduran passport boarded an El Al 707 en route to New York. She and her handsome male companion took their seats and waited for friends. The friends did not arrive. As the woman paced up and down the aisles, looking vainly for her expected companions, many of the men on the flight couldn't take their eyes off this bombshell. Was she ever! No sooner had the 707 taken off than the woman pulled a grenade out of each of the cups of her brassiere, and with a war whoop, she and her seatmate, brandishing a gun, made a dash for the cockpit, which, unique on El Al, was bulletproof and locked. The quick-thinking El Al pilot, noting the commotion, put the 707 into a dramatic dive that threw the would-be hijackers off their feet, allowing passengers to secure the woman with their neckties, while an onboard Israeli security agent shot the male attacker in the stomach. Their grenades had failed to detonate.

The plane made an emergency landing at London Heathrow, where police swarmed the plane. The bombshell turned out to be, like the thwarted Athens hijacker, a Lebanese former schoolteacher turned Marxist PFLP radical. Her name was Leila Khaled. She was twenty-four. A year before, in August 1969, carrying a book called *My Friend Che,* she had hijacked a TWA 707 between Rome and Tel Aviv and diverted the plane to Damascus, where she blew up the cockpit though spared the passengers' lives, again as a warning to TWA to stay out of Israel. Having captured the imagination of the world press as the "deadly beauty," Khaled had undergone extensive plastic surgery so she could strike again, not that there was much effective security in place to stop her. This was before the age of screeners and pat-downs. All you had to do was show your passport, and on the plane you went.

In London, Khaled's companion was pronounced dead of his gun-shot wound. He was identified as Patrick Argüello, a Nicaraguan Sandinista living in San Francisco and, like Khaled, traveling on a Honduran passport. His was a very jet-setty bio, a sign of the international times. His politics were international as well. He was part of a Central American terrorist group that, like the Red Brigades in Italy, the Baader-Meinhof Gang in Germany, and the Basque ETA in Spain, were brothers-in-arms with their Palestinian comrades, all dedicated to bringing down capitalism and bringing down the planes.

Just as Khaled was being transported to captivity in London, that same morning, three more PFLP terrorist groups struck again and simultaneously. A TWA 707, just having taken off from Frankfurt to New York, was ascending over the North Sea when two skyjackers took the captain hostage and had him reverse course for the Middle East and rename the flight Gaza One. And a Swissair DC-8 leaving Zurich for New York became Haifa One when still another female terrorist announced to the passengers, "This is your new captain speaking." An American feminist capable of dark humor joked to her seatmate how remarkable it was to be skyjacked by a woman. They'd come a long way, baby.

But the biggest PFLP "get" that morning was one of Juan Trippe's new 747s. Pan Am's flight from Brussels to New York was known among travelers as the "Wall Street Express" because it carried so many bankers doing business at Common Market headquarters in Belgium. On its one stop in Amsterdam, it was boarded by two European-looking men with passports from Senegal who had seats in first class. Presumably, they were international bankers, like most of the other capitalists up front. Such a presumption was terribly wrong. In fact, the men were the "friends" of Leila Khaled, who had not shown up for the El Al flight she had just tried to hijack. Sharp-eyed El Al security knew bankers when they saw them, and these men seemed too young. Furthermore, they had bought their first-class tickets with cash, another red flag. So El Al bumped them from the flight, into the welcoming arms of Pan Am, whose current marketing motto was "The World's Most Experienced Airline." Alas, that experience did not extend to terrorism. After takeoff, the two "Senegalese," who were actually Lebanese and had casually hidden their weapons under their seats, calmly took the circular staircase up to the unlocked cockpit, put their guns to the captain's head, and had him change course to the Holy Land.

The terrorists took the TWA and Swissair flights, now Gaza One and Haifa One, to a flat part of the Jordanian desert twenty-five miles outside Amman, to an old World War II British training airstrip called Dawson's Field. The place had been defunct for years, with no electricity, and had been used only for small craft that weighed a fraction of the 180,000 pounds of the 707. It was a tribute to the skill of the two pilots that they were able to land their craft by the light of oil drums set ablaze on the tarmac of what the PFLP had rechristened "Revolution Airport."

No pilot, however, would have been able to land the 500,000-pound 747 at Revolution. In fact, no one expected to. The Palestinians didn't want the 747 precisely *because* of its size. They wanted to have three imperialist aircraft lined up side by side in the Arab desert, so they could blow them all up, all together, for all the world to see. But El Al had foiled these plans, leading the faux-Senegalese to act on their own, without considering landing logistics. Besides, better a jumbo somewhere else than no jet at all. So they ordered the plane to Beirut, which, despite being considered the Paris of the Middle East, did not have a big modern airport like Orly that could accommodate the 747. They weren't Dawson's Field, but Beirut's runways weren't all that much longer; nor were they reinforced to bear the 747's tonnage. Beirut air controllers tried to scare the skyjackers off, to no avail. This pilot, too, did a great job and feathered the giant plane down.

Not for long. The PFLP quickly decided that Beirut lacked shock value. They now wanted Cairo, just to show Egypt's President Nasser the Palestinians' displeasure for his agreeing with President Nixon, Secretary of State William Rogers, and his top aide Henry Kissinger to a cease-fire with Israel and Middle East peace talks. Cairo had the biggest airport in the Arab world, so landing was no problem. But as soon as the plane touched down, the terrorists evacuated all 180 crew and passengers and blasted the $25 million technological marvel into oblivion, in perhaps the largest, most dramatic fireball the Mideast had ever seen. Take that, Nasser, was the idea. The explosion would be a painful thorn in the mind of travelers who might be contemplating a once-in-a lifetime trip to see the Pyramids. Not in this lifetime. Not now. The desperately needed foreign exchange from tourist dollars, Egypt's chief source of revenue, was certain to dry up.

Because of the ongoing travel recession, which was sure to grow to crisis proportions with this cataclysm, the three hijacked planes had been flying at less than half capacity. But there were still more than three hundred hostages to deal with, most of whom were Americans. Back in Jordan at Revolution Airport, the morning desert sun was rising, and by noon, the temperature outside was 120 degrees. Inside the aircraft, with no power for air-conditioning, the effect was like broiling in the metal shed used by the Japanese to torture Alec Guinness's Lieutenant Colonel Nicholson in *The Bridge on the River Kwai*. The planes' toilets were quickly fouled beyond usability, and the water provided by the self-declared "humanitarian" terrorists had so much chlorine that some hostages complained that it was like drinking from a swimming pool. Soon the targeted airlines were flying in thousands of packaged meals to vast makeshift desert kitchens; portable toilets were set up for the hostages in what came to look like a film set, a space-age *Lawrence of Arabia,* which actually was shot in this very desert.

Discomforts aside, the fear factor was overwhelming, particularly for the Jewish passengers, quickly identified by last names and Israeli passport stamps, if not by self-declaration. The Jews, in particular, were designated as the bargaining chips for the release of PFLP prisoners incarcerated in Europe and Israel. On September 7, 127 of the hostages— the non-Jewish females and children—were released, taken off the planes and transferred to Pan Am's Hotel InterContinental in Amman. Meanwhile, the rest of the men and all the Jews sat and baked in their jet ovens and worried that their end was near.

The world's press descended on Jordan. This was something no one had ever seen, and it was blockbuster news, televised across the planet, live from Revolution Field. If the Palestinians had felt they'd been ignored, they were now getting their compensatory close-up and then some. But the picture was anything but flattering, particularly three days later on September 9, when a fourth plane—a BOAC jet en route from Bombay to London—was hijacked and brought to Revolution. The PFLP leaders had wanted three planes in the desert to blow up. Two, they thought, wouldn't be a big enough spectacle. They also needed more British subjects to bargain with to secure the London release of Leila Khaled and to retrieve the body of Patrick Argüello. The plane they took was a Vickers VC-10, a beautiful rear-engined craft that was none-theless too little and too late to compete with the jets of Boeing and Douglas and represented the long frustrations of the British aviation industry. Here they all were, the 707, the DC-8, and the VC-10, the wings of man in the land of God, the Holy Land, which at the time seemed like the lowest and hottest circle of hell. The soaring brilliance of modern technology had been brought to this precipice by the savagery of man's oldest and most primitive emotions.

Back in America, President Nixon was getting trigger-happy for a direct military response. He wanted to storm Revolution Airport and bomb all of Jordan, if need be, to wipe out the PFLP. The Sixth Fleet was poised in the Mediterranean, off Jordan; military aircraft and transports were readied in Turkey. Luckily for the hostages, Nixon's defense secretary, Melvin Laird, opposed to the use of force, told the commander in chief that the weather was too overcast for an attack, and the plan was dropped. Negotiations, conducted through the neutral Red Cross, were a farce. There was no single or reliable spokesperson for the PFLP, and some of the demands—like the release of Robert Kennedy's assassin, Sirhan Sirhan—were proferred, then dropped. The talks dragged on for several more days, until Friday, September 11. Then the planes were wired with explosives. This 9/11 was the hostages' darkest hour.

But Nixon's warmongering stance had its effect. The Palestinians began to fear their own obliteration. The scattered PFLP turned over all negotiating to the PLO's leader, Yasser Arafat, who, compared to every-one else on his side, was a voice of relative reason. A deal was made. In return for Nixon's not pulling the trigger, all hostages except for Israelis

BLACK SEPTEMBER. Arab terrorists deal the jet age a crippling blow when they hijack and destroy three Western commercial airliners in the Jordanian desert, 1970.

"with military capability" would be freed, as would all the Palestinian prisoners currently being held in jails of European countries whose citizens were hostages. The remaining Israelis, forty of them, would be traded for Palestinians being held in Israel, if Israel could come to terms.

The commandos evacuated the planes, and the hostages were driven away to Amman in convoys. When the next dawn broke, the three planes were blown up, $50 million worth of "capitalist-imperialist" aircraft, in probably the greatest sound-and-light spectacle the modern press had ever witnessed. The towering columns of smoke were visible as far away as Amman, but it was an explosion seen on television around the world.

Jordan's very Westernized and pro-American King Hussein was appalled at the horrid public relations the Palestinians had wreaked on his country. He finally snapped and commenced a war against the PLO, the PFLP, and any related terrorist group within Jordan's borders. The campaign, which lasted barely a month, was known as Black September, and it succeeded in purging Jordan of the PLO and nearly half of its entire Palestinian population. An estimated 20,000 Palestinians were killed in the war, compared to fewer than 100 Jordanians. Hussein's offensive also forced the freeing of the remaining Jewish/Israeli hostages, in return for Leila Khaled, after which the PFLP—as well as its disapproving parent PLO—relocated to Lebanon.

Richard Nixon was just as outraged as King Hussein. On September 11, at the height of the terrorists' intransigence, Nixon issued an order to combat "air piracy" that included following Israel's successful lead of assigning armed sky marshals to random American flights. An initial team of one hundred federal agents was organized for this task. When the last hostages were finally released on September 28 and flown via Cyprus to Leonardo da Vinci Airport in Rome, Nixon, who was in Italy visiting the pope, came out to welcome them. He made it clear to the world that America's stance on skyjacking terrorism would be the toughest on earth. X-ray machines and metal detectors were also part of Nixon's decree. The age of airport anxiety had begun.

The excess capacity of the new 747s had never seemed like such a terrible idea. First the economy had taken its toll; now it was the human factor, the fear factor. For Pan Am, skyjacking was the coup de grâce from which it would never recover. Planes that previously had been half filled were emptier than ever. The glamour days of flying truly went up in smoke that hot September at Revolution Airport. Nearly overnight, the jet set had become the fret set.

14

The Last Playboys

THE DECLINE OF THE JET SET HAD AS MUCH TO DO WITH THE RISE OF THE TERROR-ist as it did with the fall of the playboy. The scandals involving Eddie Gilbert and Igor Cassini accelerated the extinction of this unique midcentury species of male hedonist, those high-profile lady-killing high livers who inspired the classic nomad-chic lifestyle of the 707 era. American youth was no longer aspiring to ape the Jet Set and follow their gilded footsteps. Being a playboy of the old school, the Ian Fleming James Bond school, was suddenly unhip. Being a gangster like the ones Alain Delon played, or a hippie like the protagonists of 1969's global smash *Easy Rider,* was vastly cooler, and changing the world was cooler still. The Peace Corps was, in many ways, the new Jet Set.

Ah, Delon, and ah, Paris. As Bogart said to Bergman in *Casablanca,* "We'll always have Paris." Or would we? Paris was the spiritual home of the playboy. Now both Paris and playboys were on the ropes. While the Sorbonne riots of May 1968 may have scared away their parents and the Temple Fielding set and decimated the first-class cabins of the new 747s,

American students, clutch-
ing their Frommer's and
Harvard *Let's Go* budget
guidebooks, heard the siren
call of the barricades and
began packing $200 round-
trip student charters or
$129 Icelandic Air prop jets
to make the trip to a promised continent, symbolized
by open-air-tolerated pot
smoking in Amsterdam, fabulous cheap peasant food in
Florence, and easy, if not
free, love everywhere from
Sweden to the Balearic Isles.

PRETTY BOY. Euro screen heartthrob Alain Delon,
who was involved in a French version of the Profumo
scandal, 1965.

Before the skyjackings
began in deadly earnest, and before the markets began their seemingly
permanent decline, when travelers planned for Europe in the late sixties,
London had already eclipsed Paris as the El Dorado of travel fantasies.
The youthquake that had spawned all kinds of alluring creative and artistic ferment throughout the world had in Paris spawned only revolution and unrest, Danny the Red instead of Mick Jagger. Daniel
Cohn-Bendit was the Jewish Marxist free-love-espousing radical who
forged an alliance of students and workers at the barricades of the Sorbonne in May 1968 to protest what was to them the archaic reactionary
rule of Charles de Gaulle.

The resulting violent Paris riots, like their sister riots at Columbia
University the same month, had global publicity but little effect. By
June, the Gaullists had retaken a three-quarter majority in the French
National Assembly. The riots were simply bad publicity, antitourism that
even the wizards of Doyle Dane Bernbach couldn't turn on its head into
a clever come-on, something like "Come to Paris and Get Bombed" or
"Radical Chic," before Tom Wolfe coined the phrase. Instead, Doyle

Dane gave up the French account in 1969, a year before De Gaulle died, but the Gaullists continued to rule.

One of the precipitants of the youthful unrest in France and its hatred of the ancient regime was a 1968–69 scandal that was France's version of England's Profumo Affair. The Markovic Affair, as the French contretemps was known, was as damaging to the mystique of the Jet Set as Danny the Red's Sorbonne riots were to the occupancy of Juan Trippe's 747s. While the Profumo Affair led to the emasculation of the British aristocracy and the rise of a new Cockney street elite of talent and cheek, the Markovic Affair led to nothing but a creeping malaise and a sad realization that *la gloire de la France* was less glorious than Doyle Dane had painted it.

Profumo was about sex, Markovic about death. Sex at least may have sold tickets; death was terrible for tourism. Because the scandal took place on two continents, with movie stars, rock stars, presidents, models, gangsters, French, Americans, Corsicans, and Serbians, the Markovic Affair, like Profumo's, was a dramatic testament to the incredible mobility that the 707 had wrought. Here the heady stuff of gossip columns mixed with the murky stuff of true crime. Yet the overwhelming impression was an underlying rot that raised serious doubts in the minds of a newly financially pressed American travel population whether the Old World they were thinking of escaping to was any better than the troubled one they were leaving behind. In the European collision between fantasy and reality, the big victim would be the big new 747.

In October 1968, a body was found wrapped in a plastic mattress cover in a garbage dump in Elancourt, a poor suburb of Paris—a city, if you believed Doyle Dane, that didn't possess such unromantic venues. The body seemed Parisian enough; it was even rakishly dressed in a Pierre Cardin suit. There was a bullet in the corpse's brain, and his severed penis was in his mouth. When the initial investigators determined that the dead man was the valet, body double, and dead ringer for the biggest movie star in France, Alain Delon, the case was taken upstairs to the highest levels at the Élysée Palace. This was no time for some Inspecteur Clouseau to muck up a very sensitive situation.

The victim's name was Stevan Markovic, and he was not the first but the second of Delon's dashing-looking Yugoslav doubles to meet a grisly end in the last two years. The first was Markovic's cousin, Milos Milosevic, twenty-four, who in 1966 was found shot to death beside his lover, the estranged model wife of Mickey Rooney, in Mrs. Rooney's home in Brentwood, the tony star-filled subdivision of Los Angeles near the Pacific beaches. The sixties were still close enough to Rooney's heyday with Judy Garland and his marriage to Ava Gardner that he was considered a legend in Hollywood, not a candidate for *Hollywood Squares*. Barbara Ann Thomason, twenty-nine, was a Phoenix-born beauty-pageant blonde who had played on-screen in a low-budget film with Jack Nicholson (*Cry Baby Killer*) and had played offscreen with Cary Grant. She and Mickey had become friends with Alain Delon when "the prettiest man in Europe," as he was known, came to Hollywood from Paris trying to ignite an American stardom off the fuse of his French celebrity as the "French James Dean" or, as others called him, "the male Brigitte Bardot." The attempt fizzled when the best Delon could do was *Texas Across the River,* a 1966 flop comedy western with Dean Martin and Joey Bishop, past their Rat Pack sell-by date with JFK dead.

Delon cut his losses and went back to Paris. However, his look-alike and best pal, Milosevic, decided to stay behind. He was having too much fun in Hollywood to return to the Old World. Milosevic had his own cinema dreams and began to realize them when he was cast as a Russian submarine commander in Norman Jewison's *The Russians Are Coming, the Russians Are Coming*. Mickey Rooney returned from a location shoot of a war movie in the Philippines to find out he was being cuckolded by his new friend. Adding injury to insult, Rooney had come down with a rare tropical disease and had to check in to Saint John's Hospital in Santa Monica.

With Mickey on his sickbed, the lovers went dancing at the Daisy, the Régine's/Le Club of Beverly Hills, then went home to Brentwood, where, the morning after, they were found dead. Barbara Rooney had a bullet in her jaw; Milos Milosevic had a bullet in his temple. The murder weapon was Mickey Rooney's chrome-plated .38-caliber revolver.

Mickey had the perfect alibi of being in the hospital, where he remained, in shock, after he heard the news. Just as they had with the nearby Brentwood death of Marilyn Monroe in 1962, the LAPD quickly closed the books on the case, declaring it a murder-suicide. As with Marilyn, no one ever believed it.

Two years later, the plot thickened with the discovery of the buff and toned body of Stevan Markovic, then thirty-one, in that Cardin suit, which probably belonged to his famous boss. While Delon was away making films and generally jet-setting around Europe, Markovic had been getting into more than Delon's clothes. He was living in Delon's art-filled luxe apartment on the Avenue de Messine, near the Parc Monceau. He had been having an affair with Delon's goddess wife, Nathalie. He was hosting orgies at Delon's flat for *le tout* Paris, a Claude Terrail crowd whose biggest trophy was supposedly Claude Pompidou (lots of Claudes in this crowd), the tall, blond, bronze, and superchic wife of De Gaulle's prime minister, the man most likely to succeed him. And he was secretly filming the sex parties and threatening to use these home movies to make him as rich by blackmail as Delon was by acting. In short, Markovic was leading an even faster life in Paris than the one that probably got his cousin Milos Milosevic killed in Los Angeles.

The Delon-Markovic relationship was something out of the Joseph Losey/Harold Pinter movie *The Servant,* wherein a valet covets and eventually takes over the life of his master. Delon's was a life well worth stealing. The son of a suburban butcher, Alain Delon was born in 1935. He dropped out of school at fourteen and eventually went to Indochina with the French navy. He spent nearly a year of his four-year tour of duty in the brig for insubordination. Back in France, Delon worked as a vegetable porter in Les Halles, then bummed around the Riviera on the eve of the jet age, trading on his amazing looks to seduce women and impress men. One of the latter was *Gone with the Wind*'s David O. Selznick, who offered him a Hollywood contract, voice unheard. Selznick's only precondition was that his discovery learn English, but the indolent, unacademic Delon preferred to coast on his beauty.

Luckily, he was also discovered by two famous *auteurs,* René Clément, who cast him as Tom Ripley in *Purple Noon,* the adaptation of a Patricia Highsmith thriller; and Count Luchino Visconti, who starred him in *Rocco and His Brothers.* Almost overnight, Delon became a huge star, carving out a niche as a tragic, moody gangster. Art was imitating life, because Delon was deeply attracted to the lower depths, and not merely as homework for his roles in the arty underworld films of Jean-Pierre Melville. One of his best friends was François Marcantoni, the godfather of the Corsican Mafia. Marcantoni lived in a ghetto of the Riviera town of Toulon so tough that it was called Chicago, after Al Capone.

Delon flitted effortlessly between underworld and haut monde, marrying movie star Romy Schneider before leaving her for the Moroccan-born, Bardot-esque Francine Canovas, who would change her first name to Nathalie and later would be linked romantically to both Keith Richards and Mick Jagger. In a sign of the wide-open times, Nathalie was maid of honor at Jagger's wedding to Bianca. Alain Delon had met Milos Milosevic in Belgrade in 1963, when he was filming *Marco Polo,* a production that went bankrupt. When Milosevic decided to remain in Hollywood, he convinced the narcissistic Delon to accept his cousin Markovic as his replacement, for only a tough cool guy who looked exactly like Delon would do. Delon had already met Markovic in 1964 when Milosevic got Delon to bail his cousin out of jail, where he was languishing under suspicion of masterminding a jewel robbery. Delon seamlessly switched doppelgängers to Markovic, a compulsively ruthless man without legitimate options for whom the stolen-identity game became one of double or nothing.

When Delon discovered Markovic's treachery with his wife, compounded with his huge betting losses on horses and cards, the star angrily cut his double loose. Markovic returned to his gangland milieu, the Paris branch of the Yugoslav underworld. His only real assets were his orgy photos, which could have been far more damaging to the ancien régime than any general strike masterminded by Danny the Red. Alain Delon was questioned but never charged. Claude Pompidou was questioned and denied everything. The public may not have believed her, but this was France, sophisticated France, and the public shrugged off the orgies. Claude's husband became president when De Gaulle died in 1970.

The orgy films were never found. Alain Delon went on to another star marriage and more big hits, while Nathalie Delon continued to be the muse of the Rolling Stones, inspiring their hit "Exile on Main Street," the perfect example of a Jet Set album, its tracks recorded between 1968 and 1972 in Jagger's English stately home and Richards's French Riviera villa, amid entourages of the decadently famous. The murders of the Delonian Yugoslavs were never solved. Nevertheless, from a Jet Set perspective, the case was a testament to the changes in society, even the stratified traditional class society of Europe. Here, two Balkan hustlers who heretofore would have been lucky to even *visit* Paris or Beverly Hills and, if so, to work as menials, suddenly found themselves rubbing far more than shoulders with the giants of two continents. That they both ended up dead for their upward mobility is a testament to the wages of overly ambitious sin.

If the Markovic affair greatly tarnished the allure of the Jet Set as the public aspired to it, the death knell for glamour as Igor Cassini had created it was the 1973 dissolution of the marriage between perhaps the best-credentialed Euro-playboy of the entire era, Roger Vadim, with the preeminent Hollywood-American object of lust, Jane Fonda. The Jet Set judged men by the distaff company they kept. By that standard, Roger Vadim was the lord of this ring. He was to the Jet Set what Porfirio Rubirosa had been to Café Society. While Rubirosa had hit the financial daily double by marrying the two top heiresses of his time, Doris Duke and Barbara Hutton, Roger Vadim won the pulchritude trifecta in his unions with the three supergoddesses of the sixties: Brigitte Bardot, Catherine Deneuve, and finally, Fonda. Roger Vadim *was* James Bond, minus the gun. His was a license to thrill, not kill. Until the upheavals of the late sixties trashed the old ideal of suavity in favor of cool rebellion and drastically devalued the currency of playboys, as well as that of Hugh Hefner's Playboy empire, Roger Vadim seemed like the Man to Be.

Vadim's only real competitors in the Jet Stud department were Claude Terrail and Oleg Cassini. However, for Terrail, the Tour d'Argent was a

JOLLY ROGER. French playboy-director Roger Vadim, with Jane Fonda, the third of his movie star wives, 1968.

far more jealous mistress than Ava Gardner or Rita Hayworth, and status, rather than sex, seemed to be the prime allure. Like his brother, Igor, Oleg Cassini was always too motivated by making money and achieving the security lost by his noble family to take sex as anything more than a gentleman's diversion, like polo or shooting. Yes, he was great at it, but the Cassinis were great at everything, and look what it had gotten Igor— nearly deported. Chasing the American Dream was far more exhilarating than chasing celebrity skirt.

What in the world did Vadim have? He had *movies*. Sam Spiegel had movies, too. But Spiegel was a producer, *the* producer, the creator of the stereotype, with the fat cigars and the harem of wannabe actresses and the yacht and the Rollses and the criminal record. In short, he was half genie but half ogre. Vadim, on the other hand, was a director, an artist, sensitive and smart, even if his films were duds. Plus, he was tall, handsome, charming, debonair, international.

Vadim wasn't by any means the stereotypical director, if there was such a thing. Orson Welles had a lot of the same Vadim allures but created great movies. He was more interested in making film than making love. Also, Welles's beauty had only a narrow window, until he got as fat as the great Alfred Hitchcock, that stalker of icy blondes. No ladies' man, either, was Federico Fellini, although Vadim was more in the mold of the

Marcello Mastroianni director character in Fellini's *8½*. That film was pure fiction; Roger Vadim was stranger than fiction, the stuff of novels and of adolescent male dreams.

Roger Vadim was short for Roger Vadim Plemiannikov. He always bragged of being a direct descendant of Genghis Khan, genetics accounting for his savage Mongol brio in the boudoir. His Russian descent was no mere invention but truly a fact of his life. Lesser aristocrats, Vadim's family, like the Cassinis, were uprooted by the Bolshevik Revolution. In the Jet Set, a time of travel and eros, multiple nationalities seemed to have an aphrodisiac effect. The Plemiannikovs ended up in Paris, where Vadim's father took a French wife, passed the civil service exam, and was posted to the French consulate in Alexandria, Egypt. He died of a coronary at thirty-four in 1937, in front of a nine-year-old Roger, who returned with his mother to Europe, where she managed an alpine chalet hotel that hid Jews fleeing France and the onrushing Nazis. She remarried to an architect in the cabinet of Le Corbusier, but Roger left home to be on his own at sixteen.

After dropping out of the Sorbonne and washing out as an actor, Vadim (as everyone called him, like Liberace) found a mentor/father figure in the French *auteur* Marc Allégret, who made Vadim his assistant director on a film he shot in London starring Valerie Hobson, the wife of John Profumo of the eponymous scandal. A precursor of Jet Set morality, Allégret was polymorphously perverse. He had been the gay lover of Jean Cocteau and André Gide, but on a trip to Africa with Gide, he discovered Congolese women and went straight.

Most famous for directing the film of Marcel Pagnol's Marseilles-docks love story *Fanny*, Allégret still had an eye for the boys and discovered both Louis Jourdan and Jean-Paul Belmondo, not to mention Vadim, who himself discovered Audrey Hepburn, as a swimsuited chorus girl in a seedy London private club, shades of Christine Keeler and Mandy Rice-Davies and *Expresso Bongo*. *Comme le Jet Set était petit!* Vadim, the truffle hound of star-level beauty, was also in on the ground floor of the careers of Leslie Caron and Ursula Andress.

Vadim met Bardot in 1950 when he was all of twenty-two. She was all of fifteen. They married in 1952 and were divorced in 1957, before the first 707 ever landed in Paris. However, the couple basically invented Saint-Tropez and set the standard of decadence and license that so many of Juan Trippe's customers bought tickets to Europe just to experience, however fifth-hand. France's Power Couple had used the then-sleepy and cheap Saint-Tropez as the location for their low-budget film *And God Created Woman,* an underground smash that was to the fifties, with sex, what *Easy Rider* was to the sixties, with drugs.

Woman didn't happen overnight. In fact, it was Bardot's seventeenth film. She had helped earn the rent by dancing on cruise ships. She didn't exactly emerge spontaneously as the French Marilyn Monroe. Vadim was also struggling. Despite having been a minor celebrity as the youngest screenwriter in France, Vadim had been forced to get a day job as a reporter for *Paris Match,* the French *Life,* and was in danger of ending up in total obscurity. What he had were his looks—very tall, lean, and lupine, with big glasses for his hypnotic green eyes, as needed for the left bank intellectual effect—and his charm. And his voice was a sex organ.

Vadim was the ostensible Galahad of the Jet Set. Yet if one looked closely at the man, he wasn't exactly a role model for the red-blooded aspiring playboys who were Hugh Hefner's audience. To begin with, his first three great Euro-conquests were teenagers, and Jane Fonda was barely in her twenties when she became the fourth famous actress to fall under his spell. Vadim was arguably a pedophile. He was also an addict—of gambling, drinking, drugs, and prostitutes, whom he hired both independently and as marital aids. He was also kind of a geek, obsessed with reading *MAD* magazine. And he was a financial disaster and a parasite, if not a pimp, living off the earnings of his star child brides. In short, Vadim was about as much a credit to his race of lotharios as Eddie Gilbert was to his race of high financiers.

Woman made a man, a world-famous man, out of Roger Vadim. Even if it didn't put him in the Godard-Truffaut pantheon, the film was the most successful of all the French films of the *nouvelle vague,* surely because it showed the most flesh. The log line for the movie, about the amours of an oversexed teenage orphan, could have been "Lolita in Saint-Tropez." Vadim was hoisted on the petard of his success. Bardot had an affair with costar Jean-Louis Trintignant, who left his own star wife, Stéphane Audran, for her, until Bardot dumped him for singer Gilbert Bécaud.

Bardot and Vadim divorced just before the film's 1957 premiere in New York, but, now rich and able to indulge his playboy passions like racing Ferraris, he moved on quickly to stunning

TOPLESS. French bombshell Brigitte Bardot, on the Saint-Tropez set of the scandalous *And God Created Woman*, directed by her husband, Roger Vadim, 1956.

Danish actress Annette Stroyberg, aged nineteen. The short-attention-span Vadim quickly left Stroyberg in 1960 for Catherine Deneuve, the seventeen-year-old daughter of esteemed Comédie-Française thespians. Under his tutelage, Deneuve bleached her brown hair blond and immediately became an icon, the icy goddess of Gaullist France. They lasted three years, until her hits *The Umbrellas of Cherbourg* and *Repulsion* propelled her onward. She married Swinging London's top photographer, David Bailey, who traded in Jean Shrimpton for her. Jane Fonda would become the flavor of Vadim's next decade.

It was very *Liaisons Dangereuses,* or low French farce, depending on one's perspective. Whatever, the six degrees of Roger Vadim filled the gossip columns and fan magazines on both sides of the Atlantic, year after year. A big touch of class was contributed by Simone de Beauvoir, who bestowed upon Bardot the ultimate encomium, declaring her the first liberated woman of France, a genuine "locomotif" of feminism. All aboard the Eros Express!

The Beauvoir validation must have made its impression on young Jane Fonda, who would become America's sex symbol of liberation, if only by eventually throwing off the yoke of marriage to the sexist, dominant Svengali who was Vadim. He had earned the reputation as the greatest seducer Europe had seen since Casanova, albeit with a helping hand from Paris's top procuress, Madame Claude, who dispatched her *filles de joie* for the Vadim-Fonda sex orgies, with Jane—rich from her film roles and her late socialite mother's inheritance—picking up Madame's hefty tabs. It was an investment in Method acting research that she would recoup in 1971 when she won her first Oscar for playing a fancy call girl in *Klute*.

If Vadim's other great conquests were vulnerable to him because of their age and adolescent ambitions, Jane Fonda, seemingly untouchable Hollywood royalty who hardly needed a foreign operator like Vadim, turned out to be far more vulnerable than Bardot, Stroyberg, and Deneuve combined. Key to her sensitivity was the suicide of her mother, who slashed her own throat when Jane was twelve. Then there was the iconic but unloving father, whose fame was a seemingly impossible act to follow. Jane had, like Jackie Bouvier, gone to Vassar but just dropped out. Forsaking academe for showbiz appeared at first to be a misbegotten attempt to compete with her father, especially when the Harvard Hasty Pudding Club gave Jane the anti-Oscar as Worst Actress of 1962 for *The Chapman Report*.

So off in 1963 Jane went to Europe, at the time when the siren call was loudest. Henry Fonda had heeded that same call in 1957, marrying a Venetian-Jewish socialite named Afdera Franchetti, decades his junior and just a few years older than Jane. To spite her father, Jane had begun an affair with one of Afdera's recent lovers, Sandy Whitelaw, a young former Harvard skiing champion and Hasty Pudding member who had become a junior executive for David O. Selznick. It was Jane's revenge on Harvard and Henry. However, it wasn't enough. She needed Roger

Vadim. He was the kind of lover guaranteed to give Henry Fonda, the symbol of American virtue and righteousness, apoplexy.

After Whitelaw and before Vadim, there was Alain Delon, pre-Markovic. Jane got her first European film role in the 1964 mystery *Joy House,* directed by René Clément, who had showcased Delon in the estimable thriller *Purple Noon* (1960), one of the greatest cinematic advertisements for Jet Set European travel. *Joy House,* which divided its locations between a château and a Salvation Army mission, was the opposite of glamorous; plus, it made no sense, not even in the artiest way. Whatever heat was generated with Jane by Delon, who was even more beautiful than she, was dissipated by the anemic box office. The film was barely shown in America, except at a few art houses in New York. No stroke for Henry Fonda from this one.

Waiting in the wings was Roger Vadim. He had met Jane once before, in 1958. She had just left Vassar and come to France in a desultory effort to become an artist, a female Gene Kelly in *An American in Paris.* Because she had better connections than any other American art student in the city, she spent much more of her time on the Régine's/Tour d'Argent circuit than at the École des Beaux-Arts. One night at Maxim's, on a date with actor Christian Marquand, she met Vadim, at the height of his Bardot Svengalihood.

Jane was impressed. Vadim was not. He sent his friend and amorous rival Marquand a note making fun of Jane's fat ankles, a note that Jane found and read when Marquand went table-hopping. Jane's ankles were, forgive the expression, the Achilles' heel of her beauty, her one bodily feature that wasn't perfect and that she couldn't change. Vadim had hit the G-spot of her insecurity. Was that his genius with women? Vadim's misogynistic cruelty proved to be an aphrodisiac that would simmer for years, until they met again, in 1962. Then it boiled over into Europe's most celebrated affair.

By the time of *Klute,* the honeymoon with Vadim was over, though they would not divorce until 1973. Thanks in part to Vadim's sexism and in part to the times, Jane had become radicalized and would abandon Maxim's for Hanoi. Until she did, she and Vadim were the Jet Set's prime power couple, dividing their time between Malibu and St. Moritz, Paris and Saint-Tropez, with Jane experiencing a schizophrenic career that was half Hollywood ingenue and half Euro sex goddess. On the American side were wholesome confections like *Barefoot in the Park;* on the continental side were X-rated romps like *The Game Is Over,* which could have been retitled as "Bareassed in the Parc Monceau."

And then there was *Barbarella,* shot in Rome in the last gasp of the Dolce Vita, before that sweet life turned sour with the Red Brigade's kidnappings and bombings. The Vadims' Roman lifestyle was basically Malibu on the Via Appia Antica, their villa a crash pad of druggie Hollywood hippies like Jane's brother, Peter, and his *Easy Rider* (and *Dr. Strangelove*) screenwriter Terry Southern, who wrote the *Barbarella* script with Vadim. Not even Southern could save this porno comic book of a film, which many cultists have subsequently embraced as way ahead of its time—by forty years. Luckily for Jane, her Hollywood attempt to atone by "getting serious" in the 1969 *They Shoot Horses, Don't They?* got her an Oscar nomination and broke Vadim's Euro curse.

If Vadim could have gotten work in America, he surely would have turned Jane into a Hollywood sex goddess before she did it for herself in *Klute,* but nobody here would hire him, symbolic of this country's growing disenchantment with Europe in the late sixties. This was a terrible sign for the new 747s, which needed all the European enchantment Mary Wells Lawrence and Madison Avenue could possibly muster. Alas, all those babes in Pucci minis had lost their mystique, replaced as sex symbols by tie-dyed slum goddesses. The glamour that was the Jet Set had become passé, almost Nixonian. Chic wasn't chic anymore. After Haight-Ashbury and the Summer of Love, radical was the new chic. The Jet Set lost its groove, if it ever had one. *Easy Rider* made the American South the hip destination; nothing in Provence or Tuscany seemed nearly as exotic. Juan Trippe's high-speed jet travel was no longer cool. The trips that mattered were Timothy Leary's.

Perhaps the saddest of all commentaries on the Jet Set and the most vivid symbol of its decline was the mésalliance between Oleg Cassini and Bernie Cornfeld. The Russian count and the Brooklyn socialist were the odd couple of the decade, the ties that bound being funny money and fading elegance. By the end of the sixties, Oleg Cassini, in his midfifties, was a man alone. His post as "Secretary of Style" in the Kennedy cabinet was long gone, as was his top client. When Jackie Kennedy married Aristotle Onassis in 1968, the pretense and patriotism of using an "American" designer had gone by the wayside. There was no need for Jackie to get Oleg to do Givenchy for her. Givenchy could do it himself, and Ari would pay.

Losing Jackie wasn't half as bad as losing Igor. Igor had thought the trials over his Dominican misadventures would end with the nolo contendere plea. He was vastly overoptimistic, for his next menace after the Justice Department was the Internal Revenue Service, who ultimately assessed Igor for nearly three quarters of a million dollars in tax evasion. Meanwhile, he kept partying as if the Jet Set would last forever. He got involved with a *Playboy* centerfold named Connie Mason, another Virginia belle like the one who had gotten him tarred and feathered as a young gossip columnist, which was nothing compared to what Bobby Kennedy had done to him. He turned Mason into a Ford model and then a horror-movie star before she dumped Igor to wed a powerful Hollywood lawyer.

Igor also started his own magazine, called *Status*. He dubbed it "the magazine for the restless," but despite a prestigious list of contributors that included Graham Greene, Salvador Dalí, James Baldwin, Art Buchwald, and Gloria Steinem, the most restless people involved in the venture were its investors. *Status* closed shop in under three years, in 1968. All the while Igor was bunking with Oleg, in the latter's Renaissance townhouse off Gramercy Park. But the brothers' bromance ended in a brutal fistfight at La Côte Basque, site of the Truman Capote spill-all *Esquire* story that ended his own romance with the swans of the Jet Set. The altercation was over Igor's detestation of Oleg's fatal attraction to Bernie Cornfeld, the pied piper of mutual funds and a man who made the Cassinis' formerly favorite funny financier, Eddie Gilbert—still fighting his way through the courts for his defalcations—look like a pillar of fiscal rectitude.

The tiny, plump, red-bearded Cornfeld resembled a lapsed Hasidic rabbi decked out in Cardin and Hermès. He was the visual antithesis of the sleek, perfect Oleg Cassini. Cornfeld's legendary pitch line in recruiting his mutual fund salesmen was "Do you sincerely want to be rich?" He obviously used it on Oleg Cassini, and it worked. Oleg sincerely believed Bernie would make him the global king of fashion that he always dreamed of being and, had JFK not been assassinated, he might have become on his own. Igor did not believe anything Bernie promised. He knew a con man when he saw one, even if it was every time he looked in the mirror. He wanted to save his brother, but Oleg was one of many thousands who could not resist Bernie's unique call of the wild.

Like the Cassinis and so many of the leaders of the Jet Set, Bernie Cornfeld was born on the run—in his case, in Istanbul in 1927, to a Romanian father who was an early film producer and a Russian mother, a nurse. Bernie's lifelong interest in show business was thus genetic; he would turn high finance *into* show business, which was the key to his success. His parents had met in Vienna and then together immigrated once more, to Providence and then to Brooklyn in the early thirties, in the depths of the Depression. Bernie, who loved being a Boy Scout, overcame a severe stutter and joined the merchant marine to travel the world. In 1948, he entered Brooklyn College and eventually made it through Columbia's School of Social Work. Bernie was both a social worker and a socialist, becoming an active member of the Trotskyite Socialist Youth League. The young idealist soon found that if he wanted to redistribute the wealth of the world, politics were not the answer. He would have to do it himself.

Bernie became a mutual fund salesman on Wall Street, and in spite of his former stutter, he was immediately good at it. He was passionate, not at helping the rich get richer but at helping average people make money. However, as much as Bernie liked selling funds in New York, the magic of postwar Europe that had beckoned Temple Fielding beckoned him as well. He had a half brother who'd become a vice president in 20th Century Fox's Paris office, in the years when studio head Darryl Zanuck was basically living in the George V and ruling Fox by long-distance phone. In 1955, Bernie Cornfeld, with a few hundred dollars, took a Pan Am flight to Paris that would change his life and high finance as well.

Bernie quickly discovered that there were two main constituencies of the approximately 700,000 Americans in pre-jet Europe, a major segment of the more than three million Americans then living abroad. One was the "exiles," neo–Lost Generation types, educated, bohemian, people like Bernie himself who wanted something more out of life than Eisenhower suburbia. The second, much larger group (more than 600,000) was made up of the American servicemen and their families, there to fight the Cold War. This latter group would have done anything to be back in Eisenhower suburbia, but Uncle Sam wouldn't let them go. These soldiers stayed close to the bases. Bernie didn't see many of them at the Café Flore or Les Deux Magots. It was Bernie's genius to put these two groups together by turning the usually unemployed but ever hungry educated exiles into mutual fund salesmen to peddle Wall Street products to the homesick servicemen. To the joint benefit of the salesmen and Bernie's own fortune, the pitch was that once the soldiers got home, they would be able to afford that slice of the suburbia of their dreams.

Bernie bought a used Simca, found a cheap apartment in the monied 16th arrondissement, and started taking out ads in the *Herald Tribune* offering ambitious Yanks the chance to make the then-princely sum of over $10,000 a year selling mutual funds. The requirements? Sales ability, hustle, and, rare in an ad for salespeople, "a sense of humor." Funny money was, from the beginning, what Bernie Cornfeld was all about. He found a lot of wannabe writers, artists, and musicians, gave them a five-day crash course in finance, and then sent them out to make their fortunes, so they could trade up from *saucisson* to foie gras.

Off the record, Bernie promised all his recruits that he would make them millionaires. By 1962, he was keeping his word. He had moved his company, called Investors Overseas Services, to Calvinist Geneva, in the land of a thousand banks. He had been pretty much run out of Paris by Charles de Gaulle, who was as suspicious of American mutual funds as he was of Conrad Hilton's running ice water, even though IOS wasn't selling to French citizens, only expat Americans. De Gaulle basically tried to kill Bernie by regulating him to death. Now that Bernie had become fluent in French and Francophile in his tastes, by reorganizing in nearby Geneva, he could have his gâteau and eat it, too.

By 1962, IOS had expanded way beyond GIs, with 20,000 clients in over sixty countries. Bernie charmed Wall Street's Jack Dreyfus into letting him be the exclusive overseas agent for the prestigious Dreyfus Fund, then created his own "Fund of Funds," a blend of numerous other stock vehicles. He called his sales force his "piece corps," referring to his piece of the industry, but also to his growing harem of aspiring models, actresses, and assorted gold diggers who flocked to his thirteenth-century French château, just across the Swiss border, complete with moat and drawbridge, and his Lake Geneva villa that had been built for Josephine by Napoléon.

Bernie became known as the Hugh Hefner of Europe. In fact, Hefner became one of super-bachelor Bernie's best friends, along with Tony Curtis and George Hamilton. The socialist social worker was the most ambitious man in finance since Eddie Gilbert fled to Brazil. He claimed, however, that what he was doing was social work. "We find people before they're destitute," he said, "and do something about it." What he did was generate excellent returns of over 20 percent a year for his customers, but vastly more for his salesmen, many of whom became sincerely rich, with châteaux of their own. But Bernie never forgot where he came from, flying in planeloads of New York delicatessen fare from the Stage Deli on Seventh Avenue, hot dogs from Nathan's of Coney Island, and frozen Sara Lee cheesecake.

Aside from his Brooklyn diet, no socialist ever lived so grandly and capitalistically. Bernie had a Chinese houseboy, two Great Danes, ten saddle horses, and never fewer than a dozen big blondes in tow—a living Helmut Newton album. Pure Jet Set, he had a helicopter, a Convair turboprop, and a Dassault Falcon private jet, which took him between his European properties and his suite at New York's Carlyle, just a few floors away from the Kennedy pied-à-terre. It was in New York that he met Oleg Cassini, at Le Club, through its manager, Bobby Friedman,

who was the city's only rival to Hollywood producer Robert Evans in the
who-knows-the-most-models sweepstakes. Oleg without Jackie, business-
wise, was very much like Antony without Cleopatra. Notwithstanding
his White House profile, American memories were short, and the styles,
like the times, were changing, influenced by the rise of Brit-rock, Carnaby Street, and the hippie movement. Even Oleg had started dressing
like Jimi Hendrix.

It was time to go back to Europe, Bernie convinced Oleg. Bernie's
idea was to turn Oleg into the first Giorgio Armani, long before Armani
ever hit the scene. Forget Paris, Bernie said. Rome was wide open; plus,
there was no chauvinistic De Gaulle to block their path and no Danny
the Red to shut down their factories—not yet, at least. Oleg would become the first great Roman couturier, the Christian Dior of the Dolce
Vita. He would be much bigger than Igor's University of Georgia classmate Emilio Pucci. Pucci dressed Braniff air hostesses; Oleg dressed first
ladies. Bernie, the master of the pitch, convinced Oleg that the new
House of Cassini would be a sure thing. Headquarters would be in the
Palazzo Ruspoli, one of Rome's grandest edifices, at the end of the Via
Condotti, which had just been acquired by one of Bernie's partners, a
shady millionaire Italian manufacturer named Roberto Memmo. Memmo's factories employed six thousand Italian artisans who would make
all the clothes.

Alas, just at the moment of truth, when the deal was nearly done,
Bernie and Oleg were done in by the same plunging American economy
and crashing Wall Street that would do in Juan Trippe and his 747. In
1970, Bernie was thrown out of IOS by all the salesmen whom he had
made rich, replaced by the scoundrel adventure capitalist Robert Vesco,
who himself would soon take the money and run to Costa Rica. Bernie
would spend a year in a Swiss jail until he got the financial fraud charges
against him dropped. Then he moved to Los Angeles, to be near Hefner
and his new Playboy Mansion.

Poor Oleg, with nowhere to go in Rome, tried Milan, to no avail.
Never saying die, he made his next move into creating a line of Native
American print dresses. As a boy, he was always fascinated by Indians,

and now he would try a second childhood. When that failed, he decided to return to New York. To that end, he threw himself on the lavish mercy of Imelda Marcos, who, as the patron saint of distressed playboys, would later come to the aid and comfort of George Hamilton, who had sold his Beverly Hills estate, Grayhall, to Bernie Cornfeld. The Jet Set may have been sputtering, but, ties still binding, they sputtered together.

Hef and Bernie, with their nonstop cocaine-and-champagne-fueled topless pool parties in their neighboring palaces, were making a joint and valiant attempt to rescue both *Playboy*, the brand, and playboy, the lifestyle, from irrelevance and looming extinction. They seemed to be trying to prove that even if Europe had become passé, playboydom itself had no borders. Alas, all their revelries were for a lost cause. Playboys were riding off into the sunset, and not the Pacific beaches at the end of Sunset Boulevard. Some, like the Cassinis, were fading away. Others had crashed and burned. In 1960, Prince Aly Khan died when he totaled his new Lancia in Paris's Bois de Boulogne. In 1965, near the very same deadly curve, Porfirio Rubirosa perished when he totaled his new Ferrari. Khan had just gotten engaged; Rubirosa had gotten married. Their playboy heydays were well behind them even before Juan Trippe's 707s took to the skies.

That other postwar icon of male prerogative, Gianni Agnelli, had married a Neapolitan princess back in 1953, long before Café Society sped itself up and transformed into the Jet Set. The royal marriage didn't exactly take Agnelli off the market; he had a famous three-year affair with bombshell Anita Ekberg at the height of her *La Dolce Vita* fame, as well as a hotly rumored one with Jackie Kennedy at the height of her Camelot hegemony. But the "King of Italy," as the auto tycoon was known, had left his playboy image behind with his youth. His famous romance with Pamela Digby Churchill began back in 1948, when he was twenty-seven and before she moved on to Hayward and Harriman. But that affair was less about sex than status. Bedding Winston Churchill's former daughter-in-law was of inestimable value to young Agnelli in expunging the shameful stain of his country's wartime defeat. The adult

Agnelli was known far more for his vast corporate power and his high style than for his wild oats.

Even the ultimate flyboy Frank Sinatra, who turned fifty in 1965, when fifty was *old,* took himself off the party market when he married twenty-one-year-old Mia Farrow in 1966. That union may have seemed like a merger of the Jet Set and Flower Power. Instead, it was living proof of a generation gap that could never be bridged, a twain that could never meet. The tabloid fantasy marriage between the ultimate Swinger and the ultimate Hippie was a front-page disaster that lasted under two years.

Farrow's rejection of Sinatra mirrored the baby boomers' rejection of their parents' male-supremacist, martini-fueled, conspicuous-consumption, gray-flannel culture, a culture that had spawned the Jet Set. What really was the playboy but the Eisenhower husband unchained? By the time Pan Am's 747 made its maiden commercial flight in 1970, Europe, which had provided the glamorous and sophisticated context for the rise of the playboy mystique, was rapidly losing its Old World gloss and floss, and the playboys themselves were either down for the count or knocked out of the ring altogether. And without the playboys fueling the image and the dream, no amount of Pratt & Whitney horsepower could keep the Jet Set aloft.

15

Final Destinations

THE ADVENT OF THE 747 MARKED THE END OF THE JET SET AS A SOCIOLOGICAL phenomenon that had been the quintessence of its time and was now out of time. The 747 itself, on the other hand, was a technological phenomenon that was ahead of its time, way ahead, by a decade. Until the times, Ronald Reagan flush times, caught up with the 747 and made it the most successful plane in history, it seemed that very same jumbo jet was going to be history's biggest flop, that the wings of man had been clipped by the scissors of economics and slashed by the daggers of terrorism.

The most powerful and sustained headwind that the 747 would face was the economic downturn that followed the Eisenhower-Kennedy postwar boom. This slump is known to economists as the "Secular Bear Market, 1966–1982." It wasn't that the stock market actually crashed, like it did in 1929; it just went sideways, which, to investors, was nowhere. Over that sixteen-year period, the Dow Jones Industrial Average lost a grand total of 1.18 percent. But to investors like the burgeoning ranks of mutual fund owners, who had savored returns of 30 to 40 percent a year in the Kennedy bull market, these were the times that tried Americans' souls and certainly did not encourage them to buy the latest Fielding *Guide* and plan a European blowout.

The Dow continually flirted with the magic number of 1,000, but that number was the world's biggest tease. Every time the market made an upward move, something terrible in geopolitics would hurl it back to earth—Vietnam, the assassinations of Martin Luther King, Jr., and Robert Kennedy, the Kent State murders, the invasion of Cambodia, Watergate, the Arab oil crisis. Even when America pulled out of Vietnam in 1975, the Dow went up to 1,004, but it couldn't stay there. The new Democratic president, Jimmy Carter, did not live up to the popular hope that he would be a Kennedy with a Dixie drawl. Instead, he was done in by stagflation, that reverse speedball (a slowball) of stagnation and inflation, highlighted by low growth, high unemployment, and high inflation.

Pity the poor 747 and pity the poor Skycoons. Aside from the high-profile hijacking and destruction of the Pan Am 747 in Cairo in 1970's Black September, Palestinian guerrillas were the least of the jumbo jet's jumbo problems. The biggest were the Pratt & Whitney jet engines, which, in the plane's first few years of service, broke down so many times, in potentially fatally inconvenient locations like midocean, that a massive three-way lawsuit among Pan Am, Boeing, and Pratt & Whitney (with airline suing plane maker suing engine maker) was averted only by the most delicate corporate diplomacy and quietly vast settlement amounts. Pan Am's Juan Trippe officially retired in 1968, the same year Boeing's Bill Allen stepped down as Boeing's president. The two Skycoons kicked themselves upstairs and became the chairmen of their respective boards, at an appropriately Olympian remove from the impending fray. That both leaders got out of the chief-executive line of fire before the planes entered service and the troubles began spoke volumes to plane watchers: The Big Boys knew something no one else did.

With the captains abandoning ship, the replacement crew did their best to put on a brave face. Even though the twenty-five 747s Trippe had originally ordered from Boeing seemed like the height of unfounded optimism, his successor Najeeb Halaby stuck with the program. Halaby's bullishness on the 747 was unshakable. In 1970, he exercised an option for eight more of the behemoths, even in the face of cabins with pathetic handfuls of passengers. In 1971, Pan Am posted a staggering loss of $50 million, and its annual report dropped the brave face and admitted that the next year's picture was unlikely to be much brighter. At one point in 1971, Halaby even considered the drastic step of grounding the airline's entire fleet of 747s, it being cheaper to warehouse them than fly them.

The step was aborted, but in 1972, so was Halaby. With the company's $300 million–plus loss and its debts approaching $1 billion, Halaby was replaced by World War II hero Brigadier General William Seawell, who was also a Harvard Law School graduate skilled in navigating the shoals of bankruptcy on which Pan Am was about to run aground. By 1977, after 30 percent cuts to its workforce and a 25 percent reduction of its routes, plus lots of fancy fiscal footwork, Pan Am avoided extinction and turned its first profit, small though it was, in years.

The good news didn't last long. Seawell knew Pan Am's glory days as the international Jet Set airline were as over as the Jet Set itself. Juan Trippe had already divined this in the late sixties; his bright idea had been to take *normal* people to Europe. Seawell's idea now was to take them to Florida. The Jimmy Carter brainstorm, the 1978 Airline Deregulation Act—which renounced the traditional conception of the business as a public utility in favor of a free-market "open skies" approach—liberated Pan Am from its once vaunted foreign-routes-only status, an exclusivity that had become an albatross. Pan Am now could have national routes; it could become, at long last, an *American* airline. So, greedily eyeing its New York–Miami service, Seawell bought National Airlines. To get it, he defeated Eastern Airlines in a heated bidding war. The former general was ready to hang up his wings on a high note.

It was not to be. The corporate cultures of the two companies did not jell; Pan Am snobbishly looked down on National as a "backwoods" regional carrier. Nor did National's American routes "feed" passengers to Pan Am's international flights the way Seawell had hoped. The losses began to mount. Seawell was forced to sell off the Pan Am Building to Metropolitan Life and unload its InterContinental Hotels chain, along with its half-ownership of the Dassault Falcon Jet Corporation, which manufactured the Ferrari of private jets.

No sooner had Seawell stepped down in 1981 than Pan Am ended its fabled round-the-world service, then began selling off all its international routes. In December 1991, the unthinkable occurred: Pan Am went out of business. Its final flight was that of the *Clipper Goodwill*, a Boeing 727 from Barbados to Miami, one of the airline's earliest Caribbean runs that Juan Trippe had used as a springboard to conquer the world. Now Juan Trippe was gone, and so was his world.

In his place was Freddie Laker. And a very different place it was. Laker, a British swashbuckling entrepreneur born in Canterbury in 1922, had spent his whole business life in the bargain-basement aviation business. A pilot in World War II, he then sold surplus planes in the postwar era before starting to fly supplies into Berlin in 1948 to circumvent the Soviet blockade. In 1966, seeing the same budget market that Arthur Frommer did, Laker started his own charter airline, Laker Airways, with two used turboprops he bought for a song from BOAC. By 1972, he was doing so well, and Pan Am and company were doing so badly, that he launched his famous Skytrain, no-reservations service between London and New York. The ticket price was under $100 each way. Laker was able to go cut-rate because his was a British company unfettered by American price controls. His vast success was a key factor in Jimmy Carter's deregulating the crumbling industry.

Skytrain was an idea whose time had truly come, and Laker became Sir Freddie in 1978, knighted by the queen for his service to Britain and to the sub–Jet Set mass public. At last, after all the failures of the De Havilland jets and of British aviation to compete with America in general, England had its own folk hero of the skies. But Laker turned out to have Icarus within him. His fatal flaw was that of eschewing the bug-plagued 747 and choosing for his fleet the new Douglas DC-10, a trijet plane that seated 300, somewhere between the 707 and the 747, and seemed just the right size to meet the recession-terrorist-reduced demand for international travel. Lockheed had its own rival in this category, the L-1011, while Boeing stubbornly stuck to its guns with the 747.

If Laker had known how successful he would be, he would have realized he could have filled the 747s with no problem. But for once, he sold himself short. In May 1979, after a spectacular American Airlines disaster in Chicago, the entire fleet of DC-10s was grounded worldwide. This tragedy, which killed 273 people and was the culmination of a skein of fatal DC-10 accidents that had started in 1974 with the crash in Paris of a brand-new Turkish Airlines jet, created the stigma that the plane was "unsafe."

All the testing and recertification by the Federal Aviation Administration couldn't erase the stain on the plane's reputation. Meanwhile, unleashed by the 1978 deregulation act, the American airlines began cutting their own prices to match Sir Freddie's, as did most of the European carriers. Why fly a "discount" airline, as Sir Freddie's was sneered at, when you could fly Pan Am or TWA or Air France for the same price? Laker cried foul. He also cried conspiracy, and he took his rivals to court in the largest aviation antitrust case of all time. The case was eventually settled, but the damage was done. Skytrain went bankrupt in 1982, a year after Juan Trippe succumbed to a stroke at eighty-two. Since his retirement from Pan Am, Trippe had spent the entire time enjoying himself, game fishing in the Bahamas and playing golf in Greenwich. He had nothing left to prove. He had done it all.

Trippe's great partner in the skies, Bill Allen, a sport fisherman himself, had a much harder time of his golden years. He developed Alzheimer's disease and wasted away, dying in 1985 at eighty-five. But he was conscious enough to see his 747 vindicated. It took about five years, but by the midseventies, the 747's engine kinks had been ironed out, and airports around the world had completed facilities that would accommodate the jumbo. As the competing widebodies, the DC-10 and the L-1011, began to show their fatal flaws, the 747 proved to be the safest aircraft ever created.

When Reagan took office in 1981 and the long recession finally ended, Carter's deregulation had made flying so cheap that the public began buying tickets in the droves that would get Freddie Laker rich and titled. Consequently, the 747s began to fill up, and they became the mainstay of long-distance travel around the world. Ironically, Pan Am, once the international leader, could no longer compete on price, only on class and image, and those were Jet Set qualities that spelled nothing but vanished grandeur and eventual extinction. When Boeing unveiled the 747, it was expected to become obsolete after 400 of them were sold. Instead, it just keeps on flying. By 2013, over 1,500 of the planes had been manufactured, compared to 1,000 707s. But the 707 is a museum item now, while the 747 is still very much up in the air. The leviathan is no longer a monster; it is the hero of the skies.

Although the 747 managed to rise from the dead, the remarkable resurrection of the big jet did not extend to the Jet Set. The Reagan money era definitely got lots of people back on the planes, but the new generation of first-class fliers had less in common, style-wise, with James Bond than with some of his super-rich villains, Auric Goldfinger in particular. The Reagan years were all about flash and bling, the White House as *Dynasty* on Pennsylvania Avenue, with the Hollywood Kitchen Cabinet setting the tone, and the brash tycoon Walter Annenberg at the Court of St. James's, much to the dismay of snobby Albion. Afterward, the Clinton/Bush Wall Street free-for-all created a new jet set of Gulfstreams for often uncouth and uncultured Masters of the Universe who sneered at first class as infra dig.

The problem for the Jet Set was that, at least as it was conceived by Igor Cassini, it was simply too aristocratic for an increasingly democratic and meritocratic world. Cassini not only conceptualized the Jet Set; he basically embodied it, as a European, titled, cultured, and ultimately monied aristo-playboy. Igor and Oleg Cassini and their friends were precisely the kind of beautiful people Juan Trippe's 707 ticket buyers wanted to travel to meet and, in their dreams, *to be*. America's evolving upper class had always needed an offshore role model, particularly in the post–Civil War robber-baron era, when America's great fortunes were made and became the capitalist fantasy of a tabloid-reading mass public. That model was the European, preferably British, aristocrat, who, for all of America's brief history, had set the standards of style and etiquette—first for the self-styled grandees on the gracious plantations of Dixie, then for the Old Guard in Mrs. Astor's ballroom, afterward for the more permeable Café Society of the Jazz Age to the Eisenhower fifties, and finally, for the new Jet Set.

Nobody played the all-American plutocrat-as-aristocrat game better than the Kennedys; hence JFK's perfectly Jet Set presidency and the permanent void of glamour that followed it. When movie stars entered Café Society, they behaved like aristocrats. Or perhaps, given the power of movies, aristocrats behaved like *them,* viz Gary Cooper, William Powell, Cary Grant, David Niven, Bing Crosby, and many more, who all embodied the smooth-as-silk old-boy ethos. Even Frank Sinatra, for all his Mafia associations and occasional thuggery, aspired to the "class" that corresponded to his elegant singing.

And then came Elvis. The 707 and DC-8 were launched simultaneously with the emergence of a youth culture that changed the world as much as the jets did. These new kids didn't care about being *smooth* anymore. They wanted to be *cool.* Hence the rise of a new idol class of anti-stars—Robert De Niro, Al Pacino, Dustin Hoffman—sprouting from subversive seeds planted in the fifties by James Dean and Marlon Brando. Even Ian Fleming's effete James Bond was roughened up and turned into a film icon by the tough and tattooed Sean Connery. The English upper class who had been aped socially by an insecure America ever since our Revolution was put aside at last. Still, the Brits were being aped; only now it was the newly hip English lower-class model that was copied, syncopated to the Mersey beat.

After the sixties, the only Jet Set–y actor left in America seemed to be George Hamilton, and he was regarded as far less a character than a caricature. Most important to this sea change of role models was the post-Elvis rise of musicians into gods of rock, pop, and soul. Aside from the brief early confusion of Mick Jagger over whether he wanted to be

Lord Snowdon or Chuck Berry, there were no aristocratic traditions anywhere in these emerging legends' DNA. Even when the Beatles and the
Stones and the rest of the rockocracy bought stately homes, they lived
like hippie squatters, hardly to these manors born.

The generational contempt for materialism, the ubiquity of drugs,
and the embrace of the 1967 San Francisco Summer of Love–inspired
New Bohemia didn't exactly result in making poverty chic, but rather,
elegance passé, the stuff of out-of-it parents. Yet the baby boomers
wanted to go to Europe as much as the Fielding-toting old folks did,
albeit for different reasons, like getting high on the Acropolis or walking
stoned through the Louvre or just grooving on Carnaby Street and waiting in the hour-long lines at the Hard Rock Café. Yet thanks to the giant
jets and the lower and lower airfares and the budget guidance of Arthur
Frommer, the boomers, unlike previous generations, could afford to
turn Europe into their own playground, and they did. Slim Aarons
might not have taken their photos for *Holiday,* nor were they likely to be
seated in prime tables by Claude Terrail, but they still had high times.

In the contest for the hearts and minds of American travelers between Temple Fielding and Arthur Frommer, mass overwhelmed class.
Although Frommer never made the cover of *Time,* and existed more as a
brand name than as a Fielding-esque oracle and personality, that *Time*
cover might well have been Fielding's bad-luck charm. The rich still traveled, and they still bought his annual *Guide,* but the middle class found
its travel aspirations trending downward toward Frommer rather than
upward toward Fielding. It was a sign of Fielding's desperation that in
1978 he broke down, swallowed his loathing for landmarks and museums, and published *Fielding's Sightseeing Guide to Europe.*

Guidesters could not live by foie gras alone, Fielding was forced to
admit. He suffered the dietary consequences. After a massive heart attack
and two major surgeries that left him unable to make his annual syba-
ritic rounds, he sold his book company to William Morrow in 1983 and
died three months later at his home in Majorca. He was sixty-nine. Arthur Frommer, on the other hand, was still traveling in his eighties,

though his company, with individual guides to much of the world, was sold to Google in 2012 for a reported $25 million. For him, living cheaply was obviously the best revenge.

Conrad Hilton, that avatar of the American way of travel, died peacefully at ninety-one in 1979. A devout Catholic to the end, he not only stayed with his faith but returned to his southwestern roots, after decades of living in Beverly Hills, to be buried in a Catholic cemetery in Dallas. He left a huge estate but only $500,000 to each of his surviving sons (Nick died at forty-two in 1969, of alcoholism) and a devastating mere $10,000 to Francesca, his daughter by Zsa Zsa Gabor, Conrad's undying hatred for whom was the motivation for Francesca's testamentary shortfall. The bulk of the fortune went to the Conrad Hilton Foundation, dedicated to Catholic charities and "the alleviation of human suffering worldwide." The foundation has a special mission to improve water safety around the globe, an echo from the grave of Conrad's obsession with running ice water in all his lodgings.

Hilton's alter ego, Claude Terrail, the avatar of ancien régime European playboyism, basically died kissing heiresses on both cheeks at the Tour d'Argent in 2006. He was eighty-eight. The Tour had lost two of its *Michelin* stars over the years but never its cachet as the ultimate French dining experience. Despite a diagnosis of macular degeneration, Terrail played polo until he could no longer see, and even after he had lost his vision, he insisted on being led around by two of his captains to welcome every single table, continuing his nightly tour of the Tour that he had conducted for over fifty years. His son, André, named after Claude's innkeeping impresario father and armed with an American-textbook education in hospitality from Babson College's MBA program, has stepped into his father's custom shoes. The Jet Set may have passed on, but its grandsons and granddaughters, wanting to get some sense of what it was all about, keep the Tour booked months in advance.

And the other Lotharios of yesteryear? Victor Lownes, *Playboy*'s man in England, is in his eighties, living in a stately home as an unlikely paragon of marital domesticity: He has remained married to 1973's Playmate of the Year Marilyn Cole since 1984. His business union with

Hugh Hefner was less blessed. In 1981, Lownes was the highest-paid executive in England. He earned his keep by making a fortune for Playboy casinos around the world. But when Lownes was called on the carpet by British gaming authorities for alleged irregularities, Hefner threw his main man under the London bus and summarily fired his longtime friend and colleague. The investigation cleared Lownes, who got the last several laughs, first by watching *Playboy*'s $30 million profit turn into a $50 million loss the year after he was canned, and then by besting Hef for the affections of Cole, who smoothly transitioned from centerfold to journalist.

The James Bondsmen Broccoli and Saltzman had their own competition, not over a woman but over Bond. After coproducing nine Bonds, the pair split in 1975. The artier of the two, Saltzman—never wanting to be defined by Bond alone—early on in the partnership branched out into other ventures, purchasing the Technicolor company, blowing two fortunes on *Toomorrow*, a flop sci-fi musical starring Olivia Newton-John, and *Nijinsky*, a flop biopic starring Alan Bates, and blowing a third on the development of still another sci-fi effort, *The Micronauts*, which would have starred Gregory Peck as a shrinking man had it not died in development. Then his wife developed cancer, and an overextended Saltzman had no choice but to sell his half of Bond to his partner. He died brokenhearted in Paris at seventy-eight in 1994.

Cubby Broccoli was more than delighted to stick to James Bond and be defined by the most successful film franchise of all time. He died, happy and with an Irving G. Thalberg Memorial Award from the Film Academy and a star on Hollywood Boulevard, at eighty-seven in 1996. The only thing missing in his storied career was Sean Connery at his funeral at Forest Lawn. The other Bonds were all there, but Connery, the Bond of Bonds, never wanted to be typecast by the role that made him— and helped set the tone of the Jet Set.

Another Thalberg recipient, the great London-based Hollywood producer Sam Spiegel, had predeceased the Bondsmen in 1986, at eighty-four. He was a playboy to the end, expiring on the Caribbean island of St. Martin, in a suite at the super-posh La Samanna resort. Other guests there at the time included Richard Avedon, Mary Tyler Moore, and Peter Ustinov, not to mention a gaggle of New York and London socialites, all of whom clamored for Spiegel to join them on what would have been his last supper. However, like his pal Greta Garbo, who traveled on his yacht, he said he wanted to be alone. Spiegel may have died, but the rumors never did. Sam Spiegel, as those who knew him would attest, *never* liked to be alone. With him when he died were said to be two, and possibly four, of Madame Claude's finest *filles de joie* airlifted to the tropics. If true, Spiegel went out in the style to which he had been long accustomed.

Spiegel's fellow Madame Claude confidant and London neighbor Tom Corbally, the man at the heart of the Profumo Affair, stayed in the heart of glamorous darkness until his own exit, in 2004 in New York at age eighty-three. He was the key man of the powerful corporate detective agency Kroll Associates. On the fringe of one scandal after another involving the Jet Set's less stylish fat-cat corporate successors, the private-jet set, Corbally, the Teflon spy, went to his grave unscathed. Corbally's two prime British mates and conduits to the deep-pocketed Euro merchant class, gambling king John Aspinall and nightlife king Mark Birley, both died deposed from their respective thrones, Aspinall at seventy-four in 2000, Birley at seventy-seven in 2007.

Just before Birley died, he sold Annabel's and his other super-exclusive clubs in London, the last redoubt of the survivors of the Jet Set, for $150 million to Richard Caring, a Hong Kong garment billionaire who has moved into the hospitality business. Caring's conversion came when he purchased England's tony Wentworth Golf Club, which is to the sport what Wimbledon is to tennis, and saw how much he enjoyed improving the facilities, especially the kitchen. Caring is an unusual collector. Instead of paintings or sculpture or exotic cars, he collects Jet Set clubs and restaurants, both old and new, from Annabel's to Le Caprice to the burgeoning Soho House chain. He doesn't do it for love. He does it for money, selling nostalgic status, somewhat like the Orient-Express train and hotel empire. In many ways, he has become the Colonel Sanders of exclusivity.

Richard Caring can be seen as a contemporary incarnation of a Jet

Setter. As such, he is part of a new club of global bon vivants who would include fellow Englishman Sir Richard Branson, founder of Virgin Airways, who is seriously investing to take the Jet Set model to its outer limits in outer space; designer Ralph Lauren, who has turned the world into preppies; movie star George Clooney, with his Cary Grant aura, his Lake Como villa, and his serial goddess girlfriends; Sean Combs, who is globalizing rap the way Lauren has globalized prep; and Paul Allen, with his vast yacht *Octopus* and his vaster philanthropies, a James Bond character with a generous heart.

Richard Caring's background is certainly international enough. He is the son of an Italian-American GI, Lou Caringi, whose father was an immigrant factory worker at Bethlehem Steel. Caringi stayed in London after World War II and married a local Jewish nurse who had cared for his war wounds. Caringi anglicized his name and moved to the Scarsdalian Jewish suburb of Finchley, in North London. A golf star at the posh school Millfield, Richard Caring, a classic baby boomer born in 1948, dropped out and joined his father in the rag trade, in which he had made a small fortune manufacturing deep-discount miniskirts in the Mary Quant swinging sixties.

Richard Caring's great discovery was outsourcing dress manufacturing to Hong Kong, which, given the endless number of fittings needed by English colonials to correctly duplicate a Western suit or dress, previously had never been trusted to get fashion right. But Caring mastered the art and science of standardization, providing much of the affordably priced stock of Marks & Spencer, and has now applied it to hospitality. He has assembled, in addition to the Birley collection, the Caprice, the Ivy, J. Sheekey's, and seemingly most of the rest of London's most vaunted dining spots, all of whose menus are distressingly similar, franchised and standardized poshery for rich but often clueless merchant bankers. Claude Terrail would not have approved, but Conrad Hilton would have loved it.

The one original Jet Setter whom Richard Caring most evokes is Eddie Gilbert, that outsider whose desperation to be "in" ultimately put him behind bars. Caring married a model and commutes between homes in Hong Kong and Marbella in a private jet. He sails on a 200-foot yacht. He has a stately home in Somerset and a mansion in London (with ballroom and cinema) that is known as "the Versailles of Hampstead." He gives stupendous parties, particularly one at the tsarist-era Catherine Palace in St. Petersburg whose $12 million cost went for ferrying an army of 450 guests, topped by Bill Clinton, on private jets to Russia. Caring enlisted Elton John and Bob Geldof to entertain the rich and famous, who admittedly were dunned $7,500 each for Caring's pet children's charity as part of the pleasure of their company, making the event turn a profit.

That profit motive is the key difference between Gilbert and Caring, and between the old Jet Set and the new Gulfstream generation. Gilbert's motivation to be rich was a means to be *accepted,* while Caring's ambitions, like those of many of his contemporary tycoon cohorts, are primarily financial. Whether making miniskirts in Hong Kong or making martinis at Annabel's, Caring is a brilliant businessman who never runs at a loss. The result is a bottom line–conscious standardization, wherein a meal at Annabel's can be identical to one at Mark's Club, or to one at the Ivy. This Hiltonization of luxury is as anathema today to purists raised on the Jet Set cult of personality and eccentricity-driven hospitality, costs be damned, as it was to Europe's establishment when Conrad Hilton invaded the continent with his hotel chain. Nonetheless, the bottom line seems more important to Richard Caring than a listing in *Burke's Peerage* or a membership of his own at a St. James's men's club like White's or Boodle's. In his glory days, Hilton felt just the same way.

Perhaps "society," be it Astor-ian or Trippe-ian, is simply dead. So, without social lionhood as a goal, what else can Caring aspire to other than wealth and the toys it can buy? Or perhaps the social pinnacle in England, as entrenched as its class system still is, is a much tougher nut to crack than anything in America, so Caring's attitude may be "why bother to try?" If he lived in New York, where what constitutes "high society" seems to correlate with high net worth and a concomitant propensity to make vast charitable contributions, Caring surely could donate his way onto Gotham's most prestigious boards, like those of the

Metropolitan Museum or the Metropolitan Opera, or even get a library or two renamed after him.

In England, the path to social prominence is littered with the bear traps of ancient snobbery. For Caring's bold self-making in the ever-scorned rag trade and for "stealing" their institutions, the upper crust of England despise and ridicule him as beyond nouveau with a hauteur that only the English upper crust can muster. *Tatler* ran a caricature of Caring as James Bond nemesis Ernst Stavro Blofeld, stroking a white cat. Then again, the Cassini brothers were also sneered at by British nobility, who cast doubts on the authenticity of the Cassinis' Russian royal pedigree. Displaced Russian counts were a ruble a dozen. It says something about the state of things that Mark Birley's son, Robin—an Old Etonian, of course—has opened a chain of low-cost sandwich shops for the "people," while new-money Caring has taken over Robin's ostensible birthright in Annabel's, the asylum of the elite.

Surely Caring would be thrilled to welcome Eddie Gilbert back to Annabel's, if he has not already done so; and surely Gilbert would admire Caring as a fellow arriviste who bought his clubs just as Eddie built Le Club. The close friend of John Aspinall and Mark Birley, Gilbert—who was much more interested in playing the social game than Caring—was an original Annabel's member. His disco days seemed over when, in 1967, after dragging out the legal process for five years following his flight to Rio, he finally pleaded guilty to three of the twelve New York State counts against him involving the grand larceny of $2 million from his family hardwood company, E. L. Bruce; he faced thirty years in prison. He also pleaded guilty to three more of the fifteen federal charges stemming from the escapade, facing an additional seventeen years.

Despite mobilizing a *Who's Who* of the nation's criminal bar, a dream team of lawyers, New York gave him six years, the feds four more. He was taken first to do his state time at Ossining, famous as Sing Sing, and the setting for James Cagney's classic *Angels with Dirty Faces*. One of his first visitors there was the true-blue blue blood John Aspinall, who jetted over from London. Gilbert's good behavior was so good that he was released from Sing Sing after only sixteen months and then moved up to the relatively cushy federal penitentiary at Danbury, Connecticut. After eight months of his sentence, he was released in 1969 to a waiting Cadillac limousine and his loyal Pan Am stewardess and now wife, Turid Holtan, whom he had married just before his sentencing.

To say there are no second acts in American life would have been to grossly underestimate Eddie Gilbert. Like a boomerang, Gilbert resumed his offshore partying, now in Marbella, which had become the headquarters for a new generation of wild and high-rolling sybarites spawned by the seventies oil crises and led by Saudi arms dealer Adnan Khashoggi. This largely Middle Eastern neo-version of the Jet Set might be dubbed the Pet Set, "pet" being short for "petroleum." To fund his revels, Gilbert went straight back to Wall Street and began to make a new fortune to recoup the one he had lost. In the process, he once more ran afoul of the Securities and Exchange Commission, which charged him in 1977 with manipulating the stock of the Conrac Corporation, a manufacturer of electronic instruments. Thus began another endless legal process, during which Turid, having endured enough trials, divorced Eddie in 1979.

During the divorce process, Eddie, who was jetting back and forth to the West Coast on a prospective movie deal with Martin Bregman, the producer of *Serpico* and *Dog Day Afternoon,* met another beauty, a successful soap-opera actress, in the TWA first-class cabin. The movie investment was a disaster. Eddie had expected to be making a film with Bregman's client Al Pacino. Instead, he got Sean Connery. But not as James Bond. The film, *The Next Man,* was Connery's unsuccessful attempt to escape from the Bond tuxedo, which he found to be a straitjacket. On their first date, Eddie took the actress to Le Club, even though the Cassinis no longer co-owned it. They were soon married, in Eddie's Jet Set tradition, at the chic Habitation Leclerc in Haiti and began breeding Arabian stallions on a horse farm in Goshen, New York.

To his many glamorous incarnations, Eddie had added film producer and gentleman farmer before he was forced to resume that of gentleman crook. In 1981, there was another day of reckoning when Eddie Gilbert was convicted by a federal jury on all thirty-four of the government's charges of stock fraud. He was sentenced to concurrent terms on the charges, which totaled four years; after losing an appeal, he began serving in Allenwood, a "country-club" federal prison in Pennsylvania, a white-collar paradise compared to his previous lodgings at Sing Sing and Danbury.

After more good behavior, Eddie was released two years later in 1983, only to find himself divorced and back in federal court in 1989 for violating his long probation by making money giving financial advice. He was found guilty, but this time there was no prison, just six months of consecutive weekends in a Brooklyn halfway house. For once, Eddie Gilbert realized that Wall Street was a dangerous addiction. Not so, sex. At sixty-eight he got married a fourth time, to a model who was a cousin of Al Gore, moved to Santa Fe, and proceeded to become a multimillionaire once again, this time in commercial real estate. In his nineties, the ungroundable Jet Setter was still wheeling and dealing.

Roger Vadim, the Jet Set's most famously conjugal playboy, was one filmmaker without a happy ending. He had followed Jane Fonda to Hollywood but, once they divorced in 1973, was unable to follow her success. His last cinematic gasp was a 1988 remake of the film that had made him famous, *And God Created Woman*, with Rebecca De Mornay trying to channel Brigitte Bardot. The film was a flop. Vadim did marry one more star, Marie-Christine Barrault, and had returned to his Jet Set cradle of Saint-Tropez when he died in 2000 at seventy-two.

Bernie Cornfeld, who went to Los Angeles around the same time as Vadim to recoup the fortunes that he lost in Europe, like Vadim never regained his Midas touch. He embraced the Hollywood scene, giving legendary parties at his Grayhall mansion and becoming the boyfriend of the notorious Hollywood madam Heidi Fleiss. He also decided to go the Hollywood longevity route. Forswearing his beloved pastrami sandwiches, all other red meat, and alcohol, he became a health nut. It didn't work. In 1995, he died of a stroke at sixty-seven.

Jet Set men may come and go, but, like the nine-lived Eddie Gilbert, the handful of Jet Set women seem to go on forever. In England, Mary Quant in her eighties is nearly Twiggy-thin enough to wear one of her classic miniskirts, if not her hot pants. She sold her company to a Japanese conglomerate in 2000, which has two hundred Mary Quant outlets in Japan alone. She still holds forth on Britain's glory days of fashion, when she broke all the French rules and hired "streety" girls to model her outrageous fashions in the equally outrageous legs-astride pose she called the "wet knicker stance." Despite her marriage to the aristocratic Alexander Plunket Greene, who died in 1991, Quant never forgot her Welsh coal-mining roots; her clothes did as much to shake up, if not tear down, the British class system as the Beatles' music. "I love vulgarity," she has famously declared. "Good taste is death, vulgarity is life."

Across the Channel, Régine, eighty-four, who made her name and fame catering to the aristocracy rather than defying it, is still revered as the Queen of the Night. Although her once vast overseas empire of art deco clubs is down to one—the Régine's of Astana, the capital of Kazakhstan—the latest Paris relocation of Régine's, just behind the Champs-Élysées, is still dancing until dawn. When Régine, who sold out years ago but remains a consultant, drops by to sing and dance, the frenzied waters part. Crediting her vibrant longevity to her very un-French lifelong abstinence from tobacco and alcohol, she remains one of France's iconic celebrities, the Maurice Chevalier of the jet age.

In her eighties, Mary Wells Lawrence no longer rules Madison Avenue. She spends most of her year sailing on her yacht in the Caribbean. A one-woman rebuttal to the despair of Betty Friedan's *The Feminist Mystique,* Lawrence remains a beacon to desperate housewives everywhere, notwithstanding some feminist ire raised at the way her campaigns put sex into flying. Her autobiography *A Big Life,* which she published in 2002 following the death of her husband, Harding Lawrence, is nothing but truth in advertising. It recounts her great campaigns until she sold Wells, Rich, Greene to the French agency BDDP. Lacking the founder's touch, the new company let the accounts all drift away. Wells, Rich, Greene ceased to exist in 1998. The book also openly discusses her brave campaigns against cancer. Unlike her agency, Mary Wells Lawrence is a survivor.

And then there were, or are, the Cassini brothers, the two lead engines of the Jet Set, its chronicler and its designer and its chief role models, whose likes we will not see again, even if Richard Caring were to come to New York and try to recycle Le Club. After Oleg's misadventures with Bernie Cornfeld in relocating to Italy and becoming the pre-Armani Armani, Igor, who had been at his own loose ends all over Europe, forgave his brother the seduction by Cornfeld, and together, they came back to New York in the midseventies.

While in Europe, Igor seemed to have repudiated all the conventions of class and taste befitting an Old World count or a smooth Jet Set playboy. Instead, he embraced an alternate-universe adolescence that flaunted all the rules, just as the hippies were doing in America. Igor had taken a fourth wife, an oft-topless photographed German-Sicilian sex-kitten starlet named Gianni Lou Muller, who milked being Countess Cassini for all the scandal it was worth. Although he no longer wrote the columns, Igor was the subject—and laughingstock—of them. Only eighteen when they wed, Muller was nicknamed by the European tabloids "Countess Culo" for her posterior endowment, flaunted on the most exclusive beaches of the Mediterranean. After she very publicly cuckolded Igor with a struggling Greek actor close to her age, she became entwined in one of the early-seventies drug scandals that was paraded as proof that the Jet Set was bankrupt and la dolce vita had turned sour. This one centered around Number One, Rome's answer to Le Club, which was more like Studio 54 to come, with even more cocaine consumed on the premises. It was known as Medellín on the Via Veneto.

As an habitué of Number One, leaving Igor at home to stew, the countess got involved with a drug-addicted young count, Bino Cicogna, from one of the noblest Venetian families and already a rising producer of Sergio Leone spaghetti westerns. When Cicogna was accused of being the Colombians' man in Rome, he fled (like Eddie Gilbert) to Rio, but without an Igor to rehabilitate his reputation, he committed suicide there, or was murdered. In either case, his body was found in a Rio favela with his head in the oven. Once the new Countess Cassini managed to evade conspiracy charges, she got a quickie divorce in—of all places—the Dominican Republic and married the Greek.

With his endless stories to tell, Igor, back in Manhattan, decided that if he couldn't write a column, he would tell all in a book. In 1977, Putnam published his memoir, *I'd Do It All Over Again*. A big problem with the book was that Igor, for all his unmatched adventures, hadn't written in years. In the early sixties, when he was off playing diplomat and PR man, he had hired a young Liz Smith to ghostwrite his Cholly Knickerbocker column. Now Igor hired Jeanne Molli, the right hand/ secretary of his friends Sophia Loren and Carlo Ponti, as his coauthor. The book, while written in the first person, felt secondhand, with many punches pulled, much less revealing and sensational than Igor's column in its prime. It didn't sell well and turned out to be a disappointment to Putnam.

In 1983, Igor tried again, this time all by himself, in a roman à clef called *Pay the Price,* with his antihero Ash Young a thinly veiled version of Igor's now despised father-in-law Charles Wrightsman, a very much alive and fit eighty-two at the time. Anticipating Igor's dropping the G(ossip)-bomb that would destroy society, or what was left of it, the survivors of the Jet Set were quaking in their banquettes at La Caravelle. They were still reeling from Truman Capote's own G-bomb, his notorious "La Côte Basque 1965" short story that *Esquire* had published in December 1976. That billet-doux had supposedly driven social lioness Ann Woodward to take her own life, and had subsequently ruined Capote's. Everyone knew that Igor Cassini knew far, far more, and far more firsthand, than Capote, and that his life was already ruined, so he had nothing to lose. Plus, Igor was even naughtier than Capote, and he had always been fearless. The Jet Set universe went on high alert for a suicide bomber.

The big reveal people feared was that, given his betrayal by Bobby Kennedy, Igor might open the Pandora's box of the *two* Kennedy assassinations. From his earliest days in America, the FDR-baiting Igor had been the bedfellow of the Republican elite. For all his neighborly friendship with the Kennedys in Palm Beach, Igor's father-in-law Wrightsman was an Oklahoma right-winger who regarded JFK and RFK as not far short of Communists. And wasn't it CIA chief Allen Dulles who had sent Igor to the Dominican Republic and his subsequent personal disaster? There was a whole school of thought that a CIA-Dulles right-wing cabal had targeted JFK.

Furthermore, both Igor and Oleg were close friends with their fellow White Russian aristocrat George de Mohrenschildt, the globetrotting Dallas-based petroleum engineer (and suspected secret agent) who had become Lee Harvey Oswald's mentor in the year before JFK was killed. De Morenschildt was a Jet Setter in the mode of Tom Corbally. He knew everything about everybody, but nobody knew much about him. He was great friends with the Bouviers; as a young girl, Jackie had known him as "Uncle George." In Texas, he was a friend of the Bush family, through the oil business, or the CIA, or both. However, once he appeared as a key witness for the Warren Commission, de Morenschildt began to worry that he was "the man who knew too much" and that as Oswald's perceived "handler" in Dallas, he was subject to elimination by the same forces who eliminated the Kennedys. His 1977 death by a shotgun blast to the head on a visit to Florida was ruled a suicide, but that would be more grist for Igor Cassini's conspiracy mill.

Alas, *Pay the Price* turned out to be all whimper and no bang. Perhaps because the all-powerful C. B. Wrightsman was still alive and ornery and very likely to bring a massive libel suit, not one of the major publishers in Manhattan would take Igor's novel. Igor had to settle for it to be released—without any of the fanfare or publicity expected of the ultimate PR man—as a paperback original by Zebra Books. And although people like Onassis, the shah, Dulles, and Sam Giancana put in vaguely disguised appearances in undisguised Jet Set locales across the globe, from Le Club to La Tour d'Argent, the Kennedys did not. Perhaps they were edited out. The book that was printed had no shocking hints, much less revelations. The man who did become the next Cholly Knickerbocker would not become the next Truman Capote.

If Igor could no longer set the world on fire as a writer, he sought to console himself with his other great skill, playboy-lover. He had not lost the knack. At sixty-eight, he fell in love and got married, for the fifth time, to an eighteen-year-old supermodel, Brenda Mitchell, the Oil of Olay girl from Atlanta. For Igor it was an exercise in *à la recherche du temps perdu,* bringing back his days with Emilio Pucci at the University of Georgia, where he had spent some of his happiest times teaching tennis and developed his fatal attraction for Southern belles.

After his two publishing flops in New York, Igor decided to try Europe again, taking Brenda and their two young sons, Nicholas and Dimitri, to increasingly Arabesque Marbella, where Sean Connery, who lived there for the golf, was the boys' virtual godfather. But once again, the marriage failed, and the wife brought the kids home to raise in Atlanta. Still, the Sean Connery influence had its effects. Nicholas Cassini became an all-American golfer at the University of Georgia and at one point America's highest-rated amateur. Dimitri, also a Georgia graduate and a golf star there, went into real estate, managing the Four Seasons time-share conversion of the Palazzo Tornabuoni in Florence, where Igor's mother had run a dress shop in their flight from Russia.

Igor went back to New York, where he basically lived with, and through, Oleg, who was again rich enough to support them both. Igor partied hard until the end. When he fell and broke his hip in the icy winter of 2002, he decided his time had come. He told friends that he wanted to "go out like a Roman," presumably on his shield, with honor. He stopped eating and made his exit, for the first time in his long life, without fanfare. He was eighty-six, or maybe more, as Igor Cassini never wanted to be pinned down about his age, or by it.

The equally ageless Oleg lasted four more years, until 2006. He couldn't bear a life without his brother, though in his own 1987 autobiography, *In My Own Fashion,* ghosted by political writer Joe Klein (the future "Anonymous" of *Primary Colors*), he mentioned Igor on only twenty-eight of the book's nearly four hundred breathlessly name-dropping pages, and not a word about Igor's legal troubles with Bobby Kennedy's Justice Department or the suicide of Igor's wife. That was Oleg: discreet when need be. Oleg had an image to maintain to the very end, and a key part of that image was being Jackie Kennedy's Main Man.

That image had made him rich, the first designer brand name, with an estate valued at over $50 million. If James Bond had a license to kill, Oleg Cassini had a license for everything else, from men's shirts and bath towels to luggage, perfume, car interiors, and even nail polish.

Oleg's discretion, a genetic component of his family's long diplomatic tradition, extended to his personal life. His mystique relied on the public perception of him as an unrivaled Jet Set playboy, a man for all seasons and a man for all women. Single since the late forties and his Gene Tierney days, he enabled his wannabe-playboy male clientele to live vicariously through his conquests, as chronicled by Igor in his column, and enabled his wannabe-Jackie female clientele to project their fantasies of having Oleg themselves. If they couldn't have the man, they could at least have his perfume or maybe his soap. Just as he played tennis and rode horses into his nineties, he remained publicly one of the prime bachelors in the world of celebrity. In reality, however, Oleg had been secretly married to his chief personal assistant, Marianne Nestor, since 1971. Nestor did not receive a single mention in Oleg's autobiography.

After Oleg died at ninety-two, of a sudden aneurysm at his Long Island horse farm, Marianne Nestor emerged, like a secret panelist on a game show, and unveiled her marriage certificate and Oleg's will, which left her the great bulk of his estate. It was a classic case of "If you've got it, flaunt it." Breaking over three decades of silence, Nestor certainly flaunted it, to the fury of Oleg's second daughter, Christina, from his marriage to Gene Tierney. Christina got a paltry $1 million. Her elder sister, Daria, retarded since birth and institutionalized, got $500,000. Then fifty-eight, Christina, who had dated George W. Bush at Andover and in Texas in her own gilded youth, had grown up into a divorcée who lived in Paris, but in a far from Cassini-like style. She had four children and cancer, needed the money, and felt blindsided. The story went to *Vanity Fair* and the case went to the New York courts, which overturned the will and gave Christina a quarter of Oleg's assets, or $13 million. Marianne Nestor sued her attorneys for malpractice and *Vanity Fair* for defamation, and the beat goes on. The Jet Set, ostensibly about the highest style of the twentieth century, in the bitter end reverted to the lowest common denominator.

Jet Set RIP. The Rolling Stones's 1966 song "Flight 505" was its prescient epitaph. It is the story of a man who decides to change his life by taking a jet trip. "505" was the number of the BOAC 707 service from London to New York that the Stones had flown for their first American concert tour. In the song, just as the narrator is settling in to alcoholic airborne luxury, "feeling like a king with the whole world at my feet," something goes terribly wrong. The final refrain is "they put the plane down in the sea, end of Flight Number 505."

As much as high technology, that lowest common denominator of money was key to both the rise and fall of the Jet Set. The same filthy lucre that tarnished Oleg Cassini's legacy of courtly and studly elegance was the driving force that created the fantasy of the Jet Set to begin with. When Juan Trippe launched his 707s in 1958, Europe was the grand bargain of the twentieth century. The continent was still recovering from World War II and was priced accordingly. What a lure it was, this fabulous package of the Old World and the new jets. Culture, glamour, history, fabulous food, glorious sex were only six hours from New York and at a cost the middle class could afford.

No more. With the possible exception of health care, nothing has inflated like the tariff of European travel. That $30 feast for two at Tour d'Argent in 1965 today costs $500; the $25 room at Claridge's costs $1,000. First-class round-trip airfare, then around $1,000, today would be $15,000. Furthermore, the costs far down the luxury pyramid have risen at rates nearly as shocking as those at the top. The very idea of *Europe on 5 Dollars a Day* seems preposterous, out of this world.

Given the obsessive desire of the Old World to replicate the new, Europe has vastly changed and Americanized itself. The monuments and the art are still there, but travelers have to hack their way through jungles of mediocre modernity to try to savor the continent's ancient charms. However Europe has changed, getting there has changed even more. The planes are no faster than they were fifty years ago, but the flying experience, regardless of class, has devolved from the journey of a lifetime to a Dantean descent into aviation hell. If F. Scott Fitzgerald were alive, he surely would say that the main way in which the rich are different is that they don't fly commercial.

Blame it on Wall Street. Blame it on Silicon Valley. Blame it on Hollywood. Blame it on the National Basketball Association. Blame it on Riyadh and Dubai. But look at the record. The sports hero of 1965, quarterback Joe Namath, earned $142,000. In 2005, Tiger Woods earned $87 million. In 1965, the president of General Motors earned $3.9 million. In 2012, hedge funder Ray Dalio earned $3 *billion*. There are more super-rich than ever before, and the gap between them and the rest of the population is an unbridgeable grand canyon of envy.

The classic haunts of the Jet Set are now basically off-limits to all but the 1 percent and the corporate tycoons on expense accounts who are so busy doing deals that they use the rooms at Claridge's mostly as luggage drops. In fact, the new Gulfstream set mostly avoids London and Paris except for business. For leisure, they prefer private islands or private villas and exotic destinations in the Indian Ocean or Great Barrier Reef, far from the relative hoi polloi crossing the Atlantic first class on United or British Airways.

As long as there is money, privilege, and fame, there will always be new iterations of a free-spending, high-flying, effortlessly mobile superclass. But somehow these new elites get further and further distanced from "real people" both by where they go and by the amount of money required to be one of them. During the era of the 707 and the DC-8, the wealth gap was much narrower, and the influence of the Jet Set on the general population accordingly greater. In the sixties, seemingly everyone aspired to fly off to an adventure in Europe. Now the closest most people will get to the intensely private lifestyles of the rich and famous is to watch them on tabloid television shows.

In the end, the Jet Set was a pure fantasy, as evanescent as the bubbles of the fine champagne that fueled its tantalizing idyll. But this fantasy had an enormous power in unleashing the genie of aspiration that affected the hopes and self-image of two major generations, the Eisenhower suburbanites and the baby boomers alike. Forget "Flight 505." With Sinatra crooning "Come Fly with Me" as its theme song, the Jet Set seduced a nation, and a world, into a wanderlust that no obstacles of cost, fear, or inconvenience will ever be able to quell. As long as we can dream, we'll always have Pan Am.

Acknowledgments

A world of thanks to all those around the world who have contributed to this book: The Boeing Company, Alexandra de Borchgrave, Mel Brooks, Leslie Caron, Daniel Cohen, Howie Cohen, Roger Choukroun, Renee Corbally, Tad Dowd, Francesca Drommi, Eddie Gilbert, Olivia de Havilland, Louise Duncan, Joanne and Jerry Dryansky, Ralph Elder, Dodge Fielding, Frank Filerino, Karen Mason Fitzgerald, Nandu Hinds, Barbara Warner Howard, Patricia Geoghegan, Gisele Galante, Virginie Guyonnet, Chilla Heuser, Isabelle and Marc Hotimsky, Priyanka Krishnan, Stephane Lambert, Kenneth Jay Lane, Jim Lowenstein, Jose Luna, Musée Air France, Pan Am Historical Foundation, Dr. Ivo Pitanguy, Marie-France Pochna, Michael Pochna, Rupert Prior, Eduardo Rabel, Eric Rayman, Annie Reiner, Carl Reiner, Rex USA, Victoria and Jack Risko, Dana Ruspoli, Tony Scotti, Adam Shaw, Penn Sicre, Jean Signoret, Jacques Silberstein, Nadia Stancioff, Mimi Strong, Gay Talese, André Terrail, Taki Theodoracopulos, Charles Trueheart, Sylvie Vartan, Dimitri Villard, Freck Vreeland, George Weidenfeld, Sandy Whitelaw, Ron Winston.

Special thanks to my agent, Dan Strone, an epicure in the grand Jet Set tradition, who believed in this project, with both his heart and his stomach; to his assistant Kseniya Zaslavskaya, a maestro at securing photographic permissions; and to my editor, Susanna Porter, who had a wonderful ability to keep this high-flying book grounded enough to cast its spell on both armchair dreamers who are still down on the farm as well as glittering globetrotters who've seen Par-ee and everything else.

Photo Credits

211:   REX USA/Everett Collection
217:   REX USA
227:   REX USA/Moviestore Collection/Rex
233:   REX USA/John Hodder/Associated Newspapers/Rex
237:   REX USA/Associated Newspapers/Rex
243:   The Pan Am Historical Foundation
250:   Wells, Rich, and Greene
256:   REX USA/CSU Archives/Everett Collection
265:   REX USA/Ann Ward/Daily Mail
269:   Courtesy of Renee Corbally
277:   Copyright © Boeing
297:   REX USA
300:   REX USA/Denis Cameron
306:   REX USA/CROLLALANZA
309:   REX USA/Moviestore Collection/Rex

Selected Bibliography

Abrams, Ann Uhry. *Explosion at Orly*. Atlanta: Avion Press, 2002.

Altschul, Selig, and Marilyn Bender. *The Chosen Instrument*. New York. Simon & Schuster, 1982.

Amory, Cleveland. *The Last Resorts*. New York: Harper, 1952.

Amory, Cleveland. *Who Killed Society?* New York: Harper, 1960.

Bailey, David. *Birth of the Cool*. New York: Viking Studio, 1999.

Bain, Donald. *Coffee, Tea or Me?* New York: Bartholomew House, 1967.

Barrow, Andrew. *Gossip*. London: Hamish Hamilton, 1983.

Beebe, Lucius. *The Big Spenders*. Garden City, N.Y.: Doubleday, 1966.

Bender, Marilyn. *The Beautiful People*. New York: Coward McCann. 1967.

Blond, Anthony. *Jew Made in England*. London: Timewell Press, 2004.

Bolton, Whitney. *The Silver Spade*. New York: Farrar, Straus and Young, 1954.

Boorstin, Daniel. *The Image*. New York: Atheneum, 1961.

Bosworth, Patricia. *Jane Fonda*. Houghton Mifflin Harcourt, 2011.

Broccoli, Albert, with Donald Zec. *When the Snow Melts*. London: Boxtree, 1998.

Brooks, John. *The Go-Go Years*. New York: Weybright and Talley, 1973.

Buchwald, Anne and Art. *Seems Like Yesterday*. New York: Putnam's. 1980.

Cassini, Igor. *I'd Do It All Over Again*. New York: Putnam's. 1977.

Cassini, Igor. *Pay the Price*. New York: Kensington, 1983.

Cassini, Oleg. *In My Own Fashion*. New York: Simon & Schuster, 1987.

Curtis, Charlotte. *The Rich and Other Atrocities*. New York: Harper & Row, 1976.

Daley, Robert. *An American Saga.* New York: Random House, 1980.

Davis, Deborah. *Party of the Century*. New York: Wiley, 2006.

Endy, Christopher. *Cold War Holidays*. Chapel Hill: University of North Carolina Press, 2004.

Fairchild, John. *The Fashionable Savages*. Garden City, N.Y.: Doubleday, 1965.

Fielding, Temple. *Fielding's Travel Guide to Europe*. New York: William Sloane Associates, 1959.

Fonda, Afdera. *Never Before Noon*. New York: Weidenfeld & Nicolson, 1986.

Frank, Gerold. *Zsa Zsa Gabor*. Cleveland: World Publishing Co., 1960.

Fraser-Cavassoni, Natasha. *Sam Spiegel*. New York: Simon & Schuster, 2003.

Goldsmith, Lady Annabel. *Annabel*. London: Weidenfeld & Nicolson, 2004.

Gordon, Alastair. *Naked Airport*. New York: Metropolitan Books, 2004.

Grossman, Peter Z. *American Express*. New York: Crown, 1987.

Gutowski, Gene. *With Balls and Chutzpah*. Bloomington, Ind.: iUniverse, 2003.

Halaby, Najeeb. *Crosswinds.* Garden City, N.Y.: Doubleday, 1978.

Hamilton, George, and William Stadiem. *Don't Mind If I Do*. New York: Touchstone, 2008.

Hilton, Conrad. *Be My Guest*. Englewood Cliffs, N.J.: Prentice-Hall, 1957.

Hodgson, Godfrey, Bruce Page, and Charles Raw. *Do You Sincerely Want to Be Rich?* New York: Broadway Books, 1971.

Hudson, Kenneth, and Julian Pettifer. *Diamonds in the Sky*. London: The Bodley Head, 1979.

Ingalls, Douglas J. *747.* Fallbrook, Ca.: Aero Publishers, 1970.

Irving, Clive. *Wide Body*. New York: William Morrow, 1993.

Jacobs, George, and William Stadiem. *Mr. S*. New York: Harper Entertainment, 2003.

Kaplan, Alice. *Dreaming in French*. Chicago: University of Chicago Press, 2012.

Kelly, Charles J., Jr. *The Sky's the Limit*. New York: Coward McCann, 1963.

Knightley, Phillip, and Caroline Kennedy. *An Affair of State*. New York: Atheneum, 1987.

Knox, Mickey. *The Good, the Bad and the Dolce Vita*. New York: Nation Books, 2004.

Lawrence, Mary Wells. *A Big Life*. New York: Knopf, 2002.

Levy, Shawn. *Ready, Steady, Go!* New York: Doubleday, 2002.

Lilly, Doris. *Those Fabulous Greeks*. New York: Cowles, 1970.

Lovegrove, Keith. *Airline*. Kempen, Germany: teNeues, 2000.

Lownes, Victor. *The Day the Bunny Died*. Secaucus, N.J.: Lyle Stuart, 1982.

Lycett, Andrew. *Ian Fleming*. London: Weidenfeld and Nicolson, 1995.

Margaret, Duchess of Argyll. *Forget Not*. London: Wyndham, 1975.

Marx, Arthur. *The Nine Lives of Mickey Rooney*. New York: Stein and Day, 1986.

Masters, Brian. *The Passion of John Aspinall*. London: Jonathan Cape, 1988.

Maxwell, Elsa. *R.S.V.P.* Boston: Little Brown & Co., 1954.

Mefret, Jean-Pax. *La Salle Affaire Markovic*. Paris: Pygmalion, 2007.

Miller, Russell. *Bunny*. New York: Holt, Rinehart & Winston, 1984.

Mills, C. Wright. *The Power Elite*. New York: Oxford University Press, 1959.

Musée Air France. *Un Siècle d'Aviation avec Air France*. Paris: Gallimard, 2000.

Nance, John J. *A Splash of Colors*. New York: William Morrow, 1984.

Newhouse, John. *The Sporty Game*. New York: Knopf, 1982.

Nolan, Maggie. *Champagne . . . and Real Pain*. Oakville, Ontario: Mosaic Press, 1998.

Ogden, Christopher. *Life of the Party*. Boston: Little, Brown, 1994.

Oldham, Andrew Loog. *Stoned.* London: Secker & Warburg, 2000.

Orsi, Roberto. *Rome After Dark.* New York: Macfadden Books, 1962.

Packard, Vance. *The Status Seekers.* New York: David McKay, 1959.

Pearson, John. *The Gamblers.* London: Century, 2005.

Pells, Richard. *Not Like Us.* New York: Basic Books, 1997.

Polanski, Roman. *Roman.* London: Heinemann, 1984.

Quant, Mary. *Quant by Quant.* London: Cassell, 1965.

Rasponi, Lanfranco. *The Golden Oases.* New York: Putnam's, 1968.

Rasponi, Lanfranco. *The International Nomads.* New York: Putnam's, 1966.

Sterling, Robert. *Howard Hughes' Airline.* New York: St. Martin's, 1983.

Sterling, Robert. *Maverick.* Garden City, N.Y.: Doubleday, 1974.

Shnayerson, Michael. *Irwin Shaw.* New York: Putnam's, 1989.

Smith, Liz. *Natural Blonde.* New York: Hyperion, 2000.

Solberg, Carl. *Conquest of the Skies.* Boston: little, Brown, 1979.

Stadiem, William. *Too Rich: The High Life and Tragic Death of King Farouk.* New York: Carroll & Graf, 1991.

Stadiem, William, with Mara Gibbs. *Everybody Eats There.* New York: Workman, 2007.

Terrail, Claude. *Le Roman de la Tour d'Argent.* Paris: Le Cherche Midi Éditeur, 1997.

Vadim, Roger. *Bardot, Deneuve, Fonda.* New York: Simon & Schuster, 1986.

Vartan, Sylvie. *Between Darkness and Light.* Paris: XO Editions, 2004.

Wharton, Abigail Jane. *Building the Cold War.* Chicago: University of Chicago Press, 2001.

Whittingham, Richard. *Boy Wonder of Wall Street.* New York: Texere, 2003.

Index

Numbers in *italic* type indicate illustrations.

About the Author

WILLIAM STADIEM is the author of such bestsellers as *Mr. S: My Life with Frank Sinatra, Marilyn Monroe Confidential*, and *Dear Senator: A Memoir by the Daughter of Strom Thurmond*, as well as such acclaimed works of social history as *Too Rich: The High Life and Tragic Death of King Farouk*. He writes for *Vanity Fair* and has been the Hollywood columnist for *Andy Warhol's Interview* and the restaurant critic for *Los Angeles Magazine*. A Harvard JD-MBA and former Wall Street–based International lawyer, Stadiem is also a screenwriter whose credits include Elizabeth Taylor's last starring vehicle, Franco Zeffirelli's *Young Toscanini*, and the television series *L.A. Law*.